D0204711

The Trouble with the Cong(

The Trouble with the Congo suggests a new explanation for international peacebuilding failures in civil wars. Drawing from more than 330 interviews and a year and a half of field research, it develops a case study of the international intervention during the Democratic Republic of the Congo's unsuccessful transition from war to peace and democracy (2003–2006). Grassroots rivalries over land, resources, and political power motivated widespread violence. However, a dominant peacebuilding culture shaped the intervention strategy in a way that precluded action on local conflicts, ultimately dooming the international efforts to end the deadliest conflict since World War II. Most international actors interpreted continued fighting as the consequence of national and regional tensions alone. Diplomats and United Nations staff viewed intervention at the macro levels as their only legitimate responsibility. The dominant culture constructed local peacebuilding as such an unimportant, unfamiliar, and unmanageable task that neither shocking events nor resistance from certain individuals could convince international actors to reevaluate their understanding of violence and intervention. Through this in-depth analysis, *The Trouble with the Congo* proposes innovative ways to address civil wars in Africa and beyond.

SÉVERINE AUTESSERRE is an Assistant Professor of political science, specializing in international relations and African studies, at Barnard College, Columbia University. Her research focuses on civil wars, peacebuilding and peacekeeping, humanitarian aid, and African politics, and her findings have appeared in scholarly and policy journals including *Foreign Affairs, International Organization,* the *African Studies Review,* the *Review of African Political Economy,* the *Journal of Humanitarian Affairs,* and *Birikim.* Over the past twelve years, Professor Autesserre has worked periodically for humanitarian and development agencies in Afghanistan, the Congo, India, Kosovo, and Nicaragua. She has conducted extensive fieldwork in the eastern Congo since 2001.

Cambridge Studies in International Relations: 115

Cambridge Studies in International Relations is a joint initiative of Cambridge University Press and the British International Studies Association (BISA). The series will include a wide range of material, from undergraduate textbooks and surveys to research-based monographs and collaborative volumes. The aim of the series is to publish the best new scholarship in International Studies from Europe, North America, and the rest of the world.

List of books in the series follows the Index.

The Trouble with the Congo

Local Violence and the Failure of International Peacebuilding

SÉVERINE AUTESSERRE

Barnard College, Columbia University

CAMBRIDGE
UNIVERSITY PRESS

CAMBRIDGE UNIVERSITY PRESS
Cambridge, New York, Melbourne, Madrid, Cape Town, Singapore,
São Paulo, Delhi, Dubai, Tokyo, Mexico City

Cambridge University Press
32 Avenue of the Americas, New York, NY 10013-2473, USA

www.cambridge.org
Information on this title: www.cambridge.org/9780521156011

First published 2010

Printed in the United States of America

A catalog record for this publication is available from the British Library.

Library of Congress Cataloging in Publication data
Autesserre, Séverine, 1976–
    The trouble with the Congo : local violence and the failure of international
    peacebuilding / Séverine Autesserre.
        p.   cm. – (Cambridge studies in international relations ; 115)
    Includes bibliographical references and index.
    ISBN 978-0-521-19100-5 – ISBN 978-0-521-15601-1 (pbk.)
    1. Congo (Democratic Republic)–History–1997–   2. Peace-building–Congo
    (Democratic Republic)   3. Community development–Congo (Democratic
    Republic)   4. Conflict management–Congo (Democratic Republic)   5. Internal
    security–Congo (Democratic Republic)   6. Violence–Congo (Democratic
    Republic)   7. Ethnic conflict–Congo (Democratic Republic) I. Title. II. Series.
    DT658.26.A94 2010
    967.5103′4–dc22   2010014627

ISBN 978-0-521-19100-5 Hardback
ISBN 978-0-521-15601-1 Paperback

To the victims of the Congolese conflict

Contents

Figures and Tables

Figures

Table

Glossary of Acronyms, Names, and Ethnic Terms

Throughout the book, I use the shorthand "the Congo" to refer to the book's subject, the Democratic Republic of the Congo, not to be confused with the neighboring Republic of Congo.

"Regional" in the book refers to the African Great Lakes region: Burundi, the Congo, Rwanda, and Uganda. "Local" refers to the level of the individual, the family, the clan, the municipality, the community, the district, and, occasionally, the ethnic group.

Following Congolese practice and the reference book on the topic (Willame 1997), I use the term Banyarwanda to refer to Congolese with Rwandan ancestry living in North Kivu, and Banyamulenge to refer to Congolese with Rwandan ancestry living in South Kivu. I use "Congolese of Rwandan descent," "Congolese with Rwandan ancestry," and "Kinyarwanda-speaking Congolese" interchangeably to refer to both the Banyarwanda and the Banyamulenge communities together.

In accordance with Anglophone academic texts, newspaper articles, and policy documents, I use the French acronyms for Congo-specific terms.

AFDL	Alliance des Forces Démocratiques pour la Libération du Congo-Zaïre / Alliance of Democratic Forces for the Liberation of the Congo-Zaire. Main rebel group during the 1996 war; put Kabila in power
Banyamulenge	Congolese with Rwandan ancestry living in South Kivu (literally "people from Mulenge")
Banyarwanda	Congolese with Rwandan ancestry living in North Kivu (literally "people from Rwanda")
Bemba, Jean-Pierre	President of the Congo Liberation Movement; vice president of the Congo during the transition

DDRRR	Disarmament, Demobilization, Repatriation, Reintegration and Resettlement. Program for foreign armed groups
DRC	Democratic Republic of the Congo
EU	European Union
FDLR	Forces Démocratiques de Libération du Rwanda / Democratic Forces for the Liberation of Rwanda. Rwandan rebel group composed mostly of ethnic Hutus and based in the eastern Congo
Indigenous	Term used by ethnic groups that are native to the eastern Congo to differentiate themselves from "foreign" ethnic groups, in particular the Congolese with Rwandan ancestry
Kabila, Laurent-Désiré	President of the Congo from 1997 to his assasination in 2001
Kabila, Joseph	Son of late president Laurent-Désiré Kabila; president of the Congo since 2001
Mai Mai	Local militias formed on ethnic bases throughout the eastern Congo
MLC	Mouvement de Libération du Congo / Congo Liberation Movement. Second main rebel movement during the 1998 war; allied with Uganda; transformed into political party during the transition
Mobutu, Joseph	President of the Congo from 1965 to 1997
MONUC	Mission de l'Organisation des Nations Unies au Congo / United Nations Mission in the Congo. Deployed from 1999 to the present
Nkunda, Laurent	Military officer, rebelled against the transitional authorities in May 2004 and took over Bukavu. Former colonel of the RCD-G's armed wing

ONUC   Opération des Nations Unies au Congo / United Nations Operation in the Congo. Deployed from 1960 to 1964

RCD   Rassemblement Congolais pour la Démocratie / Congolese Rally for Democracy. Initial rebel movement during the 1998 war

RCD-G   Rassemblement Congolais pour la Démocratie–Goma / Congolese Rally for Democracy–Goma. Main rebel group during the 1998 war; allied with Rwanda; controlled most of the eastern Congo; transformed into political party during the transition

UK   United Kingdom of Great Britain and Northern Ireland

UN   United Nations

U.S.   United States

Figure 1 Map of the Democratic Republic of the Congo and Its Neighbors.
This figure is based on the United Nations' map entitled *Democratic Republic
of the Congo* (no. 4007 Rev. 8, January 2004).

Preface and Acknowledgments

This book grew out of the bewilderment I felt during my first visit to the Congo. I arrived in February 2001, a young humanitarian aid worker sent by Medicos Sin Fronteras (the Spanish section of Médecins Sans Frontières) to open its mission and projects in the country. I spent six months trying to understand the Congolese context so that Medicos Sin Fronteras could best respond to the humanitarian crisis, but felt I failed to reach beneath the surface. Whenever it seemed I was beginning to grasp the dynamics of violence, I found that my brand new framework of analysis would invariably collapse the next day. Congolese friends and humanitarian colleagues usually explained the conflict through a relatively simple macro framework, as a combination of two wars: an international confrontation between the Congo and Rwanda, and an ethnic conflict that pitted indigenous Congolese against ethnic Hutus and Tutsis with Rwandan ancestry living in the Congo. Yet this analysis not only failed to explain many aspects of violence, it also rendered certain dynamics even more puzzling. For example, why did indigenous Congolese ally with Rwandan Hutu armed groups? Why did some ethnic Tutsis ally with President Kabila, the indigenous Congolese's patron, to fight other ethnic Tutsis?

From 2002 to 2004, I progressively left the humanitarian world and turned to political science, which only drew me back to the Congo. I was struck by how underanalyzed the conflict was and, after returning to the country for two months with Medicos Sin Fronteras in 2003, I decided to dedicate my research to the Congolese wars. The issues were so complex that they unceasingly sparked my interest, as they continue to do today. As my understanding of the patterns of violence on the ground increased, new puzzles appeared, centered on the international response to the conflict. It became clear to me that local agendas drove a large part of the continuing violence. Why then did diplomats, United Nations officials, and nongovernmental organization staff members continually fail to consider the local dynamics?

More broadly, why did international peacebuilders succeed in imposing peace only at the national and international levels and not at the subnational level? These questions shaped the extensive field research I conducted from 2004 to 2007. They also informed the analysis that, after years of study, several publications in policy and academic journals, and numerous briefings and invited talks, has culminated in this book.

From the first draft paper I wrote on this topic, I hoped that my scholarly inquiry could be useful to the friends, colleagues, and Congolese citizens that I had reluctantly left behind to work in New York. From the outset, I thus dedicated my research to the victims of the Congolese conflict: those killed, tortured, raped, and displaced; those forced to witness atrocities committed against their loved ones; and all of those whose lives were otherwise disrupted by the conflict. It is my aspiration to contribute to the scholarly literature on civil wars and international interventions; yet my broader wish is that this book assists all those who strive for peace in the Congo, so that eventually no woman, man, or child will suffer further from the horrific violence that has recently plagued the region.

The heart of my research, and the basis of *The Trouble with the Congo*, is the qualitative data I collected from more than 330 in-depth interviews. These interviews offer an unparalleled set of information on perceptions of violence, peace, and intervention in the Congo. My most heartfelt thanks therefore go to all of the people who took time from their busy schedules to meet with an unknown researcher. I am deeply grateful to the victims of violence for sharing their stories with me, international peacebuilders for introducing me to the inner working of their organizations, Congolese leaders for patiently answering my endless questions, and all of my other interviewees for sharing their insights and concerns about the war and peace process. I did not expect to encounter such willingness to help, such readiness to disclose potentially sensitive information, such openness regarding delicate subjects, and such interest in my work. Several Congolese and international interviewees went out of their way after our meetings to introduce me to their contacts, send articles and documents that they thought might interest me, and provide feedback on my preliminary findings. I wish I could acknowledge all of my interviewees by name, but as I promised to keep our interactions confidential, I can extend only a broad thanks; I want them to know that their kindness and the gratitude I felt for all their help was often what kept me moving forward.

Fieldwork in the midst of continuing violence is challenging. In this regard, I am greatly indebted to the Congolese and foreign teams who worked for Action Against Hunger | ACF International in the Kivus, Kinshasa, and New York from 2004 to 2007. I cannot thank them enough for leading me out of trouble the numerous times things went awry: when my fieldwork plans regularly fell apart or when the administrative, security, and logistical challenges proved too difficult to maneuver alone. I also wish to thank the staff of Medicos Sin Fronteras and Médecins Sans Frontières–Belgium for providing me with logistic, security, and administrative backup during my 2004 research in the Kivus, North Katanga, and Kinshasa. Additionally, I am much obliged to the teams of Oxfam, the Norwegian Refugee Council, and the United Nations Mission in the Congo (MONUC), for occasionally welcoming me to their homes in Goma and Bunia so that I could pursue my research in safe conditions. I owe a special thanks to the Action Against Hunger and MONUC teams stationed in Bukavu in May and June 2004, and in particular to David Blanc, for ensuring that I remained unharmed in the midst of heavy fighting.

Colleagues in North America and Europe also provided wonderful support. I am deeply indebted to Elisabeth Jean Wood and Timothy Mitchell for their guidance throughout this project. They helped me develop many ideas and navigate the research and writing process, and their advice bolstered most of the book. Jean-Claude Willame and René Lemarchand similarly acted as considerable resources. Their expertise on the Congo, in particular on the micro-level dynamics of violence in the Kivus and on international interventions in Central Africa, helped me develop a much stronger analysis. Michael Barnett, Kevin Dunn, Shepard Forman, Meghan Lynch, Stephen John Stedman, and two anonymous reviewers read the entire manuscript at different stages of the project. Their advice saved me from countless errors and helped sharpen large parts of the argument. Susanna Campbell, Christine Cheng, Alexander Cooley, Page Fortna, Joshua Goldstein, Stephen Jackson, Robert Jervis, Bruce Jones, Stathis Kalyvas, Peter Katzenstein, Zachariah Mampilly, Roland Marchal, Kimberley Marten, Michael Nest, Iver Brynild Neumann, Brett O'Bannon, William Reno, Hans Romkema, Ingrid Samset, Ole Jacob Sending, Jack Snyder, Jessica Stanton, Alex Veit, Thierry Vircoulon,

Koen Vlassenroot, and Susan Woodward also took the time to read draft texts and contributed crucial suggestions.

The audiences and participants of the numerous seminars, workshops, panels, conferences, and graduate classes at which I presented my research offered beneficial comments on versions of various chapters. Notably, the extensive feedback I received from policy makers and practitioners who worked in the Congo was invaluable, as it helped validate that I had adequately captured the international peacebuilders' views of their own situations. Anonymous reviewers for *International Organization*, the *African Studies Review*, and the *Review of African Political Economy*, as well as conversations with the editors of these various journals and of *Foreign Affairs* also provided useful guidance on articles that I later incorporated in the book. Finally, thank you to David Prout for compiling the index and to the editorial and production teams at Cambridge University Press – especially Lew Bateman, Eric Crahan, Jason Przybylski, and Joe Marwein at Newgen – for their work in transforming the raw manuscript into a real book.

I began research at New York University; conceptualized the book when in residence at the Yale University Program on Order, Conflict, and Violence; and wrote and finalized the manuscript at Barnard College, Columbia University. The three places provided wonderful intellectual environments in which to pursue this project. I am especially grateful to my Yale, Barnard, and Columbia colleagues and students for their warmth and support. Barnard and Columbia also served as an ideal place to recruit a team of superb research assistants. Sara Arrow, Danielle Boyda, Emily Crossin, Skye Tian Gao, Daniel Greenberg, Eliana Horn, Emma Impick, and Sarah Marion Shore worked tirelessly on the book during the final stretch. They edited the manuscript, ensured that it was accessible to nonspecialists, and rid it of factual errors and English infelicities.

I was fortunate to receive funding from a number of institutions, to which I am forever appreciative. They include New York University; the United States Institute of Peace; the Andrew W. Mellon Foundation (through the Inter-University Consortium on Security and Humanitarian Aid); the Yale University Program on Order, Conflict, and Violence; and Barnard College, Columbia University. I gratefully acknowledge permission to reproduce sections of the articles in which I tested preliminary versions of my argument, notably "Local

Violence, National Peace? Post-War 'Settlement' in the Eastern D.R. Congo (2003–2006)" (*African Studies Review* 49 (3): 1–29, 2006, reproduced with permission of the African Studies Association via Copyright Clearance Center); "Explaining Peace Building Failures: A Study of the Eastern D.R. Congo (2003–2006)" (*Review of African Political Economy* 34 (113): 423–42, 2006, reprinted by permission of Taylor & Francis Group, http://www.informaworld.com); "The Trouble with Congo" (*Foreign Affairs* 87 (3): 94–110, 2008; title used and portions of the article reprinted by permission of FOREIGN AFFAIRS, (87, 3); copyright 2008 by the Council on Foreign Relations, Inc); and "Hobbes and the Congo. Frames, Local Violence, and International Intervention" (*International Organization* 63: 249–80, Cambridge University Press, 2009). I also wish to thank the readers of these journals, as their feedback helped me revise and refine large parts of my analysis in preparation for this book. Of course, any errors in the book are mine alone, and the views I express do not necessarily reflect the views of any of my donors, supporting organizations, colleagues, readers, or interviewees.

Above all, I extend my great appreciation to my friends and family for providing care, humor, and much-welcomed opportunities to remember that there is a life beyond my research and a world beyond the Congo. In particular, my husband Philippe Rosen has been a constant source of support and inspiration, from when the Congo was simply the place of our next humanitarian mission to the scrutiny of this book's proofs nine years later. I thank him deeply for his insightful feedback on countless versions of my argument, for his patience when my fieldwork kept us apart for months, and for his never-faltering belief in me and my project. This book would not have existed without him.

1 | *The Peacebuilding World*

In mid-2007, in a beautiful garden overlooking Lake Kivu, I listened to an old man named Georges recall the turmoil of the mid-1990s in the eastern part of the Democratic Republic of the Congo. Before that time, he and his small circle of friends, all people of European descent but born and raised in the Congo, had been the only white people around, with the exception of the occasional development worker. This situation suddenly changed in the mid-1990s, when the Rwandan genocide sent 2 million refugees pouring into the eastern Congo. Two large-scale wars started in the massacre's wake, the first in 1996 and the second in 1998. Contingents of nongovernmental organization staff members and United Nations (UN) officials arrived, and eventually diplomats followed. The old white Congolese found them all quite amusing. "We called them 'the humanoids,'" Georges said. "It fits them very well, because they are people full of ideals, of vigor ... but they come from another planet. They are completely disoriented." I could not help but think that, in a few sentences, Georges had just encapsulated my six years of research on the international intervention in the Congo. International peacebuilders have their own world, with its own rituals, its own customs, its own beliefs, its own roles, its own stars, its own villains, its own rules, its own taboos, its own meeting places – in brief, its own culture. This peacebuilding culture shaped the intervention strategy in the Congo. And, tragically, as the Congo progressed through a transition from war to peace and democracy (2003 to 2006), the intervention failed.

An interview that I conducted in Nyunzu, a village in the jungle of the eastern province of Katanga, illustrates what this failure meant for the local population. There, I met Isabelle, a woman who had just brought her malnourished toddler to the local nutritional center. A couple of years before, she and other members of her community had fled to the bush to escape the fighting in her village. Local militias soon found her hiding place. "They were coming almost every week," she recalled, "even two to three times a week, to loot our properties, beat us, leave people naked, and make forced love to the women" – "forced love" being the standard euphemism for rape. I asked Isabelle why she did not flee again or try to find a new hiding place, and her answer has remained in my mind ever since. "We were used to it," she said. "We were near our land. We did not want to leave it."

I heard similar stories throughout my interviews with perpetrators and victims of violence. Two themes constantly recurred: the primacy of land and other micro-level issues in causing violence and producing anguish, and the unspeakable horrors perpetrated on the Congolese population. The first theme is crucial. It helps us to understand why violence started, why it became so pervasive, why it continued after the Congo embarked on a transition from war to peace and democracy, and why the efforts of international interveners failed to help the Congo build a sustainable peace.

The second theme should be familiar to anyone who has read or heard about the Congo in the past fifteen years. Scholars and policy makers consider the Congo wars of the 1990s and their aftermath as some of the most complex conflicts of our time. They are also the most terrible. Generating levels of suffering unparalleled in any recent war, they caused, directly and indirectly, the highest death toll of any conflict since World War II. An estimated one thousand civilians die every day, mostly due to malnutrition and diseases that could be easily prevented if the Congo's already weak economic and social structures had not collapsed during the conflict.[1] The wars also traumatized the population of the contested eastern provinces: 81% had to flee their homes, more than half experienced the violent death of family members or friends, more than a third were abducted for at least a week, and 16% were subject to sexual violence, usually repeatedly.[2] The atrocities that armed groups committed against the civilian population were so heinous that the Congo became a symbol of horror, even compared to such places as Darfur and the former Yugoslavia. The wars also involved up to fourteen foreign armies; they destabilized such a large part of the African continent that U.S. Assistant Secretary of State Susan Rice called them the first African World War.

---

[1] International Rescue Committee 2003, 2005, and 2007.
[2] Vinck, Pham, et al. 2008.

In order to understand how the Congo finally emerged from this disastrous and complicated situation, it is crucial to examine the international intervention conducted in support of the peace process. UN officials as well as African and Western diplomats actively supervised negotiations to end the wars. The resulting agreements produced several cease-fires and allowed for the deployment of a small UN peacekeeping force. Eventually, because of heavy international pressure, the warring parties reached a comprehensive peace settlement in 2003.

International involvement grew uncommonly robust during the three and a half years demarcated as the transitional period from war to peace and democracy, from June 2003 to December 2006 – the period on which this book focuses. The UN mission in the Congo became the largest and most expensive peacekeeping operation in the world. The European Union (EU) sent the first ever European-led peacekeeping force. The International Criminal Court chose the Congo as its historic first case, by prosecuting several militia leaders from the northeastern district of Ituri.

During the transition, diplomats and UN officials also exerted an unusually strong influence on Congolese affairs. For the first time in any conflict, the peace agreement created a specific structure, the International Committee in Support of the Transition, to institutionalize the leading role of international actors in its implementation. Foreign donors contributed more than half of the Congolese national budget. They impelled Congolese warlords through the official reunification of the country, the formation of a unified government, the preparation for democratic elections, and the progressive integration of the different armed groups into a single national army. They closely supervised the legislative, constitutional, and electoral processes. They ensured that the candidate they viewed as most able to maintain stability, President Joseph Kabila, was in the best possible position to win the elections. They made certain that troops from neighboring countries officially remained out of Congolese territory. In many places, the UN peacekeeping mission was the only force protecting the population against the remaining armed militias. During these three and a half years, the international influence was so large that numerous Congolese political leaders, international actors, and journalists equated the Congolese situation to a "protectorate."

Thanks to this heavy international pressure, neighboring countries significantly decreased both assistance to, and manipulation of,
Congolese fighters. Many national leaders also progressively switched
from the violent pursuit of power to peaceful, political competition.
As a result, life conditions dramatically improved for most Congolese.
The changes were most striking in the eastern provinces, where the
war previously had the largest impact. Families left the bush, where
they had fled to escape violence, and returned home. They rebuilt
their houses. Whole villages revived. Basic commodities such as salt
and oil became available on the local markets again. In 2006, most
Congolese enthusiastically voted for the first time in their lives to elect
provincial and national representatives. At that time, Congolese and
foreign observers hailed the peace process and the international intervention as major successes.

However, the situation in many parts of the eastern Congo, while
significantly better, continued to remain highly unstable. Throughout
the transition, unremitting clashes between various armed groups and
militias, frequent massacres of civilians, massive population displacements, and appalling human rights violations, including widespread
sexual violence, persisted in the provinces of North Kivu, South Kivu,
North Katanga, and in Oriental Province's Ituri district (see map in
Figure 1). This localized violence carried on during the postelection
period and, just as during the transition, it threatened national and
regional stability. ("Regional" in this book refers to the African Great
Lakes region: Burundi, the Congo, Rwanda, and Uganda.) In 2007
and 2008, a conflict previously confined to a small area of North
Kivu escalated into large-scale fighting, prompting 500,000 to flee
their homes. Only a flurry of diplomatic activity and a forceful inter-
position by UN peacekeepers prevented the Congo from sliding back
into a full-scale national and regional war. At the time of this writing in late 2009, however, the situation has deteriorated further. The
eastern part of the Congo, especially the Kivus and Oriental Province,
remains the theater of constant combat, which regularly threatens to
spread throughout the region. More than 80% of the inhabitants of
these places consider their living conditions to be the same as or worse
than during the wars.[3] The Congo also remains the largest ongoing

---

[3] Ibid., p. 24.

humanitarian crisis in the world. An estimated 2 million Congolese are internally displaced, and more than 360,000 linger as refugees in neighboring countries.[4]

This book is the first scholarly attempt to understand why all of the intense international peacebuilding efforts, including the largest peacekeeping mission in the world, have failed to build a sustainable peace in the Congo.

The Puzzle of Poor Strategies

The international failure to build lasting peace and security in the Congo is not unique. Most recent militarized conflicts have been internal wars, and most of these civil wars ended in negotiated peace agreements. Nonetheless, about 20% still lapsed back into large-scale violence within a few years, usually during the phase of peace agreement implementation. Recent research has shown that significant third-party involvement is critical for peace implementation to be successful, but as in the Congo case, 70% of peace processes benefiting from significant international mediation still fail to build a durable peace.[5] Why do third-party interventions often fail to secure a sustainable peace?

Understanding the reasons for these failures is more than an academic exercise. Former UN Secretary-General Kofi Annan recently emphasized the policy implications, noting that many "countries that emerge from war lapse back into violence after five years." Referring specifically to the failures of peace agreements in Angola, the Congo, Haiti, Liberia, and Rwanda, he stated, "The tragic consequences have been all too evident. ... If peace agreements had been successfully implemented from the start in just two of those war-torn

---

[4] UN Office for the Coordination of Humanitarian Affairs, 2009; and Office of the UN High Commissioner for Refugees, "Country Operations Profile," http://www.unhcr.org/cgi-bin/texis/vtx/page?page=49e45c366, accessed in October 2009.

[5] On internal wars, see Doyle and Sambanis 2006; and Fearon and Laitin 2003. On peace agreements see Woodward 2006; on their frequency see Fortna 2004a; and on their failure see Licklider 1995; Samset and Surke 2007; Walter 2002; and Weinstein 2005. On third-party involvement see Stedman, Rothchild, et al. 2002; and Walter 2002; and on its failures see Doyle and Sambanis 2006.

countries – Angola and Rwanda – [they] could have prevented millions of deaths."[6]

Recent work in international relations and comparative politics suggests a preliminary explanation for these deadly failures. Local agendas – at the level of the individual, the family, the clan, the municipality, the community, the district, or the ethnic group – at least partly drive the continuation of violence during peace agreement implementation. For example, during the late 1990s and early 2000s, after the end of the apartheid regime in South Africa, recurrent power struggles within local political parties motivated high levels of violence in KwaZulu-Natal. Likewise, in Burundi, disputes around access to land, as well as antagonisms within each ethnic group, constantly jeopardized the fragile transition to peace and democracy from 2001 to 2009. In the Maluku Islands in Indonesia, local economic, political, and ethnic agendas constantly impaired the Jakarta government's efforts to end two years of mass intercommunal violence (1999 to 2000). In Kosovo, locally derived motivations, such as occupying neighbors' apartments or seeking revenge for offenses directed at an individual or at the community, caused frequent incidents, severely affecting the peace settlement governing the province since the 1999 intervention of the North Atlantic Treaty Organization. Similarly, during the attempted transition to peace and democracy that started in 2002 in Afghanistan and in 2003 in Iraq, even a casual observer could distinguish local, national, and regional tensions, which interacted to produce violence. In Somalia, clan tensions were – and continue to be – widely acknowledged as the main source of violence, and have contributed to the failure of the numerous peace agreements negotiated since 1991.[7]

---

[6] Reported in Thalif Deen, "UN Chief Warns of Collapsing Peace Agreements," *United Nations Inter Press Service*, July 20, 2005.

[7] On South Africa: Krämer 2006 and 2007. On Burundi: personal communications from Hammache and Rosen; and BBC news report on Burundi by Robert Walker, broadcasted on December 26, 2005 on *BBC World News*. On Indonesia: International Crisis Group 2000a and personal communication from Youcef Hammache, humanitarian aid worker, December 2005. On Kosovo: personal communication from Philippe Rosen, humanitarian aid worker, September 2005; and author's field observations and interviews, 2000. On Afghanistan: author's interviews and field observations during humanitarian mission in Kabul and Hazarajat in 2002; see also Dennys and Zaman 2009 for an excellent analysis of the linkages

In the Congo as well, local antagonisms have spiraled into broader tensions before, during, and after the transition. The tensions between the Congolese of Rwandan descent (Kinyarwanda-speaking) and the so-called indigenous communities of the Kivus provide the clearest example of this dynamic. Threats against the former partly motivated the two Rwandan invasions in the late 1990s. As detailed in chapter 4, these threats were the result of a longstanding competition between the self-styled indigenous communities of the Kivus and the Congolese population with Rwandan ancestry.

After the Belgian colonizers brought people (mostly Hutu) from overpopulated Rwanda to the lightly populated Kivus in the 1930s, antagonisms over land and local social, economic, and political power emerged between a handful of villagers, with the newly arrived immigrants in opposition to the populations indigenous to the area. This grassroots conflict escalated into a national issue after the Congo's independence in 1960, because each camp recruited allies beyond the province and sent representatives to Kinshasa to advance its local agenda. These tensions caused massive violence long before the generalized wars of the 1990s started, with indigenous groups killing thousands of Kinyarwanda-speaking Congolese in North Kivu in 1963, and again in 1993. The 1994 Rwandan genocide and the subsequent arrival of 2 million Rwandan Hutu refugees in the Kivus added a regional dimension to the crisis. The Congolese of Rwandan descent allied with the new Rwandan government, which intervened in Congo to preserve its national security. Indigenous groups organized themselves into militias called Mai Mai, eventually allying with the defeated Rwandan Hutu rebels and the Congolese government. All of the grassroots fighters originally intended merely to protect their kinsfolk, but they quickly started using their military might to abuse their own communities, seize land and mining sites, or capture political power. For much of the 1990s and early 2000s, local tensions in the Kivus repeatedly prompted outbreaks of violence and fed the national and regional conflicts.

between local, provincial, national, and regional conflicts in various Afghan provinces. On Iraq: review of newspaper articles. On Somalia: Farah and Lewis 1997 and review of newspaper articles (among many others, see for example Rakiya Omaar, "Somaliland: One Thorn Bush at a Time," *Current History*, May 1994, pp. 232–236). See also Kalyvas 2003 and 2006; and Sundh 2004 for a general claim.

After the war officially ended in 2003, the same micro-level antagonisms continued to fuel the insurgencies that destabilized the Kivu
provinces. In North Kivu, Mai Mai militias remained allied with
Congolese President Joseph Kabila, as well as Rwandan Hutu militias, and fought Congolese soldiers of Rwandan descent to consol-
idate their claims over land, natural resources, and provincial and
subprovincial positions of authority. The Congolese of Rwandan
descent refused any kind of settlement because they feared revenge
killings and worried that they might lose the local economic and
political power they had acquired during the previous wars. These
conflicts fueled violence against the Kinyarwanda-speaking minority
of the Kivus and sustained the presence of Rwandan Hutu rebels in
Congolese territory, both of which remained the primary obstacles to
national and regional reconciliation from 2003 onward. As became
evident with the 2008 upsurge in violence, these grassroots issues also
had the potential to reignite the national and regional wars.

In general, during the Congolese transition, while foreign peacebuilders succeeded in imposing settlements at both the regional and
national levels, they failed to establish one at the subnational level.
Throughout the eastern Congo, bottom-up rivalries played a decisive
role in sustaining local, national, and regional violence after the conflict officially ended. These agendas pitted villagers, traditional chiefs,
community chiefs, or ethnic leaders against one another over the distribution of land, the exploitation of local mining sites, the appoint-
ment to local administrative and traditional positions of authority,
the collection of local taxes, and the relative social status of specific
groups and individuals. The resulting violence was not coordinated
on a large scale but was rather the product of fragmented, micro-level
militias, each of which tried to advance its own agenda at the level of
the village or district.

Top-down causes also sustained the violence after the generalized
conflict officially ended. Congolese and foreign politicians continued
to manipulate local leaders and militias to enrich themselves, advance
their careers, or rally support for their causes. Thus, national and
regional peacebuilding attempts were critical to deescalate some of
the ongoing conflicts. Accordingly, diplomats and UN officials organized regional dialogues and conferences to ease the tensions between
the Congo and its neighbors. In times of crises, they also put diplomatic pressure on the Rwandan and Ugandan governments to prevent

another invasion. At the national level, international interveners focused on reconstructing a unified and legitimate leadership through elections. They also tried to convince warlords to integrate their soldiers into the national army, supervised the payment of soldiers to prevent the diversion of funds, trained a few integrated brigades, and supported the Congolese authorities in their legislative and constitutional work. All of these actions significantly decreased macro-level tensions and assuaged many top-down causes of local violence.

However, as chapters 4 and 5 demonstrate, because the causes of the ongoing conflict were also distinctively local, they could be properly addressed only by combining action at the grassroots level with the intervention in the higher political spheres. Admittedly, there was tremendous variation among these locally motivated tensions. Certain grassroots conflicts (such as a dispute between two villagers vying for the same piece of land) may have been easier to address than others (such as seizing a gold mine from the hands of a local militia). Likewise, some decentralized antagonisms (such as a competition over local administrative positions) may have been more amenable to top-down interventions than others (such as a rivalry over traditional positions of authority between two clans). However, all of these grassroots conflicts had one point in common: They all required at least some bottom-up conflict-resolution processes in addition to top-down peacebuilding. This point is where the international intervention went awry. Only a few nongovernmental organizations conducted bottom-up peacebuilding in the most divided provinces. Apart from those agencies, there was no attempt to resolve land disputes, to reconstruct grassroots institutions for the peaceful resolution of conflict, or to promote reconciliation within divided villages or communities, even though international and Congolese actors could easily have done so with the resources at hand.

The Congo case is representative of a broader problem with international interventions. International peacebuilders often neglect to address the local causes of violence. As of this writing, none of the UN peacekeeping missions around the world have implemented any comprehensive grassroots conflict-resolution program.[8] No more than a handful of diplomats have tried, without success, to advocate for a

---

[8] Personal communications from UN officials, 2005 and 2008.

better approach to local issues by diplomatic groups. Even nongovernmental organizations tend to focus on regional and national sources
of tensions, with only a few exceptions. Why do interveners neglect
the micro-level causes of peace process failure, particularly when they
threaten the macro-level settlements?

The neglect of local conflicts is even more perplexing in the case of
the Congo, because we cannot attribute it to callousness, powerlessness, or inanity on the part of the foreign interveners. Admittedly, not
all of the international actors present in the Congo were concerned
about the well-being of the Congolese population. A great variety of
countries and corporations took interest in the Congo primarily for its
extraordinary mineral wealth and central strategic position in Africa.
However, these actors were in the minority. Most foreign interveners genuinely tried to end organized violence in the Congo. Far from
being callous, they usually were well-meaning individuals, who had
often devoted their lives to combating injustice, violence, and poverty. The unceasing human rights violations deeply troubled them. Far
from being intellectually limited, they were, on average, intelligent,
well-read, and well-educated people who could have understood the
importance of local conflicts. Far from being powerless, they held tremendous influence during the transition, as explained earlier. Similarly,
far from being financially limited, they spent significant resources on
the Congo (including more than a billion dollars a year on the peacekeeping mission and $670 million to organize elections). Part of these
resources could have been devoted to local conflict resolution.

This book focuses on these "international peacebuilders," meaning
the many foreign interveners (persons, countries, or organizations)
who strived to build peace in the Congo. It looks at diplomats (in
embassies, as well as in the headquarters of their respective ministries
of foreign affairs), other government officials (such as defense officers), staff of international organizations, and staff of nongovernmental organizations, all of whom shared a goal to supervise or support
the Congo in its peacebuilding efforts. Why did almost all of them
ignore the critical micro-level causes of violence?

Main Argument

I argue that a dominant international peacebuilding culture shaped
the intervention in the Congo in a way that precluded action on local

violence, ultimately dooming the international efforts. Western and African diplomats, UN peacekeepers, and the staff of nongovernmental organizations involved in conflict resolution share a set of ideologies, rules, rituals, assumptions, definitions, paradigms, and standard operating procedures. In the Congo, this culture established the parameters of acceptable action. It shaped what international actors considered at all (usually excluding continued local conflict), what they viewed as possible (excluding local conflict resolution), and what they thought was the "natural" course of action in a given situation (national and international action, in particular the organization of elections).[9] It authorized and justified specific practices and policies while excluding others, notably grassroots peacebuilding. In sum, this culture made it possible for foreign interveners to ignore the micro-level tensions that often jeopardize macro-level settlements.

The book illuminates how this peacebuilding culture operated on the ground. This culture influenced the interveners' understanding of the causes of violence. Because of earlier socialization and training processes, UN officials, diplomats, and the staff of most nongovernmental organizations interpreted continued fighting and massacres as the consequence of national and regional tensions. They viewed local conflicts as the result of insufficient state authority and of the Congolese people's inherent propensity to violence. The dominant peacebuilding culture also shaped the international actors' understanding of their role and of the paths toward peace. It constructed intervention at the national and regional levels as the only "natural" and "legitimate" task for UN staffers and diplomats. It privileged the organization of elections as the favored peace- and state-building mechanism over more effective approaches. It made diplomats and UN staff members view local conflict resolution as an unimportant, unfamiliar, and unmanageable task. The idea of becoming involved at the local level clashed so fundamentally with existing cultural norms, and so threatened key organizational interests, that neither external shocks nor resistance from certain staff members and human rights activists could convince international actors that they should reevaluate their understanding of violence and intervention.

Ultimately, this peacebuilding culture enabled foreign actors to pursue an intervention strategy that permitted, and at times even

---

[9] This sentence is a paraphrase of Neumann 2008a, p. 2.

exacerbated, fighting, massacres, and massive human rights violations during and after the transition. And it made it possible for these
actors to view their intervention as a success until war resumed in
late 2008.

Without this shared culture, the interveners' vested interests and
the existing constraints on international action would have led to a
different outcome. International actors might have located the causes
of the continuing violence at the local level. They might have contem-
plated intervention in local conflicts; they might even have considered
it one of the priorities for the Congolese transition.

It is clear that international peacebuilders are not the only, or even
the main, figures responsible for the failure of the Congolese peace
process. Certain Congolese actors at all levels; certain Rwandan,
Ugandan, and Burundian leaders; and the individuals and companies involved in arms trafficking and illegal exploitation of Congolese
resources together deserve the largest share of the blame. However,
the international peacebuilders missed an excellent opportunity to
help build peace and democracy. They enjoyed unprecedented influence on Congolese affairs during the transition because they financed
more than half the Congolese budget and controlled the only effective
military force in the country (the UN peacekeeping mission). They
also maintained great sway due to the Transitional Government's
lack of legitimacy and because the peace agreements gave them the
right to supervise the transitional process (as institutionalized by the
International Committee in Support of the Transition). By all accounts,
this influence sharply decreased with President Joseph Kabila's election and inauguration in late 2006. The three and a half years of the
transition provided a window of opportunity; this book focuses on
this specific period, referring to events that took place before June
2003 and after December 2006 only when they help explain why foreign interveners failed to seize this chance.

To develop this analysis, I build on a wealth of original data.
Between 2001 and 2007, I carried out ethnography in various parts
of the Congo. I spent fifteen months in the most violent provinces
and two months in the Congolese capital of Kinshasa. There, and in
France, Belgium, and the United States, I conducted more than 330
interviews with international peacebuilders and Congolese stakeholders. I also analyzed numerous documents, including policy papers,
agency memos, confidential reports, and news articles.

There are a number of ways to read this book. For the reader involved in conflict resolution, this book offers a new explanation for the failures of third-party interventions in civil wars: Foreign interveners neglect micro-level tensions. For the reader concerned with international relations, this book improves the theoretical understanding of international action: It identifies a dominant peacebuilding culture that shapes the interveners' views of violence, peace, and intervention, and it shows how this culture operates on the ground. For the reader interested in African studies, comparative politics, or anthropology, this book presents an in-depth study of violence in the Congo. For the reader looking for historical material, this book provides primary data that are unavailable elsewhere; I was virtually the sole academic researcher examining the international intervention who actually spent time in the unstable eastern Congo during the transition. Finally, for policy makers and practitioners, this book suggests tools and ideas with which to improve their peacekeeping and peacebuilding efforts.

There are also two ways not to read this book. First, this book is not a criticism of the UN Mission in the Congo (the Mission de l'Organisation des Nations Unies au Congo, or MONUC). The "international peacebuilders" that this book studies include not only UN peacekeepers but also other UN actors, as well as diplomats from various countries and international organizations, and many nongovernmental agencies' staff members. Reducing the analysis to a mere criticism of MONUC would thus miss one of the book's central arguments – the fact that the peacebuilding culture, as well as the understandings and actions it shapes, are spread across a variety of interveners. Additionally, as the first pages of this chapter detail and as the conclusion to the book further emphasizes, the top-down international efforts did achieve many noteworthy results. They contributed to reestablishing peace in a large part of the Congo, and they helped the Congo progress on the way to democracy. As of this writing, MONUC's presence is one of the main reasons why the Congo has not (perhaps yet) slid back into a full-scale national and regional war. The Congolese population would suffer tremendously more if it did not benefit from the peacebuilding, development, and humanitarian aid delivered by various international actors. The policy implications of this book are therefore not that donors should stop financing aid programs in the Congo and in other conflict situations because the international intervention during the Congolese transition was a resounding failure. Rather, the goal of this book is to help policy makers further boost the positive aspects of international peacebuilding interventions, in particular by including bottom-up conflict-resolution programs in their initiatives.

Second, the book does not argue that international interveners should have adopted a bottom-up approach to peacebuilding instead of their top-down strategy. Rather, it demonstrates that international actors should have used a bottom-up approach *in addition to* their top-down strategy. Just as a purely top-down intervention leads to unsustainable peace, as the following chapters show, an exclusively bottom-up strategy would only produce a very fragile and temporary settlement. Top-down explanations for violence are indeed valid and, during the Congolese transition, they were well supported by events on the ground. Top-down interventions also helped assuage some of the sources of violence on the ground. This book insists mostly on the grassroots causes of violence, because policy and scholarly writings have so far ignored them and because, like any theoretical explanation, it needs to minimize the complexity to produce a readable argument. However, this emphasis on micro-level tensions, and on the absolute need for bottom-up peacebuilding, should not be misunderstood as a dismissal of top-down causes of peace and violence.

Understanding Peacebuilding Failures

Conventional Explanations

There is a large body of literature on peace processes and, since the mid-1990s, various authors have started to analyze the implementation phase after the signing of a peace agreement. They have contributed significantly to our theoretical understanding of what determines international involvement at the stage of peace implementation, whether it makes a difference, and which types of intervention work and which do not.[10] However, these accounts often reduce the study of the "international involvement" to that of peacekeeping missions. They thus

[10] See especially Doyle and Sambanis 2006; Fortna 2004b and 2008; Gilligan and Stedman 2003; Howard 2008; Ottaway 2003; Paris 2004; Regan 2002; Stedman, Rothchild, et al. 2002; Walter 2002; and Zartman 1989.

overlook the influence of other forms of international intervention, such as that emanating from diplomatic, economic, and humanitarian actors.[11] Additionally, they usually develop large-scale statistical analyses that afford little sense to how peacebuilding actually operates in the field.[12] Finally, the focus is on macro-level variables, such as the level of violence in the target country, the interests of major powers, or the presence of national capacity for peace, ignoring the micro-level elements.[13] When looking at cases of civil war resumption, except for a few passing mentions, virtually no existing research on international interventions studies the importance of the local preconditions for peace settlements.[14] As a result, we do not know how international actors approach the micro-level dynamics of violence.

Overall, most existing studies suggest two explanations for peacebuilding failures. First, international peacebuilders may do their best to establish peace, but economic, political, legal, security, or contextual constraints may impair an adequate treatment of the problems at the root of the war.[15] These constraints can include the presence of high levels of hostility and low capacity for peace, a significant likelihood of spoilers (parties using violence expressly to undermine peace), the existence of hostile neighboring states or networks, a large number of warring parties and soldiers, demands for secession, the availability of disposable natural resources, a collapsed state, the lack of a peace agreement before intervention, or the presence of a coerced peace agreement. Other constraints could include the interveners' lack of credibility, the lack of financial and human resources for peacebuilding, ambiguous or confused mandates, an imperative to respect the host state's sovereignty, excessive bureaucracy, lack of sufficient advanced planning, very slow deployment, and an insufficient command and control structure.

[11] For example, Doyle, Johnstone, et al. 1997; Fortna 2008; Howard 2008; many of the contributors to Stedman, Rothchild, et al. 2002; and Walter 2002.

[12] For example, Doyle and Sambanis 2006; and Fortna 2008.

[13] For example, Doyle and Sambanis 2006; and Stedman, Rothchild, et al. 2002.

[14] Notable exceptions are Fetherston and Nordstrom 1995; and Lederach 1997. Lemarchand 1995; Power 2002; Richards 1996; Stedman 1997; and Wood 2000 also briefly mention such preconditions.

[15] Downs and Stedman 2002; Doyle, Johnstone, et al. 1997; Doyle and Sambanis 2000 and 2006; Kim and Metrikas 1997; Marchal and Messiant 2002; Stedman 2002; Touval and Zartman 1985; Zartman 1989; and Zartman and Rasmussen 1997. The definition of spoilers comes from Stedman 1997, p. 1.

A second reason most existing studies give for peacebuilding failures is that vested economic, political, security, or institutional interests may lead some peacebuilders to consciously encourage or ignore peace agreement violations. Major and regional powers with little or no national interest in the peace settlement will devote few or no financial, diplomatic, and military resources to peace implementation, thus failing to see the settlement through to a successful conclusion.[16] The limited and specific interests of intervening parties will also determine the level of priority that peacebuilders give to certain tasks.[17] In particular, policy makers may respond to political or economic imperatives linked to international political disputes or to the domestic situation of their respective countries rather than to developments in the peace process at stake, thus adopting inappropriate peacebuilding strategies. In rarer cases, interveners who are officially present to support the peace process may in fact have a stake in the victory of a specific warring party. To aid this party, they can directly fuel the fighting or support groups who use violence to undermine peace.[18] Finally, international peacebuilders may have a vested interest in the persistence of instability to justify their continued involvement.[19]

These explanations based on constraints and interests help account for the level and effectiveness of international involvement. However, they provide us with little theoretical understanding of whether, how, or why the existing constraints and interests lead international actors to prioritize certain peacebuilding strategies, such as the organization of elections, over others, such as local conflict resolution. To answer these questions, we need a new way to look at international interventions. In Georges' words, we need to reconstruct the world from which the "humanoids" come.

The Inadequacy of Conventional Explanations

The application of these explanations based on constraints and interests to the Congolese case perfectly illustrates both their explanatory

[16] Downs and Stedman 2002; Doyle and Sambanis 2006; Ottaway 2002; and Zartman and Touval 1996.
[17] Boulden 2001; Durch 1996; Hillen 2000; Jett 2000; and Malone 1998; as analyzed in Paris 2003, p. 442.
[18] Alao, Mackinlay, et al. 1999; and Stedman 1997, p. 51.
[19] De Waal 1997; and Rajasingham 2003.

power and their shortcomings.[20] The most popular explanation for the lack of international involvement in local conflict resolution among Congolese civilians and a handful of non-Congolese activists emphasizes Western actors' stake in the continuation of violence.[21] Western countries failed to support bottom-up peacebuilding projects because it would have counteracted their assumed war-making efforts. Indeed, in this analysis, international interveners fueled local tensions to illegally exploit the Congo's natural resources, preserve the Francophone influence in Africa or promote an Anglophone one, or maintain opportunities for sale of arms.

Popular as it may be, this explanation is deeply flawed. Admittedly, during the war, various Western actors actively aided the exploitation of the Congolese mineral resources, and therefore contributed to the violence associated with it.[22] However, no scholarly or reliable policy paper corroborates this explanation for the time of the transition. Scholars and established policy analysts rather refute it, and the data lend it very little support.[23] Six years of research and requests for supporting evidence turned up almost nothing, confirming that this hypothesis is based on a large body of unsupported accusations and only a few that are supported. The best documented charge is that, in 2005 and 2006, a handful of UN Indian and Pakistani peacekeepers struck alliances with local militias to enrich themselves through arms and resource trafficking. Some Western and African multinationals

[20] This section synthesizes all of the explanations for the lack of international action on local violence proposed by Congolese and international interviewees, developed in policy and academic writing on the Congo (in particular, Braeckman 2003; Nbanda Nzambo 2004; and Staibano 2005), raised by this book's anonymous reviewers, and suggested by academics and practitioners during the conferences and seminars in which I presented my research. The title of this section is a paraphrase of Carpenter 2003, p. 7.

[21] For public sources, see, for example, "High-Tech Genocide in Congo," *Projectcensored,* 2007 (http://www.projectcensored.org/top-stories/articles/5-high-tech-genocide-in-congo, accessed in October 2009); and "Behind the Numbers: Untold Suffering in the Congo," *ZNet,* March 1, 2006 (http://globalpolicy.igc.org/security/issues/congo/2006/0301numbers.htm, accessed in 2006).

[22] See among many others Braeckman 2003; and Lemarchand 2008, p. 5.

[23] See, for example, Boas 2008. The UN panel of experts on arm trafficking in the Congo (UN Security Council 2004b, 2005c, and 2006a) and the vast literature on the illegal exploitation of Congolese resources identify Congolese and regional actors as those fueling violence and only extremely rarely mention individuals from countries and organizations that this book labels as international peacebuilders.

such as Anvil Mining and AngloGold Ashanti were also suspected
of funding Congolese militias to secure mineral rights, and arm deal-
ers like Viktor Bout played an active role in the illegal sale of arms
to Congolese groups.[24] These, however, are only isolated cases, and
hardly suffice to support the widespread accusation that international
actors, alongside their peacebuilding efforts, also purposely fueled
local conflicts.

Outside of Congolese circles, the most frequently suggested explanation for the international neglect of local violence emphasizes that
none of the major powers had a key national interest in the Congo.
This lack of major power interest accounted for the presence of material constraints on the international intervention. These constraints
severely limited any potential action on the ground. They especially prevented international peacebuilders from addressing all of
the dimensions of the conflict and from devising new, more ambitious peacebuilding strategies. In line with this explanation, when
asked during interviews why they did not address local violence,
international interveners usually mentioned their lack of human
and financial resources, as well as the organizational, security, and
logistical hurdles they faced in their daily work. They repeatedly
emphasized that the peacekeeping operation was clearly too small to
cover the immense Congolese territory or even the unstable eastern
provinces.

This analysis is certainly correct. However, no matter how inadequate, some significant financial and human resources existed, and
part of these resources could have been devoted to local peacebuilding.
This money could have provided much-needed funding for Congolese
and international nongovernmental organizations to implement
local reconciliation projects, such as building a market, a school, or
a health center, that would reestablish social and commercial links
between two communities in conflict. These organizations could
also have helped reconstruct social mechanisms, such as local justice
institutions, for the peaceful resolution of conflict. Moreover, in each
observation site, the UN peacekeeping mission could have deployed,
alongside the military, a civilian staff member tasked with monitoring
grassroots tensions and providing suggestions for resolution. He or

---

[24] Reviews of news items, 2003–2008, as well as UN Panel of Inquiry 2002a
and 2002b; and UN Security Council 2004b, 2005c, and 2006a.

she should have had the authority to draw on existing military, diplomatic, or development resources to promote local peace.

Thus, we need to understand why international actors interpreted the lack of material and financial resources as a constraint on local peacebuilding. This book shows that it was due to the presence of a dominant international peacebuilding culture. The primary alternative answer is that international actors purposely chose to ignore local conflicts. Six distinct motivations, which draw on neorealist, neoliberal, and organizational theory, could explain why they would do so. I examine each in turn to demonstrate their shortcomings.

The first potential motivation for the international neglect of local conflicts is that foreign peacebuilders were indifferent to ending collective violence in the Congo. This explanation does not hold. It is true that no major powers had any significant national interest in the Congo, but the size and the budget of the UN peacekeeping mission underlined the presence of at least some humanitarian and geostrategic interests on the part of the UN Security Council's member states. A comparison with the 1994 UN intervention in Rwanda is illuminating. At that time, the UN leadership and the Security Council members used violence on the ground as a justification for withdrawing the peacekeeping mission. If foreign interveners had been similarly uninterested in ending collective violence in the Congo, they would have acknowledged the ongoing violence instead of ignoring it. This acknowledgment would have justified withdrawing the costly UN mission from a country in which it could never fulfill its mandated task of keeping the peace, precisely because the presence of local violence would have meant that there was no peace to keep.

In fact, chapter 6 shows that, far from being uninterested in ending organized violence, most international interveners had security, economic, and diplomatic stakes in ensuring that the instability in the Congo did not spill over its borders and contaminate its neighbors. They therefore had to contain any tension that threatened to engulf the region. Furthermore, the UN had a major organizational interest in fully pacifying the Congo. If it wanted to preserve its credibility in peacekeeping issues, it could not afford to let the Congo collapse on its watch and have its largest and most expensive mission be considered a fiasco. Most important, after the temporary deployment of European peacekeeping mission Operation Artemis to end massive violence in the Ituri district in mid-2003, Ituri and the broader Congo were perceived as a test of the UN capacity to conduct an offensive peacekeeping action by itself – and not with the support or under the direction of a specific country, as had always occurred in the past. Many UN and non-UN interviewees claimed that a MONUC failure would have negative consequences on all UN peacekeeping missions in the world.[25] As a result, the UN and the states in favor of UN peace operations had to prevent the resumption of large-scale violence, which would suggest that the world organization had failed its test.

The second potential motivation for international neglect is that the permanent members of the Security Council, which mandate the peacekeeping missions, have no interest in involving the UN missions in the messiness of local conflict. Under this assumption, the Secretary-General constrains his staff from getting tied up in local strife. The data do not support this explanation. The only mention of local conflict resolution in official UN and diplomatic documents on the Congo is in a couple of 2002 and 2003 reports of the Secretary-General on MONUC. Here, Kofi Annan officially endorsed a short-lived local peacebuilding initiative promoted by the then Deputy Special Representative for the Congo.[26] Otherwise, the issue was never on the agenda in high-level meetings, either to support or to proscribe it. During interviews, diplomats and UN officials based outside of the Congo presented local conflict resolution as an insignificant issue that had to be dealt with only in the field.

The third potential motivation is that international actors considered local conflict resolution to be an internal Congolese affair and consequently within the exclusive competence of the sovereign Congolese state. This explanation raises more questions than it answers. UN staff and diplomats overlooked Congolese sovereignty whenever they deemed it necessary to the success of the transition. For example, they closely supervised the writing of the new constitution, a matter of national sovereignty above all else. Thus, we need to understand why

---

[25] For public sources, see Refugee International 2008; "Breaching the Peace," *Africa Confidential*, June 27, 2003; Dominic Johnson, "Overburdened soldiers," *D+C*, March 2006; and Anneke Van Woudenberg, Human Rights Watch Representative, interviewed in "Can the U.N. Keep the Peace?," *PBS*, broadcasted on May 15, 2009 (transcript available at http://www.pbs.org/now/shows/520/transcript.html, accessed December 2009).

[26] See, in particular, UN Security Council 2003c. See also chapter 5 for further details.

foreign peacebuilders interpreted sovereignty as a constraint in the case of local peacebuilding and not in the case of writing the constitution. This book shows that it is because the dominant international peacebuilding culture constructed local conflict as significantly less important than national or international issues.

The fourth potential motivation for the purposeful nonengagement in local peacebuilding is that international actors pursued only specific and limited goals in the Congo, which elections could entirely achieve. Elections serve as symbolic endpoints for international interventions. They provide diplomats, international financial institutions, and bilateral donors with the partners they need, in other words, "'normal,' internationally recognized government[s]" able and willing to implement international norms and obligations.[27] In the Congo, elections also ended an ineffective transitional arrangement. This analysis is correct, but it helps explain the strategies of only some of the international actors, such as China and Russia. The most active states in the Congo during the transition (Belgium, France, South Africa, the United States, and the United Kingdom) needed to build not only an internationally recognized government but also a lasting peace, to enhance their business opportunities and protect their allied governments in the region. Similarly, as mentioned previously, because the Congo was a test case for UN peacekeeping, UN staff members knew and often emphasized that fully stabilizing the country was of the utmost importance to their organization.

A fifth and related potential motivation is that the standard operating procedures of the UN Department of Peacekeeping Operations led to reasonable successes without involving the peacekeeping missions in local tensions.[28] However, we still need to understand how "success" could be defined in a way that accommodated the continuation of violent local conflicts in parts of the country.

The last potential motivation for intentional disregard is that UN and foreign diplomatic teams had a strong organizational interest in downplaying the importance of local conflict. They needed to maintain their credibility by concealing potential evidence of failure. They wanted to avoid being drawn into a situation that could become a quagmire such as Somalia. They also believed that acknowledging

---

[27] Lyons 2004, p. 37; see also Woodward 2006.
[28] This explanation builds on Doyle and Sambanis 2006.

local violence would provide a pretext for belligerent parties to walk away from and cause a collapse of the peace process. These motivations were real, but we still need to understand why Belgian, British, French, South African, UN, and U.S. officials clung to elections when faced with overwhelming proof that this strategy was failing to end organized violence and thus jeopardizing their national and organizational interests. We also need to understand why human rights and humanitarian activists so rarely contested the focus on elections as the measure for success. This book shows that all the processes detailed in this paragraph could happen only because of the presence of a dominant peacebuilding culture. This shared culture made staff working in very different institutional spaces share an understanding of elections (as a workable and legitimate peace- and state-building strategy), of local violence (as normal), and of the persistence of localized fighting (as unrelated to the success of the transition).

Scholars familiar with the international intervention in the Congo sometimes raise what they believe to be an alternative explanation, based on organizational constraints, for the international neglect of local tensions. They emphasize that foreign and national interveners have no choice but to generalize and simplify: Interveners cannot know dozens of different local situations in depth and they have at their disposal only policies framed in general terms. This organizational issue is clearly significant and, in fact, it plays a large role in the analysis developed in this book. However, acknowledging the weight of the organizational constraint is only part of the analytical process. Instead of taking this constraint as a given, we need to study the process through which it has been constructed. Chapter 3 presents the cultural understandings that shape the international actors' views of their roles as "naturally" focused on the macro level, therefore requiring them to design and implement general policies and templates. Chapter 5 challenges this construct by showing that it would actually be possible for foreign interveners to address the myriads of local situations, as long as they worked primarily in support of Congolese grassroots actors. This chapter, then, explains the persistence of the organizational constraint and roots it in cultural issues. Overall, the book shows that explanations based on organizational constraints and cultural influence are not separate; instead, various cultural elements explain why the organizational constraint was constituted, why it persisted, and why it could hinder international action at the local level.

In sum, material constraints, lack of national interest, and organizational constraints and interests did play roles in preventing international action on local conflict. However, the following chapters demonstrate that these constraints and interests were not given, preexisting, and objective. They were rather constituted by the dominant international peacebuilding culture. This culture shaped the international understanding of violence and intervention in such a way that international actors interpreted their lack of material capabilities as obstacles to grassroots peacebuilding and viewed their national and organizational interests as compatible with continued local conflict.

Understanding How Culture Shapes Action on the Ground

For the scholarly reader, a focus on culture has the potential to answer questions and solve puzzles that other academic approaches cannot address. For this reader, and for policy makers and practitioners, the focus on culture has an added benefit: It helps us question and problematize elements that are usually taken for granted (such as that a diplomat should not work at the local level). To do this, a few theoretical remarks are necessary to explain how a dominant peacebuilding culture can shape international action on the ground. The broad process I detail in this book is that the dominant culture shapes the international understanding of the causes of violence and of the interveners' role, thus allowing for certain actions while precluding others.[29]

A culture is a social object. It is not only inside individual heads (the focus of psychological approaches), but also embedded in social routines, practices, discourses, technologies, and institutions.[30] A culture is composed of an interconnected set of collective, intersubjective

---

[29] This analysis builds on Finnemore 1996b and was largely inspired by Ferguson 1990 and Mitchell 2002. In addition to the works cited in the subsequent footnotes, Kuper 1999 provides a very helpful overview of the use of the concept of culture in anthropology, and Lapid and Kratochwil 1996 and Walker 1984 do so for international relations. See Autesserre 2009 for a preliminary version of this section.

[30] Adler 1997, p. 327.

understandings. These understandings can consist of ideologies (such as liberalism), rules (for example, international organizations should respect the sovereignty of the countries in which they intervene), rituals (national and regional conferences), "assumptions and definitions taken as given" (Congolese are inherently violent), and paradigms (the liberal peace). Paradigms often include standard operating procedures (organization of elections) and "shared definitions of the environment" (the Congo is a postconflict situation).[31]

The concept of culture does not refer only to ideas. Collective understandings frame people's interpretations of behaviors. These interpretations generate habitual actions, usually referred to as "practices." A combination of language and techniques, usually called "discourses," maintain these understandings.[32] These techniques include both ideational and physical elements. Consider the example of organizing elections. Chapter 3 shows that the liberal peace paradigm generated both an intellectual and a material toolkit with which to organize elections.[33] This paradigm spurred the development of a large body of expertise in electoral democracy building. It led to the creation of agencies and departments for electoral assistance in many international organizations and in most foreign ministries. These intellectual and physical elements constantly reinforced and co-constituted one another: The expertise informed the work of the various organizations, which in turn developed data and theory to enrich the electoral expertise. Similarly, this book shows that all of the cultural elements that influenced the peacebuilding intervention in the Congo were both intellectual and physical devices.

Cultures are not biologically given; they are socially constructed over long periods of time.[34] Anthropologists, sociologists, and political scientists have written countless books and articles on the sources of various cultures. Two findings are especially relevant for this book. To start, collective understandings can either precede action or emerge from practice.[35] This book shows that, during the Congolese transition, the dominant international peacebuilding culture was mostly an instance of the former, except for one of its central elements: the

---

[31] Weick 1995, chapter 5. Quotations from pp. 113 and 118.
[32] This is a paraphrase of Klotz and Lynch 2007.
[33] See also Swidler 1986 on the idea of culture as a toolkit.
[34] Berger and Luckmann 1967.
[35] See Weick 1995 for an overview of the sociological literature on the topic.

labeling of the Congo as a postconflict environment. Although the "postconflict" label per se, as well as the strategies it authorized, existed before the transition, it was only applied to the Congo beginning in late 2002. Through repeated interactions, UN officials and diplomats based in Kinshasa and foreign capitals constituted this shared description of the Congo as no longer at war; it had entered a "postconflict phase." Then, during the first few months of the transition, extensive communication between these actors and those deployed in the violent provinces helped to spread the label to all members of the peacebuilding field. Once applied, this label allowed for the adoption of a new set of strategies that were not necessarily appropriate for the situation on the ground. By contrast, other elements of the peacebuilding culture existed before the international intervention in the Congo. Before the transition started, a combination of training and socialization processes had already helped to spread, reproduce, and reify them.

A second debate relevant to this book is that the few authors working on the influence of discourse on peacekeeping strategies locate the sources of the dominant collective understandings at different levels. Barnett and Finnemore root them inside international bureaucracies.[36] This book similarly identifies a powerful organizational element in the peacebuilding culture: the UN and embassy staffs' understanding of their role as exclusively concerned with national and regional peace settlements. However, Barnett and Finnemore's organizational approach would expect different organizations to behave differently. It cannot explain why different actors with very distinct identities, internal cultures, and interests show puzzling behavioral similarities.[37] (Realism and liberalism, the standard approaches to international relations, similarly fail at explaining behavioral similarities for disparate actors or actors with dissimilar interests.[38])

Therefore, I also locate the sources of the dominant peacebuilding culture beyond the organization, at the levels of the world polity and the field. Following Paris and the world polity school of sociology, I argue that, for analytical purposes, we can "treat the entire world as a single society" and identify a "distinct global culture" dominant on

---

[36] Barnett 2002; and Barnett and Finnemore 2004.
[37] This criticism builds on Finnemore 1996b.   [38] Ibid, pp. 334–337.

the international scene.[39] This world polity culture "comprises the formal and informal rules of international social life," which defines "whom the principal actors in world politics should be, how these actors should organize themselves internally, and how they should behave." In the early twenty-first century, the global culture included two elements that significantly influenced the international intervention in the Congo: a veneration of elections and an understanding of violence as intrinsic to the Congo.

I also identify an intermediary level between that of the individual organization and that of the world polity: the level of the field. Following Dimaggio and Powell, I define a field as an increasingly structured set of organizations that "in the aggregate constitute a recognized area of institutional life."[40] More specifically, a field is a "semi-autonomous ... sphere of action," which is "governed by largely implicit 'rules' or 'principles of action.'" These rules and principles produce "a certain homogeneity" within the field and give it significant coherence.[41] I propose that, in the early twenty-first century, embassies based in conflict areas, parts of international organizations such as the UN and the World Bank, and nongovernmental agencies such as the International Crisis Group all belong to the same field: that of peacebuilding. Building on Bourdieu, I also show in chapter 5 that this field is structured in terms of power relationships, with dominant actors (in particular, high-ranking diplomats and UN managers), less influential ones (especially nongovernmental organizations), and actors excluded from access to the discursive space (in the case of the Congo, the inhabitants of its violent provinces).[42]

In this book, I demonstrate that cultural and normative understandings shared by the members of the peacebuilding field (such as the "postconflict" label and the perception of local conflict resolution as an unimportant task) and of the world polity (such as the understanding of extensive violence as normal for the Congo) explain why actors as different as the UN, the United States, South Africa, and many nongovernmental agencies could adopt the same understanding of the situation and similar intervention strategies. Collective

---

[39] Paris 2003, p. 442. See also Finnemore 1996b; and Richmond 2002 and 2005.
[40] DiMaggio and Powell 1983, p. 148.
[41] Benson 2006, p. 188; and Bigo 2006, p. 22.   [42] Bourdieu 1979.

understandings coming from the culture external to these organizations were translated into specific routines, rules, and procedures in different institutional spaces.

It is important to acknowledge that this peacebuilding culture was not spread across all international interveners to the same extent. Many organizations and subunits had different subcultures and distinct priorities, and some individuals or agencies actually contested various elements of the peacebuilding culture. The collective understandings that I study were thus not the only existing ones. They were the dominant ones, however, and they were dominant not only within each international organization and diplomatic mission but also across them. As a result, despite organizational differences and despite internal contestation, most of the staff located in various organizations or subunits showed a remarkable uniformity of views on two topics: the causes of violence and the appropriate strategies to end it.

For added clarity, Table 1 summarizes the sources of the peacebuilding culture that are central to the argument of this book. It shows whether these elements were – or became – part of a culture that was located inside or outside of organizations. In the latter case, the table indicates whether the culture was truly global (at the level of the world polity) or restricted to the peacebuilding field. In all cases, I distinguish whether these elements preceded the international intervention in the Congo or emerged from practice during the time of the Congolese transition.

Identifying the sources of the various collective understandings is important for better analyzing the culture studied and problematizing it, but it is only one of the many steps necessary to explain how culture shapes international action. Analyzing this process in the case of international interventions in conflict zones is especially critical because, despite a growing body of research on this topic, we still lack detailed ethnographic analysis explaining how culture operates on the ground to influence peacekeeping or peacebuilding practices. Paris leaves this topic open as an area for further research.[43] Richmond concentrates on the influence of various theoretical and ideological paradigms on peacekeeping and peacebuilding strategies in general, at a macro level.[44] Barnett focuses on elites at the UN and,

---

[43] Paris 2003.   [44] Richmond 2002, 2005, and 2008.

Table 1. *Sources of the Dominant Peacebuilding Culture's Elements*

		Preceded intervention	*Emerged from practice*
Sources external to the peacebuilding organizations	*World polity*	Violence innate to Congo Veneration of elections	
	Peacebuilding field	Top-down understanding of violence Postconflict label Strategies appropriate for postconflict environments Appropriate actors for local peacebuilding Local peacebuilding as unimportant and unmanageable task	Labeling of the Congo as a postconflict environment
Peacebuilding organizations' internal cultures		Focus on national and regional realms	

by extension, on the representatives of the few countries present in the Security Council.[45] Anthropologists have studied the influence of culture on intervention practices in the field, but they overwhelmingly focus on only one group of peacebuilders, namely, military actors. They thus often overlook the multiplicity of international interveners present on the ground.[46]

These studies provide us with fascinating insights, but explaining how culture influences action in the field also requires a consideration of all of the peacebuilders involved in a postwar setting, including the staff of various international and nongovernmental organizations, diplomats of Security Council and non-Security Council countries, and top policy makers based in headquarters as well as embassy secretaries and peacekeepers deployed in the field.

---

[45] Barnett 2002.
[46] See, among others, Avruch 2004; Duffey 2000; Fetherston and Nordstorm 1995; and Rubinstein 2008.

To explain how culture operates on the ground, I build on previous research on culture, norms, and frames. I show that people draw on collective understandings to construct roles and interpret objects.[47] In more accessible terms, culture shapes how people understand the world and, based on this understanding, what they perceive to be the appropriate action.[48]

One of the most enlightening insights in the extensive literature on culture and related concepts is that problems are not given; they have to be constructed.[49] Cultural norms shape peoples' views on what counts as a problem and what does not. For example, the understanding of significant violence as normal for a peaceful Congo prevented international actors from constructing continued fighting in the eastern provinces as a problem. Culture also affects which events will be noticed and which will not, as well as how they will be interpreted.[50] For instance, because diplomats believe that they should focus on the national and international realms, they found (or privileged) information confirming that the sources of violence lay at these macro levels.

That cultures organize knowledge in part through categories is another insight. These categories are often arbitrary and dichotomous, such as man/woman, war/peace, or barbarian/civilized. These distinctions shape how people interpret and understand objects or processes and how they act toward or within them. For example, labeling the Congo a "postconflict" situation instead of a "war" situation made a specific set of policies and procedures (such as the organization of elections) seem natural and appropriate while another set of strategies (such as work on local conflicts) seemed inappropriate and illegitimate.

Thus, while culture neither "causes" nor "determines" action, it does make some actions possible and others improbable.[51] It "establish[es] the conditions of possibility for objects or events."[52] To emphasize this point, the aim of this book is not to develop a "linear, causal analysis between independent and dependent variables" to provide lawlike statements.[53] The aim is rather to document a dispersed process,

[47] Weick 1995, p. 109.
[48] This sentence builds on Adler 1997, pp. 329–330.
[49] Barnett and Finnemore 2004; Eden 2004; and Weick 1995.
[50] Barnett and Finnemore 2004, pp. 32–33; and Weick 1995.
[51] Finnemore 1996b.   [52] Fearon and Wendt 2002, p. 58.
[53] This approach builds on Finnemore 1996b; and Klotz and Lynch 2007, p. 36.

where social objects have multiple sources, and where ideas, actions, and environmental constraints mutually constitute each other.

This book shows how the dominant peacebuilding culture constitutes specific actors (such as the UN Department of Peacekeeping Operations), identities (such as "a diplomat," as understood in the early twenty-first century), interests (such as UN organizational interests), and assumptions that are taken as truths (such as "the Congo is inherently violent").[54] Together these identities, interests, and assumptions define "legitimate or desirable goals" for the actors to pursue. They authorize, enable, and justify specific practices and policies while precluding others (for example, diplomats should work on international dialogues and not on local conflict).[55] These actions in turn reproduce and reinforce both the dominant practices and the meanings upon which they are predicated, which together constitute the dominant culture. Over time, the collective understandings and the practices that they authorize come to be taken as "natural," given, and the sole conceivable option.

Examining culture also helps explain change and resistance to it. Two mechanisms explain the latter. First, people usually tend to interpret new information as a confirmation of existing, dominant beliefs.[56] In particular, Watzlawick demonstrates that "once a tentative explanation has taken hold of our minds, information to the contrary may produce not corrections but elaborations of the explanation."[57] Second, large-scale bureaucracies (such as the UN, which was the most powerful international actor in the eastern provinces during the Congolese transition) are notoriously resistant to change because they rely on routines and stability to function and because change usually "threatens entrenched organizational culture and interests."[58] Nevertheless, organizations can and do change. Several recent studies have shown that "probably the most likely impetus to reinterpretation of the environment, or organizational mission within it," is when key actors interpret "external change or shock" as threatening organizational survival.[59]

---

[54] This paragraph builds on Klotz and Lynch 2007, p. 38.
[55] Finnemore 1996b, p. 326.
[56] See Weick 1995, chapters 4 and 6, for a review of the sociological and psychological literature on this topic.
[57] Watzlawick 1976, cited in Weick 1995, p. 84.
[58] Barnett and Finnemore 2004, p. 2; Eden 2004; and Weaver 2008.
[59] Eden 2004, p. 57.

As I show throughout this book, diplomats, international organization managers, and most international nongovernmental agencies constantly reproduced the various collective understandings constituting the dominant peacebuilding culture. There were only a few exceptions. A handful of UN staff members and diplomats, as well as certain nongovernmental agencies, questioned the dominant collective understandings. These people and agencies escaped the all-encompassing influence of the dominant culture because of various idiosyncratic elements, such as organizational or personal background, interests, and knowledge of the local language and culture.

Along with some inhabitants of the eastern Congo, these few exceptional individuals and organizations contested the strategic choices that other interveners viewed as self-evident. Their efforts succeeded only when shocking events, such as unexpected, genocidal, or particularly horrific violence took place. In these cases, UN officials reinterpreted the continued violence. It was no longer a "normal" feature of a peaceful Congo; rather, it was evidence that the war was continuing. As such, it threatened the survival of the UN peacekeeping mission and UN officials had to address it immediately.

However, this recategorization of parts of the Congo as war environments affected only one element of the peacebuilding culture (the labeling of the Congo as a postconflict environment and the strategies this labeling authorized); it did not influence the other, preexisting elements. Diplomats and UN staff members usually interpreted shocking violence as a confirmation of their beliefs that Congolese were violent by nature and that violence was a consequence of macro-level tensions. They still conceived of their role as inherently focused on the national and regional realms, and especially on elections. They never considered that micro-level conflict could be a main cause of the problem or that working at the local level could be an appropriate strategy. Thus, when they intervened to stop shocking violence, they mostly tried to bring violence back to a "normal" (meaning, less horrific and nongenocidal) level, at which point they could recategorize the targeted area as a postconflict environment.

Methodology

To show how the international peacebuilding culture shapes action on the ground, this book draws on a multisited ethnography, semistructured interviews, and document analysis. Overall, I spent a year and a half in the Congo, first as a humanitarian worker during the war (in 2001) and the first few months of the transition (in 2003), and then as an academic researcher (in 2004, 2005, 2006, and 2007). I spent most of my time in the provinces that violence continued to affect. I conducted in-depth ethnographic research in the four main towns of the eastern Congo (Goma in North Kivu, Bukavu in South Kivu, Kalemie in North Katanga, and Bunia in Ituri) and in five rural territories located in South Kivu and North Katanga (Uvira, Shabunda, Baraka, Fizi, Nyunzu, and Pweto; see map of the Congo in Figure 1). I selected these towns and villages based on their contrasting experiences of violence, the presence of different political, ethnic, and military groups on their territories, and their accessibility. I went back several times to most of these places between 2001 and 2007.

When in the Congo as an academic researcher, I remained loosely attached to various humanitarian agencies to benefit from their security backup – which became helpful many times during the course of my research – and to reach rural villages that only aid workers and military groups had the logistical means to access. I adopted various measures to minimize the extent to which this affiliation could bias my findings, notably by always making clear that I did not work for these aid agencies, by triangulating my sources, and by conducting research independently whenever security conditions allowed. I also analyzed my data in light of these potential biases.

I alternated this fieldwork in the eastern Congo with interviews in Kinshasa and in Brussels, Paris, New York, and Washington. This research design enabled me to contrast my firsthand observations of the evolution of the transition in the eastern provinces with data that showed how international peacebuilders based in Kinshasa, Europe, and the United States perceived the situation in the eastern Congo.

Thus, I marshal various kinds of evidence to support my argument. My most useful material comes from the more than 330 interviews I conducted with UN officials, Western and African diplomats, staff members of international and nongovernmental organizations, victims of violence, foreign observers, and Congolese political, military, diplomatic, and civil society actors in the Congo, France, Belgium, and the United States. Most of these interviews lasted more than two hours. When selecting my interviewees, I strove to gain exposure to the broadest possible spectrum of cultural and national backgrounds, affiliation (military or civilian), political opinions, experience of violence (as victims and as perpetrators) and, most important for this research, views on local conflict and bottom-up peacebuilding. I intentionally sought out people who were usually silent or silenced, such as indigent women in isolated rural areas and members of foreign ministries or international organizations ostracized by their colleagues. I interviewed dozens of my informants repeatedly over time, allowing me to probe more deeply into sensitive topics and to contrast the different phases of the fast-changing political environment. From 2005 onward, I disseminated my draft findings to various policy makers, practitioners, and Congolese actors, to make sure that my analysis accurately captured their understanding of their own situation. I used their feedback to revise and refine my findings on a number of critical points.

Most of my interviewees preferred to remain anonymous because of the personal risks involved in providing information on the dynamics of sustained violence in the Congo. Diplomats and UN staffers were also wary to voice their opinions openly because of the culture of secrecy pervasive in their professional circles. For this reason, I fully reference only the data obtained through on-record interviews or in public sources. In characterizing anonymous interviewees, I list only their status (such as "diplomat," "Congolese civilian," "humanitarian worker," or "UN official") and the year that the conversation occurred. Whenever it is necessary to use their names in the text, I replace them with pseudonyms.

I also draw on field observations that I conducted during the war, the transition, and the postelectoral period. During each visit to the eastern Congo, I observed how the evolution of the peace process affected the living conditions there. I specifically focused on identifying the sources of the remaining conflicts and on tracing the reasons for the various outbursts of violence. I also attended dozens of coordination meetings among international and Congolese actors and conducted numerous informal conversations with Congolese citizens and expatriates (foreigners deployed abroad, as opposed to local staffers).

Finally, I checked all this field data against public and confidential documents, such as policy papers, nongovernmental organizations' and UN reports, agency memos, and news sources. Several contacts leaked restricted documents to me and allowed me to use their contents under the condition that I would not identify my source. I treat such documents as author's anonymous interviews to protect confidentiality.

It is important to note that most of the book draws on confidential sources, be they interviews, field observations, or documents. To avoid constantly referring to my sources as "author's confidential interviews and field observations" without being able to provide more details (a practice that would rapidly make footnotes annoying to the reader), we made the editorial decision to reference only open sources. This book should therefore be read with the understanding that any information or quotation for which I do not provide a footnoted reference is based on confidential data (documents, interviews, informal conversations, and field observations). Whenever possible, I provide in the text any piece of nonconfidential information that is useful to fully appreciate the quotation or piece of information, such as the status of the interviewee I quote or the year the conversation occurred. Additionally, for the reader's convenience, I also provide references to publicly available sources when feasible, even when the information and analysis developed in the text is primarily based on confidential data.

When studying international peacebuilders, I focused my research on representatives of the countries and organizations most involved in the Congolese peace process. In terms of states, the primary actors were Belgium, France, South Africa, the United Kingdom, and the United States. In terms of organizations, key agents included the UN – and especially its peacekeeping mission, MONUC – and, to a lesser extent, the EU. Mozambique, Zambia, Canada, Gabon, the World Bank, the African Union, numerous nongovernmental organizations, and UN specialized agencies such as the UN Development Program also contributed to peacebuilding in agreement with their respective interests or mandates.

Notwithstanding the dominant cultural elements analyzed in this book, staff working in these various structures, and even different branches of the same state or organization, had very different approaches, means, goals, and work ethics. To explore and expose these differences, this book looks at both top policy makers and lower-level peacebuilders, such as embassy secretaries or peacekeepers deployed in remote areas. Thus, my analysis goes beyond the official statements and documents, to the actual practice of peacebuilding, which is often very different from the formal record. This book documents how elite instructions are contested, reinterpreted, and translated into action on the ground. It builds on the experience related by people coming from all continents and from many different national, social, and economic backgrounds, thus allowing me to claim that the culture I identify is truly a global (or field-, or organization-specific) one, and not merely a Western culture. The book also gives voice to Congolese actors, to show how they received and interpreted this international action, and why they welcomed or fought it.

This research objective presents an inherent dilemma, which Peter Uvin perfectly expressed in the introduction to his famous study of humanitarian aid in Rwanda before the 1994 genocide.[60] His words, only slightly modified, say it best: No matter how much I tried to delve into the idiosyncrasy of each organization, it is likely that for any statement I make, there have been people who acted or thought differently. Any claim about "the diplomatic community" or "the UN" is bound to do injustice to some people or organizations. The same holds true, for that matter, for statements about "Congolese politicians," "traditional leaders," or "rural inhabitants of the eastern Congo." I sought to respect the variation that exists in each group, but I probably failed to do so for everyone involved. My analysis focuses on the peacebuilding world at large, and it is therefore bound to generalize and simplify. It is my hope that what this approach offers in terms of enhanced theoretical and policy insights will offset the loss of factual minutiae.

Three last important points still need clarification. First, following the report that first popularized the concept, Boutros Ghali's *An Agenda for Peace,* peacebuilding refers to any "action to identify and support structures which will tend to strengthen and solidify peace."[61] Building on this report, this book defines "peace" as the lasting absence of organized, collective violence to attain political, social, or economic goals (see the end of chapter 2 for a further elaboration of this concept). Bottom-up peacebuilding, which I use interchangeably with local conflict resolution, entails the implementation of peacebuilding actions at the grassroots level. This strategy includes, for example, setting up local courts to adjudicate competing ownership claims over land, organizing a workshop to reconcile two villages in conflict, or building an enterprise in whose success two warring communities have a stake (see chapters 5 and 6 for more details).

[60] The entire paragraph paraphrases Uvin 1998, p. 9.
[61] Boutros-Ghali 1992, para. 21.

Second, for consistency, this book uses the name the Congo throughout, even though the Democratic Republic of the Congo – not to be confused with the neighboring Republic of Congo – changed names several times in recent history (the Belgian colonizer called it the Congo Free State and then the Belgian Congo; at independence the country kept the name of Congo; in 1971, President Mobutu renamed it Zaire; and finally in 1997, President Laurent-Désiré Kabila switched the name back to the Democratic Republic of the Congo). To avoid confusing the reader, this book also uses modern maps (as of the period of the transition) as well as the modern names of Congolese provinces and cities even when referring to colonial and postindependence times.

Third, apart from passing mentions, this book does not discuss the 1960–1964 UN Operation in the Congo (best known by its French acronym ONUC) because none of my interviewees ever referred to it, and none of the documents analyzed devoted more than a few sentences to it. The lack of influence that the first Congo mission had on the second one is surprising at first, given the apparent similarities between the two operations.[62] The UN also deployed the 1960s mission to help the newly independent Congolese state address civil war and remove foreign military elements (Belgians at the time). Just as its successor, ONUC was also a very large and costly mission, with up to 20,000 troops. Though it occurred during the vastly different political climate of the Cold War and the early years of Africa's decolonization, it faced challenges remarkably similar to those of the early 2000s, including restoring "the legitimacy, territorial integrity, and internal sovereignty of the state."[63] Finally, as with MONUC forty years later, many observers considered ONUC a major failure. In the UN Secretariat and among the UN member states, ONUC in fact became *the* example of what peacekeeping missions should not do. UN missions should not become a party in a war and interfere in the domestic affairs of UN member states. Peacekeeping missions should not engage in combat operations, because doing so jeopardizes the lives of UN troops and staff members.

---

[62] For more on the ONUC and the history of peacekeeping, see Carayannis forthcoming; Daase 1999; Mortimer 1998; and the official Web page of the mission (http://www.un.org/depts/DPKO/Missions/onuc.htm).
[63] Lemarchand 2008, p. 249.

These lessons persisted until the end of the Cold War removed some of the impediments to peace enforcement missions. In the early 1990s, the Rwandan and Somali disasters replaced the ONUC fiasco in the UN's hall of shame. These failed interventions became the reference points that UN officials and various diplomats mentioned during interviews, when they discussed what UN missions should or should not do. Eventually, by the time the UN deployed a new mission in the Congo once again, ONUC was forgotten history, with virtually no influence on the collective understanding of the causes of violence and the role of foreign interveners.

Overview of the Book

The following chapters reconstruct the international peacebuilders' world to illuminate why they failed to build a sustainable peace in the Congo, and to explain what role the dominant peacebuilding culture played in the process.

Chapter 2 focuses on how international peacebuilders understood the continuing violence during the Congolese transition. UN staff and diplomats were – and continue to be – trained to analyze conflicts from a top-down perspective. As a result, they identified national and regional tensions as the causes of the continued fighting and massacres in the eastern Congolese provinces. The main difference between the war and the transition period was the meaning of continued violence in this dominant narrative. From 2003 onward, UN staff and diplomats defined the Congolese context as a "postconflict" environment; the various bouts of large-scale fighting thus became mere "crises" rather than evidence that the war was continuing. To explain the violence that they could not relate to any national or regional antagonisms, international peacebuilders used several interrelated frameworks of analysis. In their view, local violence was private and criminal, and was the consequence of the lack of state authority in the Congo. More important, because the image of the Congolese's "inherent savagery" had persisted since the Belgian colonizers constructed it a century ago, foreign actors usually saw extensive local violence as a normal feature of life in a peaceful Congo.

Chapter 3 explains why the international peacebuilding strategy used during the Congolese transition made perfect sense in the eyes of its implementers, even though its inadequacy quickly became

apparent. In addition to their assessment of violence detailed in chapter 2, UN officials, diplomats, and nongovernmental organization
officials shared three beliefs that shaped their view of what constituted the most appropriate type of foreign intervention. To start with,
international actors perceived themselves as working in the face of
multiple and almost insurmountable constraints, which severely limited their peacebuilding options. As a result, they had to prioritize.
Two other dominant understandings oriented which strategy took
precedence: Diplomats and UN staff members are trained to work
on superstructures, such as national and international negotiations,
and they are socialized in focusing on predefined tasks and performance guidelines that fail to consider local violence. They therefore
believed that their only legitimate role was to intervene at the macro
levels. Additionally, because they labeled the Congolese transition
as a postconflict situation, they concluded that they should adopt
different strategies from those that they had used when the Congo
was at war.

  These three beliefs shaped the intervention strategy. International
peacebuilders approached all of their tasks in a top-down fashion.
Influenced by the ideological environment of the post-Cold War era,
diplomats and UN staff members especially focused on organizing
general elections. They saw other peace- and state-building tasks as
secondary, still approaching them, when at all, in a top-down fashion.
There was only one exception to this top-down approach: humanitarian aid, which interveners perceived as an apolitical solution to an
apolitical problem (the continuation of violence on the ground).

  Chapter 4 develops an alternative analysis of violence, which in part
explains why the international efforts failed to build a sustainable
peace. Local violence was motivated not only by top-down causes,
regional or national, but also by bottom-up tensions. Local agendas
have held tremendous influence throughout modern Congolese history, and they have often been intertwined with macro-level dimensions. Likewise, during the transition, many conflicts revolved around
political, social, and economic stakes that were distinctively local.
These decentralized conflicts often jeopardized the national and
regional reconciliation processes, for example by motivating violence against Congolese of Rwandan descent or by allowing a strong
Rwandan Hutu presence in the Kivus. In its final section, this chapter

analyzes the situations in the most violent areas of the Congo during the transition – the two Kivus, North Katanga, and Ituri – to explain how local dynamics interacted with the national and regional dimensions. I demonstrate that, after a national and regional settlement was reached, some local conflicts over land and political power became increasingly self-sustaining and autonomous from the national and regional developments, most notably in South Kivu, North Katanga, and Ituri, while in North Kivu they fueled the existing tensions to the point of jeopardizing the broader settlements.

Chapter 5 considers why attempts at promoting the analysis developed in chapter 4, and at adopting a bottom-up peacebuilding strategy in addition to the top-down one, failed throughout the transition. I first show how international interveners could have boosted local peacebuilding initiatives with the resources at hand. I next trace how isolated members of MONUC and of diplomatic missions, as well as certain nongovernmental organizations, tried to convince their colleagues to adopt such a bottom-up approach, and I show that these attempts were largely unsuccessful. I explain that the largest peacebuilding bureaucracies rejected these opportunities for change because the potential reforms clashed with deeply entrenched cultural norms and jeopardized numerous organizational interests. As a result, neither contestation nor the occurrence of unexpected, genocidal, or particularly gruesome or spectacular events ever became sufficient to prompt diplomats and UN staff to reevaluate their understanding of violence and intervention. Instead, a vicious circle developed, in which the perception of local conflict resolution as a long-term, unfamiliar, and illegitimate task turned local level "constraints" on international action into insurmountable obstacles, a process that in turn reinforced the perception of bottom-up peacebuilding as a negligible issue.

The concluding chapter starts by explaining why the intervention strategy could not build either peace or democracy in the Congo. It presents the standard macro-level arguments, insisting on the drawbacks of the electoral tool. It then suggests a new theoretical approach to the study of international peacebuilding failures in the Congo, in the rest of Africa, and beyond. The dominant international peacebuilding culture shapes the interveners' understanding of peace, violence, and intervention in a way that overlooks the micro-foundations necessary for sustainable peace. The resulting inattention to local conflict leads to unsustainable peacebuilding in the short term and potential war resumption in the long term. The book ends by briefly detailing the policy implications of this analysis and offering recommendations to improve international interventions in civil wars.

2 | A Top-Down Problem

In May 2004, large-scale fighting broke out in the eastern city of Bukavu. When rebel troops took over the city, they went on a looting, raping, and killing spree. In a well-populated neighborhood located not far from a United Nations (UN) peacekeeping base, a boy and his mother watched several soldiers enter their neighbor's house. From what they could see and hear, they understood that their neighbor was about to be raped. The boy ran to look for help at the UN peacekeeping base, but when he arrived at the checkpoint of the base, the Uruguayan soldier on duty spoke neither Swahili nor French. The boy tried to explain several times what was happening, but he could not make himself understood. Finally, the soldier broke into a large smile, made a sign to say that he had comprehended and went inside the camp. He came back a few minutes later with a pack of cookies, which he handed to the boy.

This appalling anecdote, narrated two years later by a furious and ashamed UN military officer, points to more than just a language problem. In the middle of fighting, bombing, and raping, it seems rather evident that when a boy tries to attract the attention of a UN peacekeeper, whose mandate includes the protection of the population, there is a high chance that the boy is asking for help. However, in this case, the peacekeeper's ingrained perception of what Congolese children want (cookies or water bottles, for which they often ask when they see foreigners) overcame his common sense. In a similar way, the international peacebuilders' entrenched understandings of peace, war, and the Congo overcame the commonsense idea that local conflict quite possibly matters.

This chapter reconstructs how three shared cultural understandings shaped the way most international interveners comprehended continued fighting during the transition: first, an exclusive focus on macro-level causes of tensions; second, the labeling of the Congo as a "postconflict" situation; and third, the view of the Congo as

inherently violent. I initially argue that members of the peacebuilding field usually approach conflict from a top-down perspective.
Accordingly, they understood violence in the Congo as the result of
regional and national tensions, certainly not local ones. There was one
major difference between the war and the transition period: During
the transition, most international peacebuilders labeled the Congolese
context as a "postconflict" environment. This redefinition changed
the meaning of continued violence in the dominant narrative. The
various bouts of large-scale fighting thus became mere "crises" rather
than evidence that the war was continuing. Less extreme violence,
though still serious, developed into a normal feature of a peaceful
Congo. In this dominant narrative, several interrelated frameworks of
analysis accounted for the hostilities that were impossible to connect
to any macro-level antagonisms. International peacebuilders viewed
decentralized conflicts as a Hobbesian challenge: They were private
and criminal, and they resulted from the lack of state authority in
the eastern provinces. Additionally, the narrative included language
implying that the Congolese were innately barbaric and it was this
barbarism that further spurred pervasive violence.

This dominant narrative included some extremely convincing elements. Top-down manipulation was certainly an important cause of
fighting throughout the transition, and the lack of state authority in
the eastern provinces significantly facilitated the continuation of violent conflicts. However, this chapter also shows that, no matter how
popular, this dominant narrative has major logical flaws, and it is
insufficient to fully understand persistent violence.

From the Top, Down: A Story

The Dominant Framework of Analysis

Most academics, policy makers, and practitioners interested in questions of war and peace share a remarkably similar approach to their
topic; they look for the causes of violence at the regional and national
levels, and not in the realm of the local.[1] Through an extensive review

---

[1] Bush 2003; Kalyvas 2003 and 2006, chapter 2. Examples include all the
texts quoted in footnotes 2 to 10 and in the first part of footnote 12;
exceptions are noted in footnote 11 and in the last sentence of footnote 12.

of the scholarly and policy literature on armed conflict, Kalyvas demonstrates that the standard analyses of war politics focus not on ordinary people but on elites – the governments of different countries in the case of international wars, or the government and the rebel leaders in the case of civil wars. These standard analyses stress high-level international politics, elite interactions, and diplomatic history. They infer local and individual identities and action from the war's master cleavage, meaning the overarching issue dimensions (such as government versus rebel, Hutu versus Tutsi, or Christian versus Muslim), which analysts usually use to explain a crisis. They perceive local dynamics as "mere (and rather irrelevant) local manifestations of the central cleavage" and local actors as mere "replicas of central actors."[2]

Ignoring the subnational dynamics is so ingrained that, in policy discourse, "local" usually means national (in opposition to international), and not subprovincial, as in this book. Since the late 1990s, "local ownership" has become a buzzword in international organizations, but it means ownership by the central government, not by people on the ground. During my interviews in various conflict zones (the Congo, Afghanistan, and Kosovo), virtually all diplomats and UN officials used the phrase "local actors" to refer to the national leaders – and not to provincial chiefs or villagers – and "local conflicts" to refer to national tensions (usually among the various members of a government), not to district- or village-specific issues.

This widespread top-down approach is partly due to what Kalyvas calls an urban bias: "Studies of civil war violence are produced by urban intellectuals," while civil wars are primarily fought in rural areas. Because information on rural areas is notoriously difficult to obtain during wars (especially when researching violence), and many prejudices still inform people's understanding of rural politics as backward and primitive, most analysts tend to interpret civil wars "acontextually and in an exclusively top-down manner."[3]

Since the late 1990s, research on ethnic wars has further reinforced the tendency to explain violence through a focus on elite actions, providing a key intellectual tool to approach the unfolding events in

---

[2] Kalyvas 2006, chapter 2. See also Kalyvas 2003 (quotation from pp. 480–481).
[3] Kalyvas 2003 and 2006, chapter 2 (quotations from pp. 38–39).

Central Africa and around the world.[4] Previously, in the mid-1990s, the primordial approach was dominant in policy circles. It portrayed ethnic hostility as eternal, ordinary people as inherently filled with hate against other identity groups, and civil wars as therefore inevitable.[5] This leading understanding was notably one basis for Bill Clinton's policy in the Balkans: From this point of view, the United States could do little to prevent the massacres since people in this part of the world had been killing one another for centuries.[6]

To refute the primordial approach, research on the civil conflicts in the former Yugoslavia suggested an approach to ethnic wars that eventually became very influential in policy and academic circles; nonetheless, as I show at the end of this chapter, the idea that some people (Africans or Yugoslavs) inherently hate one another to the point of using violence still lingers.[7] According to the new approach, ordinary people are neither inherently filled with hate toward their neighbors nor responsible for ethnic conflict. They wage violence only when incited by "ethnic entrepreneurs": elites – usually provincial or national politicians – who manipulate racial or ethnic identities in their struggle for political and economic power. From this point of view, elites manufacture tensions and corrupt the thoughts of their ethnic groups to attract supporters. Because of them, ordinary people come to view their neighbors as enemies.[8]

This framework of analysis was appealing not only because it provided an analytical grip on extremely complex conflicts, but also because it enabled action. Once the war was over, peacebuilders simply needed to weed out the extremists, the small groups of very guilty perpetrators. Left to their own devices, the masses of innocent, ordinary people would be at peace. Thus, policy makers and practitioners, in addition to numerous scholars, quickly applied this framework to

[4] I thank David Chuter, a British diplomat interviewed in Pretoria (May 2008), for first pointing this out to me, and for mentioning several ideas that I develop in the next three paragraphs.

[5] Huntington 1993; Kaplan 1994a, 1994b, and 1996.

[6] This was reported in many press articles at the time and in Drew 1994, pp. 157–158; Hansen 2006, pp. 6 and 149; and Holbrooke 1998, p. 22.

[7] With reference to Yugoslavia, see Holbrooke 1998, pp. 21–23.

[8] See, for an academic view, Denich 1994; Sells 1996; and Silber and Little 1996; for a journalistic presentation, Berkeley 2001; for a policy perspective, Holbrooke 1998; and Zimmerman 1996 (cited in Holbrooke 1998); and for a critical analysis, Bax 2000.

many conflicts, such as the 1994 Rwandan genocide and the wars in Sudan and Uganda.[9] The standard account of violence in Rwanda, for instance, emphasized the critical role of manipulation by the Hutu elite, which mobilized the masses through hate medias.[10] Thus, elite manipulation became a central element of the top-down narrative.

Of course, there are exceptions. Anthropologists, as well as a few journalists, historians, and political scientists, have long used grass-roots approaches to analyze wars.[11] However, their findings have not yet informed the dominant understanding of violence. During my research, an official from the United Nations Mission in the Congo (MONUC) reported that most UN workers never considered that local events could have a national or regional impact. According to a Western donor at the time of our interview in late 2004, the idea that local, national, and regional violence could interact was still a novel concept in diplomatic circles. Indeed, a diplomat I interviewed during the same period, who had extensive knowledge of the regional and national dimensions of the Congolese conflict, confirmed this claim. He was surprised by the very idea that micro-level agendas could affect the macro-level settlements; he reacted to a brief presentation of my ideas on this issue by saying, "It is very interesting. It is probably true. I have never thought about the [Congo's] situation in these terms!" These statements encapsulated a common theme that I encountered throughout my research: During the Congolese wars and subsequent transition, international actors were still quite unfamiliar with the theories and concepts that could have enabled them to grasp bottom-up dynamics of violence.

Almost all of the international interveners understood violence in the Congo as a top-down problem. In this narrative, regional and national tensions determined local dynamics, and regional and national actors manipulated local entities. This framework of analysis informed most

---

[9] On Rwanda: Chrétien 1995; Des Forges 1999; and Prunier 1995. On Sudan: Deng 1995; Hutchinson 2001; Lesch 1998; and Rothchild 1997, chapter 8. On Uganda, see Behrend 1999; and Doom and Vlassenroot 1999 for examples of top-down analyses, and for an alternative analysis see Perrot 2008.

[10] See Straus 2006 for a critical view.

[11] Kalyvas 2003, p. 480. Examples include Abdullah 1997; Bangura 1997; Fanthrope 2001; Fujii 2008; Jackson 2000; Lederach 1995 and 1997; Maindo Monga Ngonga 2000; Mamdani 2001; Muana 1997; Straus 2006; Van Acker and Vlassenroot 2000; Van Hoyweghen and Vlassenroot 2000; and Vlassenroot 2000.

accounts of the crises, including those written in the UN Secretary-General's reports on the Congo, in UN Security Council resolutions, in internal humanitarian agencies' reports, in news articles, and in many scholarly studies (although the latter usually painted a much more complex picture of the situation).[12] It was also the dominant interpretation that UN managers and field workers, diplomats in the Congo and in national headquarters, and humanitarian and human rights activists provided during interviews. It was the leading narrative, no matter the author's or interviewee's regional origin (African, North American, or European), current geographical position (Goma, Kinshasa, Paris, New York, etc.), or organizational affiliation (UN, diplomatic missions, or nongovernmental organizations), with only a few exceptions, which are analyzed in chapter 5.

To present the dominant, top-down understanding of violence, the following sections draw on the documents and interviews mentioned earlier, as well as on some of the best research on the Congo.[13] According to this view, regional and national tensions explain why wars took place in the late 1990s and early 2000s and why violence continued during the transition from 2003 to 2006. It is valuable to develop the dominant interpretation in some detail for three reasons. First, it was one of the bases of the top-down strategy that international interveners adopted to end the Congolese crisis. Second, the

[12] For policy and journalistic analyses, see, among many others, UN Security Council 2003–2006a; UN Security Council 2003–2006b; the "DRC Profile" posted on the MONUC Web site (http://www.monuc.org/news.aspx?newsID=885, section "Why are the problems still continuing today?" accessed in October 2007); Berkeley 2001; Braeckman 1999; Brittain and Conchiglia 2004; International Crisis Group 1999, 2000b, 2001, 2002, 2004a, 2005b, 2006a, and 2006b; and most news items on the Great Lakes, 2001–2008. For the best scholarly studies that mention the bottom-up causes of the conflict but nevertheless focus on the regional and national dynamics, see Carayannis and Weiss 2003; Prunier 2008; Reyntjens 2007; and Willame 2007. For scholarly studies that emphasize both top-down and bottom-up dynamics, and are thus closer to the analysis presented in this book, see Banegas and Jewsiewicki 2000; Lemarchand 2008; Maindo Monga Ngonga 2007; Mamdani 2001; Reyntjens 1999b and 2009; Turner 2007; and Vlassenroot and Raeymaekers 2004a.

[13] Because other authors have already developed this top-down narrative at length, this book presents it very briefly, keeping only the elements necessary to understand the rest of the argument. Readers interested in more details on the events mentioned in the following sections can find them in the sources listed in footnote 12.

dominant narrative correctly identifies some of the most significant causes for prewar, war, and postwar tensions and is therefore central to our understanding of the Congolese conflict. Finally, familiarity with the narrative is critical for the reader to appreciate its central flaw: It does not explain why ordinary people followed the regional and national elites' appeals. Because it insists exclusively on macro-level elements, it neglects the critical role of bottom-up agendas, which chapter 4 illuminates.

Brief Historical Context

For the benefit of those readers who are not familiar with recent Congolese history, a brief overview of the main factual events emphasized in the dominant narrative is necessary. As opposed to the bottom-up story presented in chapter 4, which starts long before colonization, the dominant narrative on the recent Congolese wars usually begins with the spillover of the Rwandan genocide. From April to July 1994, Hutu extremists massacred more than 800,000 Tutsis and moderate Hutus. When the Tutsi-led Rwandan Patriotic Front seized power in Kigali and ended the genocide, about 2 million (mainly Hutu) Rwandan refugees flooded the eastern Congo to avoid persecution from their new Tutsi government. The refugees, along with more than 50,000 armed Rwandan Hutus responsible for the massacres, congregated in large refugee camps located near the border in North and South Kivu. The combatants formed enormous armed groups who based their survival on violence and looting, and used the refugee camps as rear bases from which to launch raids on Rwanda.

The new Tutsi regime in Rwanda had to find a way to dismantle these rebel groups. At the same time, the reign of President Joseph Mobutu – the dictator who had ruled the Congo since 1965 – was becoming increasingly unpopular both among neighboring countries and in the West. In response, the Rwandan, Ugandan, Angolan, and Burundian governments, as well as South Sudanese rebel forces, formed an anti-Mobutu coalition, which engineered, armed, and supervised various Congolese rebel groups and local militias. In particular, with the support of this coalition, disparate anti-Mobutu forces from the Congo formed the rebel movement Alliance of Democratic Forces for the Liberation of the Congo-Zaire (Alliance des Forces Démocratiques pour la Libération du Congo-Zaïre, AFDL). Between September and November 1996, the rebellion progressively evolved into a full-scale national and regional conflict, now known as the First Congo War.

A peace process mediated by Nelson Mandela started early in the first war, but the AFDL's military superiority was so significant that the war ended in a clear victory, not through negotiations. In May 1997, the AFDL toppled Mobutu to install their spokesman, Laurent-Désiré Kabila. The new president did not have much time to savor his victory, though. Tensions soon arose between Kabila and his foreign backers over his dismissal of Rwandan military advisors, alleged support of Rwandan rebel groups, and incitement of violence against Rwandans and Congolese with Rwandan ancestry. The governments of Rwanda, Uganda, and to a more limited extent Burundi, engineered a new rebel movement, the Congolese Rally for Democracy (Rassemblement Congolais pour la Démocratie, RCD). In August 1998, the RCD launched an attack on Kabila's government, thus initiating what has become known as the Second Congo War.

This new rebellion was supposed to conquer the Congo in a few months, in part through support from the neighboring countries that had backed the AFDL. However, it met an unexpected opposition of forces from Zimbabwe, Angola, Namibia, and, to a lesser extent, Chad and Sudan; each sided with Kabila for different political, security, or economic reasons.[14]

Rebel movements quickly multiplied. In September 1998, the Congolese businessman Jean-Pierre Bemba created a second rebel group, the Congo Liberation Movement (Mouvement pour la Libération du Congo, MLC), based in the northern Equator province and including mostly former Mobutists. In November 1998, with the support of Uganda, the MLC launched a new rebellion against Kabila. Then, in 1999, a dispute between Uganda and Rwanda led Ugandan President Museveni to withdraw his country's support from the RCD and ally exclusively with the MLC. Several months later, the Rwanda–Uganda fallout generated a split within the RCD. Two movements were created: the RCD-Goma (RCD-G), backed by Rwanda, and the RCD-Kisangani/Liberation Movement, supported by Uganda. Due to internal struggles for leadership, further splits within both

---

[14] International Crisis Group 2000b provides an excellent overview of these countries' motivations for supporting Kabila.

movements later generated three smaller splinter groups: the RCD-Original, the RCD-National, and the RCD-Populaire. The RCD-G and MLC nevertheless remained the two most powerful rebel groups for the rest of the war.

In mid-1999 Kabila's troops managed to halt the rebels' advances. The stalled peace process, which had resumed a few days after the beginning of the 1998 war, delved into action at this time. The United States, UN, European Union (EU), and several of its member states (notably France, Belgium, and the United Kingdom), as well as the Organization of African Unity and several African countries (in particular South Africa, Zambia, and Libya) acted as mediators, even while in some cases supporting one of the Congolese armed groups.[15] These mediators took advantage of the stalemate that had emerged, and Angola, the Congo, Namibia, Rwanda, and Zimbabwe signed a cease-fire agreement in Lusaka in July 1999. In addition to the cease-fire, the agreement notably included the holding of a national dialogue, the establishment of a disarmament mechanism, and the creation of a UN peacekeeping force. Accordingly, in late 1999 the UN began, very slowly, to deploy a small observatory force to the Congo called MONUC, which was tasked with verifying the Lusaka cease-fire, overseeing the voluntary disarmament and repatriation of foreign militias, and supervising the withdrawals of foreign troops. As with the other measures identified in the Lusaka agreement, it took several years for the UN to fully complete MONUC's deployment (and, once this was achieved, the mission continued to expand both in size and mandate).

Despite the ceasefire, between 1999 and 2003, up to fourteen foreign armies actively fought on Congolese territory, each supporting one or more of the many Congolese armed groups. The combat eventually resulted in a country divided into five main areas of control: The government controlled the southern and western parts, and various rebel groups controlled and took over all state functions in the other four areas (see map of the partition of the Congo during the war in Figure 2).

[15] For further information on the peace process, see International Crisis Group 1999, 2000b, 2001, and 2002; Staibano 2005, pp. 22–23; and Willame 2002.

Figure 2 Partition of the Congo during the Second Congo War. This figure is based on the map entitled "Congo" drawn by the UN Mission in the Congo (MONUC), dated June 2003 and formerly available on MONUC's website. *The different shadings correspond to the territory of each armed group. The wide grey band across the country marks the ceasefire line and the demilitarized zones following the 1999 Lusaka agreement.*

The proliferation of armed groups unevenly affected the various parts of the Congo. The government and MLC areas (respectively, the southern and western parts of the country and the northern provinces) remained calm and relatively free from war-related violence. Major fighting also almost never took place across the national front lines. However, a proxy war raged in the eastern provinces, behind the cease-fire line mandated by the Lusaka agreement. South Kivu, most of North Kivu, Maniema, north of Katanga, and part of Kasai

Oriental, which the RCD-G supposedly controlled, were in fact a mosaic of enclaves under the control of competing armed bands. The RCD-G and the Rwandan army held the main towns, such as Goma, Uvira, and Bukavu. Meanwhile, local ethnic militias, called Mai Mai, and the Rwandan Hutu rebels (both of whom fought on behalf of President Kabila in the dominant narrative), as well as Burundian rebels and various other military and paramilitary groups, controlled pieces of the countryside in an ever-changing pattern (see map of armed groups' deployment in Figure 3). Severe violence also affected Ituri, a mineral-rich district in the northeastern Oriental Province, which the MLC and Uganda controlled during the first years of the war.

By all accounts, the delay in the implementation of the peace agreement largely stemmed from the poor quality of the relationships between the new Congolese president, Laurent-Désiré Kabila, and the international mediators. However, the president's assassination in 2001 by one of his bodyguards, in what remains a mysterious incident, eliminated this hurdle. His son, Joseph Kabila, took over as president and eventually secured the trust of most Western powers. The warring parties finally implemented several measures of the Lusaka accord, including the withdrawal of all armed groups to fifteen kilometers behind the cease-fire lines and the beginning of the Inter-Congolese Dialogue.

The Inter-Congolese Dialogue aimed to bring together leaders of the main Congolese armed factions, as well as unarmed groups, to design a peace plan and discuss the future of the country. After months of arguments over logistical and substantive concerns, the Dialogue finally began in April 2002. Before the signing of its Final Act in April 2003, the talks produced a series of agreements, notably the Global and All-Inclusive Agreement on the Transition in the Democratic Republic of the Congo (December 2002), which outlined a framework for the upcoming transition and the formation of a transitional government. Meanwhile, still under international pressure, two other agreements – the Pretoria agreement between the Congo and Rwanda (July 2002) and the Luanda agreement between the Congo and Uganda (September 2002) – also achieved a regional settlement. As stipulated in these agreements, most foreign troops officially withdrew from Congolese territory by the end of 2002.

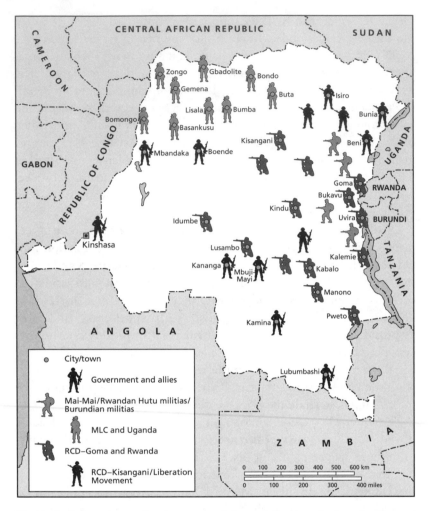

Figure 3 Approximate Deployment of Armed Groups during the Second Congo War. This figure is based on the map "Approximate Deployment of Armed Groups in DRC" by IRIN-CEA (United Nations), dated 28 March 2000.

The installation of the Transitional Government on June 30, 2003, marked the official beginning of the transition from war to peace and democracy. As mandated in the Global and All-Inclusive Agreement, "the 1+4 model" ("le schéma 1+4") structured the transitional government. The administration included one president (Joseph Kabila) and four vice presidents drawn from the RCD-G (Azarias Ruberwa), the MLC (Jean-Pierre Bemba), Kabila's former government (Abdoulaye Yerodia Ndombasi), and a coalition of unarmed parties gathered under the name the Political Opposition (Arthur Z'ahidi Ngoma). In the lower echelons, such as the ministries, the parliament, and other administrative capacities (like the governorship of a province), representation was supposedly equally divided among the eight "components of the transition," corresponding to the eight most powerful political or military groups turned political parties at the outset of the civil war: Kabila's former government, the Mai Mai, the MLC, the Political Opposition, the RCD-G, the RCD-Kisangani/Liberation Movement, the RCD-National, and the movement entitled the Civil Society.

As stipulated in the Global and All-Inclusive Agreement, the transition's main goals were to reunify the Congo, promote national reconciliation, and organize general elections. The Transitional Government was to integrate the various armed groups into the national army, the Armed Forces of the Democratic Republic of the Congo. It also was to ensure that there would be a unitary administration and police force throughout all provinces. Initially, the Transitional Government had two years (until June 2005) to complete this plan, but the provisional constitution allowed the government to request up to two extensions of the transition by six months (until June 2006) in case they did not manage to fulfill the stipulated plan by the deadline, a fact that did occur.

Many Congolese and international interviewees emphasized that the Transitional Government exceeded their expectations at the outset of the transition by succeeding in reunifying the Congo. As of late 2003, with a few exceptions, front lines ceased to divide the country, and traveling from one part of the Congo to another became feasible again. The Transitional Government also successfully organized general elections: a referendum on the new constitution of the country in December 2005, legislative elections and the first round of the presidential elections in July 2006, and provincial elections and the second round of the presidential elections (a run-off between the top two candidates) in October 2006. The new National Assembly was installed on September 22, 2006, and the other newly elected officials eventually took power throughout the country. President Kabila's inauguration on December 6, 2006 symbolized the successful completion of this lengthy peace process. In the words of the UN Secretary-General at the time, the president's induction brought "the transition process envisaged by the Global and All-Inclusive Agreement of 2002 to a formal conclusion."[16]

However, throughout the transition, massive violence continued across the eastern provinces to such an extent that Congolese officials still referred to the area between the cities of Kindu (Maniema), Kalemie (North Katanga), and Ituri as the "fatal triangle" of the country. As the following sections detail, in the dominant narrative, just as regional and national tensions had caused the wars, the remnants of unresolved regional and national hostilities caused the postwar violence. In this story, local actors were mere proxies, manipulated by regional and national elites, rather than endowed with proper agency. A diplomat based in Europe whom I interviewed in 2005 best summarized what his diplomatic and UN colleagues believed: "The main leaders of the different rebellions and the neighboring states" are behind the local crises. He added, "It is true that the concrete manifestation of these recurrent crises may give the impression that they are born from [the local level]. But I am convinced that the real causes belong to the macro, not to the micro."[17]

National Tensions

National Antagonisms. International and Congolese actors unanimously emphasized how persisting tensions at the very top of the Congolese government caused violence in the eastern provinces.[18] As with most peace agreements, the Congolese settlement relied on power sharing among the main warlords, who had fought each other for the previous five years. And, as in many such situations, power sharing and trust building proved particularly challenging.[19]

The political and military unification at the top level, in the government and in the leadership of the army, was a smokescreen. Behind this façade, each component tried to retain extragovernmental military and administrative structures to maintain its territorial control to the furthest extent possible. In the administration, the strategic

[16] UN Security Council 2006f, para. 2.
[17] For a public source, see UN Security Council 2004a, para. 38.
[18] Autesserre 2006 and 2007 include preliminary versions of the following three sections.
[19] See Tull and Mehler 2005 for a broader analysis of power-sharing agreements.

departments – police, security services, taxes, and so on – continued to operate largely along party lines throughout the transition, although some social services departments – health, social affairs, and education – began to function under the national authority in late 2003.[20] Additionally, each component strived to control its former military assets under the tenuous umbrella of the newly unified army. In particular, the antagonism between the RCD-G and Kabila fueled the resistance of most Kivu armed groups to the army integration process, because each party wanted to maintain separate control over its allies on the ground in case the war resumed. The persistent distrust and lack of integration generated a highly volatile situation in the territories controlled by troops affiliated with different factions; it led to countless small-scale battles and to several bouts of large-scale fighting.

During interviews, diplomats and high-ranking UN actors explained at length how national elites manipulated and fueled local tensions in the Kivus to attain better positions within the transitional institutions. International interveners also blamed the most acute outbreaks of violence in the eastern provinces during the transition – such as the fighting in Bukavu (South Kivu, May 2004), Kanyabayonga (North Kivu, December 2004), Rutshuru (North Kivu, February 2006), Sake (North Kivu, November 2006) and the war resumption in 2008 – on "spoilers," leaders and parties who used violence to undermine peace.[21] The three main former warring parties – the Kabila government, the RCD-G, and Bemba's Congo Liberation Movement – were indeed each split between two sides: the legitimists, who wanted to play the game of the transition, and the warmongers, who either had everything to lose with peace or had too much to gain from war to accept a settlement to the conflict.

All international actors emphasized that the local population was the first to suffer from this fighting, for two reasons. Each armed group used violence to deter villagers from supporting some other faction, or to punish them for having done so. Additionally, all soldiers, in all components, preyed on local villages to make up for receiving

---

[20] Romkema 2004; UN Security Council 2004d, para. 12; and UN Security Council 2004c.

[21] This sentence is a paraphrase of the classic definition of spoilers in Stedman 1997, p. 1.

little or no income. (Even members of the national army received only $10 to $23 a month, which was ten times less than they required to cover their basic needs. To make matters worse, this sum was usually further reduced by commanders at all levels, who diverted a large portion of the funds designated for the soldiers' pay and army supplies.) Nearly all soldiers thus extorted the local residents, stealing all kinds of valuables, such as money or mobile phones in urban areas and harvests or cattle in rural areas. Along with stealing, they often beat, jailed, raped, tortured, or killed those who refused to comply.

Mobilization of Local Actors Through Ethnic Entrepreneurs. In this story, local villagers who waged violence were mere followers who had been mobilized by a series of ethnic entrepreneurs, the first of whom was President Mobutu.[22] In the early 1990s, Mobutu faced three new developments that jeopardized his hold on power. Foreign aid dwindled due to the end of the Cold War, his domestic revenues decreased because of a worsening economic crisis, and Western pressure forced him to launch a movement of democratization. Mobutu and his cronies decided to exacerbate ethnic tensions to stay in power. They promoted the principle of "indigeneity," which stipulated that "all positions of authority [issued in the coming elections] could only be awarded to those indigenous to the region concerned."[23] This principle enabled the president and his allies to divide broad cross-ethnic coalitions that could have formed to oppose them and to deflect the hatred directed toward their regime onto the "nonindigenous," who served as scapegoats. This strategy also helped compensate for missing financial resources: Instead of paying his armed forces, Mobutu encouraged them to remunerate themselves through looting the scapegoats' properties – in addition to conducting clandestine trade and attacking humanitarian aid assets.[24]

This new patronage strategy caused massive instability throughout the entire Congo, but especially in Katanga and the Kivus.[25] The latter provinces are the particular focus of the dominant narrative.

<hr />

[22] For the best presentation of these events, see Berkeley 2001, chapter 3; Mamdani 2001, chapter 8; Reno 1998, chapter 5; Reyntjens 1999b; and Willame 1997 pp. 62–68 and 124–131.

[23] Vlassenroot 2000, p. 79.

[24] Reno 1998, chapter 5 and Van Acker and Vlassenroot 2000, para. 13.

[25] Berkeley 2001; and Willame 1997, p. 101, provide an excellent overview of the events in Katanga.

In the Kivus, Mobutu and his provincial allies encouraged the "indigenous" communities' resentment of the Congolese people with Rwandan ancestry, called the Banyarwanda (in North Kivu) and the Banyamulenge (in South Kivu). Rwandan Hutus and Tutsis had come to the Kivus in several waves: the first long before colonization; the second in the early part of the twentieth century, to provide laborers for Belgian colonial plantations; and the third in the 1960s and 1970s, when tens of thousands of Tutsis crossed the border to escape massacres in the newly independent Rwanda. In the early 1990s, Congolese Tutsis made ideal scapegoats. Their relatively small numbers prevented them from properly defending themselves. The rest of the population disliked them because they were occupying land and positions of authority that indigenous communities claimed as their own. Additionally, Rwandan president Habyarimana, a long-time ally of Mobutu, needed to boost the Tutsis' unpopularity to undermine the North Kivu rear base of the rebel movement (the Rwandan Patriotic Front, which was composed mostly of Rwandan Tutsi refugees) that threatened his power.

In the dominant narrative, the Rwandan genocide, and the subsequent arrival of 2 million Rwandan refugees and large armed groups in the Kivus, was the breaking point. (Note that this interpretation is, again, different from the bottom-up story presented in chapter 4, which emphasizes that violence started *before* the arrival of Rwandan Hutu refugees.) The transition parliament, created as part of Mobutu's democratization efforts, sent a commission "stacked with anti-Banyarwanda extremists" to review the situation in the Kivus in 1994.[26] The verdict was harsh: It ordered all people with Rwandan ancestry – Hutus and Tutsis, ancient and recent refugees – to return to Rwanda. Scores of refugees tried to avoid this fate by leaving the camps and settling in rural areas. Tensions flared, first in North Kivu, then in South Kivu, leading to large-scale massacres of Hutus and Tutsis, mass displacement of the population, and an eventual alliance between Congolese with Rwandan ancestry and foreign powers determined to depose Mobutu.

In the dominant account, this manipulation of ethnic tensions carried over to the war and the transition period, and it explained the

---

[26] Reyntjens 1999b, pp. 17–18.

ordinary individuals' use of violence. According to this story, persisting antagonisms between indigenous people and Congolese with
Rwandan ancestry accounted for most of the localized violence in the
Kivus during the war. During the transition, leaders from all sides
of the political spectrum, as well as the newspapers they controlled,
continued to fuel ethnic hatred against the Congolese of Rwandan
descent for the sake of electoral advantages. They presented this
minority as the source of the war and of all of the transition's problems, as well as the "Trojan horse" behind the destabilizing efforts of
the abhorred Rwandans. Fueling ethnic hatred spared politicians the
need to develop real political platforms. Vilifying the Kinyarwanda-
speaking minority, and questioning its right to Congolese citizenship,
was an easy way to show one's patriotism and to appeal to the majority of the Congolese population. A vicious circle developed: Existing
ethnic tensions encouraged national politicians to use rhetoric against
Congolese with Rwandan ancestry, thus further stirring ethnic hatred,
a process that enhanced the effectiveness of ethnic entrepreneurship.

As the story continues, the top-down manipulation of ethnic antagonisms provided national elites not only with political power, but also
with economic benefits. Kinshasa- and Goma-based companies tried
to force each other out of business by exploiting the tensions between
indigenous communities and Congolese of Rwandan descent. For
example, after the May 2004 fighting in Bukavu, the Kinshasa-based
phone companies Vodacom and Celtel mobilized the army's and the
Bukavian population's resentment against Kinyarwanda-speakers in
order to close down their rival, Supercell, a company managed by
Congolese with Rwandan ancestry. Similar problems arose in various
provinces throughout the transition.

The leading explanation for the conflict in Ituri during the war
and the transition involved slightly different actors from those in
the Kivus, yet it also underscored that ethnic entrepreneurs were
responsible for engineering tensions.[27] Ituri became the site of clashes
between Rwandan, Ugandan, and different Congolese armed groups,
who manipulated the latent ethnic conflict between the Hema and
Lendu communities. Just as in the other eastern provinces, regional

----

[27] See, for example, International Crisis Group 2003a; Staibano 2005, pp.
6–7 and 22–23; and Wolters and Boshoff 2006, p. 7. Chapter 4 in this book
explores the Ituri conflict in greater depth.

and national actors supervised the creation of numerous ethnic militias, leading to an escalation of violence and a series of massacres between the two local ethnic groups.

Regional Combat

In addition to these national antagonisms, the dominant narrative emphasized that a large part of the violence also resulted from a regional fight, waged by foreign actors on Congolese territory. In the early stage of the transition, many international reports and interviewees emphasized that Rwanda and Uganda remained physically present in the Congo. In particular, the Rwandan army carried out hit-and-run operations against Rwandan rebels and patrolled selected areas of the Kivus.[28] International actors also noted that these unofficial military operations progressively decreased during the transition, but not to the point of a discontinuation of regional involvement in Congolese affairs. Sections of the establishment in both countries continued to support several Congolese spoiler groups responsible for much of the violence in the eastern provinces, such as Eugène Serufuli's local defense militias, Laurent Nkunda's National Congress for the Defense of the People (Congrès National pour la Défense du Peuple), and various rebel groups in Ituri.[29]

To account for this sustained regional involvement, the dominant narrative stressed three major interests: a professed security concern over rebel groups, a desire to exploit the Congolese natural resources, and for Rwanda, a sense of duty toward ethnic kin. Rwanda stressed that the Congolese with Rwandan ancestry, both Hutus and Tutsis, experienced considerable discrimination and abuse. Allegedly fearing a "genocide" of Congolese of Rwandan descent, Rwanda regularly threatened to reintervene in the Congo during the transition if Kabila

---

[28] Concerning Rwanda, see Global Witness 2005; International Crisis Group 2005a, pp. 21–22; Romkema 2004; Prunier 2008, pp. 298–299 and 309; and UN Security Council 2004b and 2006d. There are fewer publicly available reports of Uganda's military incursions into Congolese territory; one such source is Wolters 2004.

[29] Amnesty International 2005; Fahey 2009; International Crisis Group 2004a; Prunier 2008, chapter 9; UN Security Council 2004b, 2004c, 2005a (para. 27), and 2008; U.S. Department of State's Congo Country Profile, www.state.gov/r/pa/ei/bgn/2823.htm, accessed in October 2007; and Wolters and Boshoff 2006, p. 3.

did not act appropriately to protect this minority. It is important to
note that, because the Congolese felt deep resentment toward Rwanda
due to its lengthy occupation of the eastern provinces, these threats
in fact reinforced the hatred against the Kinyarwanda-speaking community among the vast majority of the Congolese people and led to
further discrimination and violence.

International actors acknowledged Rwanda's concerns on behalf
of the Congolese population of Rwandan descent; however, they
usually emphasized that security and economic motivations best
accounted for both Rwanda's and Uganda's involvement in the
eastern Congo. The issue of foreign rebel groups on Congolese territory was particularly prominent. Ever since Rwandan Hutu militias
crossed the border in 1994, they began collaborating with various
Congolese armed groups and professed their desire to regain power
in Rwanda, through military means should negotiations prove impossible. Though the Rwandan army hunted these militias throughout
the war, these groups still numbered 7,000 to 10,000 combatants and
20,000 to 30,000 dependents during the transition. (The dependents
included family members of the combatants, refugees, and political opponents forced to flee by President Kagame's crackdown on
opposition parties). Additionally, Kagame rightly had considerable
doubts about the capacity of the Congolese army and MONUC to
secure the Rwandan–Congolese border against Hutu militia attacks.
Congolese soldiers were, indeed, highly disorganized and ineffective,
and MONUC provided only voluntary repatriation of militiamen (in
2004) or minimal support to Congolese troops hunting them (in late
2005 and 2006).

According to many military experts, however, the Rwandan Hutu
combatants remaining in the Congolese forests were too few to pose
a real danger to Rwanda.[30] The rebel group had ceased attacking
Rwanda and it only rarely infiltrated the country since its last major
assault in early 2001. Furthermore, many interviewees noted that
only a small number of the combatants had actively participated in
the 1994 massacres, and only a handful of those were among the most
wanted – those who had planned and organized the genocide. Most
of the Rwandan Hutu rebels arrived in the Congo when they were

[30] For public sources, see UN Security Council 2003–2006a; and Synergie Vie
2004.

young; they grew up as refugees, and used violence because they had no other means of subsistence.

Many Congolese and international observers therefore questioned the sincerity of Kagame's worry over the Rwandan rebel presence in the Congo, and of his desire to have them return to Rwanda. These analysts noted that Kagame's behavior during the war and the transition showed that he preferred either their extermination or their continued roaming in the Congo. Keeping the Rwandan Hutu rebels out of Rwanda ensured that their main political movement, the Democratic Forces for the Liberation of Rwanda, (Forces Démocratiques de Libération du Rwanda or FDLR), could not become an official, recognized opposition to the Rwandan ruling party. Yet, leaving these Hutu rebels close by in the Congo also allowed Kagame to maintain a permanent quasi-state of war in Rwanda. He could therefore restrict civil rights and clamp down on opposition parties. Finally, the Hutu rebels' presence in the Congo provided Kigali with an excellent pretext for coming back into the Kivus to pursue Rwanda's other interests: the illegal exploitation of Congolese mineral resources and the protection of the Congolese population with Rwandan ancestry.

The dominant narrative treated Uganda's protests about its own rebel groups stationed in Ituri and the northern part of North Kivu as it did Rwanda's complaints.[31] Most foreign interveners suspected that Uganda remained informally involved in the Congo not primarily to pursue rebel groups who threatened its security, but rather to exploit the Congolese resources.

Every interviewee emphasized, though, that even if these insurgent groups presented only minimal threats to Rwanda or Uganda, they, along with Burundian rebel groups, were a major danger to the Congolese people. The Rwandan rebels were particularly notorious for the horrors that they committed against the communities in areas under their control. They were also a latent threat to the Congolese Tutsis, who feared that, given the chance, the Hutu militias would subject them to the same fate that their Rwandan kin had suffered in 1994. Accordingly, many of the reports on MONUC presented by the UN Secretary-General to the Security Council identify the Rwandan Hutu rebels as the main source of instability in the Kivus during the

[31] See, for example, Wolters and Boshoff 2006, p. 7.

transition.[32] The 18th Report (August 2005) carries this interpretation to an extreme. Its entire subsection devoted to the "security situation in the Kivus" mentions only the Rwandan Hutu militias, and not once does it refer to the various Congolese armed groups that continued to cause violence.[33]

Thus, during interviews and in written reports, international peace-builders painted an adverse picture of the Rwandan Hutu rebels as a whole. They considered the Hutu combatants to be purely predatory militias, who exploited the local population until they could finally win back Rwanda. They also noted that the dictatorial nature of the Kigali regime, its harsh treatment of political opponents, and its categorical refusal to make any concession to Hutu rebel demands gave the refugees in the Congo little hope for livable conditions in Rwanda. As a result, many Rwandan Hutu commanders intimidated and sometimes executed the potential deserters in their ranks; they knew that they themselves would be killed if they ever laid down their arms or lost their combatants.[34] In comparison, life in the Kivus was much easier: The Rwandan rebel militias could live off the local population and enrich themselves through the illegal exploitation of resources.

Illegal Exploitation of Natural Resources

In the dominant narrative, the illegal exploitation of Congolese mineral resources thus holds a central place as one of the primary motivations for violence waged by regional and national actors.[35] In this part of the story, local actors were again only proxies, supervised and manipulated by regional and national elites.

The Congo has massive reserves of gold and diamonds, most of the world's reserves of columbo-tantalite (an essential material for most electronic equipment), numerous mines of silver, cadmium, copper, and zinc, and rare minerals such as cobalt, nickel, niobium, tantalum, beryl, cassiterite, and wolfram (used in high-technology industries). Many of these resources are located in the eastern provinces of the

---

[32] UN Security Council 2003–2006a.
[33] UN Security Council 2005a.
[34] Synergie Vie 2004.
[35] See, for example, Lemarchand 2008, p. 276; Nest, Grignon, and Kisangani 2006; Prunier 2008, pp. 291–292; UN Panel of Inquiry 2001a, para. 218; and "Illicit gold finances weapons," *News24.com*, April 8, 2005.

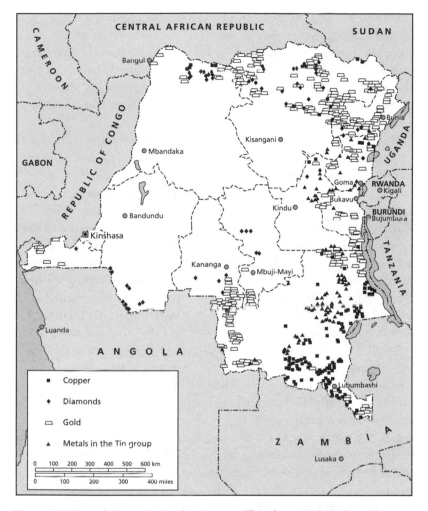

Figure 4 Mineral Deposits in the Congo. This figure is based on the map "Mineral Deposits in the Congo" in Global Witness 2005, p. 7.

Kivus, Katanga, Kasai, and Maniema (see map of mineral deposits in the Congo in Figure 4), and most of them have not yet been tapped.[36]

---

[36] Braeckman 1999, pp. 161–162; Global Witness 2005, p. 13; and "A Golden Age for the Congo," by Jim Jones, *Mineweb*, posted on August 21, 2005 (http://www.mineweb.com/mineweb/view/mineweb/en/ page15831?oid=4039&sn=Detail).

During the war, Rwanda and Uganda had established a monopoly on trade in the zones they controlled.[37] State officials of all ranks, from the highest national authorities, including Presidents Kagame and Museveni, to the lowest rank-and-file soldiers, benefited from the trafficking. In addition to the two governments, Rwandan, Burundian, and Ugandan rebel militias were similarly involved in resource exploitation.

During the transition, UN and nongovernmental sources continued to provide ample evidence of Ugandan and Rwandan involvement in the illegal exploitation of the eastern provinces' mineral resources.[38] However, in contrast to the war period, this involvement was sporadic and aimed at influencing or supervising Congolese allies. The seven-year conflict had enabled foreign countries to set up systems of exploitation that could continue to function through Congolese proxies even after the Rwandan or Ugandan armies had withdrawn. Most documents and interviewees also noted that, just as during the war, Rwandan, Ugandan, and Burundian rebel movements continued to control many mineral-rich areas of the Kivus, often in collaboration with Mai Mai groups.[39]

By all accounts, national actors also often participated in the illegal exploitation of natural resources in the eastern provinces. In partnership with complicit administrative officials, the RCD-G troops, and subsequently the troops of General Nkunda, secured, taxed, and supervised the exploitation and transportation of the valuable raw materials in their area of control to Rwanda. On their arrival in the eastern provinces, a number of Congolese army brigades also became involved in mining. Soldiers either dug minerals or taxed the local production, while the officers both facilitated and benefited from illegal exportation to Rwanda, Tanzania, or Uganda.[40]

---

[37] UN Panel of Inquiry 2001a, 2001b, 2002a, 2002b, and 2003. See also, Global Witness 2005, p. 13.

[38] Global Witness 2005, pp. 4, 24–26; International Crisis Group 2005a; Pourtier 2004, p. 4; Romkema 2004; UN Panel of Inquiry 2003; UN Security Council 2004b, 2005b, 2005c, 2006a, and 2007a; and Wolters and Boshoff 2006, p. 7.

[39] Global Witness 2005, pp. 4 and 20–21; UN Mission in the Democratic Republic of Congo (MONUC) 2004; UN Panel of Inquiry 2003; UN Security Council 2004b, 2005c, 2005i (para. 39), 2006a, and 2007a.

[40] Global Witness 2005.

In the dominant narrative, this regional and national involvement in illegal mining generated violence in three ways. First, national and foreign actors, as well as their local proxies, competed for the control of mining sites, over which fighting frequently broke out in the eastern provinces. Second, illicit exploitation of resources enabled all armed groups to finance their war efforts. Third, all armed groups employed extreme violence against civilians – including "killing, rape, torture, arbitrary arrests, intimidation, mutilation, the destruction or pillage of private property ... [and] mass displacement" – to "gain control either over resource-rich areas or over the ability to [exploit them]."[41]

In sum, consistent with the standard scholarly and policy analyses of conflict from a top-down perspective, international peacebuilders saw very clear regional and national causes for the continuation of violence in the Congo between 1994 and 2006. Despite the similarities, there was a key difference in how the international interveners understood the fighting during the war and during the transition. From late 2002 onward, international actors labeled the Congo as a "postconflict" situation. The application of this label transformed the meaning of the continued violence in the dominant narrative. During the transition, even though violence was allegedly still caused by the same top-down tensions as before, it was no longer interpreted as evidence that the war was continuing.

A "Postconflict" Environment

Contrary to the other cultural elements documented in this book, the interveners' shared definition of the Congolese situation as "postconflict" did not precede intervention. The "postconflict" label itself, as well as the strategies it allowed, was already part of the existing peacebuilding culture; but the application of this label to the Congo was constructed through practice and spread among members of the peacebuilding field. As this section shows, the construction followed the same process that Porac et al. illuminated: "Subjective interpretations of externally situated information [became] themselves objectified via behavior. ... This continual objective-subjective-objective

[41] Ibid, p. 10.

transformation [made] it possible eventually to generate interpretations that [were] shared by several people."[42]

That is, many diplomats and civil servants based outside of the Congo interpreted the signing of the various peace agreements in late 2002 as the end of the Congolese war. A UN official later explained to me that it was a simple matter of definition. Postconflict countries are countries that have undergone wars. The Congo had undergone a civil and international war, so when regional and national peace agreements ended these wars, the Congo became a postconflict environment.

This redefinition had practical consequences. Diplomats based outside the Congo concretely enacted their interpretation of the country as in a postconflict situation. Belgium reviewed its priorities: Economic and political matters became more important than security issues. Donors such as the EU began disbursing development aid, which they usually do not give to countries at war. The UN mission, MONUC, was from that time forward considered a "peace*keeping*" and not a peace-enforcement mission.

At first, most field-based actors contested this new categorization. In mid-2003, for example, a Europe-based donor visited Goma and met with the international nongovernmental organizations working there. He told them that, because the Congo was finally at peace, they must get outside of the wartime frame of mind and start conducting activities across the front lines. The field workers found this statement ludicrous and widely challenged it; at that time, heavy fighting had just resumed in North Kivu.

Despite the situation, however, all actors of the peacebuilding field – donors, journalists, and even humanitarian agencies confronting violence on a daily basis – progressively adopted the postconflict language. In a process very similar to that which organizational theorist Weick describes, foreign and Congolese nongovernmental organizations "noticed the changes" in the diplomats and donors' strategies and interpreted them as cues that the Congo had entered a postconflict phase.[43] They "act[ed] on these new interpretations in ways that

---

[42] Porac et al. 1989, pp. 398–399, cited in Weick 1995, p. 79. See also, Berger and Luckmann 1967.
[43] All quotations in the rest of this paragraph come from Weick 1995, pp. 79–80.

verif[ied] the original interpretation" by initiating development and postconflict reconstruction programs. These actions "constrained the information" that the different organizations extracted from their environment. This information, in turn, reinforced the interveners' belief that the Congo was indeed a postconflict situation, and it thus "affected the next round of choices." At the same time, extensive formal and informal communication among international peacebuilders (during meetings, afterwork drinks, parties, and through e-mail exchanges) helped spread this interpretation. Simultaneously, as chapter 5 details, people affected by violence lacked the discursive space to challenge this dominant discourse. Eventually, the label became "objectified" and "widely internalized" into a shared understanding of the situation.

From 2004 until the resumption of large-scale fighting and the threat of regional war in late 2008, almost all international interviewees and many Congolese elites, as well as press reports, used the "postconflict" label to refer to the ongoing situation. The language of war progressively disappeared. During the transition, there were no more "rebel" leaders; instead, there were "renegade" officers, such as the "renegade" officer Laurent Nkunda. There were no more rebel armed groups or militias; rather, there were "units of the Congolese army" not yet integrated. In place of war violence, there were now "crises," such as the "Bukavu crisis" (May–June 2004), the "Kanyabayonga crisis" (December 2005), the "Rutshuru crisis" (January 2006), and the "Sake crisis" (November 2006; see the timeline in the appendix). Even though these events saw large-scale fighting between "former" war enemies, led to the deaths of hundreds of combatants and civilians, the displacement of hundreds of thousands, and very nearly caused a collapse of the regional and national peace processes, they were not considered evidence of a continued war. Furthermore, because such small and large-scale crises were omnipresent in the eastern provinces, international peacebuilders stationed there worked, as many of them phrased it, "in constant crisis mode" – but, again, not in war mode.

This interpretation could remain dominant despite the continuation of massive violence due only to the presence of other shared understandings: the view of the eastern Congo as a Hobbesian environment and the related perception of violence as a normal feature of a peaceful Congo. Analyzing these two collective understandings helps illuminate the major flaw in the dominant narrative. The narrative was incomplete, because it did not take into account the local causes of violence.

Although top-down actions did contribute to violence, they are not the entire story. The dominant narrative failed to acknowledge the presence of decentralized conflicts over land, mineral resources, traditional power, taxes, and the relative social status of specific groups and individuals. It presented micro-level conflicts as mere consequences of broader tensions, while they were in fact motivated by distinctively local causes. It pictured local actors as manipulated by regional and national elites, while they often refused enduring allegiance to these macro-level actors. It portrayed the Mai Mai, the Rwandan Hutu militias, and the population with Rwandan ancestry as unified groups, when these "groups" recognized no central command system and were in fact extremely fragmented. The result, as the following sections detail, is that the conventional story went awry when it considered violence not motivated by macro-level tensions: International peacebuilders presented such violence as extremely limited, residual, criminal, and unworthy of international attention – a view that chapter 4 thoroughly refutes.

In the Eastern Provinces, a Hobbesian World

In interviews, most international actors agreed that some instances of violence independent from regional and national tensions occurred, but interviewees talked about these only in response to a direct question. Reports by the UN Secretary-General also offered glimpses of violence unrelated to the macro levels in their sections on human rights or humanitarian aid, but these sections usually mentioned only the consequences of conflicts, not their causes. This neglect of localized conflict is not surprising, given that international actors only had the intellectual tools (concepts, theories) to understand top-down dynamics, not grassroots ones.

Pieced together, the fragmentary and dispersed statements that I collected on non-macro-level conflicts during formal interviews, in informal conversations, and from public or confidential reports showed that international actors drew on several cultural elements to approach such decentralized conflicts. These collective understandings notably included the use of a Hobbesian framework to analyze the situation in the eastern provinces, the view of recent wars as private and criminal, and the perception of violence as innate to the Congo.

The Missing Leviathan

International peacebuilders usually saw decentralized violence as a Hobbesian problem. A Western diplomat, for example, claimed to have seen parts of the Congo where "Hobbes would have been right at home." During other interviews, several diplomats similarly used Hobbesian terms to describe the conflict. Along the same lines, a British journalist wrote a long article on the Congo filled with statements such as, "Thomas Hobbes was right."[44] Mampilly introduces his analysis of rebel governance in the Congo by noting how people usually compare the situation there to "the anarchy envisioned by Thomas Hobbes."[45] In this view, as Kalyvas has best stated, civil wars are "characterized by the breakdown of authority and subsequent anarchy"; they foster the privatization of violence, and they are motivated by greed and the possibility of looting.[46]

True to Hobbes, international actors understood localized violence in the eastern provinces as the consequence of a lack of state authority. A 2005 report of the Secretary-General to the Security Council, for example, identifies "law and order problems" as the main causes of the "fragile security situation" in Katanga.[47] A high-ranking diplomat similarly explained to me that the effective vacuum of authority was the primary underlying condition that allowed for active conflict. Another claimed that the problems of local violence in the eastern provinces were "all linked to the absence of the state." More broadly, many interviewees identified the Transitional Government's failure to extend its authority in the eastern provinces as the most important obstacle to a resolution of the Congolese crisis.

Once again, this analysis included very convincing elements. State authority was, indeed, mostly absent from the eastern provinces, where it could have helped peacefully resolve many localized

---

[44] "Congo's tragedy: the war the world forgot," by Johann Hari, *The Independent*, May 5, 2006.
[45] Mampilly 2007, pp. 194–195.
[46] Kalyvas 2003, p. 475.
[47] UN Security Council 2005b, para. 24–25.

conflicts. Under President Mobutu, the state had gradually retreated from the provinces. Because he received significant foreign aid to run the mining industry, Mobutu never depended on the population to generate resources. His internal regime was devoid of the political mechanisms that might have forced him to be accountable to his subjects. In the 1980s, Mobutu therefore cut funding for public services such as health care, education, and infrastructure. The retreat of the state touched the whole country, but it affected the eastern provinces most acutely.[48] The central power perceived the Kivus and Katanga, which had been the theater of multiple insurgencies since independence, as rebel areas to be treated differently from the rest of the country. Mobutu therefore invested almost nothing in infrastructure or development in these provinces despite continued taxation. As a result, a significant cleavage developed between the Kivus and the capital, which eastern Congolese perceived as predatory, and eventually led to a virtual disconnection of the eastern provinces from the central authorities.

The problem worsened in the 1990s. When foreign aid dwindled, Mobutu decided to reward his local allies by allowing them to found "virtually autonomous fiefdoms organized around commerce in diamonds, gold, coffee, timber, cobalt, and arms."[49] This strategy boosted the autonomy of local entities. The ongoing economic crisis further compounded the situation. Deprived of resources, state bureaucracies completely collapsed and public services ground to a halt.

The eight years of war in the late 1990s and early 2000s did very little to reestablish state authority. It is true that state functions operated at a prewar level throughout the government-controlled areas and that the Congo Liberation Movement zone also benefited from some real administrative structures. However, the war further decreased state presence in the eastern provinces. This part of the country fell under the control of various rebel groups, whose attempts at reestablishing a state bureaucracy remained quite limited.[50] Some state functions did exist, in particular taxation and tight control on the movement of Congolese citizens and expatriates, including from one city to another. Certain services, such as health care, functioned in the main urban centers, usually because of the support of international humanitarian

[48] Tull 2005; and Bayart 1996, p. 46.   [49] Reno 1998, pp. 148–149.
[50] For excellent analyses of rebel governance during the war see Tull 2005; and Mampilly 2007.

organizations. Each province also had a governorate, while each town or village retained some administrative buildings usually belonging to the police and the administrator. Yet, the core law and order departments, such as the justice system and the police, were either nonexistent or mere outgrowths of the military. Furthermore, in many places one wondered how state agents could work in such conditions: The offices were decrepit, and most lacked even basic supplies (typewriters, electricity, phones or other means of communication). Above all, Congolese and expatriates widely perceived state officials as mostly interested in extorting money rather than providing public services.

The situation did not improve substantially after the war officially ended. The slow pace of the transition, the presence of parallel administrative and military structures, and the existence of Congolese and foreign militias perpetuated the absence of state authority in the eastern provinces, especially in the rural areas. Continued bias, corruption, and inefficiency in the justice and police systems were so widespread that these sectors had no credibility among the population. This continuing lack of state authority in the eastern provinces resulted in the Belgian foreign minister declaring, in February 2005, that the Congo remained a "failed state." Three years later, the *Index of State Weakness in the Developing World* still identified the Congo as the third weakest state in the world.[51]

Despite the clear vacuum of state authority in the eastern provinces, this part of the dominant narrative included several problematic elements. A lack of authority does not mean people will immediately begin killing and raping each other. As Kalyvas emphasizes, mechanisms of social control (aside from the state) prevent the translation of tensions into intense fighting and, "even in the context of civil wars, such conflicts do not always result in violence."[52] Another, complementary explanation is needed to understand why ordinary people enroll in militias or support violent groups. The dominant discourse on the Congo, however, did not acknowledge this point. Rather, international interveners often presented violence as a direct consequence of the lack of state authority. Those who went deeper in their analysis pointed to criminal agendas to explain why local conflict would erupt into violence in the context of a state authority vacuum. The others

[51] Patrick and Rice 2008.   [52] Kalyvas 2003, p. 485.

implicitly relied on the widespread belief that Congolese were inherently violent.

"Local" Means "Criminal"

International interveners who unpacked the causal link between lack of state authority and decentralized violence usually viewed the latter as a criminal problem. In the prevailing narrative, greed, in particular the control of minerals, motivated local groups. As a UN official explained, "The local agenda? It's resources!" A high-ranking French diplomat concurred: At the provincial level, it is a "mafia problem." Other UN and diplomatic interviewees made similar statements. This part of the narrative built on two very popular ideas in the peacebuilding field: that post-Cold War conflicts are different from previous forms of organized violence, and that today armed groups are motivated by "greed" rather than by "grievances."

Kalyvas found that before the 1990s, most policy analysts perceived wars as "ideological, political, collective, and even noble," motivated by collective grievances to be redressed in a search for "justice." Seemingly unified warring parties, which leaders tightly controlled, vied for control of the central power. At least one side enjoyed broad popular support, and the violence was supposedly controlled and disciplined. By contrast, since the 1990s, international actors began facing the presence of what they perceived as "new" forms of violence, such as terrorism and warlordism. They also confronted increasing difficulties in finding a master cleavage that could explain continuing civil wars. Violence became seen as criminal, depoliticized, private, predatory – closely tied to the looting of personal property, crops, or mining resources – and gratuitous.[53]

In the press and during many of my interviews, the Congolese wars, and especially the situation in the rebel areas, usually appeared as *the* example of such "new wars." In addition to emphasizing the presence of a large-scale illegal exploitation of natural resources, as detailed earlier, international interviewees stressed the dire economic conditions in the eastern provinces, which rendered petty criminality all the more attractive. Most international peacebuilders used this reasoning to explain, for example, why soldiers in the Congolese army perpetrated such widespread human rights violations. In the

[53] Kalyvas 2001, quotation from p. 100.

words of Henry Boshoff, a prominent military analyst, "The delay and frequent failure to pay military salaries [was] a major problem that [resulted] in soldiers engaging in banditry and violence against the civilian population."[54] International peacebuilders also analyzed Mai Mai violence in this way. To a Western diplomat, this violence was "not linked to any kind of political project"; it was purely private and criminal. A high-ranking French official concurred: Mai Mai were mere bandits. UN actors often voiced a similar perception.

Once again, part of this story was very convincing. To start with, in the eastern Congo, economic conditions were indeed miserable. Mobutu's rule not only weakened the state, but it also impoverished the Congolese population. Mobutu's strategy of control was built on patronage (paying substantive sums to ensure the loyalty of the army and buying off opposition politicians through distribution of state economic assets), which he financed by hoarding state resources; eventually Mobutu held up to 95% of the Congo's budget,[55] This system diverted the resources that would have been necessary to develop the productive capacity of the country. It also meant that the existing industries, factories, and productive land were distributed to cronies who often had no managerial experience. As a result, the national revenue shrank from $377 per capita in 1958, right before independence, to $117 per capita in 1993.[56] The reduction of the private sector, the disintegration of the public sector, and the lack of education produced "thousands of marginalized young people with no social support, poor education, and few possibilities of employment," especially in rural areas.[57]

In the eastern provinces, the lack of economic opportunity worsened during the war. The fighting left most infrastructures destroyed, and occupying soldiers often subsequently dismantled the few remaining working factories and transported them to Rwanda.[58] Mining areas fell under the control of militarized networks, thus depriving local civilians of this last potential source of income. The situation barely improved during the transition. Children and teenagers who grew up

---

[54] Boshoff 2005. See also, UN Security Council 2004d.
[55] Reno 1998, pp. 152–154.
[56] Van Acker and Vlassenroot 2000, para. 13.
[57] Van Hoyweghen and Vlassenroot 2000, para. 94; and Bayart 1989, pp. 93–94.
[58] See UN Panel of Inquiry 2001a for a public source.

during the war rarely received proper schooling and thus were not well prepared to pursue peaceful and productive activities. Land was scarce, so young people could not easily acquire fields for farming.[59] The economic infrastructure was nonexistent, and outside intervention in the eastern provinces continued to focus on humanitarian issues, funding only very few development projects. Inhabitants of the Kivus, North Katanga, and Ituri therefore faced extreme poverty.

Additionally, large-scale criminal activities were indeed widespread in the eastern Congo. As detailed previously, countless regional, national, and local groups remained involved in illegal mining. This situation in turn fueled the absence of state authority in the eastern provinces in two ways. First, it reinforced the reluctance of many local strongmen to work in good faith with the central authorities. Second, it deprived the Transitional Government of important resources that could have helped the state extend its authority.[60] Reports by the UN Secretary-General as well as visit reports and resolutions by the UN Security Council also often emphasized the "linkage between the illegal exploitation of natural resources, illicit trade in such resources, and the proliferation and trafficking of arms as one of the factors fuelling and exacerbating conflicts in the Great Lakes region."[61]

There are two problems with this narrative, though. First, as chapter 4 demonstrates, not all (or even most) of localized violence was linked to criminal agendas. Local violence was, rather, motivated by identifiable political, social, military, or economic causes. Second, poverty does not necessarily produce criminality or violence. And the only remaining element of the dominant narrative that explained why poverty and the lack of state authority resulted in violence was particularly unconvincing: It built on the widespread belief that Congolese are inherently violent.

An Inherently Violent Country

International actors usually pictured the Congo as an inherently turbulent country where violence was expected even in times of peace. To

---

[59] See chapter 4 for an explanation on the scarcity of land despite the Congo's immense size.

[60] UN Security Council 2004c (para. 44 and 73) and 2004d (para. 114) contain publicly available data on this topic.

[61] Quotation from UN Security Council 2007b.

many international interviewees, the situation had not changed much since Joseph Conrad wrote his famous novel; the Congo was still a *Heart of Darkness* in the center of Africa.[62] A UN peacekeeper, originally from North Africa, lectured me once on how to understand the situation in the Congo. In essence, he warned: Do not come here with your European sensibilities and your European ideas. Violence and corporal punishments are a part of the life here. The Congolese are used to it. Whipping people is the way of the Congo. The Congolese do not feel it the same way we do, he explained. A Western diplomat to whom I relayed this story found such normalization of violence a quite "legitimate" phenomenon. "It's a human tragedy," he said, "but ... it is a country that has been through, certainly since 1996, a decade of pretty serious ongoing violence, and people become somewhat numb to that, such as the level of shooting [in a large US city] would seem intolerable in Tokyo, but [in that US city] it is part of the background."

To elaborate, during interviews and in press articles, a widespread explanation for the persistence of local fighting, massacres, and human rights violations after the beginning of the transition dictated that extensive violence had always existed in the Congo. It was therefore normal for the country, and it would be completely understandable if it were to continue. In the words of a UN official, violence was the "usual mode of relations between the Congolese state and its population." The Congo was "a country with a history of abuses" and "a constant pattern of violence against the population by people in power." Therefore, the violence and the "armed men ... preying on the population" observable during the transition were present "in the same way" as they had "always" been before. Along the same lines, another UN official conjectured that the mounting violence in the Kivus in 2007 might have been just the "typical state of affairs" for these provinces. A Western diplomat qualified the same situation as "more of the same in a terrible part of the world" and as an "inevitable" problem. An experienced aid worker explained to me that a high level of rape had always existed in the Congolese society: "For generations, eight women out of ten have been raped by their father, their uncle, or a neighbor." A French diplomat further claimed that rape perpetrators considered sexual

---

[62] Conrad 1971 [1902].

violence to be natural because the Congolese population's approach to violence was essentially identical to that of European citizens in the Middle Ages.

Extreme violence has certainly been part of Congolese life for most of the country's recent history. At least since the arrival of the white traders – and probably since the beginning of the Arab slave trade – violence was part of the daily life. Both during colonization and after independence, the central power strategically organized the use of violence, and provincial state officials and traditional chiefs implemented this tactic at the local level. According to Hochschild, terror was central under Belgian colonial rule.[63] "Terrorizing people [was] part of [the] conquest"; Belgian rulers officially sanctioned it as *the* way to control the native population. When the Congo was the personal property of Belgian King Leopold II (1885–1908), colonial officers usually maimed unproductive workers and frequently killed or tortured the rest of the population. Even after the Congo became a colony of the Belgian state (1908–1960), use of the "chicotte" (leather whip) was so widespread that it became, in the minds of the Congolese population, as associated "with white rule as the steamboat or the rifle." According to Hochschild's sources, about 10 million Congolese died of forced labor, massacres, burned villages, malnutrition, and the chicotte under colonial rule.

State violence continued at a high level after Congolese independence. Like its colonial predecessor, the newly independent state used coercion extensively, including forced labor, beatings, massacres, torture, public executions, and forced displacements.[64] Mobutu relied primarily on patron-client networks rather than on violence; yet coercion forces – especially the infamous Presidential Special Division – were a crucial instrument when clientelism failed. These forces played such an important role that Bayart identifies them as "one of the main channels of interaction between state and society."[65] As a result, Mobutu's regime very soon came to be described as "Bula-Matari" ("he who breaks the rock"), a metaphor that originally referred to explorer Henry Morton Stanley's regime of terror and was later extended to designate the Belgian colonial state.[66]

---

[63] Hochschild 1998. Quotations from pp. 123 and 120, and statistic from p. 282.
[64] Bayart 1989.   [65] Ibid., p. 300.
[66] Turner and Young 1985, pp. 30–31.

The wars of the 1990s only worsened the situation. In the eastern provinces, violence against the Congolese population, including the widespread use of sexual violence against women and girls, was omnipresent. Violence against the population was not only extensive; it also took particularly gruesome forms. In Shabunda (South Kivu) for example, many horrific events occurred throughout the seven years during which Mai Mai and RCD-G forces fought over the village of 10,000 people. A humanitarian worker based there reported that once armed people "took a family, they killed the father, they took the mother, they told the children to support the mama while they were raping her. They took out the heart and the liver of the father, and they told the children to eat them." She heard of "many cases like that." She also knew of many women "who went to the forest, were kidnapped, and became the 'wives' of 20 or 30 soldiers." I heard similar testimonies throughout my fieldwork, in all of the villages where I worked. All journalists, humanitarian aid workers, and human rights activists working in the eastern provinces reported equally appalling stories. These reports may seem unbelievable but, during the war, doctors and nurses testified that horrible torture permanently mutilated countless victims.[67] Even Congolese living in places less affected by war, such as Kinshasa, faced multifaceted violence in their daily lives, although it was much less intense and less widespread than in the eastern provinces.[68]

Extreme and horrific violence has thus clearly been present in the Congo at least since the late nineteenth century. However, understanding the Congo's history of violence as evidence of a higher "normal" violence threshold in Congolese society as opposed to others overlooks a central element of Conrad's *Heart of Darkness* and of Hochschild's analysis of colonization: Both authors assigned barbarism and inherent savagery to the Europeans, at least as much as to the Congolese. Violence reached an unprecedented scale and intensity after the arrival of the colonizers, and Mobutu was able to use extensive violence to control his population in large part because of the

---

[67] Reliable data on the horrific aspects of violence during the war can be found in the many (confidential) situation reports written by humanitarian medical organizations based in the eastern Congo at that time, as well as in most of the human rights reports published between 1996 and 2003 (see, for example, Human Rights Watch 2000 and 2002).

[68] Trefon 2004, chapters 11 and 12.

perpetuation of modern forms of state power. From this perspective, extreme violence and "savagery" are not part of the Congo's "nature," nor are they atavistic or primordial. Rather, they are imported and products of modernity.[69]

Furthermore, the extent of the disaster in the Congo during the war does not explain why international peacebuilders should have understood violence in a way that blatantly contravened all norms of human rights, humanitarian values, and conceptions of people's equality regardless of race or ethnicity, principles to which the immense majority of peacebuilders said they subscribed.

In fact, the very idea that extreme violence is inherent to various parts of the world, such as the Congo or the former Yugoslavia, should be questioned. Admittedly, conflict is inherent to social life, and all societies experience a certain level of violence even in times of peace. War and peace are not mutually exclusive categories.[70] Rather, they are two ideal types, one referring to a situation mostly devoid of violence, the other to a situation mostly governed by violence. In this manner, the labels "war" and "peace" are most useful when conceptualized as points toward the two extremes of a continuum from a total absence of violence to a constant presence of violence. Nowhere in the world can we find a situation that meets the criteria for either extreme. While it is difficult to determine where each society should be located on the continuum, we can use approximations. Countries considered at peace should be placed somewhere toward the "no violence" end of the continuum, while countries at war should be placed somewhere toward the "constant violence" end of the continuum, as depicted in Figure 5.

As many people noted in response to my argument, certain societies are more violent than others, and the presence of violence in a country does not necessarily mean that the situation is abnormal or close to war. In favor of this argument, we can concede that, in the early twenty-first century, the United States, South Africa, and the western Congo are more violent than Switzerland and Sweden. We can likewise acknowledge that, in the Congo, the eastern provinces are more violent than the rest of the country.

[69] Young 1994.
[70] See Richards 2005; and Richmond 2005 for a similar point.

Figure 5 Continuum of Violence.

However, it would be difficult to defend a definition of "peace" and "normality" that includes levels of violence similar to those experienced by the inhabitants of the eastern Congo during the transition. When violence reaches the scale and intensity that it has in this region, with regular fighting among organized armed groups, torture and killing of civilians by soldiers, and a frequent use of sexual violence against noncombatants, it is very difficult to conceptualize such violence as a "normal" feature of peaceful life, as implied by the international discourse on the Congolese transition. Rather, such high levels of violence must be taken as evidence that war has resumed, rendering the postconflict label no longer appropriate for the eastern provinces.

Furthermore, Congolese citizens themselves, as opposed to outside observers, can best determine which level of violence is normal for their society. All of my eastern Congolese interviewees regarded the ongoing bloodshed as being, without question, out of the norm. Their reactions to incidents of torture, fighting, and massacres clearly showed that they were far from habituated or "numb" to such events. Even perpetrators did not consider the violence that they committed as "normal" or "natural." Rather they presented it either as a means to achieve military goals or as the unfortunate result of their own "suffering" and of "poor leadership."[71]

A comparison with the Mobutu era, itself a violent period of Congolese history, is also illuminating. Mobutu did use tremendous brutality to suppress dissent, and violence did become a mode of production and a way of living for several groups who inhabited the border areas of the eastern Congo. However, according to all sources, written documents as well as interviews with Congolese and foreign actors, the level and intensity of violence during Mobutu's rule was never comparable to what it became during the transition, even in the unstable eastern provinces. Almost all of the local and national

[71] Baaz and Stern 2008, p. 81.

conflicts were either suppressed (by Mobutu's law and order forces) or resolved peacefully (by the local and national justice system and by various traditional and modern conflict-resolution institutions). Although it is impossible to obtain reliable data on the numbers of killings, rapes, or instances of torture for both periods, the rough estimates available show a tremendous difference between the Congo in the 1970s and 1980s and the Congo post-2003.

In fact, the understanding of violence against the Congolese population as normal and acceptable even in times of peace is a historical construct that dates back to the nineteenth century.[72] Through cartoons, novels, movies, museum displays, documentaries, policy discourse, and newspaper articles, Belgian colonizers built up the image of the Congolese "inherent savagery" to enable intervention and colonial conquest.[73] This understanding quickly became dominant and persisted throughout the twentieth century. Dunn documents how this established rhetoric influenced U.S. action during Africa's decolonization, and how it partly accounts for the United States' lack of engagement in the Congo in the 1990s despite intervention in Haiti and Kosovo. Westerners did not know the dynamics of the Great Lakes due to the dearth of in-depth research on the region, but a century of powerful imagery enabled them to feel that they knew it well. As Dunn explains, "what was 'known' was that Zaire/Congo was a land of ... inherent savagery, and barbarism, an apolitical chaos beyond the rational comprehension of the 'civilized' West."[74]

In the early twenty-first century, many policy makers, journalists, and most Western and African individuals perpetuated the image of Congolese as brutal, barbarous, and savage "by nature." They suggested that perpetrators waged violence for violence's sake, as pure madness. When discussing the Congolese conflict, they usually emphasized the unending, puzzling, and gruesome character of the violence; the state of quasi-anarchy and chaos; the polarization of the society according to ethnic issues; and the "folkloric" aspects of the Mai Mai militias, such as reliance on supernatural powers and a

---

[72] Dunn 2003.
[73] Hergé's *Tintin au Congo* (Tintin in the Congo, published in 1930–1931) provides an excellent illustration of how this process played out in popular culture.
[74] Dunn 2003, p. 165.

tendency to fight naked.[75] Writer John Le Carré best summarized this widespread perception of the Congo when he explained why he chose to set his 2006 novel, *The Mission Song*, in this country: "The novel isn't really set in Congo at all," he said, "Congo is just backcloth, an abstraction, a symbol of perpetual colonial exploitation, slaughter, famine and disorder."[76]

The belief that the Congo was an inherently turbulent environment enabled international actors to consider that violence not motivated by national or regional tensions was a normal feature of life in a postconflict environment. This dominant narrative did not construct local conflict as a problem that international peacebuilders themselves might be required to address. Intense violence had always been there; it was part of the culture of the country. The only political dimension of this hostility that international actors did have to tackle was the lack of state authority, which enabled a high level of violent criminality. Otherwise, localized violence was devoid of economic, political, military, or social dimensions. A conversation I had with a UN field official prior to an interview perfectly illustrates this point. In passing, he warned me that he probably could not tell me much about local conflict "because [he] covered mainly political and military issues," thus implying that decentralized violence was neither political nor military related. In the dominant narrative, local violence was a mere law and order problem, to be addressed by national authorities once the state had been reconstructed.

Conclusion

The international understanding of the situation in North Katanga provides a perfect illustration of the different trends analyzed in this chapter. Widespread violence persisted in this province throughout

---

[75] See, for example, "Heart of Darkness," a documentary series broadcasted by ABC (USA), January–February 2002; "La malédiction de Kurtz," by Karel de Gucht, *Le Soir*, February 14, 2005; "DR Congo's atrocious secret," by Hilary Andersson, *BBC*, April 9, 2005; "Congo's Conflict: Heart of Darkness," by Sarah J Coleman, *Beliefnet*, June 2, 2005; and "Politics – DRC: Making order out of chaos for the 2006 election," by Anjan Sundaram, *All Africa Global Media*, September 9, 2005. See also the excellent analysis of the media's framing of violence in Baaz and Stern 2008, pp. 58–60.

[76] John Le Carrré, "Congo Journey," *The Nation*, October 2, 2006.

the transition. Yet official documents on the Congo, such as reports of the Secretary-General to the Security Council, reports of the UN Security Council visits to the Great Lakes region, or UN resolutions, as well as international interviewees, very rarely mentioned this fact. When they did, it was to emphasize that Kabila's advisors manipulated North Katangan Mai Mai groups in order to pursue economic or political agendas. In this narrative, when Kabila's advisors feared that the transition process was depriving them of their power, they decided to derail the peace process. This top-down manipulation caused large-scale combat between various Mai Mai groups and units of the integrated Congolese army in mid-2005. It also explained why tensions in the province subsided in 2006: Kabila's advisors saw that they were going to win the elections, and they therefore could allow the transitional process to reach its end.[77] Violence in North Katanga was thus a consequence of macro-level tensions, which would end once national conflicts had disappeared and national actors had agreed to integrate their local proxies into the unified Congolese army.

When I asked international interveners how they explained instances of violence that they could not link to Kabila's advisors, the response was unanimous: Mai Mai violence was "linked to the absence of the state." Criminal agendas, such as controlling mining sites, collecting illegal taxes, and looting the population, were the prime motivation for the militias' actions. The violent nature of Congolese militiamen explained why they committed massive human rights violations – cannibalism, rape, torture, murder – to pursue their criminal activities. Because it was criminal and barbarous, this violence could not and should not have been interpreted as a political project and, as a high-ranking UN military official most strikingly put it, it "was not a major security problem."

Thus, in Katanga and the other eastern provinces, international peacebuilders (with only a few exceptions that chapter 5 analyzes) linked most of the continuing violence during the transition to macro-level antagonisms. In the dominant narrative, regional and national dynamics started the two large-scale conflicts of the late 1990s; these conflicts and the subsequent peace process thoroughly assuaged the main sources of tensions (thus enabling the Congo to enter a

---

[77] For a public source, see Wolters and Boshoff 2006, p. 2.

"postconflict" phase), but many antagonisms remained. Violence continued in the eastern Congo during the transition because regional and national elites manipulated local actors to fulfill their macro-level agendas. Violence noticeably not related to top-down cleavages was a Hobbesian problem. It was the consequence of the lack of state authority in the eastern provinces, itself the result of decades of poor management by the central government. Decentralized conflicts were private and criminal, and grassroots violence was a normal feature of life in a peaceful Congo.

This understanding of violence shaped the strategy that international actors used to support the Congo in its efforts to build peace and democracy. The dominant narrative positioned international actors to work on the regional and national levels. Furthermore, because local conflict was either a consequence of top-down tensions or a normal feature of life in a peaceful Congo (only compounded by the lack of state authority), there was no need to intervene at the local level.

3 | A Top-Down Solution

A story circulates in the small circle of aid workers who spend their lives working in various war environments. Depending on whether I was in Kosovo, the Congo, or Afghanistan, I heard different versions of it applied to the World Bank, the United Nations (UN), or the International Monetary Fund, but its basic components remained the same. In the Congo, for example, the story ran along the following lines. The UN recently published a report on its action in the country. Surprisingly enough, entire sections of this document focused on East Timor. The organization launched an internal inquiry to determine the reasons behind this puzzling discrepancy. It discovered that the staff member who had prepared the report had just been redeployed from East Timor to the Congo. On arrival in his new position, he implemented the exact same strategies in the exact same way he had done in all his previous postings. As usual, when reporting time arrived, he took his template report, hit "search and find," and replaced "East Timor" with "the Congo." This time, he simply missed a few occurrences.

This anecdote encapsulates a complaint that I frequently heard while conducting fieldwork in the Congo. In the words of a local peacebuilder, "there is a tendency for foreign interveners at different levels to arrive with their baggage, their methodology; sometimes they call it their 'toolkit.'" A diplomat based in Kinshasa similarly observed that most UN officials use the same strategy, write the same reports, and organize their lives similarly, regardless of where they are in the world. Most do not even try to contextualize their actions. "It would not change anything for them if, during the night, you transposed them [from the Congo] to Afghanistan," he said. A UN official agreed, deploring the fact that his colleagues had forced a template on the Congo in which elections were key but not necessarily suitable for the circumstances. Each of these interviewees, and many of their colleagues, emphasized that UN staff, diplomats, and nongovernmental organization officials often approached the problems of the Congolese transition though a series of standardized, technical tasks.

This common criticism of international interventions raises a fascinating puzzle. Why do intelligent, well-read, and well-trained people, genuinely moved by Congolese suffering and committed to ending it, still adopt a one-size-fits-all approach to peacebuilding, especially when it has often proved inadequate in the past? The answer lies in the dominant international peacebuilding culture.

In this chapter, I trace how international peacebuilders understood their role as foreign interveners and how this understanding, in turn, shaped their evaluation of which actions and strategies would be appropriate. I identify four central elements of the dominant peacebuilding culture: the conception of the UN and diplomatic staff's role as "naturally" focused on the regional and national realms, the belief that specific strategies are appropriate for "postconflict" environments, the veneration of elections, and the view of humanitarian and development aid as an ideal solution to local conflict. I locate the sources of these dominant understandings, respectively, in the organizational cultures of international bureaucracies, the peacebuilding field, the world polity, and again the peacebuilding field. I show how these four dominant understandings have shaped the material and intellectual "toolkit" that international actors have developed for their interventions in postconflict environments. I also delineate how, during the Congolese transition, these collective understandings influenced intervention on the ground. In doing so, I illuminate why the international peacebuilding strategy of the Congolese transition was perfectly sensible to its implementers even though events on the ground quickly established its inadequacy.

The chapter first shows that, in addition to their assessment of violence detailed in chapter 2, UN staff, diplomats, and nongovernmental organization officials shared three beliefs that shaped their view of how foreign interventions should be conducted. To start with, international actors perceived themselves as working in the face of multiple almost insurmountable constraints that prevented them from addressing all of the dimensions of the Congolese crisis. To prioritize, they relied on two other dominant understandings central to the prevailing peacebuilding culture. Due to training and socialization processes, UN officials and diplomats believed their only legitimate role was to intervene at the regional and national levels. Additionally, because they defined the Congolese transition as a postconflict situation, they judged that they should adopt strategies different from those that they had used when the Congo was at war.

Beyond shaping the overall intervention strategy, these three shared understandings directly influenced the international actors' choice of which specific tools to employ during the Congolese transition. All of these tools had to be macro-level instruments. Influenced by the ideological environment of the post-Cold War era, diplomats, UN staff members, and nongovernmental organization officials focused on the organization of general elections. They saw other state- and peacebuilding tasks as secondary, still approaching them, if at all, in a top-down fashion. Humanitarian and development aid, which they perceived as an apolitical solution to an apolitical problem (the continuation of violence on the ground), was the only exception to this macro-level approach.[1]

Three Shared Understandings

An Impossible Mission

The international peacebuilders I interviewed and the documents I analyzed emphasized one central claim: Diplomats, UN staff members, and nongovernmental organization officials saw themselves as working in an extremely difficult environment, riddled with innumerable almost insurmountable constraints.[2]

Peacebuilding in countries emerging from war is generally an enormous endeavor. As former UN Secretary-General Kofi Annan has noted, it requires many tasks, including "the creation or strengthening of national institutions, monitoring elections, promoting human rights, providing for reintegration and rehabilitation programs, and creating conditions for resumed development."[3] In the Congo, international actors viewed their task as even more difficult than usual. At the onset of the transition, the Secretary-General emphasized the "magnitude of the challenges" that the UN mission had to overcome:

---

[1] Some material in this chapter is revised and expanded from Autesserre 2009.
[2] See Staibano 2005 for a public source on many of the points developed in this section.
[3] UN Secretary-General 1998, para. 63.

The political arrangements underlying the transition process are complex, the country lacks a strong and efficient public administration, and many of the political actors have little direct experience in democratic practices. Basic mechanisms for the functioning of a modern state (such as a statewide banking system) are often non-existent. ... The country is still divided, military hostilities continue in the east, the population is traumatized by years of conflict, the country is poverty stricken and State services and infrastructure are non-existent.[4]

In a later report, he added, "It should also be remembered that the country has suffered from four decades of corrupt governance and has never enjoyed true democracy."[5] All of these conditions made peacebuilding seem particularly challenging, if not impossible, to the international interveners involved in the Congo.

UN, diplomatic, and nongovernmental staff members constantly enumerated the obstacles that they met in their daily work during the transition. They deplored the presence of spoilers, the continued involvement of Rwanda and Uganda, the national and foreign interests in the looting of natural resources, the collapsed state, the unceasing security problems that rendered many areas inaccessible to almost all international actors, and the tremendous logistical hurdles. The lack of roads and communication infrastructures meant that the interveners had to carry out most excursions by plane, even if only over short distances, and this logistical burden was extremely costly. International actors also worried that, after seven years of war, Congolese society was so polarized that the population viewed any peacebuilding action suspiciously. Congolese often considered peacebuilders either as manipulated by one of the warring parties or as the puppets of foreign powers and potential spies.

Additionally, almost all of the officials of the United Nations Mission in the Congo (MONUC) I interviewed, in both the Congo and New York, at the bottom and at the top of the hierarchy, deplored a lack of financial resources. Such complaints could seem preposterous given that MONUC enjoys the highest budget of any peacekeeping mission (reaching more than $1.1 billion per year during the transition, and continuing at that level at the time of this writing in 2009). However,

---

[4] UN Security Council 2003c, paras. 67 and 92.
[5] UN Security Council 2004d, para. 108.

this budget was "primarily concerned with the mission's logistical needs," especially transportation. The amount available for financing other activities was, therefore, "minimal."[6]

Moreover, diplomatic and UN interviewees repeatedly mentioned the endless bureaucratic impediments they faced. MONUC interviewees particularly emphasized hurdles rooted in bureaucratic red tape, conflicting loyalties, and antagonistic interpersonal relationships. They regretted spending too much valuable time filling out request forms, waiting for countless intermediaries to approve their requests, and attempting to comply with the numerous UN standard operating procedures. Military staff members lamented UN regulations concerning the use of troops and equipment, which hindered their combat efforts. Furthermore, many countries tried to pursue their own interests through the UN mission by swaying its mandate or influencing the nationals they had within the organization; consequently, they ended up damaging MONUC's internal cohesion. According to diplomatic and UN interviewees, the loyalty of many MONUC staff was primarily to their nation state and not to the UN. These issues were problematic for the civilian side of the mission and far worse for the military side. Different contingents reportedly consulted with their capitals before deciding whether they would obey the orders of their UN Force Commanders. The UN itself identified this problem as one of the main causes for the MONUC troops' failure to respond adequately to the May–June 2004 large-scale fighting in Bukavu.[7]

Most interviewees also lamented the lack of coordination among different sections and departments, as well as between civilian and military staff, which impaired work within their organizations. Lines or fractures of a more personal nature reinforced this lack of internal cohesion. According to many MONUC officials, the UN mission "swarmed with" personal conflicts rooted in discrimination or favoritism according to gender, age, nationality, race, religion, language, or culture. Similarly, diplomatic missions suffered from a lack of coordination and rivalry among ministries active in the Congo (such as

---

[6] Sundh 2004. For primary evidence in support of this statement, see the various UN general assembly resolutions on "Financing of the United Nations Organization Mission in the Democratic Republic of the Congo" (2004–2006).
[7] UN Mission in the Democratic Republic of Congo (MONUC) 2005b.

the ministries of foreign affairs, defense, and cooperation and development), decision centers (such as the presidency and Foreign Affairs ministry in France, or the National Security Council and the State Department in the United States), or administrative levels (such as embassies and capitals). Nongovernmental organizations were no exception; they, too, suffered from a lack of coordination among field offices, capitals, and headquarters. These internal fractures regularly hampered the peacebuilding efforts of each of these bureaucracies. For example, MONUC military and civilian personnel often protested that they were never informed of each other's actions, including when these actions could have jeopardized their own projects.[8] If internal cohesion was thus lacking, coordination with other organizations was even more problematic: Many interviewees complained that their peacebuilding partners refused to share information and to assist them in their work.

Diplomats, UN staff, and nongovernmental organization officials also often complained of human resource constraints, as all encountered difficulties in recruiting qualified staff willing to work or stay in the Congo. Many seasoned expatriates viewed the Congo as a highly dangerous place and a difficult posting, one to avoid at all costs. Moreover, the recruitment of people proficient in at least either French or one of the local languages proved problematic. Finally, previous knowledge of the country was usually not a criterion for recruitment, thus diminishing the likelihood of skillful analysis by new arrivals.

By all accounts, the UN peacekeeping mission was most affected by these human resources problems. To begin with, many MONUC staff members, including those within the top management, spoke only English, and not any of the languages widely used in the Congo such as French, Swahili, or Lingala. Ironically, those who did know a language widely used in the Congo often did not speak English sufficiently well to communicate with their colleagues. Furthermore, not only were MONUC troops too few to cover the immense Congolese territory, but they often had inadequate training or insufficient experience in war situations. Congolese and international actors alike (including many MONUC officials themselves) considered many

[8] For public sources on this topic, see Staibano 2005, p. 13; and "Congo: Deal with the FDLR threat now," International Crisis Group's Media Release, Brussels, 14 September 2005.

battalions incompetent, cowardly, and unmotivated. To add to these challenges, the civilian side of the mission was constantly under-staffed. In 2005, for example, the vacancy rate reached 27%.[9] Many interviewees, both within and outside of MONUC, also emphasized that the mission's civilian staff often lacked the competence, train-ing, capability, experience, or motivation necessary to fulfill their tasks.

According to many Congolese interviewees, this human resource problem fueled the foreign peacebuilders' already high unpopu-larity among the local population, a fact that many international interveners did not fully realize. The UN had a dubious history of involvement in the region, due to its failure to respond to both the Rwandan genocide and the subsequent massacres of Hutu refugees by the Rwandan army in the Congo. Moreover, in the minds of many Congolese, the UN was present during – and therefore likely impli-cated in – the darkest pages of their history: the secession of Katanga and South Kasai in 1960, the assassination of the beloved Prime Minister Patrice Lumumba in 1961, the massive influx of Rwandan refugees in 1994 and the subsequent Rwandan invasion in 1996, as well as the assassination of President Laurent-Désiré Kabila in 2001. The behavior of MONUC staff during the war and the transition did very little to improve the UN's image in the eyes of the local popula-tion. To the Congolese, the peacekeepers wasted the Congo's money (or money that international actors had earmarked for the Congo) on large cars, high salaries, and beautiful houses. They failed to ful-fill some of their duties, in particular the protection of the popula-tion – most saliently in Kisangani in 2002, in Bunia in 2003, and in Bukavu in 2004. In 2005, a major sexual exploitation scandal involv-ing a number of MONUC civilian and military staff members dealt a final blow to the UN mission's popularity. Overall, the Congolese often saw MONUC staff as useless parasites, whom they nicknamed "tourists in a war zone."[10]

MONUC's unpopularity not only affected its ability to pursue peacebuilding programs, but also negatively impacted the popularity and credibility of other international interveners. Most Congolese,

[9] UN Security Council 2005k.
[10] Nickname reported in "UN takes fight to DR Congo militia," *BBC*, 2 March 2005.

not aware of the subtle differences between the various expatriates present in the Congo, usually considered all foreigners – UN, nongovernmental organizations, diplomatic staff, and academic researchers – to be "MONUC staff" and heaped on them all of the negative connotations that the phrase carried. This categorization, combined with a widespread perception that the peacebuilders were unsuccessful – confirmed by the continuation of violence in the eastern provinces – resulted in a growing antiforeigner sentiment that reached higher levels than ever during the transition.

This shared understanding of the peacebuilding environment as a particularly difficult one, fraught with multiple logistic, security, human, and financial constraints, was the first of the three main collective understandings that shaped the overall intervention strategy. As numerous interviewees explained, international actors could not undertake every single peacebuilding task because they faced so many obstacles. Rather, they had to concentrate their limited resources on a select number of top priorities.

It is important to note that these numerous constraints could have prompted international interveners to adopt many different approaches. For instance, international actors might have abandoned the Congo, as is often the case with African conflicts, to avoid facing these obstacles. They might have, as the UN charter mandates, established a UN trusteeship for the country to give the UN as much power as possible to overcome the existing limitations. Alternatively, they might have focused on bottom-up peacebuilding to circumvent the inefficient and corrupt Transitional Government. Instead, because of their socialization and training processes, virtually all international peacebuilders believed that the only legitimate approach they could employ had to center on interactions with regional and national leaders.

A Top-Down Approach

Though certain international peacebuilders sometimes made minimal attempts at intervention at the local and provincial levels, extremely varied actors – including MONUC military contingents and UN civilians, diplomats from various countries and continents, World Bank employees, and staffs of many nongovernmental organizations – shared one significant characteristic. They focused almost exclusively on the macro level.

UN Security Council resolutions, for example, always called for action at the regional and national levels. The same is true for the reports on MONUC that the UN Secretary-General delivered to the Security Council. The 15th Report, dated March 2004, for instance, lists the Secretary-General's recommendations to strengthen the peace process, none of which go below the national level. The 16th Report, dated December 2004, presents MONUC's two-pronged strategy for the remaining part of the transition as "helping the Government to draft essential legislation and hold credible elections" and "creat[ing] concrete leverage ... that can lead to internationally sanctioned actions aimed at neutralizing spoilers."[11] None of the subsequent reports mention action at the local level. Likewise, throughout the transition, the most powerful peacebuilders – diplomats, donors, and international organizations such as MONUC and the World Bank – spent their time mediating and, when necessary, pressuring the main Congolese, Rwandan, and Ugandan political and military leaders, while disregarding grassroots actors.

There are two reasons for this overall focus. First, peacebuilders understood the continuing violence as a top-down problem. Second, they understood their role as exclusively concerned with top-down intervention. In this framework, "top-down" did not mean a top-down approach at the provincial or local level, such as working with local warlords, provincial governors, or village and community chiefs. Rather, it meant working at the regional and national levels (regional still meaning at the level of the Great Lakes region).

An "Automatic and Intuitive" Strategy. As detailed in chapter 2, international peacebuilders located the causes of continued violence in the regional and national realms. Following this diagnosis, it made perfect sense for them to focus their efforts at the macro level. Because regional and national tensions generated most of the persisting violence in the eastern provinces, assuaging these tensions would end the continued fighting. Because antagonisms among the leaders of the former warring parties accounted for the slow progress of the transition – especially in terms of the reunification of the country, the army integration, and the enactment of essential legislation – reconciling these leaders would help achieve the objectives of

---

[11] UN Security Council 2004c, para. 30.

the transition. Finally, because the residual, grassroots violence was due to the absence of state authority, state reconstruction would end it. As a UN official described, a state-building process oriented at the macro level would provide the Congo with legitimate state authorities who would subsequently address the "law and order" problems in the eastern provinces. Local violence would then "taper downwards as the transition was consolidated and as the state extended." Many Western diplomats similarly claimed that "helping Congolese build up a state" and reconstruct the rule of law was the best way to end violence by armed groups.

As a result, several diplomats and UN staff members explained to me that they and their colleagues had decided not to focus on local conflicts for the time being, following a "sound analysis and decision-making" process. A high-ranking diplomat stated that "the international community looked at international, national, and local issues and concluded that it wanted to put an emphasis on the main external and national issues." In justifying this decision, he offered that working at the local level would result only in a "short-term assuaging of local violence," while efforts at the national and international levels would result in a "long-term peaceful [solution for] the Congo." Another diplomat concurred and added that regional and national endeavors in fact constituted the first part of a sequence of actions that began at the macro level and then moved down to the local level. Actions at the macro level were supposed to create an "enabling environment," "solidify the state," and allow the overall situation to evolve from emergency to rehabilitation and development. Only when these top-down actions had succeeded would the political and economic context be fit for bottom up work. He regarded the idea of working at the local level before solving the national and regional problems as a waste of time, because "all the efforts at the bottom would always be jeopardized by problems at the top." For both of the above-mentioned interviewees, and for a few of their colleagues within diplomatic missions and in the UN, action at the grassroots level would be appropriate and constructive only once they had stabilized the regional and national levels.

However, the vast majority of my interviewees did not say they had intentionally decided to ignore local tensions, as did those discussed earlier. Rather, they painted a much more complex picture of the situation. To them, not addressing local problems was rarely a conscious "decision." Instead, electing to work exclusively on the regional and national levels, and not on local conflict, was "automatic and intuitive." Most interviewees took this decision for granted, to such an extent that many acknowledged that they had not even considered the possibility of working on local issues. In sum, the decision to focus on the macro level was largely not the result of rational decision making, but the product of a shared understanding of what appropriate peacebuilding strategies could include. This understanding was rooted in the identities and organizational cultures of the main international bureaucracies involved in the Congo.

Organizational Cultures. Peacebuilding agencies in the Congo each had its own organizational culture, which shaped its actions and which most staff members saw as fixed and unquestionable. In particular, the most powerful of these organizations, the diplomatic missions and the UN, defined their role as exclusively concerned with regional and national matters, and not with subnational ones. This shared understanding had been constructed and reproduced over decades, or in the case of diplomatic missions, sometimes hundreds of years, and was thus already deeply ingrained by the time the Congolese transition started.

Since diplomacy's origins in classical antiquity, the diplomat's role has been to develop good relationships with host governments, to gather information, and to protect one's nationals. It was not to get involved with subnational actors. The development of a system of sovereign states, which upheld the doctrine of nonintervention in the domestic affairs of other states and was codified in the 1648 treaty of Westphalia, reinforced the diplomats' tendency to interact primarily with state representatives. Many features of diplomacy changed dramatically between the seventeenth and the twentieth centuries (notably criteria for recruitment and staff's techniques for gathering and transmitting information), but one characteristic remained. Diplomats focused on relationships among central governments and, by extension, among governing elites.[12] Indeed, *Satow's Guide to Diplomatic Practice*, the diplomats' handbook in the twentieth century, still defined diplomacy as "the application of intelligence and tact to the conduct of official relations between the governments of

---

[12] Hamilton and Langhorne 1995; and Neumann 2008b.

independent states, extending sometimes also to their relations with vassal states."[13] Being a diplomat still meant working almost exclusively with state representatives and other economic and political leaders, although there was always some contact with other groups.[14]

The rise of international organizations such as the League of Nations and the UN as important diplomatic forums profoundly changed the practice of diplomacy but, because such institutions gathered only diplomats and international civil servants, they only reinforced diplomats' tendency to work at the macro level.[15] After World War II, important developments took place in the world polity culture.[16] Largely as a result of the decolonization process, the norm of discouraging international interference in the domestic affairs of a sovereign state became very influential on the international scene.[17] This norm influenced all international actors to varying extents, but its effect on diplomats was clear: It reinforced the diplomatic tendency to focus on macro-level developments. At the same time, the Cold War strategic framework of U.S.–Soviet relations led both superpowers to resolve conflicts in their zones of influence. As the Assistant Secretary of State for African Affairs under the administration of George H.W. Bush recalled, this course of action invariably resulted in a top-down approach to conflict resolution.[18]

The classic diplomatic ethos was so hierarchical and so focused on top-down strategies that a new kind of approach, called "Track II diplomacy," developed in the 1960s. Nondiplomatic actors, such as religious and nongovernmental organizations, would complement traditional diplomatic work by adopting a bottom-up (or rather a decentralized top-down) approach.[19] This development is particularly interesting because it did not change the practice of diplomacy itself, although it represented an acknowledgment that working at

---

[13] Satow 1979, p. 3; and Neumann 2002, p. 639.
[14] Neumann 2002, p. 639; see also Barston 1988; Hamilton and Langhorne 1995; Jönsson and Hall 2005; Nicolson 1988; Simpson 1972; and Watson 1991.
[15] Hamilton and Langhorne 1995; and Jönsson and Hall 2005.
[16] Paris 2003; see also Richmond 2002, chapter 2.
[17] See Vincent 1974 for a fascinating history of the nonintervention norm, in particular prior to the Cold War and during its early years.
[18] Cited in Schraeder 2003.
[19] Lewer 1999; see also Richmond 2002, especially pp. 9–11 and chapters 2 and 4.

the local level could be crucial. Diplomacy remained a hierarchical, top-down endeavor, and bottom-up work became the prerogative of other, decentralized actors.

Similarly, in recent years, foreign ministries have increasingly acknowledged that diplomats should engage with nonstate actors, and they have developed pilot projects to give subnational state representatives a diplomatic function. However, the traditional model of diplomacy, which stresses the centrality of intergovernmental relations and emphasizes top-down processes, has remained dominant.[20] One needs only consider the many memoirs published by diplomats in recent years – or interview other diplomats – for evidence of this persisting ethos: Diplomats seem to spend their lives in meetings with government representatives, journalists, and the occasional Western aid worker. If they do engage with local people, such encounters are rarely significant enough to warrant mention. Just as was true a century ago, diplomats still regard their interactions with governing elites as the only meaningful part of their daily work.[21]

Like diplomatic missions, the most influential international organizations in the Congo have, ever since their founding, cultivated internal cultures that were macro-level oriented. The UN was created in 1945 as an international organization tasked with intergovernmental work, and its charter prohibited it from intervening in "matters which are essentially within the domestic jurisdiction of any state."[22] Many UN-affiliated organizations, such as the World Bank and the International Monetary Fund, have a similar statutory obligation to work through the national government in their countries of intervention and to respect the countries' sovereignty on internal matters. Moreover, as diplomats staffed these organizations from the very beginning, the diplomatic culture – and especially the diplomats' understanding of their role as focused on government-to-government, elite-to-elite, top-down interactions – influenced the constitution of these bureaucracies' cultures from the start.[23]

Although these international organizations quickly established recruitment channels independent of their member states, "recruitment remained in a very high degree the [prerogative] of the world's foreign

---

[20] Hocking 2004; Lewer 1999; and Neumann 2002, pp. 641–644.
[21] See, for example, Grove 2005; Holbrooke 1998; and Thayer 1974.
[22] UN Charter, Chapter 1, Article 2, point 7.   [23] Watson 1991, pp. 28–29.

ministries," and thus the diplomatic ethos persisted.[24] The two post-World War II trends mentioned previously further reinforced the tendencies of international organizations' staff to focus on the macro level. Because of the diplomatic tensions between the West and the Communist bloc during the Cold War, the two superpowers regularly prevented the UN from intervening in the subnational affairs of any state for fear that it would jeopardize their control over their allies. Furthermore, the noninterference norm deeply influenced the UN, which was committed to upholding this principle as well as that of self-determination.[25] Even when the UN needed to intervene militarily, peacekeeping missions identified and employed strategies that "emphasize[d] the fastest possible transfer of governmental power to [national] actors and the expeditious departure of the peacekeepers from the country in order to minimize the degree of external interference in the country."[26]

Before and during the Congolese transition, two main mechanisms helped spread these collective understandings of the "legitimate" role of each international intervener among and within organizations. First, many diplomats moved back and forth between international organizations and their foreign ministries. Second, diplomats and UN officials moved from headquarters to the field or from one field mission to the next every couple of years. With each move, these actors brought to their new positions the knowledge they had acquired in previous postings, including an implicit understanding of their new organizations' role.

Practical Implications. During the Congolese transition, UN actors and diplomats interpreted the prohibition of international interference in the domestic affairs of states as forbidding action at the subnational level. According to most UN, diplomatic, and nongovernmental interviewees, such subnational intervention would be a paternalist, neocolonial, or neoimperial endeavor. In contrast, international actors considered interference legitimate as long as they worked with, and filtered their demands through, national representatives. For example, the diplomats and UN staff I interviewed did not perceive their efforts to influence the Congolese constitution as paternalist, neocolonial,

---

[24] Neumann 2008b, p. 6.
[25] Paris 2003; see also Richmond 2002, chapter 2.
[26] Paris 2003, p. 462. See Fetherston and Nordstrom 1995 for an analysis of UN peacekeepers' consistent top-down approach to violence in the mid-1990s.

or neoimperial, even though they put tremendous pressure on the transitional representatives, wrote part of the constitution, and then threatened to cut funding if the parliament did not adopt a document satisfactory to Western powers. International interveners deemed these and other actions, such as pressuring Congolese legislators as the laws on elections and citizenship were being written, acceptable because they remained at the macro level.

The shared understanding that the UN and diplomatic missions' identities and roles were exclusively focused on national and international matters also influenced the structure of these organizations. The departments within foreign ministries and international organizations were arranged along international, regional, or national lines (for example, "UN desk," "Africa bureau," or "Congo desk"). Similarly, within the UN peacekeeping operation deployed in the Congo, the various departments were organized around national- or regional-level themes: elections; civil affairs; disarmament, demobilization, repatriation, reintegration, and resettlement of foreign combatants; and so on. Finally, with only a few exceptions, diplomats and experts deployed abroad were usually based in the capital of the host state.

In keeping with this tradition, on the rare occasions that diplomats working on the Congo from their national capitals or the international organizations' headquarters traveled to the field, they usually went to the Congolese capital. Likewise, with the exception of the South African and Belgian consuls in Lubumbashi (Katanga), all diplomats stationed on the ground were based in Kinshasa, and they seldom visited the interior of the country more than a couple of times a year. The European Union (EU) and Belgium deployed a few representatives of their aid departments to the eastern provinces, but these officials focused only on aid issues (which, as I explain below, were considered to be apolitical), and they did not have diplomatic status. While the UN did deploy many civilians and military representatives to the provinces, almost all of the top management staff were based in the Kinshasa headquarters and seldom traveled beyond the capital.

This geographical bias further reinforced the international actors' tendency to focus on capital-centered developments. For example, a Belgian diplomat explained that, during the transition, "the reports written by the [Belgian] embassy that were devoted to the provinces, or to a specific province" were only about 10 or 15% of all the "reports, mail, and electronic communications" that were sent to Brussels each day.[27] He emphasized that, as a result, his colleagues in Brussels, just like those in Kinshasa, "tended to perceive the country through its capital." Several diplomats and UN officials I interviewed similarly explained that being based in Kinshasa tainted their view of the Congolese transition and strengthened their propensity to concentrate on events unfolding in the capital – such as the legislative and constitutional process or the tensions within the Transitional Government – rather than on events occurring elsewhere in the country.

Last, the diplomatic and UN staffs' shared understanding of their identities and roles influenced the expertise that was available in each bureaucracy. Long formal training (for diplomats) or a short induction course (for MONUC staff), as well as everyday interactions with other staff members, helped socialize newcomers within their organizations' cultures.[28] Both categories of actors learned to consider diplomatic solutions (meaning solutions based on negotiations with top political leaders) to any kind of problem they encountered. Diplomats also studied how to develop good relationships with presidents or ministers, including those who were corrupt and involved in violence, and how to maintain these relationships even in the most difficult circumstances. Finally, though each country and organization had different additional priorities, such as economic and trade issues for Belgium and maintaining peace and security for the UN, all their training processes focused on macro-level actions. Would-be Belgian diplomats visited central banks to learn how to finance exportations. UN officials similarly learned to find state-centered responses to security problems. Overall, UN and diplomatic interveners became used to framing their policies in general terms, which were perfectly appropriate for action on the regional and national scenes but not for work at the grassroots level.

As a result of these various diffusion, training, and socialization processes, virtually all foreign government officials, diplomats, and staff of international organizations posted in the Congo claimed their

[27] Author's interview with Jozef Smets, Belgian Ministry of Foreign Affairs, Africa department, Brussels, May 2005. Smets excludes from this statistic the specific case of Katanga, where Belgium had a consulate.

[28] Weick 1995 provides an overview of how socialization produces similar views among professionals. Barnett 2002, Barnett and Finnemore 2004, and Eden 2004 present fascinating case studies of such processes within national and international bureaucracies.

organizations had always focused on superstructures, such as states, international organizations, or regional and national dialogues. Notwithstanding rare attempts at contesting this (documented in chapter 5), international peacebuilders thus concluded that focusing their overall approach on the macro level was the only "natural" and "appropriate" course of action.

A *"Postconflict" Intervention*

A macro-level focus was thus a standard rule, deeply rooted in the UN and embassies' organizational cultures. In practice, however, international actors could abstain from subnational intervention only because, during the transition, they labeled the Congo a "postconflict" situation. During a time of war, involvement with at least some subnational actors is inevitable. For example, during the Congolese wars of the 1990s, UN staff and diplomats had to convince the various rebel leaders to agree to peace negotiations and sign peace settlements. UN actors also sometimes needed to mediate local ceasefires. The U.S. government toyed with the idea of organizing a "Kivu dialogue" to resolve the tensions between the various communities of this province. Then, as detailed in chapter 2, in late 2002, international interveners recategorized the Congo as a postconflict situation. The label "postconflict" signals a return to some kind of normality, notably the decline of violence throughout the country as well as the presence of a unified government that supposedly controls the state's territory. This labeling thus ushered in a change in the material and intellectual tools that international actors used to understand the Congolese situation and to act within it. Although the tools each organization used were different, they shared two characteristics: They were top-down and they were appropriate for stable environments rather than for those in conflict. As a Western government official recalled, from the point the situation was redefined, he and his colleagues "started working in another framework: the implementation of the peace process, of peace. [They] were no longer in a conflict zone."

This shift halted the few efforts at subnational conflict resolution that interveners had previously considered. High-ranking diplomats as well as MONUC's top managers began considering local conflict as an exclusively internal matter that fell within the expertise of the Transitional Government. As a high-ranking UN official recalled,

"The structures that had been able to deal with [warring] parties as [legitimate] parties disappeared" when the transition started. The UN officially started working "in support of the Transitional Government," through the International Committee in Support of the Transition (a formal structure created by the peace agreement to institutionalize the leading role of the international community in its implementation) and through three joint commissions on the legislative process, security-sector reform, and electoral agendas.[29] Diplomats became wary of antagonizing the president and vice presidents for fear of failing in their most essential duty: maintaining good relationships with the host government. Diplomats and international organization staff members were especially cautious with the president because, as a diplomat temporarily dispatched to MONUC explained to me, "instinctively, as a diplomat, you are taught that you don't argue with presidents." Therefore, "something changed" with the formation of the Transitional Government: Diplomats respected the president more than the vice presidents even though they were constitutionally his equivalents, so "the parties were not equal" in practice. Because of this preferential attitude, in late 2003, when Kabila refused to let Congolese Rally for Democracy-Goma (RCD-G) general Laurent Nkunda assume the military leadership position that the peace agreements allocated to him (thus sowing the seeds for subsequent large-scale fighting), diplomats and UN management staff did not pressure Kabila as much as they could have because "a president is a president," and diplomats do not second-guess presidents.

Furthermore, as mentioned earlier, from the moment of the postconflict recategorization, the UN mission was considered a peace*keeping* and not peace enforcement mission. As a result, soldiers deployed to the Congo did not arrive with any expectation of fighting, and combat material was not always available.[30] MONUC civilian officials similarly stated that they came to help solidify peace, not to work in a war zone. The 2004 fighting in Bukavu and the subsequent anti-MONUC protests therefore took many peacekeepers by surprise, to such an extent that several wondered how their roles might alter in this "changed," violent environment.

[29] UN Security Council 2004d, para. 119.
[30] For a public source, see Cowan 2005.

The postconflict designation also created an additional constraint on UN staff and diplomats. Because the Congo was not at war, subnational actors could no longer be considered "rebels" or "warring parties." Instead, the label "postconflict" ushered in a distinction between parties that could be seen as legitimate partners and those that could not. This differentiation separated those with whom diplomats could meet and negotiate (the actors participating in the transition) from those with whom discussions were now considered "illegal" (the actors continuing to commit violence and not participating in the transition). Diplomats and UN staff were not supposed to meet with the "illegal" actors officially; it would risk legitimizing and reinforcing them. As a result, the option of mediating between different combatants disappeared, because at least one of the parties was now considered illegitimate.

The illegal status ascribed to "renegade leader" Laurent Nkunda and the subsequent problems it caused clearly illustrate the consequences of this new constraint. In the first months of 2004, when warning signs of an impending crisis were developing, the MONUC leadership categorized Nkunda as an illegal actor whom its staff members were forbidden from meeting. The logic of exclusion continued until it was too late: Nkunda took over the eastern city of Bukavu (South Kivu) in May 2004, and MONUC officials were forced to negotiate with him. Then again, in 2006 to 2007, when it became obvious that Nkunda was building a quasi-independent state in the territory under his control in North Kivu, the top UN hierarchy similarly prevented its staff from meeting with the agitator. The setbacks of this strategy became evident in late 2007 and in 2008, when heavy fighting resumed between Nkunda and the Congolese army.

The Intervention Tools

These three dominant understandings guided which tools international interveners would employ during the Congolese transition. Regarding the region and nation as the only legitimate levels for their actions, UN staff members and diplomats could use only macro-level instruments. Yet interveners could not employ their entire toolkit at once, as they faced so many constraints that it was impossible to tackle all the dimensions of the Congolese crisis. In prioritizing, a dominant world polity ideology oriented their choice toward a standard instrument used in "postconflict" environments: the organization of elections. With the notable exception of humanitarian aid, international interveners saw other peace- and state-building tasks as secondary, still to be approached in a top-down manner and only in response to acute crises or to ensure favorable conditions for the polls.

The Election Fetish

A Favorite Tool. As Paris and Richmond have demonstrated, after the Cold War, a "generally unstated but widely accepted theory of conflict management," the liberal peace thesis, came to dominate the world polity.[31] At the core of this thesis is the belief that states founded on liberal democracy ensure both domestic and international peace, as democracy has the means to resolve antagonisms relatively peacefully and democracies do not fight each other. In the late twentieth century, these shared beliefs quickly evolved into a global norm that most policy makers took for granted

Elections were a central element of the liberal peace paradigm since they represented an essential trait of liberal democracies. Thus, in the 1990s, holding regular elections became the key to domestic and international legitimacy.[32] Major international organizations such as the UN, the Organization for Security and Cooperation in Europe, the Organization of American States, the World Bank, the International Monetary Fund, and virtually all donor governments began to insist that "elections were the only legitimate basis for governmental authorities within states."[33]

In dealing with war-torn and postwar countries, a consensus emerged: Any state that Western powers rebuild *must* be democratic.[34] Thus, the "democratic reconstruction model" was born.[35] This model progressively included so many prescriptions and demands – reform of the entire security sector, reconstruction of the entire political system, and transformation of the entire economic environment – that the endeavor was unlikely to succeed.[36] Elections offered a simple and

---

[31] Guilhot 2005; Paris 2003 and 2004; and Richmond 2005. Quotation from Paris 2004, p. 5.
[32] Paris 2003 and 2004.   [33] Paris 2003, p. 446.   [34] Ottaway 2002.
[35] Ottaway 2003.   [36] Ottaway 2002, pp. 1006–1007; and Ottaway 2003.

straightforward solution to this problem.[37] In the eyes of most policy makers, elections simultaneously worked toward the imperatives
of democratization, legitimation, and war termination. They transformed institutions of war into vehicles for peace and democratization: They represented a return to constitutional rule and established
new political institutions and rules of competition.[38] Elections also
supposedly gave crucial momentum to further democratic reforms
by legitimizing new governments and "broaden[ing] and deepen[ing]
political participation and the democratic accountability of the state to
its citizens."[39] They offered reassurance that peace agreements could
be implemented successfully.[40] In brief, as a landmark UN document
on peacekeeping operations explained, elections "replace[d] a violent
contest for political power with a non-violent one."[41]

Additionally, elections enabled international peacebuilders to act,
because interveners could organize provincial, legislative, and national
polls while remaining in the capital and interacting with national counterparts. Organizing elections had one final advantage. Eventually,
the process would provide international financial institutions and
bilateral donors with the national partners they needed – namely, a
central leadership through which to implement their top-down strategies. These leaders would be "'normal,' internationally-recognized
government[s]," able and willing to implement international norms
and obligations, such as consenting to the presence of peacekeeping
missions, signing memoranda of understanding, or taking responsibility for the money loaned to their country.[42]

Thus, elections became a standard task for postconflict reconstruction worldwide. Beginning in the 1990s, "internationally monitored
elections ... [were] routinely used to validate the political institutions
of states that [were] undergoing regime transitions or emerging from
crises."[43] International organizations and virtually all donor governments saw elections as the prerequisite for development, human rights,

---

[37] The following development builds on Lyons 2004 and 2005; Paris 2003
and 2004; Ottaway 2003; and Youngs 2004. See also Carothers 2002 for a
fascinating analysis of the false assumptions that boost the use of electoral
remedies.
[38] Lyons 2004 and 2005.   [39] Carothers 2002, p. 8.   [40] Lyons 2004.
[41] UN Best Practice Unit 2003, p. 147.
[42] Lyons 2004, p. 37, and 2005; and Woodward 2006.
[43] Paris 2003, p. 445.

peace, security, and justice.[44] Elections, rather than achievements such as the end of large-scale violence or the successful reconstruction of the state, became the symbolic endpoints for UN peacekeeping. As soon as the first postwar voting had transpired, the peace operation was declared successful and began to draw to a close, as occurred in Cambodia in 1993 and in Liberia in 1997.[45]

Holding elections even became equated with establishing democracy. This simplification of democracy was a sharp break from previous conceptions that envisioned a complex system growing out of a long history, often of centuries, and dependent on the idiosyncratic conditions of a country.[46] In this new conception, the success or failure of democracy relied not on deep-rooted, long-term trends but on pacts among elites, which a technical device (elections) could help make or break.[47] Democracy was no longer a contingent, complex, long-term historical process; it was a matter of short-term engineering. It had a clear beginning, the opening of the election campaign, and a clear end, the election of all necessary officials. International peacebuilders no longer needed to worry about creating the broader preconditions that make the electoral process meaningful, such as freedom of speech or freedom of the press. They could build democracy by completing a series of technical tasks.

As a result, very different organizations – including the UN, Western foreign ministries, and many nongovernmental organizations – developed standard operating procedures, a stock of expertise, specialized bureaucracies, and well trained staff to organize elections in postconflict states.[48] Experts developed concrete, quantifiable indicators to calculate the extent to which the vote was democratic, free, and fair, and thus measure the success or failure of the international intervention. Electoral processes became routinized. International interveners could now organize elections by bringing in specialists who would implement voting procedures in all countries following the same specific, predefined strategy.

---

[44] Ibid., p. 445.   [45] Paris 2004, especially chapter 5. See also Lyons 2005.

[46] See, for example, Moore 1966; and Putnam, Leonardi, et al. 1993. I thank Timothy Mitchell for mentioning this idea to me and for providing several of the arguments that I develop in this paragraph.

[47] See Przeworski 1999 for a social science defense of this conception, and Held 2006 for a critical view.

[48] Paris 2003; and Guilhot 2005.

Using the Election Tool in the Congolese Transition. This collective understanding of elections as a standard tool for postconflict reconstruction largely informed the international peacebuilders' decision of how to proceed during the Congolese transition. For almost all the international actors I interviewed, whether high-level diplomats based in their national capitals or low-ranking UN workers deployed in the field, the focus on elections in the "postconflict" Congo was the "natural," "obvious," and "normal" way to proceed.

During formal interviews and informal conversations, when I asked whether, beyond being a standard postconflict reconstruction task, elections were actually suited for the immediate postwar Congo, international actors raised two kinds of arguments. First, they presented elections as a prime peacebuilding mechanism. Because they considered the wars to be consequences of the Congolese government's crisis of legitimacy, they believed elections would play a critical stabilizing role. Elections would help reestablish a legitimate government.[49] They would select a winner among the various warlords who vied for control of the central state, and produce a parliament that represented the entire population. They would even help placate Rwanda and Uganda by giving their alleged proxies an opportunity to contend for national leadership positions.

Second, international actors emphasized that elections were a prime state-building mechanism. The official MONUC Web site, for example, claimed that the mission was working "to establish a lawful state through the organization of multiparty, free, and transparent elections."[50] Security Council members "insisted a lot on the respect of the electoral calendar because it [was] essential that the [Congo] got a real state."[51] It is important to note that, because international actors considered part of the ongoing violence to be a Hobbesian problem, they viewed state reconstruction through elections as the best way to end this continued violence. Overall, as reiterated in

---

[49] For a public source, see International Crisis Group 2007a, p. 2.

[50] See http://www.monuc.org/news.aspx?newsID=742, accessed several times between 2006 and 2008.

[51] Declaration from Jean-Marc de la Sablière, French ambassador to the UN, on behalf of the Security Council delegation that visited the Congo in November 2004. Reported in "Le Conseil de sécurité salue des 'progrès importants' pour la paix en RDC," *AFP*, November 23, 2004. UN Security Council 2005j, p. 3, provides another good example of this widespread conception.

various UN documents, elections marked a "turning point in the history of the Congo" and heralded an era of peace, democracy, and social development.[52]

In addition to providing these rational justifications for their focus on elections, during interviews, most international interveners also voiced a puzzling but widespread belief (or hope) that somehow "things would go better after the elections." Without ever providing much support for their claim, they said that the elections would break the vicious circle of arbitrariness and self-destruction in Congolese political and military life, or solve the problems posed by the Rwandan Hutu militias, the lack of army integration, and the political conflicts among Congolese, Ugandan, and Rwandan actors.[53] All five UN Security Council resolutions concerning the Congo between September 2005 and September 2006 also "underlin[ed] the importance of elections as the foundation for the longer term restoration of peace and stability, national reconciliation and establishment of the rule of law in the Democratic Republic of the Congo."[54] International interveners expected that even the humanitarian situation would improve after the elections.[55]

Beyond these expected benefits for the Congo, according to various interviews and public documents, elections had other concrete advantages for UN contributors and for MONUC itself. The UN Secretary-General presented elections as a central element of MONUC's exit strategy.[56] Elections supposedly determined the length of the transition by marking its end, its "culmination."[57] This benefit was especially important given the financial burden that MONUC represented for UN contributors, the United States in particular. The funding commitment was so significant that it prompted some donors to look

---

[52] UN Security Council 2003a (para. 70), 2004d (para. 110), and 2005j (para. 65).

[53] On the first item, see Karel de Gucht, "La malédiction de Kurtz," *Le Soir*, February 14, 2005.

[54] UN Security Council 2005f, 2005g, 2005h, 2006b, and 2006c. See also "Le Conseil de sécurité salue des 'progrès importants' pour la paix en RDC," AFP, *Kinshasa*, November 23, 2004, for a similar point.

[55] UN Security Council 2005k, para. 57.

[56] UN Security Council 2003c, para. 29; see also Ken Bacon (president of Refugee International), "RI letter to MONUC regarding exit strategy," 2004, http://www.refugeesinternational.org/content/article/detail/1007/.

[57] UN Security Council 2005j (first sentence) and 2003c (para. 81).

for justification to pull the peacekeepers out of the Congo as quickly as possible. Field-based interviewees also emphasized that elections provided them with a concrete outcome (the number of elected officials and the participation rate of the population in the polls) that they could show donors to prove effective use of funds. Last, elections provided a clear means of evaluating the success or failure of the transition. If international observers judged the electoral process as mostly free, fair, and transparent (using indicators developed by electoral experts based on their experience in other countries), they could call the international intervention a success. During interviews, several UN, diplomatic, and nongovernmental organization officials often emphasized that this formulaic approach with its focus on elections was much easier to use than a yet-to-be-developed, situation-specific evaluation of the international intervention based, for example, on the progress that the Congo had made toward state reconstruction or community reconciliation.

This understanding of elections as the natural focus of the international intervention was especially attractive to the peacebuilders deployed in the Congo, not because it offered the only possible reading of the situation, but because it overcame a number of organizational constraints and therefore allowed UN staff and diplomats to act in this otherwise "impossible" situation.[58] Organizing elections did not require any in-depth knowledge of Congolese issues. It could be arranged primarily at the national level, in collaboration with national counterparts. It was a well-rehearsed task, for which the tools, procedures, and expertise were readily available.

At this point in the analysis, we should note that it is only because international actors understood democracy building as a technical, mechanical, and short-term endeavor that they could use this preexisting, acontextual formula to focus their intervention, evaluate their success, and judge whether it was appropriate to withdraw MONUC. It is true that, in theory, international actors acknowledged that a democratic Congo needed much more than just elections. Immediately prior to the transition, for example, the UN Secretary-General report

---

[58] This sentence, just as the process analyzed in this paragraph, builds on Barnett and Finnemore's 2004 study of the development of analytic tools by staff of the International Monetary Fund in the early days of the organization.

on MONUC listed a host of "conditions" viewed as prerequisites to any free and fair elections: security-sector reform; disarmament, demobilization, and reintegration of Congolese and foreign combatants; and the creation of a lawful state, including the organization of a civilian police force. The provision of technical assistance for elections was only one of these many prerequisites, and it was the very last one listed.[59] However, ignoring the necessary preconditions, international peacebuilders used the expertise available to them and focused on the technical dimensions of organizing elections.

A Congolese contact reported an anecdote that exemplifies this process. During a conference, an angry Congolese citizen challenged William Swing, the Special Representative of the UN Secretary-General in the Congo, by saying that free and fair elections could never be organized throughout the Congo during the short period of the transition. Swing answered that the UN had been able to organize a vaccination campaign over the whole territory, so there was no reason why it could not organize elections for the entire country. Whether or not this anecdote is true, it provides a useful comparison. Throughout the transition, international peacebuilders approached the organization of elections in a very similar way to how they approached vaccination campaigns. It was a matter of training facilitators (nurses or voting station clerks), identifying the targets (children under five or Congolese citizens over eighteen), moving the necessary materials (vaccines or ballot boxes), and using predetermined indicators to measure the success of the operation (the percentage of children immunized or the percentage of Congolese citizens who voted). From this point of view, the electoral process was simply, as some of my interviewees put it, "a logistics problem." During the first year and a half of the transition, international actors focused on these logistical challenges to such a point that, in February 2005, they suddenly realized they had overlooked the other critical measures necessary for the elections to take place, such as training Congolese political actors in democratic practices.[60] They financed a few such projects from then on, but the international electoral assistance program nonetheless remained focused on logistical matters.

---

[59] UN Security Council 2003d, para. 59.
[60] Former U.S. Senator Howard Wolpe, Panel on "War Again in the Eastern Congo: International Engagement," Washington, D.C., January 2009.

Admittedly, there was much to overcome logistically. The physical organization of the elections in an immense territory (roughly the size of western Europe or the United States east of the Mississippi) practically devoid of infrastructure and with "a population without identity cards and no census since 1984" required massive financial and logistical resources.[61] Security hurdles were enormous. There was no legal framework for the electoral process when the transition began. As many interviewees concluded, these logistical challenges rendered the Congo host to "the largest and most challenging electoral process ever conducted with UN support."[62]

The size and number of these obstacles might have convinced peacebuilders that they should have devoted their resources to other peace- or state-building priorities. However, the two dominant collective understandings documented in this section help explain why international peacebuilders never considered other alternatives. The focus on elections in postconflict environments was so "natural," so taken for granted, that it was beyond questioning. Likewise, the association of elections with democracy was so strong that questioning the organization of elections would seem as if one was questioning whether the Congolese deserved democracy. Furthermore, in the case of the elections, international peacebuilders were willing to face the obstacles because they were familiar with the tool: They relied on a stock of existing intellectual and material resources for electoral engineering. In the words of a Western diplomat, "If you focus on ending violence, [you are] looking at a problem that people are not able to solve. If you look at elections, you know the steps that you have to take, the things that you have to do." Organizing elections was a feasible, workable task, no matter how severe the constraints and how large the obstacles.

Using the Tool on the Ground: Elections as the Transition's First Priority. The organization of elections thus quickly became the focus of the international intervention in the Congo. As early as mid-2004, all diplomatic and UN interviewees emphasized that the organization of free, democratic, and transparent elections was "the number one priority," the "main goal of the transition." The Secretary-General's 16th Report on MONUC (December 2004) stated that "the overall goal of MONUC in the Democratic Republic of the Congo is

---

[61] Quotation from UN Security Council 2005j, para. 2.
[62] UN Security Council 2006d, para. 69.

the holding of credible elections *followed* by a stable and sustainable peace."[63] The Secretary-General's reports on MONUC started to address the "electoral process" before attending to the "security situation."[64] The amount of space devoted to the electoral process in these reports increased as time passed, eventually taking up more than a third of the 21st and 22nd reports (the last two reports of the transition, dated 2006).[65] By way of comparison, the latter report devoted only one paragraph (out of ninety-eight) to the security situation in North Kivu and one to the security situation in South Kivu.[66] The UN's focus on elections was such that a MONUC manager, reflecting on his organization's work during the transition, concluded that everything done was in the pursuit of general elections. The fifteen member states of the UN Security Council were on the same wavelength, as an analysis of its resolutions, reports, and press releases indicates.[67] More broadly, elections were so central to the peacebuilding strategy that they structured the way international actors, even nongovernmental organizations' staff members, talked about time: In interviews, they organized their thoughts in terms of "preelections" and "postelections."

Accordingly, foreign embassies, many UN agencies and, most important, MONUC devoted the largest part of their human, logistical, military, and financial resources to the organization of elections (with the only exception being humanitarian and development aid, analyzed later in this chapter).[68] While lack of funding constantly held up programs for local peacebuilding, security-sector reform, economic development, and humanitarian aid, international donors managed to fill all funding gaps for the expensive election process.[69] The UN, the EU, and state donors disbursed more than $670 million to cover just the logistical and security costs for the

---

[63] UN Security Council 2004c, para. 29, my emphasis. Most other Secretary-General reports on MONUC written during the transition contain similar statements.
[64] See, for example, UN Security Council 2004d.
[65] UN Security Council 2003–2006a.
[66] UN Security Council 2006e.
[67] See, for example, UN Security Council 2005d and 2005e (para. 2); and Security Council, "Résolution 1565 du Conseil de sécurité prorogeant la MONUC jusqu'au 31 mars 2005," October 1, 2004, Communiqué de presse SC/8203.
[68] For a public source, see International Crisis Group 2006b.
[69] UN Security Council 2003–2006a.

polls.[70] In addition to this already large amount, interveners met the massive indirect costs of the electoral process, such as the numerous "development" projects aimed at preparing the population for the voting and the many measures adopted to secure the country in order to hold elections. In contrast, other contributions to peace and state building were negligible.[71]

While the direct and indirect costs of the electoral process were enormous, the opportunity costs were even larger. Because international actors upheld such a strict focus, they diverted much-needed financial, human, logistical, and military resources – which they could have used to help secure the unstable eastern provinces – to the election process.[72] Moreover, most MONUC staff and diplomats subordinated other state reconstruction and peacebuilding tasks to the organization of elections. Most significant for this book is how the focus on elections influenced the way international actors evaluated continuing violence. For example, in his reports to the Security Council, the Secretary-General regularly emphasized the threat posed by Rwandan Hutu militias and various Congolese armed groups "to the security of the [Congolese] electoral process," as if the soldiers' threats to the election process eclipsed the horrors these combatants perpetrated on the Congolese population.[73] The UN Security Council, the MONUC desk officer for the Congo, and the UN Special Representative for the Congo often presented security problems similarly.[74] Toward the

---

[70] Journalists and researchers usually report a figure of $585 million. This estimate, however, fails to include two major EU contributions: $75 million disbursed to deploy 2,000 EU troops for the 2006 general elections, and over $11 million spent on election observation missions.

[71] International Crisis Group 2006b provides the most comprehensive source of data on this topic. For additional sources, see the financial reports by the Congo's ministry of budget and by the Congo's foreign donors.

[72] See Human Rights Watch 2007, p. 114, for a similar claim, and UN Security Council 2005b (para. 64), 2006e (para. 81), and 2005k (para. 67); and MONUC press briefing, August 31, 2005 (sent by e-mail by the MONUC Public Information Office), for details on this distribution of resources within MONUC.

[73] See, for example, UN Security Council 2004d (para. 117) and 2005b (para. 25).

[74] See, for example, UN Security Council 2005g; William Lacy Swing, "War, peace and international engagement in the Congo," *Statement to the US Institute for Peace, Washington,* 2006, cited in Katz-Lavigne 2008; and "R.D. du Congo: bilan des préparatifs des élections pour le printemps 2006," ONU News Center, August 17, 2005.

end of the transition, the obsession with elections became so great that interviewed diplomats and UN staff members would state that the Congolese transition was aimed at organizing general elections; they often forgot to mention that the transition was also supposed to ensure that violence ceased throughout the Congolese territory. Several countries actually argued that the elections should proceed even if large-scale fighting resumed in the eastern provinces, because these provinces were marginal compared to the rest of the country and the inevitability of the elections would have a deterrent effect on spoilers. Clearly, the psychological disconnect between elections and peace had become such that diplomats envisioned the possibility of a successful completion of the "transition to peace and democracy" even in the event of renewed war.

International actors therefore oriented their military strategy toward the organization of the elections rather than ending collective violence. In mid-2005, for instance, the UN Secretary-General requested additional troops for Katanga not to secure the province – where large-scale fighting between Mai Mai and governmental troops was ongoing – but rather to ensure the security of elections. The UN Security Council finally authorized this troop deployment in 2006, but only for the duration of the electoral period, and only to provide support for the elections.[75] There, and in the rest of the country, MONUC expected to dramatically decrease its support for the integrated Congolese army and its actions against militias once the elections had transpired.[76] Just like the international military strategy, the Congolese security-sector reform came to have one main strategic orientation: providing security for the elections. The first phase of the plan was to create and train eighteen army brigades by June 2006 in an effort to safeguard the electoral process, rather than protect the Congolese territory and population.[77] The reform of the police was similarly oriented toward providing election security.[78] In 2007, a French diplomat looking back on the transition summarized the overall approach used during the previous years: "The objective was not

---

[75] UN Security Council 2004d, 2005j, 2005b, and 2005g. See also UN Security Council 2005k, para. 28.
[76] Wolters and Boshoff 2006.
[77] For a public source, see ibid., p. 8.
[78] UN Security Council 2004d (para. 104), 2005b (para. 39), and 2007c (para. 34). See also UN Security Council 2005f.

merely to fight against violence; it was mostly to fight against violence to allow the elections to take place in good conditions." Therefore, as would be expected, when asked about MONUC's support of bottom-up peacebuilding, one staff member told me that the organization worked "according to its priority: resolving local conflicts with a view to the preparation of the elections."

Working "in Constant Crisis Mode"

Given the constraints on international action, this almost exclusive focus on elections left international actors with little time and few resources to devote to other issues. The UN and most states involved in the Congolese peace process made a rhetorical commitment to all of the usual concerns of the time, such as ending gender-based violence, reinstituting the rule of law, protecting human rights, ensuring sustainable development, and promoting good governance. In practice, however, the pattern was clear: International actors devoted time and money to peace- and state-building tasks only when doing so could contribute to the success of the electoral process, or when not doing so had triggered – or had the potential to trigger – "crises." Either way, because of the shared understandings detailed earlier, international actors mostly approached the task at hand in a top-down fashion, by working with the Transitional Government, leaders and representatives of the Congo's neighboring countries, and various other international actors. There was only one exception to the top-down approach: humanitarian and development aid, which interveners perceived as an apolitical solution to an apolitical problem (the continuation of violence on the ground).

Responding to Crises. Generally speaking, international peacebuilders worked reactively to address the numerous "crises" that marred the transition. A discursive analysis of how international actors conferred this label, either during interviews or in official documents, reveals that a "crisis" referred to one of two situations: particularly shocking violence, or events that international actors interpreted as threatening the national or regional settlements.

Throughout the transition, international peacebuilders continually categorized the situation in Ituri (a northeastern Congolese district, see map in Figure 1) as a crisis because uncontrolled militias continued to commit appalling amounts of horrific torture, rape, and killing there. Ituri in fact functioned as the symbol of continued violence in the Congo. During formal interviews and informal conversations, when I mentioned that my research concentrated on "violence in the eastern Congo," many diplomats, UN officials, and nongovernmental organizations staff members started discussing violence in Ituri. In advocacy agencies' statements and newspaper articles, (faulty) declarations, such as "the current conflict in the Democratic Republic of the Congo ... is mainly based in the district of Ituri" or "the fighting is largely limited to the still-dangerous Ituri region in the northeast," frequently appeared.[79] Similarly, although most sexual violence occurred in South Kivu, most press articles focused on the sexual violence in Ituri. The equating of Ituri with violence was so strong that, in an attempt to draw attention to the humanitarian crisis unfolding in South Kivu in early 2005, the UN Office for the Coordination of Humanitarian Affairs published a press release entitled "the threat of an Iturization of South Kivu."[80]

As a result, Ituri enjoyed a special status during the Congolese transition. As chapter 5 will explain, this small district received a disproportionate share of the human and financial resources that the UN and foreign donors devoted to the stabilization of the eastern provinces. Most important, because of the shocking nature of the violence there, Ituri was also the theater of some of the only international peacebuilding programs at the local level.

Beyond Ituri, international actors devoted most of their remaining resources and attention to events that they interpreted as threatening to the national or regional settlements. In particular, they focused on the following episodes (see the chronology in the appendix): the large-scale fighting in Bukavu (May–June 2004), the ensuing protests, and the attempted coup d'état in Kinshasa; the massacre of Congolese of Rwandan descent in the Burundian refugee camp of Gatumba (August 2004), which provoked threats of Rwandan invasions and a RCD-G temporary withdrawal from the Transitional Government;

---

[79] Respectively, "Campaign to end the genocide," World Federalist Association, www.wfa.org (accessed in 2005); and John Donnelly, "Rising from chaos, isolation war-ravaged nation edges toward stability," *The Boston Globe*, July 10, 2005.

[80] "RDC: La menace de 'l'Iturisation' du Sud Kivu inquiète les humanitaires," Office for the Coordination of Humanitarian Affairs – Democratic Republic of the Congo, March 2005.

the large-scale fighting in Kanyabayonga (December 2004), Rutshuru (January 2006), and Sake (November 2006), which similarly increased the threat of renewed regional and national conflicts; and the armed struggle in Kinshasa between the two top presidential candidates, Kabila and Bemba, when the results of the first round of the elections were announced (August 2006). These "crisis interventions" usually included three components: one political, directed at the regional and national elite; one military, consisting of the emergency deployment of peacekeeping troops to impose a cease-fire on the ground; and one humanitarian, aimed at alleviating the consequences of the fighting on the population.

The political and military components of the crisis interventions remained top-down, geared at high-level elites and only rarely at select provincial elites. For example, during the Bukavu crisis, the UN Secretary-General "maintained close contact with regional and international leaders and members of the Security Council and encouraged them to do all that they could to de-escalate the tension."[81] Diplomats similarly pressured the Congolese and Rwandan governments and the main leaders of the largest militias, met with all national representatives to ensure their continued participation in the transition process, and tried to address the various concerns of all these actors. Meanwhile, MONUC troops on the ground attempted to stop the rebels' advance. International action to defuse the Gatumba, Kanyabayonga, Rutshuru, and Sake crises similarly centered on applying pressure on Kinshasa, Kigali, and the rebel leaders and, in the last three cases, deploying peacekeeping troops.[82]

The Exception: Development and Humanitarian Aid. The provision of aid to affected populations, the third component of the "crisis interventions," was the main form of international engagement in the eastern provinces throughout the transition. Most aid programs in these provinces concentrated on emergency relief such as nutritional assistance, primary care, and water and sanitation projects to prevent excess mortality; distribution of blankets and cooking items to refugees and displaced people; and medical and psychological assistance to the victims of sexual violence. Slowly, as the transition progressed, donors and aid agencies also started implementing development

[81] UN Security Council 2004d, para. 40.
[82] For a public source, see International Crisis Group 2007a, p. 2.

programs in the Kivus and Ituri, such as rebuilding roads and schools, jump-starting small businesses, and promoting good governance, although these remained much rarer than humanitarian projects.

Significantly, these programs were the only exceptions to the taboo on international interference at the subnational level, aside from the rare attempts at contestation analyzed in chapter 5. International relief workers dealt directly with decentralized authorities and local militia leaders to negotiate access to the population and to ensure the security of their staff and beneficiaries. Development officials theoretically implemented their programs via national authorities but, in practice, they often negotiated directly with subnational representatives regarding daily tasks.

Numerous scholars have extensively studied why most international and local actors would see these actions as perfectly acceptable forms of subnational interventions.[83] Although humanitarian and development aid is inherently political, humanitarian and development agencies have constructed their work as a neutral, apolitical endeavor. The charters of most international nongovernmental organizations, such as (among many others) the International Committee of the Red Cross, Doctors Without Borders, Oxfam, the International Rescue Committee, and Action Against Hunger, define humanitarian and development aid as necessarily separate from politics. It is a matter of charity, of alleviating the suffering of the most vulnerable, irrespective of gender, age, race, or creed. Because international aid workers do nothing political, they can work at the local level and associate with subnational actors without being accused of neocolonialism or breaching the host state's sovereignty. This image of pure, apolitical charity has another consequence of significance: It renders humanitarian aid, as opposed to measures such as financing the reform of a foreign army or subsidizing a corrupt government, especially palatable in the eyes of the donors' domestic populations.

Humanitarian and development aid was especially important during the Congolese transition because international media and policy makers framed the situation in the eastern provinces as a

---

[83] This paragraph builds on Anderson 1999; Curtis 2001; Duffield 2001; Ferguson 1990; Macrae and Leader 2000; Prendergast 1996; Rieff 2002; and Uvin 1998.

humanitarian rather than a security or political crisis. Press articles and policy speeches emphasized the humanitarian disaster (the
number killed, raped, or maimed) more than the political and social
dimensions. Most countries, as well as the UN, claimed to be involved
in the Congo primarily out of humanitarian interest. They accordingly devoted most of their bilateral aid for the Congo to humanitarian or development projects rather than to political or security ones.
The United States, for example, provided approximately $125 million
per year in bilateral aid to the Congo during the transition, more than
75% of which went to humanitarian or development assistance.[84]
Similarly, the EU financed various missions in the Congo for a total
amount of more than €1 billion, close to 75% of which was devoted to
development or humanitarian projects.[85] Foreign states also deployed
many more humanitarian and development staff to the Congo than
political staff.

The leading understanding of local violence reinforced the framing
of the Congolese crisis as a humanitarian problem. As detailed in chapter 2, the dominant narrative presented decentralized violence as an
apolitical problem. Consequently, in this narrative, there was nothing
political and military actors could or should do about it; local problems required an apolitical response, such as humanitarian and development aid. Donors, diplomats, and UN officials usually explained
to me that, because humanitarian and development aid workers are
used to dealing with subnational actors, they are best equipped to
address local tensions. Humanitarian assistance would assuage the
consequences of ongoing violence on the population. Additionally,
national development programs, and a few local development projects, would improve the living conditions of the Congolese population, promote economic recovery, and thus diminish the appeal of
economically motivated criminality.

Accordingly, when I asked diplomats and UN actors what actions
they took to end decentralized violence, they generally answered that
their respective countries or organizations had "many programs"
addressing local conflicts, advising me to speak with their aid department – or with the humanitarian nongovernmental organizations that

---

[84] Gambino 2008, p. 89, confirmed by analysis of U.S. budgetary documents.
[85] Hoebeke, Carette, et al. 2007, p. 16.

this department financed – if I wanted more information. For example, a diplomat who had identified the issues of nationality, army integration, ethnic tensions, and the state of the justice system as the roots of the problems in the Kivus said that the aid department of his embassy was solving these problems by sponsoring a project to heal female victims of sexual violence, alongside a broader humanitarian program. Another concluded our one-hour conversation on the political character of local conflict by saying that "working with local actors ... [was] a typical development issue." Likewise, when questioned about UN action on local conflict, a UN official said that he could not tell me much about local violence because he was not following humanitarian issues. Just like his colleagues, he claimed that tackling local violence was the responsibility of specialized humanitarian agencies of the UN. In general, it was so obvious to my diplomatic and UN interviewees that dealing with local violence was a core responsibility of humanitarian actors that they often did not even understand why I asked what they, as political actors, were doing to assuage local conflict.

It would hardly be correct to say, however, that the resources devoted to the humanitarian and development response were sufficient. Surprisingly, given the scale of the disaster, the Congolese crisis was not even on the top of the humanitarian agenda. From the beginning of the 1990 wars to the end of the transition, other more high-profile emergencies such as Kosovo, Afghanistan, Iraq, the East Asian tsunami, and Darfur, continually superseded the Congo. The Congo was actually one of Doctors Without Borders' "10 most unreported humanitarian stories of the year" from 1998 onward, and in 2005 it was Reuters' top "forgotten crisis" and the UN Under-Secretary-General for Humanitarian Affairs' "biggest, most neglected humanitarian emergency in the world."[86] With the exception of Belgian newspapers, which regularly ran stories on the Congolese transition, the Congo only hit the news in times of catastrophe. In the words of Andrew Stroehlein, media director for the International Crisis Group, "even a nonlethal car bombing in Iraq or a kidnapping in Afghanistan

---

[86] Doctors Without Borders, "Top 10 most underreported humanitarian stories, Annual listings," http://www.doctorswithoutborders.org/publications/reports; and Ruth Gidley, "Congo war tops AlertNet poll of 'forgotten' crises," March 9, 2005.

[got] more Western media coverage in a day than Congo [got] in a typical month of 30,000 dead."[87]

Stroehlein then offered a convincing explanation for the media's puzzling neglect of the Congo. "News editors have long assumed 'no one is interested in Africa,' supposing their audience sees only hopeless African problems eternally defying solution and thus not worth attention."[88] This perception, again, is a legacy of long-standing discursive constructions about Africa in general and the Congo in particular: Violence is inherent to Africa (and to the Congo), and the continent is a hopeless place where nothing can be done to improve the situation.[89] As a result, despite the framing of the Congolese war as a humanitarian crisis, the resources for the humanitarian emergency remained paltry compared to the needs.

Beyond Crises: The Standard, Macro Approach

Beyond such emergency interventions, international actors devoted their (very limited) remaining time, resources, and attention to addressing what they identified as the root causes of the crises: regional antagonisms and national sources of tensions (see chapter 2). In all of these cases, in accordance with the dominant understanding of the international role, foreign interveners made sure to work in a top-down fashion, through regional and national elites, and to limit their interference at the subnational level as much as possible.[90]

Alleviating Regional Tensions. To reestablish good neighbor relations in the Great Lakes region, international interveners focused their efforts on four main issues. First, they organized regional conferences to help former combatants find solutions to the presence of foreign armed groups in the Congo and the illegal exploitation of the Congo's

---

[87] Andrew Stroehlein, "In Congo, 1,000 die per day: Why isn't it a media story?" *The Christian Science Monitor*, June 14, 2005.

[88] Ibid.

[89] Dunn 2003; and Shaw 2007; see also chapter 2 in this book.

[90] De Goede and Van der Borgh 2008, Lemarchand 2008, Prunier 2008, and Reyntjens 2009 present a lot of data, along with fascinating details, on these regional and national actions. This section thus provides only a very brief overview, which includes exclusively the elements necessary to understand the rest of the book. Interested readers can find more information on these topics in the writings mentioned above and in the various reports released by the International Crisis Group throughout the transition.

natural resources by its neighbors. The conferences were also meant to help restore diplomatic relationships, promote economic collaboration and trade, prepare for the return of refugees, and establish collaborative security institutions. Second, diplomats representing their countries at the UN Security Council established a panel of experts to monitor the illegal exploitation of Congolese natural resources. They also set up an arms embargo to prevent regional and Congolese actors from arming militias in Ituri and the Kivus.

Third, diplomats and UN officials tried to convince the leaders of foreign armed groups present in the Kivus and Ituri to officially renounce the armed struggle. At the same time, they sought to persuade the rebels' home governments (Rwanda, Uganda, or Burundi) to let them return home safely and peacefully. Whenever relevant, diplomatic and UN staff also attempted to induce the Congolese government to stop supporting these militias. In addition to these actions, MONUC ran a program of voluntary Disarmament, Demobilization, Repatriation, Reintegration, and Resettlement of foreign combatants (called DDRRR in UN parlance). In an uncharacteristically bottom-up fashion, DDRRR experts negotiated with local militia leaders to convince them to return home with their troops, or at least to let their troops return if they wanted. When the leaders proved inflexible, as they usually did, MONUC staff members strove to convince the lower-ranked soldiers to desert. MONUC also occasionally provided logistical and training support to units of the Congolese army that tried, usually unsuccessfully, to forcibly disarm Rwandan and Ugandan rebels and destroy their bases.

The fourth and last international action to assuage regional sources of tensions – and national ones simultaneously – was to closely monitor the discrimination against Kinyarwanda-speaking Congolese, which international actors saw as triggering most large-scale crises. Efforts included mediating between the RCD-G (which defended the interests of the Congolese of Rwandan descent) and the other actors of the transition, putting significant pressure on Congolese parliamentarians to ensure that they wrote a new nationality law guaranteeing sufficient protection for this minority, and strongly condemning aggression toward people with Rwandan ancestry whenever it occurred. At the height of the worst crises, a handful of diplomats even went so far as to call personally key provincial officials in the hope of helping to deescalate the tensions between the communities in conflict.

Addressing National Problems. Just as the international action to assuage regional tensions was mostly top-down, so, too, was the international attempt to resolve national antagonisms. As already discussed, international peacebuilders concentrated on organization of general elections and devoted most of their remaining time and resources to the management of crises. International interveners allocated the small amount of time and resources left to two areas: supervising selected legislative matters and reforming the security sector.

For the first task, a select number of diplomats and MONUC officials closely supervised the writing of the constitution, as well as the formulation of the various laws that might affect initiatives otherwise under their purview – notably the electoral laws, the legislation on determining nationality, and the security sector reform.[91] This task was well rehearsed and, in line with the collective understandings detailed earlier in this chapter, foreign interveners saw this interference in Congolese domestic affairs as perfectly legitimate, because it took place through interactions with Congolese governmental elites.

International interveners viewed the second task, security-sector reform, as much more problematic. They considered it an internal matter in which they should not interfere; it would mean trampling on Congolese sovereignty, and hence it would be an illegitimate, neocolonial endeavor. They also considered it complex and unfamiliar, since they could draw only on limited expertise and few standard operating procedures – in other words, they had no "toolkit" to reform the security sector in a postconflict country. Moreover, donors were as usual reluctant to fund a foreign army. They were afraid (with good reason) that they would be held accountable for training and supporting an army of thugs and that their programs would only serve to make Congolese soldiers more effective perpetrators of atrocities. As a result, international actors devoted very few financial, logistical, and human resources to security-sector reform.[92] And they did so only late in the transition process, after the May–June 2004 fighting

---

[91] For public sources on the electoral law, see UN Security Council 2005a, para. 9, and on the constitution, see James Traub, "The Congo Case," *The New York Times*, July 3, 2005; as well as the interview of the UN Under-Secretary-General for Peacekeeping Operations Jean-Marie Guéheno, broadcast on Radio France International on April 29, 2005.

[92] Boshoff 2005, Kasongo and Sebahara 2006, and Wolters and Boshoff 2006 provide some excellent analyses of the security-sector reform process.

in Bukavu had demonstrated that, if left to fester, army integration problems had serious potential to jeopardize the regional and national settlements.

Diplomats, as well as UN and World Bank officials, focused on the one component of the process that was most familiar to them: the integration of the army. True to these actors' conceptions of their role, the whole process remained top-down and centered on interactions with macro-level elites. Interveners pressured Congolese leaders to convince them to demobilize and integrate their troops, provided technical assistance to the general staff of the army, and supervised the use of funds for army integration. Several countries risked training a few brigades and offered limited financial support to the centers that attempted to unite soldiers of various armed groups in a single army. By all accounts, this international support always fell short of what was needed to complete the army integration process successfully.[93] At the end of the transition, only fourteen integrated brigades (out of an expected eighteen) existed, and they were among the worst perpetrators of human rights violations in the Congo. Lacking adequate equipment, these brigades were incapable of working without MONUC support. More than 100,000 soldiers still needed to be either integrated into the army or disarmed, demobilized, and reintegrated into civilian life.[94] Those who had already been demobilized rarely received adequate support.

Moreover, while the international technical and financial backing for the army integration process was insufficient, the problem was far worse for the other components of security-sector reform: the civilian police and the justice system. The number of police officers trained was woefully inadequate, ultimately amounting to fewer than 55,000 individuals for a population of about 66 million, only 40% of the internationally recommended ratio of police to civilians.[95] Furthermore, the training remained basic and concentrated on election security. It focused on preparing the forces that would be deployed in Kinshasa and in the Ituri capital of Bunia, not in the

---

[93] UN Security Council 2005i (para. 77), 2005e, and 2006d.
[94] UN Security Council 2007c, paras. 29, 31–32, 49.
[95] For detailed data on this issue, see UN Security Council 2003c (para. 74), 2003a (para. 46), 2005i (paras. 42–44), 2005j (paras. 49 and 71), 2006e, and 2007c (para. 34).

rest of the country. Consequently, at the end of the transition, the police force was weak, inefficient, corrupt, inadequately equipped, and oblivious to even the most basic norms of human rights.

International support for the judiciary system was even weaker. MONUC provided some technical advice and training to a couple hundred magistrates, mostly those deployed in Bunia and, to a lesser extent, Kinshasa. Along with the French government and the EU, MONUC also started to reconstruct the justice system in Ituri by rehabilitating a few buildings and training, transporting, and paying a handful of judges.[96] Not only was this action insufficient for the provinces involved, but it also neglected the remainder of the country, including the unstable Kivus and Katanga. Consequently, the justice system remained almost nonexistent. As of March 2007, "fewer than 60 of the required 180 first-instance courts exist[ed], laws [were] obsolete and judicial facilities and prisons [were] extremely dilapidated."[97] What did exist had little independence from the executive power.[98] Furthermore, justice remained inaccessible to most ordinary Congolese; for example, it cost a woman $300 to bring a rape case to court, while the average per capita income was at most a few dozen dollars a month.[99] Judges usually ruled in favor of the party that had paid them the most, no matter who was guilty or innocent. Finally, many Congolese interviewees deplored that high-profile perpetrators of past war crimes not only enjoyed impunity, but were also rewarded with positions of authority. They lamented the broader consequences of this persisting impunity, which sustained the idea that violence was the easiest way to access power and wealth.

While international actors rhetorically supported other measures related to the rule of law, concrete actions were restricted to a few ad-hoc, limited, and ineffective initiatives to promote human rights and address issues of corruption and economic mismanagement. The protection of "civilians under imminent threat of physical violence" was similarly negligible. Though this task had been part of MONUC's mandate since February 2000, and was regularly reaffirmed and

---

[96] For public sources, see UN Security Council 2003a, 2004a (paras. 29–30), and 2007c (para. 37).
[97] UN Security Council 2007c, para. 35.
[98] UN Security Council 2007c, para. 33 and 35.
[99] UN Mission in the Democratic Republic of Congo (MONUC) 2005a.

strengthened during the transition, MONUC almost never "deemed it within its capabilities," except at times in Ituri.[100]

In sum, security-sector reform, reconstruction of the justice system, and other state-building tasks could have been international priorities during the Congolese transition, because they were both possible and essential to stability in the Congo. However, beyond interactions with state elites and a focus on elections, international actors lacked a toolkit to work on these issues. Throughout the transition, the persistence of high levels of violence in the eastern provinces regularly revealed the inadequacy of the overall intervention strategy.

Conclusion

I have so far argued that various elements of the international peacebuilding culture shaped the intervention strategy into a top-down approach. Diplomats and UN staff members are trained to work on superstructures, such as national and international negotiations, and they are socialized to focus on predefined tasks and performance guidelines that fail to take local violence into account. During the Congolese transition, they therefore believed that their only legitimate role was to intervene at the macro level, and they chose to devote their resources to working with regional and national leaders, with an emphasis on organizing general elections. Ultimately, the peacebuilding culture oriented foreign actors toward an intervention strategy that permitted, and at times even exacerbated, fighting, massacres, and massive human rights violations during and after the transition.

The next two chapters suggest an alternative analysis of violence, which in part explains why the international efforts failed to establish a sustainable peace. Chapter 4 demonstrates that grassroots issues were, in fact, the main reason why violence continued during the transition, elections increased the tensions in several provinces, Congolese officers and soldiers vigorously resisted the security-sector reform, and foreign militias continued to thrive in the Congo.

---

[100] Holt and Berkman 2006, chapter 8; and UN Security Council 2003–2006b.

4 | *A Bottom-Up Story*

A disconnect frequently surfaced between the international peace-builders' statements on the security situation in the eastern Congo and the events unfolding on the ground. On May 26, 2004, I attended a large meeting with U.S. diplomats, donors, and humanitarian actors based in South Kivu, at which everyone concluded that the province was relatively calm, except for pockets of tension in the northern and southern sections. All present agreed that the city of Bukavu, where the meeting took place, was once again stable and uneventful. A few hours later, large-scale fighting broke out in Bukavu and quickly spread to the entire province, almost causing a collapse of the national and regional peace settlements.

U.S. and humanitarian actors were not the only ones to err in their judgment. In December 2004, at the height of another major bout of fighting in the eastern provinces, the Belgian foreign minister claimed that the situation was "within reach of stabilization, of peace."[1] In May 2005, while the population of the eastern provinces lived in fear of recurring massacres, a United Nations (UN) spokesperson claimed that "overall, the situation was now well under control, but still remained quite hostile."[2] In June 2005, another UN spokesperson claimed that the security situation was "progressively returning to normal," notwithstanding the fact that, two weeks prior, UN troops had engaged in a massive "four-hour gun battle with militiamen" and that, two weeks later, UN forces and militias fought for more than eight hours.[3]

---

[1] Cited in *Le Potentiel* (Kinshasa), December 20, 2004.

[2] François Dureau, chief of the Department of Peacekeeping Operations' Situation Center, during a press briefing on "Recent developments in DR Congo," Department of Peacekeeping Operations, May 4, 2005.

[3] Citations from "La MONUC 'se focalise' sur le problème des rebelles Hutus rwandais dans l'est de la RD Congo / Six civils retrouvés massacrés par des rebelles Hutus rwandais," *Xinhuanet*, June 16, 2005 ; and "15,000 disarm but Ituri militias regrouping – UN," Reuters, June 22, 2005.

This disconnect emerged because the dominant narrative on the causes of continued conflict overlooked a critical point: the influence of bottom-up tensions. Though national and regional antagonisms often motivated manifestations of violence on the ground, a number of distinctively local agendas did as well. These decentralized agendas revolved around clearly identifiable political, military, economic, or social goals. In other words, micro-level tensions were neither purely a consequence of macro-level manipulation, nor were they merely criminal or humanitarian problems.

The significance of local agendas helps explain why the international intervention strategy presented in chapter 3 failed to build a sustainable peace. Though national and regional conflict resolution efforts assuaged macro-level tensions, and thus helped reduce the overall level of violence, these top-down efforts did not significantly impact locally motivated hostilities. As a result, micro-level agendas persisted in causing local, national, and regional violence during and after the transition.

In this chapter, I build on the body of research demonstrating that regional and national tensions are not the sole – and sometimes, not even the main – causes of violence in war and postwar environments.[4] According to Kalyvas, who launched the political science research agenda on micro-level conflicts, there is "considerable local input and initiative in the production of violence. Rather than being imposed upon communities by outsiders ... violence often (but not always) grows from within communities even when it is executed by outsiders."[5]

I use Kalyvas's framework of analysis, slightly modified to include the regional in addition to the local and national dimensions, to analyze the two mechanisms through which the various dimensions of violence interacted: cleavage and alliance. "Cleavage" refers to the "overarching issue dimension" that links actors at the center to actors on the ground – for example, ideology, ethnicity, religion, or class. As detailed in chapter 2, the dominant narrative relies exclusively on the mechanism of cleavage to explain ongoing conflict. "Alliance" is a concept that links local actors' quest for local advantages to the

---

[4] Adam 2005; Fujii 2008; Kalyvas 2003 and 2006; Krämer 2006 and 2007; and Straus 2006.
[5] Kalyvas 2003, p. 482.

central actors' quest for national power. It "entails a transaction between supralocal and local actors, whereby the former supply the latter with external muscle, thus allowing them to win decisive local advantage; in exchange the former rely on local conflicts to recruit and motivate supporters and obtain local control, resources, and information."[6] This mechanism points to the main gap in the usual interpretation of the Congolese conflict.

In this chapter, I develop an account that emphasizes the bottom-up causes of violence and their interaction with top-down dynamics, a story that is different from and complementary to the dominant narrative presented in chapter 2. I first show that local agendas have had tremendous influence throughout Congolese history and have often been intertwined with macro-level dimensions. I then detail the changes that the war produced and move on to demonstrate that, during the transition, many conflicts revolved around political, social, and economic stakes that were distinctively local. Finally, through an analysis of the situation in the most violent provinces of the Congo during the transition – the two Kivus, North Katanga, and Ituri – I explain how local dynamics interacted with national and regional tensions to produce violence.

Partnerships between local actors and national and regional actors did exist. Therefore, as the dominant narrative posits, macro-level developments often influenced micro-level activity. However, after the national and regional settlements were reached, some local conflicts over land and power became increasingly self-sustaining and autonomous from the macro-level developments, most notably in South Kivu, North Katanga, and Ituri. There, the resulting violence was not coordinated on a large scale, but was rather the product of fragmented, decentralized militias, each trying to advance its own agenda at the village or district level. Consequently, local disputes led to violent clashes that no national or regional actors could stop. Furthermore, as the North Kivu situation illustrates, grassroots tensions also had the potential to jeopardize the regional and national settlements, especially when these tensions motivated alliances between Congolese villagers and Rwandan Hutu militias or when they prompted violence against Congolese of Rwandan descent.

---

[6] Ibid. (quotations from pp. 476 and 486); and Kalyvas 2006.

As will become evident over the course of the chapter, some types of grassroots conflicts are more salient at a particular juncture and in a particular locale – such as antagonisms over land in the Kivus in the 1930s and in Ituri in the 2000s, or struggles to control the local exploitation of mineral resources in North Katanga during the transition. The respective weight of bottom-up and top-down tensions in generating violence also varies over time and place – for example, while top-down tensions were particularly influential during the wars of the 1990s, bottom-up tensions were particularly significant during the transition. Some conflicts have incited more fighting than others, but this chapter demonstrates that both macro-level and micro-level antagonisms have generated and sustained ongoing violence.

Importance of Local Conflict in Modern Congolese History

Attaining Local Citizenship: Power, Land, and Ethnicity Before the Wars of the 1990s

To understand how micro-level conflicts could jeopardize macro-level settlements during the transition, it is crucial to examine how local conflicts first acquired a national dimension. This section traces the process throughout the twentieth century. It provides an overview of the role of local identity and a case study of the tensions between the self-styled "indigenous" communities and Congolese with Rwandan ancestry. The goal is twofold: to locate the local roots of the antagonisms that eventually caused large-scale violence during and after the wars of the 1990s and to illuminate the interaction between top-down and bottom-up causes of violence.

The broad lines of this argument are simple. Throughout the twentieth century, micro-level rivalries over land, resources, and power progressively produced a series of cleavages at both the local and national levels. Most of the conflicts involved only a few villages, communities, or provincial leaders. In the case of the conflict between the Congolese with Rwandan ancestry and the indigenous communities of the Kivus, however, local actors joined with national and regional politicians from the 1960s onward. These conditions progressively led to a polarization of the indigenous Congolese society against the "nonindigenous" Congolese of Rwandan descent, which became a key national cleavage during the war. All of these local tensions caused considerable violence long before regional dynamics triggered the 1996 war. In the eastern provinces, they also laid the grounds for the national and regional factors to take effect during the generalized wars and the subsequent transition.

The Critical Role of Local Identity. Until the wars of the 1990s, access to land, political rights, and other benefits depended on one's identity as a member of a particular village or community.[7] Before colonization, being a client of a village's – or group of villages' – chief, (a Mwami) determined one's ethnicity, as well as one's access to political power and to land (the Mwami granted his subjects the temporary right to use part of the tribal land).[8] Under Belgian rule, colonial law distinguished between political citizenship, granted to Belgian residents (and, much later on, to the "évolués," the Africans who had reached the status of "civilized" human beings), and ethnic citizenship, granted to indigenous Congolese based on their membership in a local ethnic community.[9] For most Congolese, one's identity as a member of a specific ethnic or tribal group thus became the basis for receiving national rights as a citizen, in addition to remaining the key factor for access to land, wealth, and political, social, and economic power at the local level. Colonial rule introduced two other significant changes at the grassroots level. It accentuated the political division of ethnic communities by further dividing the "African race" into "multiple ethnicities, each with its own 'customary' home, 'customary' law, and a 'customary' authority to enforce it."[10] Belgium's system of indirect rule also bolstered the power of the local chiefs by granting them a local monopoly on administrative, executive, and judicial power over the ethnic groups that they were ruling, and by putting at their disposal the resources of the colonial state to assert their authority.

Additionally, the colonial state sowed the seeds of one of the main crises that developed after independence: the struggle for land.[11] The colonizers declared all uncultivated land property of the state and

---

[7] This section draws mostly on Mamdani 2001; Mathieu and Willame 1999; Van Acker and Vlassenroot 2000; and Willame 1997.

[8] Van Acker 1999a; Van Acker and Vlassenroot 2000, paras. 6 and 7; Vlassenroot 2000, pp. 61–62; and Willame 1997, p. 35.

[9] The rest of this paragraph draws mostly on Mamdani 1996, part 1. On the "évolués," see Doom and Gorus 2000, p. 57.

[10] Mamdani 2001, p. 237.

[11] Mugangu Matabaro 2008 provides the best analysis of land conflicts in the Congo.

either distributed it to colonial families, put it on the land market, or transformed it into national parks. They authorized the Congolese access to only the drastically reduced land reserved for the "native communities."[12] Access to land was crucial at that time, and it remains so now. For many people, land is the key to survival and the ability to feed one's family. For many more, it is a primary means of gaining the social capital needed for assimilation into the local community.[13] The contract by which the traditional chief granted his subjects access to land was indeed "an institution that legitimize[d] the whole social organization by absorbing all the persons living in a given area in a network of relationships of mutual dependency."[14] Finally, land is a means of securing natural resources.

Because the stakes of land ownership were so high, colonial encroachments on land tenure arrangements in the Kivus led to the formation of two grassroots militias that attempted to defend what they saw as the utmost expression of the "traditional rural order."[15] These were the first instances of what became a long tradition of local tribal militias, whose purpose was "a mix of self-defense and profit secured from pillage and cattle rustling," and who ultimately terrorized the communities they had set out to protect.[16] From the colonial reform onward, conflict over land predominantly affected the most densely inhabited parts of the eastern Congo, namely, North Kivu and the border areas of South Kivu.

The crucial role of local identity persisted after the end of colonization. In contrast to colonial politics that granted rights based on race, the independent Congo granted national citizenship, and thus civil and political rights, to all individuals according to membership in the central state. However, it kept ethnic citizenship to "preserve the authenticity of Congolese customs."[17] As during colonization, the state granted ethnic citizenship to groups based on their membership in a Native Authority and defined this citizenship as the source of

---

[12] Vlassenroot 2000, pp. 62–63; and Willame 1997, p. 40.
[13] Van Acker 1999b, pp. 6–7; and Willame 1997, p. 43.
[14] Van Acker 1999b, p. 6, my translation.
[15] Van Acker and Vlassenroot 2000, para. 25.
[16] International Crisis Group 2000b, p. 24; and Alan Riding, "Art show forces Belgium to ask hard questions about its colonial past," *New York Times*, February 9, 2005.
[17] Mamdani 1996 (pp. 128–137) and 2001 (p. 261).

economic and social rights, including the right to access land. The local customary authorities retained their monopoly over local power and thus held tremendous influence over their subjects' lives; they could "confirm ethnic belonging and … issue identity cards, oversee administration, allocate customary land for livelihood, hold tribunals through which customary justice [was] meted out, run local markets, and so on."[18]

Because these local conflicts were rooted in such vital agendas, decentralized violence continued after the end of colonization in addition to the large-scale fighting that raged during the first years of independence (notably an attempted secession of the provinces of Kasai and Katanga, and a series of rebellions in the Kivus and Maniema).[19] For example, communities such as Shis, Regas, and Kusus conflicted over provincial and national agendas, while local antagonisms emerged even within the same ethnic group.[20] When Mobutu came to power in 1965, he succeeded in ending most of this decentralized fighting through extensive military force, but sporadic rebellions continued to surface regularly in the eastern provinces, notably in South Kivu and North Katanga.

A few years later, in 1973, Mobutu passed a General Property law, which theoretically nationalized all land, vacant or not, customary or not.[21] This law transformed the "traditional" authorities into administrators of the Congolese state, thus further institutionalizing ethnicity. Most important, this process also aggravated the ongoing antagonisms. By asserting state control over customary land, it deprived these same traditional chiefs of their main source of power: their ability to give and take back the land as they wished. The nationalization process also created a new class of marginalized people, mostly young peasants who, deprived of access to the former customary land and thus of the traditional mode of integration within their communities, were left with few survival opportunities. Consequently, tensions increased at the local level. A magistrate based in the Kivus in the 1980s recalled during an interview that he "had been struck by the increasing number of murders, in North Kivu especially, that

---

[18] Mamdani 2001, p. 238.   [19] Willame 1997, pp. 45–46.   [20] Ibid., p. 45.
[21] This paragraph draws on Mamdani 2001, pp. 242–243; Mugangu Matabaro 2008; Van Acker and Vlassenroot 2000, paras. 8 and 12; Van Hoyweghen and Vlassenroot 2000, pp. 63–66; and Willame 1997. pp. 54–56.

occurred at the rate of one every three days." After some research, he had found that the "main causes" of this constant, very small-scale violence "were conflicts over land, followed by ... the gross injustice ... of certain court decisions that the losing side did not accept."[22]

Given the already tense situation, Mobutu's new strategy of control in the 1990s, which aggravated ethnic rivalries by redirecting the hatred of his regime (as detailed in chapter 2), could only further compound the micro-level antagonisms. Mobutu and his cronies' promotion of the principle of "indigeneity" was especially influential, as it enhanced antagonisms between many communities and enabled indigenous groups to settle conflicts over land and local power favorably.

In sum, decentralized conflicts over land and grassroots power had generated deep-seated antagonisms between various eastern communities long before the wars of the 1990s. The following section presents a detailed case study to help the reader understand in greater depth how grassroots and national dynamics interacted in such a way that local tensions eventually escalated into a national and regional conflict. This case study focuses on one specific local conflict, the tensions between indigenous Congolese and the Kinyarwanda-speaking population of the Kivus. However, it is important to note from the start that the dynamics of grassroots antagonisms creating deeply entrenched cleavages at the local level and the dynamics of local actors engaging national actors in their fight were replicated between many other communities and in many other places, such as in Ituri.[23]

A Textbook Case: The Tensions Between Indigenous Communities and Congolese of Rwandan Descent. In the 1930s, Belgium created the Mission for the Immigration of the Banyarwanda (Mission d'Immigration des Banyarwanda), a structure that would transfer tens of thousands of people from Rwanda to the Congo to provide workers for the plantations of the Kivus and the mines of Katanga.[24] The status

---

[22] See also Willame 1997, pp. 55–56.

[23] International Crisis Group 2008; and Vlassenroot and Raeymaekers 2004b provide an excellent overview of the Ituri case.

[24] The remaining part of this paragraph is based on Willame 1997, p. 41. This entire section builds on Mamdani 2001; Mathieu and Willame 1999; Van Acker and Vlassenroot 2000; and Willame 1997 (the reference text on the topic). See also Jackson 2006 for an excellent analysis of the interaction between the local, national, and regional dimensions of this conflict in the past century.

of this immigrant group in the Congo quickly became ambiguous. On the one hand, the colonizers denied most Kinyarwanda-speaking people an "indigenous" status and thus a Native Authority with its own customary land. On the other hand, Belgian officials appointed more people with Rwandan ancestry to the local administration, providing the whole group with better access to political and economic power than the indigenous Congolese received. Tensions therefore developed between indigenous and Kinyarwanda-speaking elites. The latter claimed that they were entitled to land and traditional representation, while the former complained that people of Rwandan descent enjoyed too much power in administrative and business circles.

At the time of the Congo's independence, the debate about the Kinyarwanda-speaking minority's legal status was so sensitive and complicated that the 1960 Fundamental Law, the Congolese constitution, left it unresolved.[25] As a result, most people of Rwandan descent living on Congolese territory were considered citizens of the Congolese state, but still not "indigenous." They remained under the jurisdiction of indigenous native authorities and had no access to land as a community (they could only temporarily use land allocated by their indigenous chiefs). At that time, the arrival in the Kivus of up to 60,000 Tutsi refugees fleeing the massacres occasioned by the independence and revolution in neighboring Rwanda (from 1959 to 1962) further complicated the situation. A few years later, the status of the population with Rwandan ancestry became even more precarious. The 1964 constitution granted Congolese citizenship only to those individuals whose ancestors were members of a tribe living on Congolese territory before 1908, the date when the Congo Free State, which had formerly been the personal property of Belgian King Leopold II, came under the control of the Belgian parliament. This constitution, therefore, denied national citizenship to the individuals whose ancestors had been "imported" by the colonizers in the 1930s.

In North Kivu, the most densely populated eastern province and thus the place where land was the scarcest, tensions over citizenship soon evolved into a full-blown crisis.[26] At independence, the elite of the Banyarwanda (as Congolese now call people with Rwandan

---

[25] Mamdani 2001, pp. 239 and 242.
[26] This paragraph is based on ibid., pp. 235–245; Van Hoyweghen and Vlassenroot 2000, paras. 67–69; and Willame 1997, pp. 44–52.

ancestry living in North Kivu) strived to maintain their economic and political power over the province. Principally, they facilitated illegal immigration from Rwanda and expelled indigenous chiefs from the Rutshuru territory (see map of North Kivu in Figure 6). The indigenous communities used similar methods to oppose Banyarwandan power and reestablish political and economic control over the population of the Masisi territory. In late 1963, these antagonisms erupted in the first open conflict between Banyarwanda and indigenous Congolese. Known as the war of the Kanyarwanda (the war of the sons of Rwanda), this conflict led to tremendous violence on both sides, including torture, murders, and forced displacement.

Blocked from access to land and political power at the local level, the Banyarwanda looked to the national sphere for an alternative strategy. At the same time, indigenous communities contested the nationality of the Banyarwanda to undermine their local elite and their claims on land. These new strategies launched the "spiraling crisis of citizenship" that fed the insecurity of the Congolese of Rwandan descent and escalated from a local issue into a national and regional conflict, eventually causing massive violence during the 1990s wars and the subsequent transition to peace.[27]

In the late 1960s, the Banyarwanda won the backing of then President Mobutu, who favored promoting ethnic minorities because they could help him govern without threatening his regime.[28] This presidential support manifested itself principally in two ways, both of which reinforced grassroots tensions. First, Mobutu promoted the immigration of Tutsi pastoralists to the Congo, a policy that the colonizers had previously discouraged. This influx intensified the conflict between farmers (mostly indigenous) and livestock herders (mostly Tutsi Banyarwanda), whose cattle grazed on large portions of land previously devoted to crops. Second, Mobutu granted top political positions to several individuals of Rwandan descent, particularly in the security and the party apparatuses, two key institutions at that time. These politicians exploited their influence to help other Congolese of Rwandan descent increase their economic, political, and social power, notably in the Kivus.

[27] Quotation from Mamdani 2001, p. 243.
[28] The following development is based on ibid. and Willame 1997.

In 1972, the Kinyarwanda-speaking politicians succeeded in per-
suading the government to enact a law granting citizenship to the
Rwandan refugees who had arrived in the Congo before 1950. This
legislative reform enabled the Banyarwanda to have a greater influence over North Kivu's social, economic, and political life. For example, it granted citizenship to so many Banyarwanda that they became
the majority in the Masisi territory, and could from then on outvote
the indigenous communities.

Furthermore, the previously mentioned 1973 General Property
Law, whose chief architect (Barthélémy Bisengimana) was a Tutsi
with Rwandan ancestry, increased the Banyarwandan control over
lands the indigenous communities deemed their own, thus intensify-
ing resentment against the "immigrants."[29] Mobutu distributed the
settler-controlled land he had nationalized as a reward for political
loyalty and, in the Kivus, the Banyarwanda were his main beneficiaries. Furthermore, although Mobutu did not succeed in national-
izing the customary land, the possibility of economic profit enticed
many North Kivu traditional chiefs to sell off sections under their
control. This practice gave the wealthiest Banyarwanda an opportunity to buy large chunks of land, especially in Masisi and Rutshuru.
The transactions were usually so murky, however, that they created
overlapping ownership claims based on both modern and traditional
law, generating a new layer of antagonisms. For example, the previously mentioned magistrate based in the Kivus in the 1980s observed
traditional authorities illegally selling the lands already cultivated by
their subjects to the Tutsis, and the land formerly owned by Congolese
Hutus to rich Hutus who had recently emigrated from Rwanda. These
dealings created conflict between the new owners and the people who
had cultivated the land prior to the sale, eventually leading to further
contestation between indigenous and Banyarwanda communities as
well as between "old" and "new" Rwandan immigrants.

From then on, local and national rivalries remained deeply entan-
gled. Some Banyarwanda families used their connections with
Barthélémy Bisengimana, Mobutu's principal secretary, to continue to

---

[29] Unless otherwise indicated, the remaining part of the analysis on North
Kivu is based on Mamdani 2001, pp. 242–243; Van Acker and Vlassenroot
2000, paras. 8 and 12; Van Hoyweghen and Vlassenroot 2000, pp. 63–66;
Willame 1997, pp. 54–56; and on author's confidential sources.

increase their economic, political, and social power. At the same time, feeling threatened by the Banyarwanda's increased control over land and local positions of authority, the indigenous populations exploited their relationships with the indigenous director of the Central Bank, a key national actor under Mobutu, to challenge their enemies' claim to citizenship. The indigenous lobby's efforts to curb the power of the Banyarwanda bore fruit in 1981: A law was passed to revoke the 1972 legislation and grant citizenship only to those who could prove that their families were in the Congo before colonization, set at 1885, the year of the Berlin Conference. Though not implemented at the time, the law facilitated denial of even more rights to the Banyarwanda, strongly reinforcing the community's fear of disenfranchisement.

In addition to these national consequences, the tensions between the indigenous people and the Banyarwanda also generated low-level violence in North Kivu throughout the 1980s. A Congolese citizen working in the Kivus for a development and peacebuilding organization at the time recalls that "in 1986 to 1987, there was already the premise of an open conflict. There was distrust, threats, isolated assassinations – ad hoc, isolated, but with a political undertone. The problem of nationality was in the air, but it was not clear, because Mobutu's dictatorship quieted everybody in the country, and people could not express themselves."[30]

According to this Congolese peacebuilder, the grievances were numerous on both sides. The Banyarwanda "felt excluded from traditional and administrative power at ... the level of the village ... [and] subject to harassment" by leaders of the indigenous Hunde ethnic group, "in Masisi especially." The indigenous communities countered that Banyarwanda should not complain about a lack of participation in local political life because, "first, they were not from there, and traditional power is hereditary and cannot be manufactured; and second, it was agreed when [the Banyarwanda] arrived that [they] would not have any political life." To support this last claim, indigenous people contended that, in 1948, the Belgian colonizers had written an official letter that "promised to the Hunde chiefs that the Banyarwanda would never take up political positions." Moreover, as my interviewee noted, the Hundes complained that the Banyarwanda prevented them from being heard at the national level. The Hundes believed that Mobutu

---

[30] Author's interview with Batabiha Bushoki, New York, February 2005.

trusted only his Hutu and Tutsi advisors on Kivu-related questions, and that the Banyarwanda had assassinated all of the indigenous actors from the Kivu who were becoming influential. As could be expected, land was another important cause of dissension. According to this interviewee, "the Hundes thought that Banyarwanda held all the land, but that it was not always legal, that sometimes lands had been acquired by administrative and judicial cheating." Additionally, the Hundes felt marginalized in terms of international aid: They protested that external donors favored the Banyarwandan community at the expense of the indigenous people. Finally, all indigenous communities complained that Banyarwanda "never acknowledged that some members of their communities had arrived only recently and were therefore not eligible for Congolese citizenship."

In addition to conflict between Banyarwanda and indigenous communities, tensions also mounted within the Banyarwanda community between Tutsis and Hutus. Until that time, despite the recurrent combat between both ethnic groups in neighboring Burundi and Rwanda, the community of Congolese with Rwandan ancestry had functioned on a "linguistic and regional" cross-ethnic basis: the Kinyarwanda speakers, both Hutus and Tutsis united.[31] In the late 1980s, this community started splitting because, in the words of the previously mentioned magistrate, "the Hutus who came to the Kivu and invested there tried to affirm their power and diminish the Tutsi influence."

In the neighboring province of South Kivu, the relationships between the Congolese of Rwandan descent and the indigenous communities experienced an evolution very similar to that of North Kivu. A micro-level conflict progressively evolved into a major cleavage, polarizing indigenous communities and people with Rwandan ancestry, contaminating national politics, and eventually jeopardizing the Kinyarwanda speakers' integration.

Tutsis from Rwanda had settled in South Kivu long before colonization. Starting in the 1960s, they progressively changed their name, and thus their political identity, from "descent-based" (Banyarwanda, "those ancestrally belonging to Rwanda") to "territorially based" (Banyamulenge, "those living in the hills of Mulenge").[32] This tactic

---

[31] Mamdani 2001, p. 235; and Willame 1997, pp. 68–69 and 87–88.
[32] Mamdani 2001, pp. 248–249; and Willame 1997, pp. 83–84.

allowed them to differentiate themselves from the unpopular Tutsi refugees who arrived in the 1960s and to maintain relatively peaceful relations with their neighbors until later in the decade, when a grass-roots conflict jeopardized the fragile equilibrium.

The history of this conflict can be traced to the early 1960s and the clash between two local leaders, Henri Simba and Simon Marandura, over the leadership of the Fulero chiefdom (South Kivu).[33] This micro-level antagonism slowly evolved into a much broader dispute, with Marandura's supporters eventually transforming into a multiethnic rebellion that opposed the government and controlled a large piece of territory around Fizi – and included future president Laurent-Désiré Kabila among its leaders.[34] Banyamulenge were initially not involved in the conflict, but several individuals supported the rebellion. The situation changed when the rebels started slaughtering the Banyamulenge's cows to feed themselves. Cattle are immensely important among pastoralists: They are the main source of wealth, determine social status, and are a source of pride in the community. Stealing and killing cows are therefore major offenses. In reprisal, Banyamulenge allied with the central government. Thanks to this Banyamulenge support, after ten years of fighting, the Mobutu government managed to end the rebellion and regain control over Fizi territory in 1977.

The Banyamulenge action added to the existing resentment that indigenous communities felt toward the population with Rwandan ancestry. This hostility had coalesced because of the latter group's use of a non-Congolese language (Kinyarwanda), their isolation on the Hauts Plateaux (High Plateaus), their success in business, and their pastoralist occupation that degraded neighboring farmland.[35] The Bembe, an ethnic group indigenous to the area, decided to exact their revenge politically and to regain power in Fizi by sidelining Banyamulenge politicians in all electoral competitions. To implement this strategy, they enlisted allies at higher levels. Due to their efforts, the ethnic discrimination against Banyamulenge spread to the southern part of South Kivu, then to the whole province, and finally to the

---

[33] This paragraph is based on Lemarchand 2008, p. 10; Prunier 2008, p. 52; Van Acker and Vlassenroot 2000, para. 25; Verhaegen 1967; Vlassenroot 2002; and Young 1967; as well as author's confidential sources.

[34] Verhaegen 1967 contains the most detailed presentation of this evolution.

[35] Willame 1997, pp. 84–86.

national level.[36] In contrast with North Kivu, however, the tensions did not generate violence in the 1980s, except once in 1989.[37]

The national and regional evolutions of the early 1990s further worsened the micro-level tensions in both Kivus; local, national, and regional conflicts eventually fused to produce the two generalized wars of the 1990s.[38] In 1991, the National Sovereign Conference, which Mobutu had established to consider potential political reforms, rejected Banyarwanda representatives. This exclusion put representatives of the indigenous communities in the best position to enroll national allies in their local fight against the Banyarwanda. It also further fed the Banyarwanda's fear of persecution. As a result, tensions increased in North Kivu. Each side felt it had lost its rightful control of land and political power and that the other side threatened its very existence. Many indigenous and Banyarwanda communities formed their own tribal militias to protect themselves.

During the same period, the progress of the civil war in neighboring Rwanda (1990–1994) also fueled local antagonisms and widened the split within the Banyarwanda community. Some Congolese Tutsis financed the war effort of the rebel Rwandan Patriotic Front, which thousands of young Congolese Tutsis crossed the Ugandan border to join. Congolese Hutus, on the other hand, saw the Rwandan Patriotic Front as a Tutsi power movement and they formed a reservoir of recruits for the (Hutu-dominated) Rwandan government of President Habyarimana.[39] The consequences were twofold.[40] First, Hutus intensified their resentment against Tutsis. Second, and concurrently, indigenous communities increasingly perceived all the Congolese with Rwandan ancestry not only as nonindigenous but also as "owing political allegiance to Rwanda."

The emerging Hutu–Tutsi antagonism corresponded with national preoccupations – the government's scapegoating of ethnic minorities – as well as with local issues. Local chiefs in North Kivu needed to dominate the Banyarwanda population, and especially the Tutsis, who increasingly questioned their authority and called for

---

[36] See ibid., part II.   [37] Ibid., p. 87.
[38] This paragraph is based on Mamdani 2001, p. 249; and Willame 1997, pp. 62–68 and 124–131.
[39] Prunier 2008, p. 50.
[40] Mamdani 2001, p. 246; and Willame 1997, pp. 68 and 87–88.

emancipation.[41] The Hutu Banyarwanda seized the opportunity and exploited the growing anti-Tutsi sentiment to defend their position. They attempted to cast themselves as "indigenous" (because they had usually arrived before 1960) in opposition to the Tutsi Banyarwanda (most of whom had come in the 1960s and 1970s).

Sporadic violent incidents between indigenous Congolese communities and Banyarwanda erupted in 1991 and 1992 in Masisi territory. Spreading in March 1993 to inflame all of North Kivu, the tension caused at least one thousand deaths on both sides and the displacement of more than 130,000 people.[42] The massacres in Masisi also marked the first armed opposition between Banyarwanda Hutus and Tutsis.[43] Only the heavy intervention of Mobutu's forces, assisted by local conflict management initiatives, succeeded in quelling the violence within the Banyarwanda group and between this community and indigenous communities.

The peace was short-lived. The arrival of 2 million Rwandan Hutu refugees after the 1994 genocide increased the pressure on land in both Kivus, thus heightening the tensions among all communities. It reinforced the Tutsis' fear of being targeted in the Congo as their ethnic kin had been in Rwanda. It also led indigenous Congolese to increasingly radicalize against all "Rwandans," Tutsis as well as Hutus, refugees or not. As detailed in chapter 2, these growing tensions, combined with deteriorating security and economic conditions and the promotion of ethnic hatred, ultimately led to large-scale violence against Tutsis and Hutus in both Kivus.

In sum, bottom-up tensions caused the eruption of violence in the Congo long before regional factors (the Rwandan genocide in 1994 and the subsequent invasion by neighboring countries) precipitated the 1996 war. Grassroots rivalries over land, resources, and political power, reinforced by national and provincial actors' top-down manipulation, produced conflict at both the micro and the macro levels. Local agendas were at the root of the ethnic tensions directed toward the people of Rwandan descent, which evolved into one of the most significant macro-level cleavages of the 1990s and became the main national cleavage of the 1998 war.

---

[41] Reyntjens 1999b, pp. 14–15.
[42] Mamdani 2001, p. 253; Willame 1997, p. 66; and Prunier 2008, p. 50.
[43] UN Mission in the Democratic Republic of Congo (MONUC) 2004.

The causation went both ways: Local tensions created national cleavages, but, at the same time, national factors set the stage for local conflicts to erupt into large-scale violence. The colonial state and the Mobutu regime perpetuated local citizenship as a key element of the political, social, and economic landscape of the Congo. Mobutu's ruling strategies largely caused the disintegration of state authority in the eastern Congo and eroded existing forms of decentralized authority. As a result, the potential for the peaceful resolution of local antagonisms at the grassroots level decreased significantly. Last, in the 1990s, Mobutu and his local allies fueled the existing bottom-up conflicts to maintain their hold on power. All of these processes prepared the ground for local agendas to play a determining role during the two wars of the late 1990s.

Local Antagonisms and Violence: What the War Changed

Interaction Between Regional, National, and Local Dimensions. Local political, economic, and social agendas contributed to the widespread and horrific violence during the two wars of the 1990s.[44] The micro-level dynamics described earlier fueled macro-level tensions and provided a foundation for the national and regional fighting that took place throughout the eastern Congo. At the same time, national and regional cleavages reinforced local antagonisms.

The interaction between local violence and the national and regional conflicts was especially obvious during the 1990s wars. From the first days of the hostilities, local Banyamulenge and Banyarwanda militias fought on the side of the Rwandan army and the main rebel movements – Alliance of Democratic Forces for the Liberation of the Congo-Zaire, then the Congolese Rally for Democracy (RCD) and the Congolese Rally for Democracy-Goma (RCD-G) – although Banyamulenge increasingly questioned this alliance throughout the war and a large Banyamulenge contingent eventually switched sides.[45] In addition to this bottom-up dimension, the relationship was also

---

[44] As in most of this book, the information presented in the remaining part of this chapter comes from author's field observations and confidential interviews. The footnotes, therefore, reference only public sources and on-record interviews.

[45] Braeckman 1999, pp. 247–249; and Lemarchand 2009, p. 8.

top-down. During the Second War, the RCD-G, on taking over an area, would organize the Congolese population into local "popular self-defense committees" tasked with attacking the Rwandan Hutu rebels. The Rwandan army used a similar strategy. When it set out to "pacify" a region – meaning to hunt down Rwandan Hutu militias – it began by occupying the territory militarily and then organizing local defense training camps, for which the population was compelled to supply the trainees and the food. In 2000, the RCD-G claimed to have 10,000 local defense force members in North Kivu and had reportedly organized local defense training camps in several places in South Kivu.[46]

The governmental side could similarly count on numerous grassroots allies. During the First War, most Mai Mai militias first sided with Mobutu and then, as the fighting progressed, switched to supporting the rebels. During the Second War, Mai Mai militias, along with the Rwandan Hutu rebels, functioned as Kabila's main proxy in his battles against the RCD-G and Rwanda. The nomination of a Mai Mai leader as chief of Kabila's ground armed forces eventually formalized this local–national alliance. Mai Mai and Rwandan Hutus also worked hand in hand throughout the eastern provinces. Rwandan Hutus were sympathetic to the Mai Mai because they shared a common enemy (the Rwandan army), and therefore the Rwandan rebels helped arm, train, and supply Mai Mai soldiers. The two groups often formed mixed armies.[47]

As a result, numerous regional, national, and local armed groups, organized in complex and often changing patterns of alliances and counteralliances, plagued the eastern provinces throughout the war. A 2003 International Crisis Group report compellingly demonstrates that, in the Kivus, the national war (between Kabila and the RCD-G) and the regional conflict (between Rwanda, Uganda, and the Congolese government) interacted with, shaped, and were in turn shaped by local tensions specific to the provinces (such as antagonisms over local power, local resources, and the status of the Kinyarwanda-speaking Congolese).[48] Studies on the Ituri district similarly illuminated that the relationships between the micro- and macro-level

---

[46] International Crisis Group 2000b, p. 16.
[47] For a public source, see Synergie Vie 2004.
[48] International Crisis Group 2003b.

dynamics of violence were not only top-down but also bottom-up.[49] Manipulation of local actors by Ugandan, Rwandan, and Congolese armed groups led to the fragmentation of local militias and to an escalation of disputes among neighboring communities. At the same time, grassroots antagonisms over local political and economic power eventually caused the dissolution of a national rebel group, the RCD-Kisangani/Liberation Movement, into three splinter groups.

It is important to understand that local agendas were not only distinct from national and regional motivations but also sometimes superseded nationally or regionally induced cleavages. New Mai Mai militias kept forming and splitting. Grassroots militias often switched sides and some Mai Mai groups, such as Mudundu 40, emerged as allies of the RCD-G in the last years of the war. In North Katanga, Mai Mai militias who were on Kabila-controlled territory fought against government forces, while Mai Mai militias who were on the other side of the national frontline fought against RCD-G troops. Most of the time, no modification of the national or regional cleavages could account for these splits and changing alliances; only local agendas could. The Mai Mai wanted to protect their communities or maintain their local control against whomever the external invader (Rwanda, RCD-G, or government soldiers) happened to be. When a local militia did collaborate with Rwandan or RCD-G troops, it was usually not out of support for these armies' goals, but rather because allying with them was the best way for the militia to advance its grassroots agenda.[50]

Thus, although in constant interaction with the national and regional cleavages, and despite frequent reinterpretation in the language of these cleavages, distinctively local military, political, economic, and social agendas fueled war violence. In turn, the generalized fighting effected three main changes in the grassroots dynamics of violence: It reinforced some preexisting local antagonisms, it led to the militarization of others, and it created new decentralized tensions.

Reinforcement of Local Antagonisms. The wars strongly reinforced existing intercommunal antagonisms. From the very beginning of the

---

[49] International Crisis Group 2008, pp. 12–20; UN Security Council 2005i, para. 11; and Vlassenroot and Raeymaekers 2004b, p. 395.
[50] The short studies of Mudundu 40 in Tull 2005, p. 197; and Turner 2007, p. 95 provide a fascinating illustration of this analysis.

generalized conflict, the Rwandan army and the RCD-G removed, often by violent means, most traditional chiefs from the areas they controlled and installed people with Rwandan ancestry (often Tutsi) in their stead.[51] In response, national, provincial, and local indigenous elites mobilized ethnic hatred to save whatever power they retained. Laurent-Désiré Kabila, and subsequently Joseph Kabila, employed the theme of ethnicity both to mobilize combatants and to join forces with the population under their enemies' control. Their strategy was to build a common front with the indigenous population of the Kivus against the Rwandan "aggressors." As early as August 1998, Laurent-Désiré Kabila called on the indigenous population to slaughter the "Rwandan invaders" along with the Tutsis, regardless of whether they were armed or unarmed. Kabila also reopened the debate over the nationality of the Congolese of Rwandan descent. He asked the governmental commission in charge of preparing the Lusaka conference to perform an exegesis of colonial archives to prove "definitively" the "exogeneity" of this minority.[52] In Mai Mai–controlled districts and villages, many traditional chiefs used this information to provoke ethnic hatred to gain support for their fight against the RCD-G.

As a result, throughout the country, ethnicity became the principal paradigm that the Congolese used to explain the wars, as well as the main perceived and stated reason for violence. In particular, the fact that Kinyarwanda-speaking Congolese took over provincial power in large parts of the eastern Congo with the support of the Rwandan army reinforced their association with Rwanda in people's minds and fueled the existing ethnic polarization. Virtually all Congolese blamed people with Rwandan ancestry, especially the Tutsis, for all of the Congo's problems, including the regional conflict and the civil war. Many people even referred to the 1998 war as "the war of the Banyamulenge." Violence against communities of Rwandan descent was especially heavy wherever they lived unprotected by RCD-G or Rwandan soldiers. Pogroms in Kinshasa and Lubumbashi in 1998 resulted in the massacre of hundreds of Tutsis. Likewise, throughout the Second War, Mai Mai carried out extreme violence against Banyamulenge, Banyarwanda, and Rwandan families living in the

---

[51] For a public source, see Roberto Garreton, the UN Special Rapporteur on the human rights situation in the Congo cited in Reyntjens 1999b, p. 178.

[52] International Crisis Group 2001, pp. 13–15.

Kivus to terrorize them into leaving the Congolese territory.[53] At that time, even though it was highly dangerous to proffer such statements when the Kivus were under RCD-G control, I heard many Congolese speak openly of their desire to commit "genocide" against the Congolese of Rwandan descent.

One ethnic antagonism that the war did not reinforce was that between the Hutus and Tutsis of Rwandan descent. During the war, these two communities banded together to defend themselves against their common enemies, the indigenous groups. Although this temporary coalition was often tense and although the Banyamulenge community was split between pro- and anti-Rwanda groups (as will be detailed in the section on South Kivu), most Congolese Hutus and Tutsis nevertheless remained allies until the last year of the transition.

Militarization of Preexisting Antagonisms: The Example of Nyunzu Territory. The wars did not simply reinforce local antagonisms. They also turned previously latent local tensions into open conflicts, as illustrated by the example of Nyunzu, a small rural town in North Katanga (see map of Katanga in Figure 8).

Two sources of tensions marred relationships in Nyunzu territory before the war. First, several families, branches of the same family, or tribes, competed around the selection of the villages, districts, and territory chiefs. Though villages were often divided, the conflict remained "cold." Even the opponents of an existing chief usually respected him and crises erupted only at his death, over the choice of his replacement. Second, for centuries, tensions had developed between the marginalized Pygmy minority and the other ethnic groups, the Baluba, Bakalanga, Bahemba, Batungo, and Baombo, who together represented about 60% of the territory's population and called themselves "Bantus." (The label "Bantu" originally refers to a diverse family of languages, not a single, unified ethnic group, but the polarization of identities progressively led these nonpygmy groups to adopt the term.)[54] Traditional law disentitled the Pygmies to land, villages, and the right to select a customary chief. They had to live attached to Bantu villages, in which Bantus barely tolerated them and

---

[53] Van Acker and Vlassenroot 2000, para. 24.
[54] See Reyntjens 1999a, p. 244, for a more detailed analysis of the Bantu label in Africa.

used them as cheap labor for agricultural chores. The dominant ethnic groups stigmatized the Pygmies as barbarous and uncivilized – in short, as one of my Bantu interviewees phrased it, as a species "somewhere in between animals and men."

When war reached Nyunzu in early 1997 because the Rwandan army and the RCD-G chased the Rwandan Hutu rebels into the territory, national and regional armed groups took advantage of these two preexisting antagonisms to enlist local allies. Local actors simultaneously used national and regional factions to advance their decentralized agendas. The Rwandan Hutus drafted Pygmies as guides or as semislaves, and tasked them with carrying their luggage, finding food, or cultivating their lands. At the same time, the Pygmies, as well as the existing chiefs' opponents, saw the Rwandan Hutus' arrival as an opportunity to obtain arms and supplies to seize power locally and take revenge on their former oppressors.

The alliances between the Rwandan rebels and frustrated local groups eventually led to the creation of local Mai Mai militias in this part of the country. Later, in 1999 to 2000, a new national actor became involved in this already complex web of alliances. Kabila reluctantly agreed to arm the North Katanga Mai Mai to facilitate the fight against the RCD-G, despite his fears that the arms distributed there would be difficult to recover afterwards. In Nyunzu territory, these interacting local, national, and regional agendas led to a reconfiguration of power among five different Mai Mai groups, mostly organized along ethnic lines. Then, in early 2003, the RCD-G tried, in turn, to enroll Mai Mai groups to weaken Kabila and obtain additional concessions during the final rounds of the peace talks. The RCD-G succeeded in attracting some splinter groups, thus multiplying the number of militias present in the area.

As a result, Nyunzu territory suffered from an extremely high level of violence throughout the war. Mai Mai and Rwandan Hutu forces, who controlled most of the countryside, regularly clashed with Rwandan and RCD-G troops, who dominated Nyunzu city's center, the territory's main roads, and several large villages along the way. Mai Mai militias also often fought with each other over land or mineral resources. All armed groups repeatedly subjected the population to massive human rights violations, including forced displacement, gang rape, killings, massacres, torture, and burning of villages.

According to interviews conducted throughout the eastern Congo, the militarization of previously contained local antagonisms over land, traditional power, ideology, and the management of public affairs recurred in many areas of the eastern Congo other than Nyunzu. Those who felt disavowed usually enlisted in an armed group during the war or had their children recruited to one of the militias. They then used the new power their arms gave them to try, in turn, to settle their accounts.

War-Induced Conflicts. The war also induced numerous new grassroots conflicts. To start with, it generated widespread resentment over the power shifts that the fighting had caused. Just as in Nyunzu, the war allowed many marginalized and previously exploited communities to gain power and exact revenge throughout the eastern Congo. The Alliance of Democratic Forces for the Liberation of the Congo-Zaire, the main rebel movement of the 1996 war, consisted mostly of alienated individuals or groups: "Kasaians" expelled from Katanga in 1992 and 1993, deserters from Mobutu's army, and unemployed Baluba from Kasai, among others.[55] All armed groups also had a large proportion of young people in their ranks. These combatants claimed that they wanted to fight the marginalization affecting them since Mobutu's policies had generated a land crisis, the collapse of the educational system, and the destruction of the country's productive capacities.[56]

Armed groups were attractive to these disenfranchised communities because they offered leadership roles and social mobility; they represented a way to upgrade their members' social status.[57] In Willame's words, for most young people, "guns [became] the only tool of promotion in a society that [could] not integrate them any more."[58] Van Acker and Vlassenroot even regard Mai Mai militias as "experiments with more egalitarian forms of social organization for self-help and protection."[59] These authors demonstrate that combatants adhered to a firm moral code, which enforced a strict egalitarianism among soldiers and linked their perceived invulnerability to spiritual fetishes.

---

[55] Willame 1997, p. 136.
[56] Van Acker and Vlassenroot 2000, pp. 2–3 and 20–22; Van Hoyweghen and Vlassenroot 2000, p. 113; and Vlassenroot 2000, p. 97.
[57] Vlassenroot 2000, pp. 95 and 97.   [58] Willame 1997, p. 137.
[59] The remaining part of this paragraph is based on Van Acker and Vlassenroot 2000. The quotations come from para. 27.

While outside all "normality" had collapsed and exclusion was standard, these militias were "enclaves" that rejected the traditional patrimonial order and proposed an alternative system. As such, they were a means to recreate trust in the social world. They provided their members with new, stringent boundaries, a simple principle for explaining the state of disorder (ethnicity), a solution to it (chasing the "foreigners" from the Congolese soil), and an everyday routine (training and violence).

Participating in militias was also a way to invert the existing social order, which placed the combatants at the bottom. The general context of conflict and impunity gave militia members the opportunity to settle previous personal conflicts, often related to land or to other grievances about discrimination or injustice.[60] Most important, the omnipresence of violence overturned the old social order and gave power to armed groups. Militia leaders were undoubtedly in a stronger position than traditional authorities to make decisions about the political affairs of the community and to carry out "justice." Militiamen also controlled access to land (which, as mentioned earlier, was the most important prerogative of traditional authorities): They were able to rape, maim, or kill those who tried to access their fields. As a result, in both the rural indigenous communities and among the people of Rwandan descent, the young generation – the generation of the combatants – eventually enjoyed the preeminent role that elder and customary chiefs formerly held. Furthermore, previously marginalized ethnic groups, such as the Pygmies in North Katanga or the people with Rwandan ancestry in the Kivus, often assumed power at the local level.

In addition to generating resentment among particular groups over power shifts, the war produced significant anger among the population over the behavior of all the armed factions. Combatants, in fact, rarely fought with each other, but rather targeted unarmed civilians, either to prevent them from collaborating with other warring parties or to punish people who had already done so. The Rwandan and RCD-G contra-guerilla warfare strategy was to attack parishes, health centers, and development projects to empty the countryside, where Mai Mai were able to blend into the population and enjoy an

---

[60] See also Van Acker and Vlassenroot 2000 as well as Vlassenroot 2000.

economic rear base and support.[61] Rwandan and RCD-G troops also
enacted extremely bloody retaliations against local villages following
any Mai Mai ambushes, a policy that only heightened the population's hatred of the "invaders."[62] Mai Mai adopted a similar terror
strategy toward civilians, carrying out killings, mass rape, beating,
and torture whenever they took over a town or village previously
occupied by enemy troops. As a result, prewar animosities turned
into deadly grudges. In Nyunzu, for example, the Bantu population
resented mistreatment by all Mai Mai groups, but was especially
ashamed by violence perpetrated by the Pygmies, because, as mentioned earlier, Pygmies were considered to be significantly inferior.
Throughout the RCD-G–controlled area, humiliations, massacres,
and countless violations of human rights greatly intensified the preexisting tensions between people of Rwandan descent and indigenous
communities as well as those between powerful and marginalized
individuals or groups.

Finally, the war added another layer of complexity to the overlapping ownership claims over land, as the situation in Ituri most clearly
illustrates. Generalized fighting broke out in the district in June 1999,
because Hema landowners had tried to appropriate Lendu-occupied
land.[63] The subsequent violence led to a long series of mutual expro-
priations and forced displacement by various armed groups. Many
displaced people settled on land left vacant by refugees or displaced
families from other communities and began to cultivate it. This practice of usurpation, which occurred in similar ways throughout the
rest of the eastern Congo, created a new division between the previous owners and the wartime land appropriators.

The interaction with regional and national cleavages during the war
thus reinforced local hostilities: It induced a series of new local cleavages, enhanced decentralized violence in places where it existed prior
to the generalized fighting, and transformed latent antagonisms into
open conflicts in places where tensions had been previously contained.
As could be expected, all of these local disputes persisted during the

---

[61] For public sources, see Braeckman 2003, pp. 165–166; and Reyntjens 1999b,
p. 185.
[62] See Human Rights Watch 1999; Kalere 2002; and Rassemblement pour le
Progrès (undated, probably 2001) among many other compelling reports on
this topic.
[63] The last section of this chapter provides more background to this conflict.

transition and continued to generate violence in the local, national, and regional realms. There was, however, an important shift during the transition period: In addition to interacting with the macro-level cleavages, some grassroots conflicts also became increasingly autonomous from the national and regional developments.[64]

Local Patterns of Violence During the Transition

Social, Political, and Economic Agendas

When describing the situation during the transition in the eastern provinces, a conflict-resolution worker based in South Kivu noted that "the most obvious division, 'everybody against the [people with Rwandan ancestry],'" was not the only problem. Rather, commanders exploited "hundreds of potential divisions, of local problems," which often erupted in violence.[65] A mosaic of alliances and counteralliances separated the numerous ethnic groups in North Kivu, South Kivu, North Katanga, and Ituri. Just as during the war, clan, political, social, and to some extent ethnic identities remained fluid and individuals often switched allegiance from one group to another as opportunities arose.

Social, economic, and political issues motivated the interclan and ethnic conflicts. These local causes of tensions were intertwined with one another (as this section shows) and with national and regional agendas (as the next section demonstrates).

The lack of social opportunities for young and disenfranchised communities persisted as a motivation for enrollment in armed groups. A donor, for example, claimed that Mai Mai remained "very hungry for some respect and some identity." Just as during the war, involvement in a militia gave its members the feeling of being "part of a thing" and a sense of being "recognized as something separate from the masses." Furthermore, previously marginalized individuals and groups, such as the youth and the Pygmies, had strong incentives to perpetuate the violent situation that had enabled them to attain a higher social status than they could have during peaceful times. Similarly, many

---

[64] Autesserre 2006 and 2007 include earlier versions of the rest of this chapter, except for the section on Ituri.

[65] Author's interview with Hans Romkema, Head of Mission, Life and Peace Institute, 2004.

Mai Mai chiefs (who were often ill trained and illiterate) knew that, should peace return to the Congo, they would lose their status as all-powerful, kinglike leaders; they would once again become mere soldiers with no rank or status, potentially subordinated to their former enemies. This concern was one of their main motivations for refusing to be integrated into the national army.

The threat of retaliation against individuals perceived to have wronged their neighbors or their communities during the war was another social cause of persisting local violence. This threat remained mostly latent throughout the transition, but it was, according to a humanitarian worker, one of the main issues that would arise from the return of refugees from Tanzania.[66] It was also the main reason why many refugees and displaced persons failed to return to their home villages in the Kivus, North Katanga, and Ituri. They were "afraid of being accused of having supported someone, or taken this or that point of view, or afraid that the mere fact that they had fled was a sign that they had a bad conscience."[67]

In addition to social issues, political antagonisms at the local level fueled significant violence. Conflicts of succession continued to generate tensions similar to those that had existed before and during the war, and the competition between new and traditional authorities added yet another layer of complexity. During the war, many customary chiefs had fled, either to escape ongoing violence or because an armed group had usurped their power. As the general conflict abated, traditional authorities returned to their territories, generating a high level of decentralized hostility. The case of Nyunzu territory (North Katanga) provides, once again, a perfect example. While conducting interviews in a camp for displaced people, I realized that, contrary to my expectations, the camp was not comprised of the lowest-ranking members of the communities, but rather of families of local traditional authorities, notably village and collectivity chiefs. Though ordinary citizens had been allowed to return to their villages, when the chiefs tried to do so, Mai Mai soldiers who had assumed power in their stead threatened them and forced them to leave again.

---

[66] Author's interview with Jean-Charles Dupin, humanitarian advisor, UN Office for the Coordination of Humanitarian Affairs, Bukavu, 2005.
[67] Author's interview with Anders Vatn, head of mission, Norwegian Refugee Council, Goma, March 2005.

Field observations, interviews, and articles in the press suggested that this situation was common throughout Katanga, the two Kivus, and Ituri.[68]

In addition to disputes over traditional power, there was widespread conflict over appointments in state institutions by transitional authorities. For example, in Shabunda territory (South Kivu, see map in Figure 7) in 2004, General Padiri, an ethnic Tembo whom transitional authorities recognized as a leading figure in the Mai Mai movement, reportedly appointed only Mai Mai Tembo to important military and administrative positions. This preferential treatment led to several small-scale fights between the Mai Mai Tembo and Mai Mai from the Rega ethnic group, until the latter retaliated by chasing the former from Shabunda territory.

In most cases, such political tensions interacted with economically motivated hostilities. Political power often guaranteed access to land and economic resources, while access to wealth in turn produced the resources to buy arms, reward troops, and secure political power. In particular, the land problems that had led to massive local violence before and during the war remained the principal source of conflict in many rural areas of the Kivus, North Katanga, and Ituri.[69] Antagonisms over land regularly erupted in open fighting. They also greatly impeded the peaceful return of displaced persons, because those who controlled the land after the war threatened to use force to maintain their possession.

In addition to providing the means of survival for most rural families, land ownership was also critical because it determined access to natural resources, which otherwise had to be acquired by force. During the transition, competition for the control of minerals remained a major cause of grassroots conflict throughout the eastern provinces. In 2005, the UN Office for the Coordination of Humanitarian Affairs claimed that this issue was becoming the driving force of the Mai Mai

---

[68] For a public source, see "Forgotten war rumbles on in South Congo Province," Reuters, September 14, 2005.

[69] Cellule Provinciale d'Appui à la Pacification and Programme des Nations Unies pour le Développement 2008 provides excellent public data on this issue. International Crisis Group 2005a, p. 14; MONUC 2004; and Mugangu Matabaro 2008 are other good public sources. The section on Understanding the Joint Production of Violence during the Transition, later in this chapter, illustrates this analysis in greater detail.

phenomenon.[70] In Nyunzu, for example, violence during the transition occurred mostly around the gold deposits of the northern part of the territory because most of the Mai Mai chiefs had regrouped there and were competing to control the mines. Mai Mai were not the only culprits, or even the main ones. All of the armed groups based in the eastern provinces used violence to access natural resources. In Shabunda (South Kivu) for instance, a Civil Society representative reported that "the armed forces" provoked conflicts among the persons who had legal claims on mineral-rich areas. When the tensions reached an alarming level and erupted in violence, armed forces usually intervened to confiscate people's weapons and mining rights. The armed forces would then either exploit the mines themselves or hand them over to a third party. They reportedly bribed provincial and national commanders into looking the other way.[71]

Economic interests in resource exploitation were sometimes so great that they superseded the national or regional cleavages. Battlefield enemies occasionally cooperated around mining sites to boost their economic benefits. A prime example is the partnership between RCD-G and Mai Mai troops over the control of columbo-tantalite and cassiterite in Walikale territory (North Kivu), which started during the war and continued until early 2004. According to Global Witness, "the deal gave control of the mine at Bisie to the Mai-Mai and control of the town of Mubi to the RCD-G. Thus, the Mai-Mai benefited by taxing the mineral trade at the mine itself and the RCD-G benefited by taxing the minerals as they were transported out of the area (and again in Goma)."[72]

Finally, the need to find a means of survival, which had pushed many civilians to enroll in armed groups during the war, remained salient during the transition.[73] Given the lack of economic opportunities in the eastern provinces, membership in an armed group was still the most profitable option. As anyone traveling through the eastern Congo at that time could observe, the continuing insecurity enabled various militiamen to set up checkpoints and demand "tolls" from

[70] UN Office for the Coordination of Humanitarian Affairs, *Pour ou contre les Civils: l'ambiguïte Mayi Mayi*, press release, Kinshasa, 2005.
[71] See UN Security Council 2005k, p. 49, for other publicly available examples.
[72] Global Witness 2005, p. 16.
[73] See also Baaz and Stern 2008.

those who came through, capture custom revenues, and make money "through looting, rackets, and blackmail."[74]

Apart from the militias, nongovernmental and UN organizations were among the only sources of jobs with a decent income available during the transition. These were legal and peaceful positions, but they were scarce, and competition over them could lead to violence and even, in South Kivu, murder. In Uvira, Baraka, and Fizi, for instance, nongovernmental organizations were threatened with the most dire consequences should they continue to hire "foreign" staff – meaning staff non-native to the city where the agencies were working. One nongovernmental organization working in Baraka even had a "foreign" staff member killed. None of the official complaints filed with the authorities achieved anything. Rather, local authorities condoned these practices of intimidation.

In sum, during the transition, just as during the war, violence was motivated not only by regional and national tensions but also by long-standing bottom-up agendas, whose main instigators were villagers, traditional authorities, administrative chiefs, or ethnic leaders. Local manifestations of violence, although often related to national or regional struggles, were also precipitated by distinctively local problems. Even issues usually presented as regional (such as the violence waged by Rwandan Hutu militias in the Congo) or national (such as ethnic tensions between indigenous Congolese and people of Rwandan descent) had significant local components, which fueled and reinforced the regional and national dimensions. The first part of this chapter has already explained that tensions between indigenous Congolese and Congolese of Rwandan descent were rooted in long-standing, bottom-up conflicts over power and land. The following sections on North and South Kivu demonstrate that, during the transition, similar grassroots demands made by people with Rwandan ancestry continued to fuel hatred and generate widespread violence. Before turning to this analysis, however, a case study on the Rwandan Hutu militia provides another prime example of the extent to which grassroots agendas impacted macro-level dynamics during the transition,

---

[74] Quotation from Rony Brauman, director of research at the Médecins Sans Frontières Foundation, reported in "Violence ignored in Congo's Katanga– MSF," Reuters, July 24, 2005.

and therefore how problematic the ignorance of local issues in the dominant narrative presented in chapter 2 is.

A Closer Look: Local Dimensions of the Rwandan Hutu Militias' Presence

Decentralized economic, political, and social conflicts often motivated grassroots alliances with the Rwandan Hutu militias. For example, in an interview, Ignace Murwanashyaka, the president of the main politicomilitary movement representing the Rwandan Hutus in exile, the Democratic Forces for the Liberation of Rwanda (FDLR), claimed that some traditional chiefs were "very favorable" to his people, and that Rwandan Hutu refugees had been "welcomed" by several Congolese ethnic groups. He added that Rwandan Hutus had been able to mix with the local population in most places, and that many of the refugees had become so well integrated that it was "very difficult to distinguish them from the locals."[75] During another 2005 interview, a high-ranking official from an FDLR splinter group similarly explained to me that his people had "developed very good relationships with the natives" and that they had even "received some land from the [chiefs]." Given the number of atrocities for which Rwandan Hutu militias were responsible, and consequently the high level of resentment amongst most Congolese people, these claims may have sounded like mere propaganda. However, Rwandan Hutus did in fact benefit from the support of various local strongmen, and many were indeed integrated in Congolese villages.[76]

Many Mai Mai militias continued to collaborate with the Rwandan Hutus (who, as explained previously, had been their wartime allies) in both Kivus during the transition. In South Kivu, for instance, Mai Mai support ranged from hiding Rwandan Hutu combatants, to sharing the profits amassed from the control of marketplaces and mining areas, and even to forming a mixed Mai Mai–Rwandan Hutu armed group called the Rastas. In exchange, the Rwandan Hutus assisted their Mai Mai allies in their factional fighting against other Mai Mai militias.[77]

---

[75] Author's phone interview, 2005.

[76] See Life and Peace Institute 2006 for a public source on this issue.

[77] Global Witness 2005, pp. 4 and 20; UN Mission in the Democratic Republic of Congo (MONUC) 2004; and UN Security Council 2005i, para. 39,

During the transition, the Rwandan Hutus even enrolled new allies: soldiers originally from Bemba's or Kabila's forces and now part of the Congolese integrated army. According to a UN official working with them, Congolese soldiers were afraid of Rwandan Hutu combatants and therefore refused to attack them. Furthermore, because the integrated army failed to pay and discipline its soldiers adequately, Rwandan Hutus could easily bribe the troops to assist them in taxing and looting the Congolese population. The situation in Shabunda exemplifies this alliance, which also existed in slightly different forms in various locations of South Kivu and southern North Kivu.[78] In Shabunda, the FDLR controlled the northern part of the territory. Rwandan Hutu families peacefully cultivated their fields and regularly sold their products to the local market. Rwandan Hutu combatants were reportedly on very good terms with the Congolese army brigades that were supposed to prevent them from raiding the local population. Together, they jointly controlled and taxed the local inhabitants.

Beyond Shabunda, certain local administrative authorities and populations of North and South Kivu tolerated the presence of Rwandan Hutus, as long as they refrained from the most blatant human rights violations.[79] Many other local authorities and population abhorred the Rwandan rebels' presence; however, even the most violent splinter group of the FDLR, the Rastas, which became notorious for the atrocities it committed between 2004 and 2008 in the area around Bunyakiri (South Kivu), benefited from some local support. A handful of villagers provided Rastas with the information necessary for their operations: for example, whom to kidnap and hold for ransom (such as a farmer who was about to marry off his daughter and had just finished gathering the dowry) or whom to torture and kill (such as a family who wanted to prevent one of their daughters from trafficking with the militia).[80]

The presence of Rwandan Hutu militias in the Congo, usually understood as a regional or national problem, was thus very much

---

provide excellent examples of the Mai Mai–FDLR collaboration around mining sites.

[78] For a public source, see UN Security Council 2004c.

[79] For a public source, see the news report by Ghislaine Dupont, *Radio France International*, broadcast on August 12, 2005, 6:30 a.m.

[80] For a public source, see Union Paysanne pour le Développement Intégral 2007; and Life and Peace Institute 2007.

grounded in local dynamics. Grassroots alliances were key to perpetuating the Rwandan Hutus' presence on Congolese territory and
the violence associated with it. As the leader of the Rally–FDLR, one
of the main FDLR splinter groups, acknowledged, Rwandan Hutu
refugees "would not have been able to survive" without the relationships they had developed with some local populations. Rwandan
Hutu groups were too small and too internally divided to fight the
Congolese military forces on their own. By contrast, local armed
groups' support enabled the Rwandan combatants to recruit allies,
repel their opponents, and hide from enemy soldiers (usually RCD-G
and sometimes integrated units) determined to attack them. Likewise,
the Rwandan Hutu militias were able to obtain the economic resources
they needed to buy arms and continue fighting because some local
authorities tolerated – and some grassroots militias supported – their
presence around mining sites. Finally, the very fact that Rwandan
rebels could live near Congolese villages enhanced their quality of
life on Congolese territory and, therefore, diminished their incentives
to return peacefully to Rwanda. Wherever decentralized authorities,
grassroots forces, and local communities provided robust support,
Rwandan Hutu families were able to trade goods and services with the
surrounding population. In other places, Rwandan Hutu combatants
could at least live off the surrounding Congolese residents through
looting.

Understanding the Joint Production of Violence during the Transition

Decentralized agendas thus played a critical role in sustaining instability during the transition. It is now important to understand how
these micro-level agendas interacted with the national and regional
conflicts to jointly produce violence. During the transition, the pattern of interactions varied within each of the most violent provinces,
and often within each territory. To generalize, national and regional
cleavages were as influential as local rifts in engendering fighting in
North Kivu. By contrast, grassroots agendas were more influential
than national or regional tensions in producing violence in South
Kivu, North Katanga, and Ituri. However, the nature of the most
significant micro-level tensions, the relative autonomy of grassroots

disputes from national and regional conflicts, and the manner in which bottom-up antagonisms influenced macro-level problems differed among these three provinces.[81]

North Kivu: Master Cleavages and Local Alliances

As detailed in chapter 2, international peacebuilders attributed the violence in North Kivu to the master ethnic cleavage (people of Rwandan descent versus "native" communities), neatly superimposed and on the same dividing line as the national and regional political cleavage (President Kabila versus the RCD-G and later versus Nkunda's National Congress for the Defense of the People, both supported by Rwanda).

It is true that, after large-scale fighting took place around Bukavu in May to June 2004 and the RCD-G lost control of South Kivu, the military dimension of the countrywide political conflict between Kabila and the RCD-G continued in one last place: North Kivu. The "*Petit Nord*" (the southern part of North Kivu, including Walikale, Rutshuru, and Masisi territories; see map in Figure 6) remained the last stronghold of the RCD-G, which maintained absolute control there. In violation of one of the transition's rules, both the governor and the regional military commander were RCD-G officials. Up until 2006, the integrated army brigades in the province did not enlist rank-and-file soldiers from each of the armed groups that had participated in the Inter-Congolese Dialogue, but instead relied exclusively on former RCD-G soldiers. The governor also maintained his 3,000-strong Local Defense Forces, a predominantly Congolese Hutu militia that he had created during the war and that Rwandan forces had trained. Additionally, North Kivu retained its own "financial coordinator," akin to a finance minister, instead of relying on the national minister in Kinshasa. Its tax services still reported to the provincial capital Goma, not to their hierarchical superiors in Kinshasa. Instead of going to the capital, revenues remained in the province. As a result, from the "Bukavu crisis" onward, national politicians – except for

---

[81] Van Acker and Vlassenroot 2000, Vlassenroot and Raeymaekers 2004a, Vlassenroot and Romkema 2002, and Willame 1997 provide excellent background information for the two Kivu case studies.

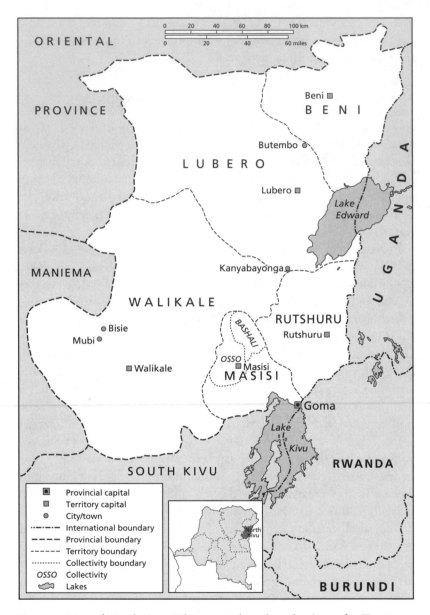

Figure 6 Map of North Kivu. This map is based on the *Carte des Territoires du Nord Kivu* by OCHA DRC Geographic (WGS84), dated April 2002.

those belonging to the RCD-G – thought of North Kivu as an exception: The province least integrated into the transition process and the last holdout, the place Kabila needed to control in order to unify the entire country.

It is also true that the regional dimension was present during the transition, although less so than during the wars. Rwanda reportedly supported the RCD-G (and later Nkunda's forces) with its financial, military, and political might and engaged in fighting against Mai Mai and Rwandan Hutu militias alongside RCD-G (and later Nkunda's) troops.[82]

However, this reading of the conflict overlooked the key role of local tensions. The Kabila government's strength in its struggle against the RCD-G in North Kivu depended on the allies it had there: The members of the former Congolese Rally for Democracy–Kisangani/Liberation Movement, which fought against the RCD-G from the outside (on the northern front, along the same front line as during the war), and the Mai Mai, which waged war against the RCD-G from within the RCD-G's area of control. During the transition, both of these allies fought with the RCD-G (and later Nkunda) over provincial and local issues rather than over national or regional agendas.

As previously discussed, ever since colonization, North Kivu had seen a strong polarization develop between its two most populous ethnic groups, the Banyarwanda and the Nandes, due to conflict over provincial power.[83] During the war, the elites of these competing ethnic groups each controlled half of the province and allied themselves with different warring parties: the Banyarwanda with the RCD-G, and the Nandes with the Congolese Rally for Democracy–Kisangani/Liberation Movement and Kabila. During the first months of the transition, the antagonism reached such a point that the Banyarwanda suspected the Nandes of harboring plans to eradicate them, and vice versa.[84] In May 2004, the Transitional Government finally reunified the province administratively and put it under the leadership of an RCD-G politician. Members of indigenous ethnic groups living in Goma complained that the RCD-G's rule had a strong ethnic bias

---

[82] For publicly available documents, see the sources quoted in chapter 2.

[83] See also Willame 1997 for more on this issue.

[84] For a public source on this issue, see UN Mission in the Democratic Republic of Congo (MONUC) 2004.

against them and perpetuated the dominance of the Banyarwanda, who still occupied all political, military, and business positions of authority in the province. As a result, up until the end of the transition, Nande Mai Mai groups remained active in the "Grand Nord" (the northern part of North Kivu, including Lubero and Beni territories), for fear of a potential Banyarwanda invasion from the south. Despite administrative reunification, the front line persisted between RCD-G and anti-RCD-G forces, allied respectively with Rwanda's and Kabila's troops. Numerous skirmishes took place on this front line in 2004, 2005, and 2006, and a large-scale confrontation erupted around Kanyabayonga in late 2004.

Kabila could also count on grassroots tensions between indigenous and Banyarwanda communities to help recruit local allies, both political (such as the Civil Society movement) and military (such as the Mai Mai militias) to fight against the RCD-G from within its area of control.[85] For example, in Masisi territory, Civil Society representatives and local militias had two reasons for combating anything they perceived as a Banyarwanda movement. To start with, Banyarwanda (mostly Tutsis) owned the majority of the land, as a result of transactions made under Mobutu, but the Hundes and the Nyangas claimed that it was still theirs, because nobody had the right to sell their customary land. The pattern of displacement during the war further complicated the property ownership problem. Many Tutsis fled Masisi in the 1990s to escape the ongoing massacres and abandoned their acreage or sold it at an artificially low price. When they came back after the 1996 and 1998 wars, they found their lands occupied. Allegedly, they took all of it back, by force if necessary, including the property they had sold legitimately.

Moreover, as in the 1980s, the Hundes and the Nyangas still felt they were the only communities with a rightful claim to political power, as the Hutus were only immigrants (even though they formed the majority population of Masisi territory). These positions led to major tensions over the naming of village or collectivity chiefs. For instance, in the Osso and Bashali collectivities, the Hunde population reportedly sided with the newly returned traditional chief, himself a

---

[85] Nonconfidential sources for this and the following paragraphs include ibid; author's interview with Azile Tanzi, Head of Mission, Campagne pour la Paix, Goma, 2005; and author's interview with Bushoki, 2005.

Hunde, against the Hutu chiefs who had seized power during the war; in retaliation, the Hutu chiefs committed "a lot of abuses" against their opponents' supporters.[86] Because Hutus dominated the army forces stationed in the area, the Hundes could not express their dissatisfaction for fear of reprisal from the military apparatus. However, it was clear that the Hundes would immediately take revenge on their Hutu neighbors should the local composition of the army change.

Like the indigenous groups, Banyarwanda fighters pursued local agendas that were paramount to their survival. They refused any kind of settlement because they feared revenge killings and worried that they might lose their land, as well as their local economic and political power. Their leaders also had significant personal stakes in disrupting the transition. A governmental tribunal had convicted a handful of Banyarwanda officers in absentia for the assassination of former president Laurent-Désiré Kabila in 2001. They stood at risk of imprisonment and death should they find themselves in territory under Joseph Kabila's control.

Then, during the last year of the transition, the Banyarwanda community split. In 2004, a new law on nationality regranted most Hutus in North Kivu Congolese citizenship, with rights to land ownership and political representation, because they or their ancestors had been present on Congolese territory before the 1960 independence. Feeling more secure, the Hutus progressively abandoned their alliance with the Tutsis and, in 2005, attempted to distance themselves from their former allies to better affirm their Congolese allegiance.[87] After the 2006 elections, Hutu Banyarwanda tried to ally with the Nandes, who had won the leadership of the province. This shift in the local balance of power resulted in an increased marginalization of the Tutsi minority, who did not qualify for Congolese citizenship (most had come only in the 1960s and the 1970s), lost all hope of political representation, increasingly feared for their lives and property, and became more radicalized.

Throughout the Walikale, Rutshuru, and Masisi territories, these local antagonisms over political and land issues materialized on the military stage. In particular, they fueled the conflict between Mai

---

[86] Author's interview with Tanzi, 2005.
[87] Human Rights Watch 2005; and International Crisis Group 2005a and 2007a provide excellent public data on this issue.

Mai, who represented the indigenous communities and allied with
Rwandan Hutu militias, and the Local Defense Forces, who sided
with the Banyarwanda and allied with the RCD-G. These local tensions also regularly escalated into serious threats to the national and
regional settlements. In particular, fighting became more frequent and
more violent after the May 2004 Bukavu crisis precipitated a complete
breakdown of trust between the RCD-G and the Mai Mai. In October
2004, the situation in Masisi became so tense that there was once again
a tangible front line within the province, with both groups committing
abuses against people crossing to the other side. The neighboring territory of Rutshuru was the theater of repeated clashes between Mai Mai
and RCD-G elements, and these local tensions built up and erupted
into a large-scale confrontation in January 2006. A few months later,
a new armed group, the Congrès National pour la Défense du Peuple
(National Congress for the Defense of the People), appeared under the
leadership of the Tutsi general Laurent Nkunda, purportedly to protect the people with Rwandan ancestry. Nkunda's militia progressively
took control of large parts of Rutshuru and Masisi territories and
frequently clashed with Rwandan Hutus and Mai Mai soldiers. This
renewed military threat prompted the creation of additional Mai Mai
groups, such as Pareco, which invoked a community self-protection
doctrine. After the transition officially ended, both Nkunda's followers and the Mai Mai continued to fight over the same objectives: protecting their communities and consolidating their claims over land
and provincial or subprovincial positions of authority. In 2007 and
2008, numerous clashes took place in the province, killing thousands
of fighters and civilians, displacing more than half a million people,
and eventually jeopardizing the national and regional settlements.

Local agendas regarding traditional power or land, which led to hostilities at the provincial level (Nandes versus Congolese of Rwandan
descent) and at the village level (Hutus or Tutsis versus other communities), were therefore as influential as national and regional cleavages
in generating violence in North Kivu. However, one could easily use
the macro-level ethnic and political cleavages to interpret local conflicts, and thus, as in the dominant narrative, see North Kivu politics
as a reflection of these macro-level tensions. In contrast, in South Kivu
after the Bukavu crisis, and in North Katanga and Ituri, the master
cleavages carried much less weight, and one could hardly interpret the
local agendas using the dominant top-down approach.

South Kivu: Progressively Autonomous Local Agendas

Until the Bukavu crisis, the dynamics of violence in South Kivu were similar to those in North Kivu: primarily driven by micro-level agendas but usually interpreted as revolving around the political cleavage of RCD-G versus Kabila and the ethnic cleavage of Banyamulenge versus other communities. Then, in May 2004, armed groups allied with President Kabila defeated the RCD-G troops stationed in South Kivu. Most of the RCD-G soldiers retreated to North Kivu or Rwanda, though some were integrated into the Congolese army. The RCD-G authorities lost administrative control of the province. People with Rwandan ancestry fled to North Kivu, Burundi, Rwanda, or to the Banyamulenge rural stronghold in Minembwe and the high plateaus of Itombwe (see map of South Kivu in Figure 7), and only the tensions around their potential return remained. If macro-level cleavages had been as important in causing violence as the dominant narrative contends, their quasi disappearance from South Kivu politics should have produced a pacified situation. Yet, the province remained extremely unstable. In 2005, for example, the 200-kilometer road from Kamanyola to Fizi crossed over the territory of twelve armed groups and bordered that of four other militias, some of which were allied with foreign rebel groups. All of these groups continued to commit human rights violations against the Congolese population, while the juxtaposition of RCD-G, Mai Mai, Banyamulenge, and Rwandan Hutu soldiers transformed the province into a powder keg.

Despite the quasi-disappearance of the national and regional sources of tensions, South Kivu remained fragmented due to many unresolved local conflicts. Antagonisms revolved around three main points: first, the leadership of specific militias, for example, between Mai Mai leaders such as General Dunia and Colonel Nguvu; second, opposing claims on land, mining sites, and administrative and traditional positions, as between Banyamulenge and indigenous groups around Minembwe territory (see the in-depth case study below); third, ethnic tensions – Bembes versus Banyamulenge and Buyus; Tembos or Regas versus Shis; Fuleros versus Banyamulenge – and interclan tensions – among the three main Shi subgroups, among Bembe clans, and among Banyamulenge clans. As a result, Mai Mai militias continued their armed struggle despite the fact that, by mid-2004, almost all of them had been officially integrated into the national army.

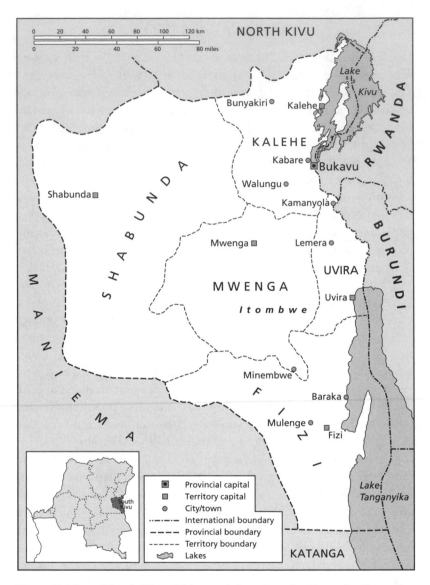

Figure 7 Map of South Kivu. This map is based on the *Carte des Territoires du Sud Kivu* by OCHA DRC Geographic (WGS84), dated April 2002.

The tensions between indigenous and Banyamulenge communities provide a prime example of how what the dominant narrative presented as the result of national and regional cleavages was actually primarily a consequence of grassroots struggles. The very existence of the Minembwe territory, which the RCD-G had carved up during the war and which indigenous communities wanted to reclaim, was one of the main sources of open fighting. Tutsi dissidents wanted to keep Minembwe as a territory according to RCD-G diagrams, so that they could remain the majority there and thus retain control over land and political power in the area. Their Mai Mai opponents mobilized around the ideas that the Tutsis wanted to "grab their land" and they had to fight to defend their ancestral rights. The Tutsi dissidents further insisted that Tutsi soldiers remain in South Kivu after being integrated into the national army. From their point of view, maintaining a military presence in the province was the only way to protect their families and ethnic kin from retaliation from indigenous communities. Mai Mai saw the situation differently; they perceived this request as a Tutsi maneuver to maintain military capacity in the province to advance their ambitions by force if they failed to realize them peacefully. These grassroots agendas generated constant low-level combat in the Minembwe area throughout the transition.

Other micro-level antagonisms also fueled hatred toward Banyamulenge in the rest of the province. In June 2004, most Banyamulenge inhabitants fled from Uvira and Bukavu to avoid retaliation for the fighting that occurred there between RCD-G troops and Kabila loyalists. By fleeing, they vacated the high positions and nice houses that they had acquired during the war. Indigenous Congolese confiscated these jobs and houses and then refused to return them to the Banyamulenge who came back. Some of the profiteers went so far as to organize riots and harassment campaigns whenever Tutsis tried to return. The most publicized episode occurred in September 2004 in the wake of the massacre of 160 Banyamulenge refugees (mostly women and children) in the Gatumba refugee camp in Burundi. When hundreds of refugees tried to return to the Congo from Burundi, they were blocked at the border for three days and remained in a no man's land between the two countries. An angry mob, which local authorities had reportedly organized, stoned the first group that succeeded in reentering the Congo. In October, a similar confrontation transpired when another group of some 1,600 Banyamulenge refugees from Burundi once again could not gain entry into the Congo for several days. After these incidents, a few Banyamulenge trickled back into South Kivu, but many stayed in Burundi, afraid to return. The Tutsi armed groups based in Minembwe thus constantly insisted on the right of all Tutsi refugees and displaced people to return and reclaim their land, houses, and jobs.

It is important to note that, contrary to the dominant narrative, neither Mai Mai nor Banyamulenge militias were coherent, unitary, or integrated armed groups. No Mai Mai hierarchy controlled all of the armed groups bearing the Mai Mai name, either nationally or even within one city. For example, according to a Congolese peacebuilder, there was no central command controlling the five Mai Mai militias present in Uvira after June 2004. Throughout South Kivu, each group was further split into subfactions to such a point that many brigade leaders seemingly could not control their battalion commanders. In brief, Mai Mai militias were micro-level armed groups that refused enduring allegiance to national and regional actors.

Similarly, the Banyamulenge community was not unified; instead it split over the role of Rwanda during the last years of the war. Seeing ethnic hatred flare up in the wake of the Rwandan invasion, many Banyamulenge maintained that Rwanda was not their best protector, as they had initially perceived, but rather that its actions undermined the interests of the community. A large group of Banyamulenge therefore defected and allied with Kabila. This split persisted throughout the transition. The Banyamulenge community of the high plateaus of Itombwe was divided between the poor and powerless clans, who followed Commandant Masunzu and allied themselves with the Kinshasa government, and the rich and powerful clans, who followed Commandant Nyamushebwa, opposed the Transitional Government, and loosely allied with Banyarwanda rebel movements from North Kivu. Periodically, the tensions between the two sides became so high that they each reportedly attempted to enlist allies among other ethnic communities, prepared for fighting and, at times, resorted to violence.

Another major amendment to the dominant narrative is that the alliance between Mai Mai and national and regional actors became increasingly weak as the transition progressed. Most Mai Mai militias stationed in South Kivu abandoned their previous alliance with president Kabila. Officially, Mai Mai were angry about not receiving the same treatment as the trained forces did during the army integration process.[88] Although it was certainly a significant grievance,

---

[88] Global Witness 2005, p. 20.

another compelling reason for the split emerged after Kabila retook control of the province in June 2004: Siding with the president would have prevented Mai Mai from furthering their local interests. Kabila needed to extend the Transitional Government's authority in the province, a process which involved imposing legitimate state and traditional authorities (often non-Mai Mai chiefs), providing security (notably by imposing strict control over all armed groups), and ending the conditions of impunity under which the Mai Mai's power had operated. In 2005, the rupture between the South Kivu Mai Mai and Kabila became increasingly clear. Mai Mai administrative authorities often refused to obey government instructions that clashed with their own interests. Similarly, many Mai Mai officers refused to obey their superiors in the Congolese military. This rupture sometimes led to fighting between Mai Mai and government-affiliated factions of the integrated army, as it did in Kabare in late January 2005. This antagonism abated in 2006, but it was merely a pause in the trend of mounting tensions, rather than a genuine settlement; conflicts froze until the upcoming local and national elections, with most groups waiting to see if the polls would satisfy their claims or if they would have to resume fighting.

Likewise, the withdrawal of foreign armies from the province in late 2002 deprived one of the master cleavages, the regional confrontation, of most of the weight it had carried during the war. Admittedly, many Mai Mai militias continued to rely on Rwandan and Burundian rebel armed groups. This partnership remained mutually beneficial, because it provided Mai Mai with additional fighters and at the same time gave foreign armed groups the local support they needed to stay on Congolese territory. However, during the transition, this alliance was no longer primarily aimed at fighting the Rwandan and Burundian state armies, but rather at asserting the various armed groups' local control over land, mining sites, goods, and populations.

In sum, from the Bukavu crisis onward, local agendas were the determining factors in generating violence in South Kivu. In accordance with the dominant narrative, we could interpret the problems caused by the return of the Banyamulenge, the Minembwe territory, and the continued Rwandan Hutu presence as the result of national or regional cleavages. However, all three issues had very strong local dimensions. Additionally, the major source of tension in 2004 and 2005 was linked to the insubordination of Mai Mai militias – which, in turn, determined their alliance with Rwandan Hutu forces – and this insubordination stemmed from purely grassroots causes.

North Katanga: Uncontrolled Militias Rejecting National Control

Micro-level factors distinct from the macro-level agendas similarly accounted for the continued insecurity in North Katanga.[89] The national political cleavage of Kabila versus RCD-G had very little influence in this province during the transition, because Kabila had ensured the loyalty of the administrative and military authorities in the region, either by replacing RCD-G elements or by letting them ally with him. The national ethnic cleavage between indigenous communities and people with Rwandan ancestry was similarly noninfluential, as there were hardly any Congolese of Rwandan descent in the province. The regional conflict carried just as little weight, since foreign armed groups had left Katanga.

As explained in the conclusion of chapter 2, the dominant narrative nevertheless blamed the continuation of violence on national agendas, maintaining that Kabila's advisors manipulated Mai Mai groups to pursue their political and economic goals. However, none of the UN and diplomatic interviewees who offered this narrative could clearly articulate the national leaders' motivations for this manipulation or provide evidence to support their claims. Katangan interviewees often identified the desire to illegally exploit natural resources as the main cause for national involvement in their province, but they similarly could provide no concrete evidence for their assertions. In fact, all the data I gathered through my fieldwork point to a different conclusion. People based in Kinshasa, some of whom were close to Kabila, were indeed involved in Katangan politics, but only in pursuit of an ad-hoc, uncoordinated, and individual search for profit (notably through the illegal exploitation of mineral resources) and local power (by supporting their own ethnic group or clan), rather than to advance any national-level political or military strategy.

To grasp the reasons behind the continuation of violence in North Katanga, we must realize that the appearance of government

---

[89] International Crisis Group 2006c provides an excellent public source of data on Katanga during the transition.

control and unification was a facade. During the transition, a rupture occurred between the North Katangan Mai Mai and the Transitional Government. Katangan Mai Mai thought that Kabila had not adequately rewarded them for saving Lubumbashi, the capital of Katanga province and the second largest city in the Congo, from the RCD-G and Rwandan troops during the war. Furthermore, Mai Mai members of the Transitional Government came from the Kivus and Maniema, so the Katangan Mai Mai felt neither represented by them nor bound by the agreements that they had signed (including the agreement to integrate Mai Mai troops into the Congolese army). The Kabila faction's reluctance to integrate the Mai Mai groups active in government-controlled territory during the war into the new national army further compounded the problem.[90] To Kabila's followers, these Mai Mai groups were enemies because, as mentioned earlier in this chapter, they had fought government forces during the war instead of helping Kabila repel the foreign invaders. The leaders of the national army nevertheless tried to convince the Mai Mai to join them but met only limited success. They therefore changed strategy and, in late 2004 and in 2005, organized military operations in many Katangan territories against the remaining nonintegrated forces. This shift led to additional skirmishes, along ensuing insecurity and violations of human rights. It also increased the fallout between the Mai Mai and the government.

As a result, in late 2004 and 2005, journalists and humanitarian workers reported continual fighting between the units of the integrated army and Katangan Mai Mai, notably around Pweto, Manono, Mitwaba, Kongolo, and Malemba Nkulu (see map of Katanga in Figure 8). In late 2005 and early 2006, the fighting around Pweto, Manono, and Mitwaba escalated to the point of displacing close to 200,000 people.[91] Eventually, state authority completely collapsed in North Katanga, creating virtually total impunity for human rights violations and illegal actions and further facilitating violence by all armed groups.

Mai Mai not only rejected the government's control but, most significantly, fought with one another to advance their grassroots agendas. At

---

[90] The rest of this paragraph draws in part on an author's interview with Nawezi Karl, University of Kinshasa, October 2004.
[91] Wolters and Boshoff 2006.

Figure 8 Map of Katanga. This map is based on the *Carte des Districts et Territoires du Katanga* by OCHA DRC Geographic (WGS84), dated April 2002. In this book, North Katanga refers to the northern part of the Katanga province, which remained violent during the transition. It includes Tanganyika territory, the northern half of Haut Lomani territory, and the part of Haut Katanga west and north of Lake Moero.

the territory or village level, Mai Mai groups strived to maintain their power over their former areas of control to dominate the administrative and traditional positions of authority, manage mineral-rich areas, divert taxes, and impose numerous fines on the population. These political and economic agendas interacted with many ethnic tensions.

Hatred of Pygmies and "Kasaian" groups remained widespread, and long-standing rivalries between northern and southern Katangans mounted in the lead-up to the elections. Meanwhile, in each district, clan, tribal, or ethnic rivalries continued to fester. The resulting fighting among Mai Mai militias produced such abuses against the local population – including massacres, torture, and mass displacement – that, near Mitwaba, villagers created a new "popular self-defense force" to protect themselves from the Mai Mai. (This development was ironic because, initially, Mai Mai militias were born as popular self-defense forces tasked with protecting their villages.) In sum, even if the security situation of many areas improved tremendously compared to the war period, micro-level, locally motivated, uncontrolled militias continued to plague most of North Katanga throughout the transition.

Ituri: The Primacy of Land

The critical role of local conflict in Ituri was similarly clear, particularly because access to land was so important.[92] Antagonisms over land had emerged long before colonization, and even as early as the arrival of Hemas and Lendus, the two largest ethnic groups in the district. Herders, usually Hemas, needed grazing pastures for their livestock while farmers, usually Lendus, wanted to retain the land for agricultural purposes. Colonial and postindependence regulations led to an overlap of legal property deeds and ancestral land rights, which exacerbated the intercommunal conflicts. Just as in the Kivus, local actors decided to recruit national allies in their fight. From the late nineteenth century onward, the Hemas took advantage of the educational, economic, and political opportunities that the Belgians and Mobutu's government offered to secure their political and economic predominance, which generated deep resentment among other communities. As explained previously, disputes over land triggered the massive violence that engulfed Ituri in 1999 and caused significant fighting throughout the generalized wars.

During the transition, militias continued to fight among themselves, primarily over land issues. They were particularly interested in

---

[92] In addition to drawing on the author's confidential sources, the analysis of Ituri politics is also based on International Crisis Group 2003a, 2004c, and 2008; Veit 2008 and 2009; and Vlassenroot and Raeymaekers 2004b.

regaining control of local mining sites or of territory that traditionally belonged to their respective ethnic groups.[93] Disputes over land, and not an ancient ethnic hatred, were the source of most antagonisms between the Hemas and the Lendus, as well as of most intraethnic fighting.[94] They were also a significant cause of tension for refugees returning to their communities, as returnees often found their land occupied by new groups (usually of a different ethnic origin) and wanted to take it back.[95] The primacy of land issues was even such that, as chapter 5 further details, Ituri was the only place where many international peacebuilders agreed local conflicts mattered. For example, the Secretary-General's reports on the Congo often mentioned this, and the last report on the United Nations Mission in the Congo (MONUC) during the transition claimed that land ownership remained "a fundamental cause of ethnic tensions in Ituri."[96]

As in the other eastern provinces, the land conflict in Ituri was intimately linked to competitions over political power, access to education, and economic opportunities.[97] Local administrative agencies, rebel militias, customary chiefs, and businessmen tried to maintain or expand their control over the district. These conflicting agendas generated countless instances of fighting, massacres, and other human rights violations.[98] From 2002 onward, in particular, militias continually splintered and fought each other over the control of timber and gold, the two main sources of revenue with which armed groups could finance their activities.[99]

The relationship between micro and macro levels here was similar to the situation described for North Katanga. During the transition, national or regional actors' manipulation of Ituri armed groups

[93] For a detailed presentation of these conflicts, see International Crisis Group 2008, pp. 10–12; and "Debating for justice," Interactive Radio for Justice project, broadcasted on October 23, 2008 (transcript available at http://www.irfj.org/Programs/DFJ/08/DFJ_prog08_english.doc).

[94] International Crisis Group 2008, p. 9.

[95] "Debating for justice"; and personal communication from Alex Veit, academic researcher, January 2009.

[96] UN Security Council 2006d, para. 34.

[97] See "Debating for justice" for a public source.

[98] Public sources include Amnesty International 2003; UN Security Council 2003c (para. 11) and 2006d (para. 34); Veit 2008 and 2009; Vlassenroot and Raeymaekers 2004b; and Wolters and Boshoff 2006.

[99] Samset and Madore 2006, p. 5.

mostly disappeared. There remained only a limited Ugandan involvement in the district, which was aimed at illegally exploiting Congolese resources.[100] Violence continued because militias rejected the attempts by the Transitional Government, the newly integrated army, and MONUC to impose state authority in the district, since it would have jeopardized their control of local economic and political positions of authority. In contrast to many Katangan Mai Mai, however, militia leaders in Ituri also attempted to gain leadership positions in the national army and government and, for those who were under threat of indictment by the International Criminal Court, to avoid being sent to The Hague.

This rejection of state authority best accounts for the last large-scale fighting during the transition between Ituri armed groups (in late 2004 and early 2005). During this time, the army started its deployment in the district, the Congolese government and MONUC launched a demobilization program for Ituri militias, the transitional authorities began reforming the local administrative and judiciary institutions, and MONUC extended its deployment to medium-sized towns. Ituri armed groups considerably escalated their attacks to prevent the state from extending its authority in the district, and thus to retain their areas of control and enlarge their territorial basis as a potential bargaining chip in future negotiations. Their attempts were mostly unsuccessful, and after that round of violence armed groups either dissolved or realigned and fought the army for their very existence.

The persisting impunity also partly explained why the militias refused to disarm and rather continued to recruit fighters. The International Criminal Court and the Congolese military prosecutor convicted only a few perpetrators of war crimes; countless others went without punishment, and many were even integrated into the local police and army units. As a result, most Ituri militias claimed that their community (whether Hema, Lendu, or any other ethnic group) still needed to protect itself from expropriation, oppression, and extermination by their local enemies. These dynamics persisted after the 2006 elections and led to yet another escalation of the conflict in late 2008.

---

[100] The rest of this and the following paragraphs are based on Alex Veit's extensive field research in Ituri (personal communications to author, 2006–2009). See Veit 2008 and 2009 for the synthesis of his findings.

Conclusion: The Need for Local Peacebuilding Programs

The eastern part of the Congo remained so violent during the transition not only because of regional and national tensions but also because of the presence of distinctively local problems. These included conflicts over land, mineral resources, traditional power, local taxes, and the relative social status of specific groups and individuals. It is true that, as stipulated in the dominant narrative on the transition, criminal agendas explained part of the continuing violence. However, the criminal dimension of the micro-level conflicts was no larger than the criminal dimension of the macro-level conflicts. Just as with top-down tensions, political, social, and economic issues also motivated grassroots antagonisms. The scale was different; the nature was not.

Local, national, and regional dimensions of violence remained closely linked in most of the eastern Congo. In line with the dominant narrative, the absence of state authority in the eastern provinces reinforced the appeal of violence and deprived local actors of established avenues for peaceful resolution of existing antagonisms. Local militias continued to ally themselves with national and regional actors during the transition, even if they did so to a much lesser extent than during the war. Local agendas provided national and regional actors with local allies, who were crucial in maintaining military control, continuing resource exploitation, and persecuting political or ethnic enemies.

However, contrary to the dominant narrative, the relationship between local and national or regional tensions was not merely top-down. Even issues usually presented as purely regional (such as the presence of Rwandan Hutu militias) or purely national (such as disputes between indigenous communities and Congolese with Rwandan ancestry) had significant local components, which fueled and reinforced the regional and national dimensions. Throughout the transition, decentralized antagonisms over land and political power motivated violence against the people of Rwandan descent and enticed some Congolese groups to allow a strong Rwandan Hutu presence in the Kivus. In turn, these two issues were the main stated motivations for the continued Rwandan involvement in the Congo, and the main reasons why Nkunda's troops and RCD-G hardliners continued to fight throughout the transition. Thus, micro-level conflicts eventually jeopardized the national and regional settlements.

Furthermore, most of the massacres, massive human rights violations, and population displacement that took place during the transition were not coordinated on a large scale. Local strongmen responsible to no one but themselves perpetrated them in pursuit of micro-level agendas. Contrary to one of the central assumptions of the dominant narrative, groups such as the Mai Mai, the Congolese with Rwandan ancestry, or the Rwandan Hutu militias were not unitary actors. National authorities did not represent their constituencies, filter their demands, control the rank-and-file, and channel messages internally and externally.

A single command structure never unified all Mai Mai militias. During the war, the only commonalities between the different Mai Mai groups were their reliance on magic-based rituals and their pretense of being destined to defend their villages. Apart from that, they fought on all sides of the war. Most, but not all, of those based in the Kivus allied with Kabila, and most, but not all, of those located on the government side of the front line in North Katanga fought against Kabila's forces. During the transition, contrary to the claims of most international peacebuilders, President Kabila did not control Mai Mai militias and their national delegates did not adequately represent them. The Mai Mai "movement" remained a loose network of very different, fragmented, micro-level armed groups following various – and often competing – leaders. These militias sometimes cohabitated peacefully with one another, as in North Kivu, but they also often fought one another, especially in North Katanga. Furthermore, although several Mai Mai leaders officially participated in the transition, many Mai Mai militias refused to obey transitional authorities, notably in South Kivu and North Katanga.

Similarly, the Rwandan Hutu combatants were organized into different, competing armed groups. The FDLR was the main faction; others included the former Rwandan Armed Forces, the Alliance for the Liberation of Rwanda, the Rally of the Democratic Forces for the Liberation of Rwanda, and smaller groups such as the Rastas, the Rally for Unity and Democracy, and Ngobo za Yezu. These groups did not have a single command structure, but were loosely coordinated with each other. Dissension over political or economic stakes was frequent. Toward the end of the transition, the Rwandan Hutu militias fractured even more, and often fought one another over the spoils of looting, leadership positions, and the decision of whether to return to Rwanda.

The people with Rwandan ancestry were not a uniform group, either. The RCD-G was split between moderates, who traveled to Kinshasa and participated in transition institutions, and hardliners, most of whom remained in North Kivu to continue fighting. In the broader population of Rwandan descent, the wartime alliance between Hutus and Tutsis crumbled toward the end of the transition. The Tutsis themselves had distinct and sometimes inconsistent agendas. North Kivu Tutsis usually aligned with Rwanda and the RDC-G or Nkunda, while many South Kivu Tutsis rejected the Rwandan alliance. Tutsi groups were not even unified within a single province. The Banyamulenge were deeply divided along class lines and between insurgent and government loyalists. Even the relations among North Kivu Tutsis could be tense.

As a result, during the transition many local conflicts became autonomous from the national and regional developments, most notably in South Kivu, North Katanga, and Ituri. There, local disputes over political power, economic resources (especially land and mining sites), and social status led to clashes that no national or regional actors could stop. The humanitarian cost was staggering.

Thus, in addition to assuaging regional and national antagonisms, international peacebuilders should also have helped address conflicts at the grassroots level. Appeasing micro-level tensions was essential to ending collective violence on the ground and to ensuring the stability of the national and regional settlements. Furthermore, because the causes of violence varied so greatly between and within each province, peacebuilders should have tailored their strategies to each specific context, instead of using a blanket approach for all areas.

5 | *The Defeat of Bottom-Up Solutions*

In 2007, I interviewed a high-ranking Western diplomat, who concluded our conversation with the statement:

I don't see this war, or most of the violence [during the transition], as being a question of conflict between communities in the Congo. Even in Ituri, the ethnic element of it was largely drummed up, provoked by politicians and leaders of groups who had a vested interest in power and the control of territories and of riches. There are some local conflicts that need to be resolved, certainly between Banyamulenge and the population in Bukavu [South Kivu], or between Tutsis and Hutus or Hunden in Masisi [North Kivu], but they are not the forces that perpetuate the chaos. The forces that keep the chaos going are the interests of various groups, both foreign and domestic [people in Uganda and Rwanda, Congolese intermediaries, Rwandan Hutu militias].... .

[In the Congo,] there was never a conflict in the first place. The war started because the Congo was invaded, because [the Rwandan and Ugandan presidents] did not want Kabila anymore ... . The Congolese were not fighting each other until Rwanda and Uganda ... paid or forced them ... to do it. ... [Land conflict, conflict around traditional power, and so on] are all minor considerations in my view ... . So I have to be very blunt about it, if I had $100 million, I would not spend [it] on local conflict resolution ... . I am telling you straightforwardly that if you are looking at local conflicts as having more than a two percent influence on violence, you are in outer space.

This quotation raises several fascinating puzzles. First, it is typical of the way most diplomatic and international organization staff members working in or on the Congo reacted to an analysis emphasizing that local conflicts sustained violence. It is also the exact opposite reaction to that of scholars and policy makers not working in or on the Congo. These individuals, in contrast, easily accepted the importance of local agendas. Why was there such discrepancy between the two groups? Why were policy makers involved in the Congo so impervious to demonstrations of the importance of local peacebuilding? Second, an erroneous historical claim – that there was no violence before the Rwandan invasion – was the basis of the analysis presented in the quotation. Despite its inaccuracy, I frequently heard this claim from international interveners based in the Congo, even from those who had developed an in-depth expertise in Congolese history. How could knowledgeable individuals perpetuate such a gross factual error?

This chapter helps resolve these two puzzles by tracing the history of contestation and failed attempts at bottom-up peacebuilding throughout the transition. In doing so, the chapter illuminates why foreign actors did not revise their overall intervention strategy when the continuation of extensive violence established its limitations, and why they did not reorient their actions toward local conflict resolution. By analyzing both opportunities for and resistance to change, this chapter elucidates how the international peacebuilding culture presented in chapters 2 and 3 could remain dominant throughout the Congolese transition.

I first develop the outlines of a workable bottom-up peacebuilding strategy to demonstrate the feasibility of local conflict resolution. I then trace various attempts to challenge the dominant narratives on the causes of violence and the role of international interveners. Isolated members of the United Nations Mission in the Congo (MONUC) and diplomatic missions, as well as certain nongovernmental organizations, tried to convince their colleagues to adopt a grassroots peacebuilding approach, yet they were largely unsuccessful. I emphasize the role of subcultures to clarify how these exceptional individuals and agencies escaped the dominant culture. I also note that the influence of shocking events explains local-level intervention by other actors.

I then analyze why the largest peacebuilding bureaucracies usually rejected these opportunities for change. The protesters were not dominant actors on the international scene, and the strategy for which they advocated clashed with deeply entrenched cultural norms and organizational interests. As a result, neither contestation nor shocking events ever became sufficient to prompt diplomats and United Nations (UN) staff to reevaluate their understandings of violence and intervention. Instead, a vicious circle developed, in which the perception of local conflict resolution as a long-term, unfamiliar, and illegitimate task turned "constraints" on international action at the local level into insurmountable obstacles. These factors, in turn, reinforced the perception of bottom-up peacebuilding as a negligible issue.

A Potential Local Conflict-Resolution Strategy

During formal interviews and informal conversations, whenever I or another proponent of local peacebuilding managed to convince international interveners that, in addition to addressing macro-level antagonisms, it was important to resolve micro-level disputes, our interlocutors would raise two related objections. First, local conflicts were so complex and widespread that it was impossible to devise a coherent and comprehensive strategy to address them. Second, even if it were possible, the financial, logistical, and political obstacles to such an intervention would be insoluble.

Admittedly, any strategy to overcome the massive upheavals of a decade of war would inevitably have been messy, imperfect, and tense, at least for a time. Nevertheless, adding a bottom-up component to the top-down intervention would have been possible.[1] International actors could have prioritized treating core problems at the local level in addition to managing their broader dimensions. Given that many Congolese government officials were weak and corrupt, and that Congolese nongovernmental organizations and civil society representatives often lacked the funding, logistical means, and technical capacity to implement effective peacebuilding programs, international actors could have played a critical role in supporting, training, financing, and advising these local actors.

To begin with, donors could have augmented the financial, logistic, and human resources devoted to local peacebuilding: either (ideally), by increasing their aid expenditures, or (if increased funding to the Congo proved impossible), by shifting their assistance priorities away from elections. It is true that the transitional Congo already received significant international resources, including MONUC's annual $1 billion in funds. The European Union (EU) also dispatched to the Congo its first military operation outside of Europe and, together with its member states, contributed $500 million to the organization of elections (the largest contribution ever dedicated by the EU to any

---

[1] The rest of this section is a revised version of policy recommendations laid out in Autesserre 2008.

electoral process). Yet, however enormous $1 billion per year sounds in absolute terms, it is derisory in relative terms. In 2008, for example, the U.S. military occupation in Iraq had an operating budget of $1 billion per every four to seven days. The ratio of resources devoted to the Congo per person appears trifling even compared to other multilateral interventions. The cost per capita of reconstruction in the Congo in 2004 was $39, whereas it was $79 for El Salvador, $129 for Afghanistan, $211 for Bosnia and Herzegovina, $240 for Kosovo, and $278 for East Timor.[2] In terms of humanitarian assistance, international aid to the Congo in 2004 averaged $3.23 per person per year, while it reached $89 for Darfur and $177 for Iraq.[3] The amount of human resources deployed to the Congo was similarly trivial. Even during the transition, when MONUC was at its peak (19,566 troops in 2006), they amounted to only 33 peacekeepers per 100,000 inhabitants, compared to 53 in the Ivory Coast (2004), 112 in Burundi (2004), 304 in Sierra Leone (2001), and 508 in Liberia (2006) – and 672 U.S. and allied troops in Iraq in 2008, a number which several analysts and generals still deemed insufficient.[4] Given the Congo's geostrategic position, its potential to destabilize all of central Africa if generalized conflict resumed, and the scale of its humanitarian crisis, it would have made sense to devote additional resources to achieve a better peacebuilding strategy.

Short of devoting additional resources, international actors could have privileged peace or justice over delusory democracy. They might have devoted, for example, the $670 million spent on elections (in addition to the hundreds of millions spent on indirect costs related to the electoral process) to security-sector reform, local conflict resolution, or a major revamping of the justice system. As I argue in chapter 6, by postponing the organization of the vote by several years, to focus first on creating an environment conducive to free, fair, and meaningful elections, interveners would have helped promote both peace and democracy in the long run.

The Congolese people would probably have agreed to such a deferral. As detailed in chapter 2, most national elites and militia leaders

---

[2] Englebert and Tull 2008, p. 130.
[3] International Rescue Committee 2005.
[4] Englebert and Tull 2008, p. 131, except for the statistics on Iraq, which comes from a review of press articles.

had vested interests in postponing elections to maintain their positions of authority. Futhermore, as Chapter 6 explains, the rural population of the eastern provinces usually had very little understanding of how elections worked and therefore felt they had little at stake in the polls. It is difficult to estimate how the rest of the population would have reacted to a longer democratization process. However, according to many interviewees, only the massive sensitization programs financed by foreign donors led urban Congolese to regard elections as *the* viable solution to the Congo's problems. Thus, another route would probably have been received well: a transition process carefully planned over ten years to build a lasting peace and democracy at all levels. This would have included: reconstructing the administrative, judicial, and economic capacities of the country; minimizing visible international interference; building the capabilities and credibility of democratically chosen leaders; guaranteeing freedom of speech and freedom of campaigning; providing rural Congolese with necessary civic education; eventually organizing the polls under good conditions; and explaining the advantages of this strategy to the population.

In the meantime, at the local level, the very first priority would have been to resolve land disputes in the eastern Congo. International peacebuilders could have supported both top-down and bottom-up measures. Diplomats and donors could have pressured the Congolese government and representatives from all of the eastern communities to expedite land reform. These interveners convinced Congolese authorities to write a constitution that promoted democracy and human rights and to elaborate a citizenship law that alleviated the fears of many Congolese with Rwandan ancestry. So, too, could they have persuaded the Congolese government to enact new land legislation that upheld the rights of vulnerable people (such as women, minorities, and returnees) and clarified when and how legal or traditional ownership rights applied. Throughout the country, but especially in the eastern provinces, the new legislation could have mandated a review of all land property deeds. Donors could also have helped by providing independent experts on land and judicial matters and insisting that the Transitional Government consult relevant stakeholders before formulating the new legislation.

In parallel, Congolese grassroots organizations and judicial employees could have traveled to explain this property law to rural populations, who generally knew little about their rights. The land reform also might have established formal mechanisms for resolving disputes through ad-hoc arrangements or local courts that would be staffed by legal employees and representatives of the affected communities. Whenever necessary to ensure fairness or prevent the creation of new resentments, the courts could have awarded money or in-kind compensation to people whose property might be confiscated. For example, they could have required the beneficiaries of redistribution to share their harvest with the former owners or to help them build another house, as happened in a few South Kivu villages. The courts could have handled all adjudications free of charge, thus allowing the most disenfranchised people a chance to claim what was theirs.

In areas where many families, clans, or ethnic groups had lost the land that they needed to survive, such as in Masisi (North Kivu) or Kabare (South Kivu), the new legislation could also have created provincial commissions to design a fair redistribution policy. These commissions would have included representatives from every local community and social group, Congolese experts on land issues, and neutral observers. The commissions could have focused on redressing injustices and finding sustainable solutions. As the International Crisis Group suggested, for example, such a commission in the territories of Masisi and Walikale (North Kivu) could have cancelled all of the title deeds for estates and ranches issued since Congo's independence.[5] It could also have compensated the former owners of expropriated land and assigned some of it to landless families (especially among the Hundes, the Hutus, the Nyangas, and the Tutsis, which are the main groups living in these territories) for individual or collective use, depending on its suitability for agriculture or animal grazing.

Just as donors had the potential to facilitate the top-down element of the land reform process, they could have made the bottom-up dimension possible as well. They might have funded the training of Congolese grassroots organizations and justice officials who would explain the law to rural populations, staff the local courts, or serve as observers to the land redistribution commissions. They might have provided for these local structures' operating costs. The donors could

---

[5] International Crisis Group 2007a.

also have disbursed funds to compensate property owners who had lost their land.

Such broad land reforms could have prevented new disputes, improved intercommunal relations, and helped extend state authority to the mining sites in the region – provided these efforts targeted all of the communities in the eastern Congo, not just the Kinyarwanda-speaking population and its traditional enemies. They could also have helped ensure that the return of Tutsi refugees to the Kivus would not trigger another major crisis.

In parallel, state and civil society agencies could have organized forums and workshops so that all local actors had a chance to express and resolve their grievances, whether about land, sharing traditional and administrative power, or anything else. Then, to ensure a lasting peace, nongovernmental organizations could have helped restore social links between communities in conflict. The most effective strategy would have been to create enterprises, health centers, markets, and schools in whose success all parties had a stake. A similar approach has worked in parts of Bosnia and Herzegovina, Cambodia, and Tajikistan, and a pilot project conducted in Ituri demonstrated its appropriateness for the Congo.[6] Community-driven economic development programs at the grassroots level could also have focused on providing alternative opportunities to local combatants, enabling them to earn a living and a respectable status in a world not governed by violence, thereby facilitating reintegration into their home villages.[7] To make all of these projects possible, donors could have offered considerably greater financial support to the Congolese nongovernmental organizations that organized peace talks and reconciliation programs, especially those involving opportunities for civilian jobs and better social services.

Enabling local populations to decide how to deal with war criminals and which transitional justice structure to use was another necessary peacebuilding measure. Nongovernmental organizations could have helped organize meetings where all stakeholders could participate in the decision and subsequently support its implementation. Reconstructing such grassroots mechanisms for the peaceful

---

[6] See Anderson 1999 on Bosnia and Herzegovina, Cambodia, and Tajikistan; and Samset and Madore 2006 on Ituri.
[7] See Samset and Madore 2006 for a public source on this topic.

resolution of conflict – for example, traditional councils or local justice institutions – would not only have helped assuage current tensions but would also have enabled communities to peacefully manage future antagonisms.

In combination with land reform, such a broad conflict-resolution program could have helped stem violence, address many of the grievances that gave rise to local militias, shrink the pool of local recruits for regional and national warlords, reintegrate refugees and displaced persons, and start rebuilding state institutions.

In addition to diplomats and donors, MONUC could also have played a significant supporting role. To obtain human, financial, and logistical assets for local conflict resolution, it could have distributed its resources according to a different framework of priorities than the one detailed in chapter 3. In the eastern provinces, MONUC could have deployed more special operations forces (small, mobile groups of commando soldiers trained in guerilla warfare and intelligence gathering) and fewer traditional troops. The former can navigate local-level action more adeptly, especially in logistically difficult environments. Additionally, in their daily work, military and civilian UN staffers could have helped provincial authorities develop their capacity to oversee the management of mining sites. MONUC, possibly in cooperation with other UN agencies, could also have recruited well-trained local civilian peacebuilders for deployment in the eastern provinces, downsizing its staff in Kinshasa if necessary. It could have tasked these new recruits with monitoring grassroots tensions and given them the authority to draw on military, diplomatic, or development resources to broker local peace. Such interventions could have helped address the broader dimensions of violence by deterring local warlords and offering them the possibility of development assistance.[8]

Of course, in the long term, local peace is sustainable only if the state is stable and its institutions are functional at all levels. It was therefore crucial that international actors maintained, as they did, or even intensified their support of the Congolese government to help it integrate the many fractionated armed groups into the national army. It was also critical for the interveners to continue and even strengthen their efforts to solve the security problem posed by the Rwandan Hutu militias. Those who were not guilty of war crimes could have,

[8] This last idea builds on Anderson 1999; and Prendergast 1996.

for example, been resettled in the Congo, but far from the Rwandan border. In parallel, the peacebuilders might have launched a joint MONUC–Congolese army campaign to capture the few Rwandans guilty of the 1994 genocide who were still present in the Kivus, as well as the major perpetrators of atrocities on the Congolese population. Additionally, peacebuilders should have increased diplomatic pressure on regional and Congolese actors to stop fighting in Congolese territory and used UN peacekeeping troops to protect those populations in immediate danger, instead of primarily protecting UN buildings and equipment. International actors should also have helped the Congolese government rebuild its national justice system, as this was an essential step toward ending impunity and thus deterring violence, assuaging communal resentment, and promoting good governance. Finally, while it was crucial to organize free and fair elections to select leaders representative of and accountable to their population, interveners should have done this only when the preconditions for a meaningful process were in place.

International interveners could have designed other local conflict-resolution strategies, some of which might have been even more effective than the program outlined in this section. For instance, they may have found a solution that gave more responsibilities to local authorities and minimized international interference. Regardless of which option they ultimately chose, one thing is clear: The interveners could have included a bottom-up peacebuilding component in their overall strategy. The logistical, financial, and human resources existed; international actors had many opportunities to become more involved in grassroots conflict resolution; and such an involvement would have helped them better support the Congo in its efforts to build peace and democracy.

Contestation and Opportunities for Change

Several international interveners actually tried to seize these opportunities. In addition to Congolese activists, a few international non-governmental organizations as well as isolated UN staff members and diplomats either implemented a bottom-up peacebuilding approach or advocated for increased international involvement at the local level. However, despite their efforts, almost all of their colleagues rebuffed the responsibility of working on decentralized violence. As a result, during the Congolese transition, international support for grassroots conflict resolution remained extremely weak, limited to a few nongovernmental organization programs and very rare and ad-hoc actions by UN staff members and diplomats.

The Limited Attempts of Nongovernmental Organizations

A handful of nongovernmental organizations implemented most of the existing local peacebuilding programs in the eastern provinces. They also most actively contested the dominant narratives on the causes of violence and the role of international actors.

During the transition, the Life and Peace Institute and Search for Common Ground were the main international agencies that facilitated and sustained decentralized conflict-resolution programs. The Life and Peace Institute mostly supported Congolese partners with funding, logistical support, and training, thus enabling them to implement projects as varied as peace talks between local elites, soccer matches between youths from communities in conflict, and micro-credit cooperatives for women from rival clans and ethnic groups in the Kivus. Search for Common Ground focused its efforts on radio and television shows promoting intercommunity reconciliation and on a traveling theater show that emphasized the benefits of peaceful grassroots collaboration. Smaller international organizations included La Benevolencia, which had a similar radio program in North Kivu; Global Rights, which implemented four micro-level projects to resolve land conflict in Masisi and Rutshuru; International Alert, which tried to reconcile indigenous communities and people of Rwandan descent; the Africa Initiative Program, which organized dialogues among elites of different Ituri communities; and the Haki na Amani Network, which supported grassroots institutions for conflict prevention and management in Ituri.

Although focused on development projects in general, Action Aid, Caritas, the Center for International Studies and Cooperation, Christian Aid, Cordaid, the International Rescue Committee, Law Group International, the Norwegian Refugee Council, Save the Children, and World Vision also conducted decentralized peacebuilding programs, but these were extremely small and limited to managing grants and subcontracting projects to local partners. Additionally, toward the end of the transition, the Interchurch Organisation for

Development Cooperation and the Initiative for a Cohesive Leadership began, respectively, to support grassroots peacebuilding associations and to organize workshops with provincial and national elites to help them resolve their differences.

A small number of other international nongovernmental organizations also addressed some local causes of violence through a development or human rights framework. For example, Soderu's infrastructure-building programs intentionally included a conflict-resolution dimension: helping reestablish contact between communities in conflict and providing militiamen with alternative, peaceful means of subsistence. Human Rights Watch had a permanent presence in North Kivu, and its human rights investigations often seemed to function as a deterrent to violence.

Overall, the few existing peacebuilding projects made a crucial contribution to local stability in the parts of the eastern Congo where they were implemented. For example, the Life and Peace Institute and its grassroots partners helped initiate a dialogue between Mai Mai and Congolese Rally for Democracy-Goma (RCD-G) soldiers in selected villages of Walikale, Masisi, and Rutshuru territories (North Kivu). These efforts eventually resulted in the merging or close collaboration of the enemy groups in these locales. In Uvira, Minembwe, and Fizi (South Kivu) as well as Masisi, Walikale, Rutshuru, Beni, and Lubero (North Kivu), grassroots organizations also reestablished communication between various warring communities and helped them design strategies for reconciliation and trust building.[9] In parts of Irummu and Djugu, the Ituri territories most affected by violence, various micro-level peacebuilding projects "enable[ed] people from different sides of the conflicts to live together peacefully."[10] These accomplishments reinforce the argument that, had international interveners adopted a comprehensive local conflict-resolution framework everywhere in the eastern provinces, the transition would have been far less violent and much more successful.

However, because most nongovernmental organizations understood intercommunal tensions in an oversimplified manner (populations of Rwandan descent versus indigenous Congolese in the Kivus; Hemas versus Lendus in Ituri), their projects disproportionately focused on

[9] Life and Peace Institute 2004.
[10] Samset and Madore 2006, quotation from p. 48.

the reconciliation of a very limited set of groups. They often neglected other kinds of ethnic tensions, as well as the political, social, and economic agendas that also motivated continued violence in the eastern provinces. Additionally, because of funding constraints, most projects focused on organizing intercommunity dialogues, without including the concrete development measures necessary to cement the benefits of reconciliation efforts.

To make matters worse, throughout the eastern provinces, there were only a handful of these local conflict-resolution initiatives and they had only a limited scope and area of implementation. As could be expected, in accordance with the dominant narrative on the role of foreign interveners, most of the peacebuilding nongovernmental organizations present in the Congo worked on the regional and national tracks. For example, the International Crisis Group lobbied both regionally and nationally and advocated for a top-down approach to local conflicts.[11] Likewise, the Belgian agency 11.11.11 worked mostly with Kinshasa actors and geared its advocacy campaigns toward these macro levels. In the eastern provinces, the vast majority of nongovernmental organizations present focused on emergency aid, in particular, medical and food assistance. They purposely avoided any kind of peacebuilding dimension in their programs, to preserve their neutrality and thus their ability to access areas controlled by all warring parties. They maintained that they did not have the mandate, the skills, the legitimacy, or the resources to work on political, economic, or social tensions. They emphasized that their role was to address the consequences of violence, and not its causes.

Not only were there too few local peacebuilding organizations to significantly reduce the violence motivated by economic or social factors, but they were also ill equipped to address the decentralized conflicts caused by military and political antagonisms or manipulated by regional and national actors. Nongovernmental officials lacked the diplomats' and UN staff's influence on grassroots military and political leaders. They could not organize a military operation to keep militias in check, as MONUC could. Their relationships with

---

[11] I thank Hans Romkema for pointing this out to me (e-mail communication, October 2004). This top-down approach to local conflict resolution is evident in all International Crisis Group reports published during the transition.

high-ranking Congolese officials were often weak or nonexistent, in contrast to those of diplomats and UN staff, who could easily request sanctions against a specific local officer from his superiors in the Congolese hierarchy. Because nongovernmental organizations were well known for their interactions with all stakeholders in their area of operations, collaborating with them did not bring any specific recognition to local elites. In contrast, a local leader with whom diplomats and UN staff negotiated became an important actor in the eyes of the population and other warring parties, because he was seen as worthy of international attention. Embassies and UN organizations also have much larger aid budgets than nongovernmental agencies, so cooperating with the former carried a much more significant financial incentive (potential aid to the population that local leaders can later tax) than dealing with the latter. As a result, warlords usually did not listen to requests to respect basic human rights when they came from nongovernmental organizations; the warlords would hear the message only if it was delivered by political or diplomatic actors.

Moreover, nongovernmental agencies did not have the resources or the ability to progress from micro-level conflict resolution to macro-level peace settlements. Because they lacked close relationships with Congolese and regional authorities, international peacebuilding nongovernmental organizations often tended to address local conflict in isolation from the national and regional tracks. For example, Hans Romkema, the Life and Peace Institute's Head of Mission, criticized the fact that "almost without exception," nongovernmental agencies "created their own peacebuilding initiatives and had difficulty connecting with other levels or neighboring locations."[12] Nongovernmental organizations could adequately address some of the local dimensions of violence, but they needed partners at the higher levels to prevent regional and national problems from reigniting the local tensions that they had just defused.

Overall, international nongovernmental organizations were not equipped to function as the sole actors aiming to prevent micro-level violence. They needed to work as part of a network of peacebuilders that included not only local counterparts (such as Congolese churches and grassroots agencies) but also other international partners, such as diplomats and UN staff. The locally focused nongovernmental

---

[12] Author's interview, Bukavu, 2004.

organizations therefore conducted advocacy campaigns, in which they contested one or more elements of the peacebuilding culture that guided international actors away from local conflict.

To start with, the few nongovernmental organizations that worked on local conflict resolution in the eastern provinces contested both the international actors' understanding of violence and their strategic focus on the macro levels. These few organizations emphasized the critical role of local tensions in sustaining violence, and they repeatedly asked MONUC and embassy staff to increase local involvement. However, their counterparts either reacted in a hostile manner, ignored them, or alternatively, agreed to give them some limited additional funding for their programs.

Additionally, human rights and humanitarian agencies, as well as various policy think tanks and Congolese civil society actors, wrote numerous reports documenting the continuation of combat in the eastern provinces, as well as the rampant human rights violations over the entire Congolese territory.[13] They implied that there was nothing normal about the continued violence and pleaded for immediate international action to end it. They ensured that all actors, including diplomats and high-ranking UN staff members based outside of the eastern provinces, were told that their peacebuilding strategy failed to end the fighting.

The Congolese went one step further and contested the "postconflict" categorization and the strategies and policies it enabled. The Kivus' inhabitants maintained that extensive combat was still under way; they called the major fighting "wars" instead of "crises," and requested military intervention and protection against warlords. However, the actions of the human rights and humanitarian advocates, both Congolese and foreign, only encouraged further humanitarian aid and increased top-down intervention in times of "crises." These actors were unable to meaningfully challenge how international interveners analyzed the continued violence.

From 2004 onward, Congolese and international peacebuilders also contested the overall intervention strategy, especially its focus

---

[13] For example, among many others: Amnesty International 2005; Human Rights Watch 2004 and 2005; International Crisis Group 2004a, 2005a, and 2006c; International Rescue Committee 2004 and 2005; Médecins Sans Frontières 2005; and Pole Institute 2004.

on the swift organization of elections. They warned that arranging elections within the short timeframe of the transition would fuel ethnic tensions, expand the audience and the power base of extremists, empower radicals bent on cleansing the Congo of its Kinyarwanda-speaking population, and generate a renewed cycle of violence, because supporters of losing candidates were likely to resume fighting. Certain Congolese civil society representatives told UN staff and diplomats that elections were not a priority and that they should, instead, first establish peace and security.[14] A few months before the 2006 presidential and legislative elections, the International Crisis Group published a report documenting the risks posed by the upcoming vote. Its predictions were grim. Violence in the Kivus was likely to increase even further because of poor electoral results for the RCD-G. Supporters of opposition leader Etienne Tshisekedi (who refused to take part in the elections) would probably cause unrest in Kinshasa and the Kasai. Finally, massive fraud would likely tarnish the legitimacy that voting was supposed to herald, generating protests and thus undermining stability in all major cities.[15] This contestation had no impact, and elections, as noted in chapter 3, transpired three years after the official end of the war.

Nongovernmental agencies were thus mostly unsuccessful both in enlisting the necessary partners for their local peacebuilding initiatives and in contesting the dominant narratives. The fact that similar contestation efforts within MONUC, diplomatic missions, or other international organizations were also unable to effect organizational change largely explains this failure.

Fleeting Scheme by MONUC

The second most extensive contestation arose within MONUC. Had it been successful, it would have perfectly met the nongovernmental organizations' expectations described earlier. The initiative occurred between late 2002 and early 2004, at the same time that UN and diplomatic actors were redefining the Congolese context as a "post-conflict" environment. Lena Sundh, a Swedish diplomat temporarily

---

[14] Audience member to panel on "Conflict and Peace Processes in the Eastern D.R. Congo," African Studies Association Conference, November 2007.

[15] International Crisis Group 2006a.

dispatched to MONUC to serve as Deputy Special Representative of the UN Secretary-General, and several of her close collaborators initiated the project. It is worth retracing this attempt in depth, as it provides invaluable insights to understanding the failure of contestation within and outside of the UN.[16]

Sundh's team analyzed the ongoing conflict as having "multiple levels": the local, provincial, national, and regional. They also recognized that the international peacebuilding system was "troublingly" fragmented between "the local and provincial levels on the one hand and the national and regional levels on the other." The team regretted that "many actors," such as "the governments and the entire UN nebula," were involved solely at the regional and national levels, while only emergency aid organizations, such as the UN High Commissioner for Refugees, the UN World Food Program, and various nongovernmental agencies were present at the provincial and local levels. From their point of view, "there was nobody to make the links and reconnect both sides, so that [the UN] could work simultaneously at different levels." Sundh's team realized that MONUC was the only actor capable of linking peacebuilding actions at the micro and macro levels.

The team also believed that MONUC had to focus its efforts mainly on the local realm because it wielded most power there. As one of the MONUC staff members involved in the process recalled, "We were wondering: Why do we work on the regional and national levels? We have little influence and we are not respected, while at the provincial level we carry some weight. So we have to position ourselves at this level." Sundh's staff argued that the UN should see the national peace process primarily as a long-term objective; meanwhile it needed to start working locally and manage the conflict from the bottom up.

For its main targets, Sundh's team identified the tensions that the Global and All-inclusive Agreement of 2002 did not address, in particular, disputes that regional or national actors manipulated or that could serve as triggers for a renewal of the broader conflict. According

---

[16] As in most of this book, all quotations in this section come from the author's confidential interviews, including numerous conversations with MONUC staff members, many of whom were not involved in the actual contestation process. It is important to note that, due to their concerns over professional repercussions and following their requests, I do not identify any interviewee by name in this section.

to a MONUC official familiar with the policy, "local conflicts" therefore meant "anything that was not really part of the national conflict." These tensions could be "very small," such as the antagonisms that groups of Tutsis returning to their communities in Kalemie (North Katanga) might trigger, or "quite big," such as the battle between Nande and Banyarwanda in North Kivu. They could be "in a village," "between two communities," or at the level of an entire province – such as the possibility of riots in Kasai if the opposition party, Union for the Progress and Democracy, lost the elections.

Working on local conflicts was such a new and controversial idea that, before proceeding further, Sundh's team first had to write a "very down to earth" document designed to signal to MONUC colleagues that addressing grassroots tensions was "part of [their] job." The team therefore put together a policy paper on local conflict, dated December 2002, which "presented [the idea by] saying that even though there was a national peace process, there were still tensions and conflict going on in different parts of the country. And if nothing was done about them, they would actually risk endangering the peace process." The main goal was to ensure that "at minimum, MONUC staff first picked up on these tensions or possible conflicts before they became violent again," and "tried to do what it could to avoid conflicts flaring up locally." The document therefore asked that the Department of Peacekeeping Operations support MONUC's research "for all provinces" on questions like "what [was] the previous history of conflict, who [were] the spoilers, ... what [were] the kinds of possibility for new tensions, who [were] the actors that [could] help, and so on," to be better prepared to prevent any potential local crisis.

The UN headquarters endorsed this policy on local conflict in mid-2003.[17] When listing his recommendations for MONUC's new mandate during the transition, the Secretary-General included as his second item the pledge "to contribute to local conflict resolution and the maintenance of security in key areas of the country."[18] (In accordance with the dominant narrative, the first item was "to provide political support to the transition by assisting the Congolese parties in the implementation of their commitments, leading to the holding

[17] Sundh 2004.
[18] All the quotations in this paragraph come from UN Security Council 2003c, paras. 29, 30, 55, 58–60, and 99.

of elections.") The same report also identified "contributing to local-level conflict resolution" and "creating peaceful solutions to local conflicts" as two of MONUC's immediate priorities, especially in the Kivus. MONUC's local strategy was to be three-pronged: "(a) crisis management to address acute security concerns between different groups; (b) post-conflict measures aimed at building confidence; and (c) conflict prevention initiatives to avoid the recurrence of violence." The UN mission was to "serve as a catalyst for international support and assist the initiatives undertaken by local religious institutions as well as Congolese ... and international non-governmental organizations." To do so, the Secretary-General planned to "expand the presence of its civilian personnel and military observers in the Kivus" and aimed to "call on donors to contribute to a special fund for local peacemaking."

The last part of these ambitious plans, notably the deployment of additional staff to work on local conflict resolution in the Kivus, never materialized. Furthermore, the initiative on local conflicts remained under Sundh's leadership. Other MONUC staff members saw it as her initiative, her pet project, and MONUC's Political Affairs Division never integrated grassroots peacebuilding into its daily work. The new strategy thus proceeded, but did so slowly. MONUC nominated a coordinator for local conflict, and several other officials, primarily from Sundh's close professional collaborators, joined the venture. The local conflict team tried to develop analyses and recommendations on how to defuse micro-level tensions, and focused its efforts on two combined actions, both of which started in mid-2003. The first was to develop a strategy for addressing local tensions in the Kivus. The second was to inform the field offices of the importance of decentralized conflicts and to provide the relevant officials with training on bottom-up peacebuilding.

The local conflict unit drafted the Kivu strategy in close partnership with the MONUC field offices in the Kivus and with some external input from embassies and donors. It aimed, in the short to mid term, to ensure the stability of the province, while in the long term it hoped to promote the extension of legitimate state authority and the rule of law.[19] The end product, finalized in February 2004, read like an action plan for local conflict prevention and, when relevant,

[19] Staibano 2005.

for crisis response.[20] It had two parts: first, an analysis of local conflicts in the Kivus from colonization to the transition, which was well documented and very convincing; second, two "regional implementation plans," which listed broad recommendations to address local problems in North and South Kivu, respectively. These recommendations were important but problematic in several ways. They lacked concrete details necessary for easy implementation, they overlooked several key causes of local conflict, and they failed to include input from Congolese grassroots actors.

Since the strategy document focused on the Kivus, the training sessions primarily included the MONUC officials based in these provinces, although several staff members deployed in North Katanga were invited. According to the UN Secretary-General's 14th Report on MONUC to the Security Council (dated November 2003), MONUC also started implementing a few bottom-up conflict-resolution initiatives in both Kivus. In the Shabunda and Walungu territories, the Uvira–Baraka area, and the Beni–Butembo area, MONUC staff facilitated local ceasefires between units of Mai Mai, RCD-G, and Kabila troops. The Secretary-General's report detailing these initiatives emphasized that they made two major contributions. First, they helped alleviate the root causes of the Congolese conflict. Second, they addressed the "heart" of the disarmament, demobilization, and reintegration of foreign and Congolese combatants, as this process was "intricately linked to local-level political and economic dynamics in the eastern part of the country."[21]

The local conflict unit planned to repeat this initiative of drafting a provincial strategy and training relevant MONUC officials for all of the provinces, starting with North Katanga. However, for several reasons, MONUC neither fully implemented the Kivu strategy nor drafted strategies for other provinces. Members of the local conflict unit had many other issues on which to work, and some of them thought that the stakes of local conflict policy were actually "not crucial." Furthermore, the initiative met with resistance, sometimes quite strong, from many other MONUC officials both in Kinshasa and in the field. When asked during interviews, MONUC staff members usually attributed this resistance to widespread personal grudges against important members of the unit, criticizing Lena Sundh or her

---

[20] UN Mission in the Democratic Republic of Congo (MONUC) 2004.
[21] UN Security Council 2003a, paras. 13–16 and 20, quotation from para. 66.

collaborators as authoritarian, arrogant, or disrespectful of their colleagues' ideas (see the section The Defeat of Contestation for a different analysis of the reasons behind this widespread resistance). As a
result, when Sundh and her close collaborators left the Congo in the
first half of 2004, the local conflict policy was discarded.

The UN Secretary-General's reports best illustrate how quickly the
local peacebuilding initiative was forgotten. Contrary to its precursor,
the 15th Report on MONUC of March 2004 had no section on local
conflict resolution. It devoted only one paragraph to "Quick Impact
Projects," whose number and budget were limited (fifty-nine projects
for $672,830), and of these, only a few supported grassroots peace-
building.[22] The Secretary-General's 3rd Special Report on MONUC,
dated August 2004, still identified "communal- and provincial-level
power" as a significant source of tensions in the Kivus, but it did so
in the military strategy section. It mentioned local peacebuilding only
once, in the section on "challenges and the way forward," describing
this as a task for the Congolese government, not for MONUC, and as
an unimportant issue (one of the many measures necessary to achieve
the territorial reunification of the country).[23] Later reports scarcely
mentioned local conflict resolution.

There was still a chance that Sundh's ideas had a legacy in the field,
though. In late 2004, the head of MONUC created a Joint Mission
Analysis Cell, aimed at centralizing information within the organization and conducting threat analysis in the mission areas.[24] The UN
recruited François Grignon to lead the cell, and asked him to develop
action plans for the Kivus as well as Maniema, Katanga, and potentially the Kasai. Grignon was the former Great Lakes analyst at the
International Crisis Group, and the main author of a report, mentioned in chapter 4, that presented the war in North and South Kivu
as the result of three overlapping and interacting levels of conflicts
(regional, national, and local).[25]

Grignon began by focusing on the Kivus and, rather than implementing the strategy previously written, developed a new one. According

[22] UN Security Council 2004a, para. 58.
[23] UN Security Council 2004d, part III and paras. 83–84.
[24] For a public source, see UN Security Council 2004c (para. 44) and 2004d
(para. 98); and the website of the UN Advisory Committee on Administrative
and Budgetary Questions, http://www.un.org/ga/acabq/topics_results.
asp?desc=131 (accessed in July 2008).
[25] International Crisis Group 2003b.

to various interviewees, the previous strategy was discarded because Sundh's approach "was based on an isolation of the local dynamics"; it was too academic, too theoretical, unfit to be translated into operational actions, and obsolete in the wake of the May 2004 Bukavu crisis. Instead, the new strategy aimed to "mobilize together the means of all the sections – political, military, humanitarian, and human rights" simultaneously at the regional level (focusing on the Congo-Rwanda relationships), in Kinshasa (working with national leaders who could influence the situation in the Kivus), and locally in the provinces. From September to November 2004, Grignon thus drafted new action plans, once again in collaboration with the Kivus' field offices and the New York headquarters.

In terms of strategy and operational approach, Grignon's documents were extremely similar to Sundh's Kivu Strategy, except in three regards. As mentioned previously, Grignon planned national, regional, and international actions in addition to local actions. His plans included much more detailed and concrete measures than the Kivu Strategy (for example, they listed potential ways to sanction spoilers). They also suggested working with Mai Mai groups and religious authorities, both of which were mostly overlooked by the first strategy.

A plan for Katanga and subsequent potential strategies for other provinces were supposed to follow the Kivu action plans. However, Grignon and his colleagues never developed strategies for other provinces, and the MONUC's field offices never implemented the Kivu action plans. In 2005, the goals of the action plans were progressively toned down to "better reflect MONUC's capabilities and objectives." As a staff member explained to me, rather than addressing the "sources of conflict that are linked to a historic heritage of thirty or forty years of manipulation of the land issue," the plans became a collection of "short-term objectives." Their goal was merely to "put out the fire, if possible throwing a bit of soil on the embers, so that they don't light up again in the following years." MONUC officials thus argued that they could only "see to it that people stop cutting each other's throats," but it was the role of "public policies, by the [Congolese] state, the UN Development Program, other UN agencies, bilateral actors, [and] non-governmental organizations" to do the long-term peacebuilding work. In North Kivu, the action plan remained one of many strategies to implement once the situation improved, which it never did. In South Kivu, the deputy head of office further developed and modified Grignon's document, but he and his colleagues accomplished little in terms of implementation.

Henceforward, the abandoned initiative on local conflict became a guarded secret within the mission. Only a few UN staff members agreed to talk about it – only after I had gained their trust through repeated interactions, and only under conditions of strict confidentiality. During our conversations on the topic, they reacted as if we were discussing something shameful. It was also very hard to get a copy of the documents Sundh's team wrote between 2002 and 2004, even though they had been discarded and never implemented, and even when I promised to treat these documents confidentially. Interestingly, fear of a breach of confidentiality did not motivate the reluctance to share the documents; most people said that the papers did not include any restricted information, and those who finally did leak them to me did not ask me to keep them private. Rather, my contacts gave me trivial pretexts such as they had "lost" the documents or they had "put them in their country house and could not dig them up" (see the section The Defeat of Contestation for a potential explanation of this reluctance). William Swing, the Special Representative of the UN Secretary-General, even told me that he "had to ask" if he could give me these records. Since he was the highest-ranking MONUC official, I wondered whose permission he had to seek.

By 2006, the local conflict initiative was defunct. Virtually all of the people previously involved in it had left the mission, for reasons unrelated to their participation in the project. None of the newcomers whom I interviewed had heard about it or knew that it had ever existed. When I broached the topic during interviews, MONUC actors said that local peacebuilding would potentially be something to consider after the elections (but, in fact, these deliberations started only very slowly in 2008). During the last year of the transition, staff members at the Joint Mission Analysis Cell remained the only people who still emphasized the role of local tensions in sustaining violence in the eastern provinces, jeopardizing the election process, and endangering the broader national and regional settlements. However, their role was limited to writing reports that their colleagues and superiors then derided or ignored. A few of their political, humanitarian, civil affairs, and human rights colleagues based in the field also sometimes pointed out the influence of specific local tensions in their areas of operation. Intermediaries between the staff on the ground and the Kinshasa and New York headquarters, however, filtered out most of this information. Field-based actors never mounted a large-scale or coordinated advocacy effort to convince their superiors to pay more attention to local conflict, nor did they contest MONUC's broader strategic orientation toward the macro levels and elections.

As a result, MONUC's overall involvement in local peacebuilding throughout the transition remained limited to ad-hoc, isolated, and uncoordinated initiatives. It is true that, when asked directly, all MONUC officials claimed that they – or their colleagues based in the provinces – were engaged in bottom-up conflict resolution. However, in direct contradiction to MONUC's overall strategy in the Congo, which assumed that there was no military solution to the conflict and focused instead on a political settlement, MONUC's main peace-building approach at the local level was military rather than diplo-matic, economic, or political.[26]

According to most interviewees, the very presence of troops and military observers in unstable places was MONUC's major contri-bution to local peace; it acted as a deterrent because potential war-ring parties could not afford to break a ceasefire under the eyes of UN staff. Additionally, UN troops stationed in the major cities of the Kivus occasionally tried to mediate local ceasefires between differ-ent militias. UN military observers could have contributed as well, because they were officially responsible for monitoring local tensions and acting as a third party if these tensions escalated; however, their local peacebuilding efforts remained sporadic and extremely rare.[27]

MONUC's civilian staff members who worked on political, human rights, humanitarian, or civil affairs implemented more diverse and concrete local-level actions, although these were still very limited in number and scope. During the first year of the transition, influenced by Sundh's efforts, the Political Affairs Division tried to organize conflict-management meetings between different ethnic communi-ties, especially in South Kivu. It quickly abandoned the initiative once the local conflict unit disappeared.[28] Afterwards, Political Affairs

---

[26] See, for example, UN Security Council 2004d, for the claim that MONUC's strategy should be political rather than military.

[27] See ibid., para. 101, for the military observers' official role.

[28] E-mail communication from Romkema, March 2005.

officers based in the eastern provinces restricted their efforts to regular appointments with provincial officials, usually to confer about the upcoming elections. They also organized a few conferences at which civilians could discuss peace and reconciliation. Finally, they mediated – or supported the nongovernmental organizations' mediation efforts – between the leaders of the population with Rwandan ancestry and their traditional enemies. Such initiatives took place mostly in times of intense crises, such as during the large-scale fighting in Bukavu (February and May 2004), Kanyabayonga (December 2004), Rutshuru (January 2006), and in the aftermath of the Gatumba massacre (August 2004).

Overall, contact between MONUC's Political Affairs officers and local actors remained very limited, as a telling anecdote reported by a Western diplomat illustrates. In 2005, this diplomat paid a visit to the Kivus with the foreign minister of his country. Upon arrival, the minister asked for the phone number of several key provincial officials. "MONUC people were all embarrassed," the diplomat reported, "as they did not even have these phone numbers!" To make matters worse, they managed to provide the requested contact information only after two hours, and only thanks to one of their Congolese staff members. Non-MONUC interviewees based in the eastern provinces, notably Congolese officials and nongovernmental peacebuilders, confirmed that they very rarely interacted with MONUC staffers.

Other MONUC departments also implemented very rare, ad-hoc conflict-resolution projects. The Human Rights Department wrote detailed reports on the ongoing human rights violations, which increased accountability and was reportedly an effective deterrent for future violence.[29] The Humanitarian Affairs Section (renamed the Civil Affairs Section in 2006) convinced several internally divided communities to set aside their differences in exchange for humanitarian aid. However, these combined humanitarian and peacebuilding projects were extremely few, and their main objective was not to build local peace but to help MONUC win the hearts and minds of the local population.[30]

MONUC's civilian and military components' overall contribution to local peacebuilding was thus negligible. To justify their lack of

[29] For a public source, see Sundh 2004.
[30] UN Security Council 2002 (paras. 66 and 67) and 2003d (para. 49).

action on grassroots conflict, MONUC officials usually claimed that working on micro-level issues was not their responsibility but rather that of nongovernmental organizations and Congolese authorities. These interviewees said that MONUC itself should not work on local violence; rather, it should facilitate the peacebuilding initiatives of other international and local agencies by providing logistical support and securing areas when necessary. However pervasive, this position was deeply flawed. As detailed in chapters 2 and 4, except for a few cases, Congolese authorities and religious leaders were either unable or unwilling to conduct local conflict-resolution programs, or they were involved in fueling the violence. Even the Truth and Reconciliation Commission mandated under the Global and All-Inclusive Agreement, which could have overseen grassroots peacebuilding efforts, became fully operational only in 2005 and never implemented any concrete projects. And, as detailed earlier, nongovernmental organizations could function effectively only if they were part of a network that included UN and diplomatic actors.

Rare Initiatives by Diplomatic Missions

Regrettably, contestation from within the foreign ministries was not only similarly unsuccessful but also very rare. It happened mostly in three diplomatic missions (from Sweden, Belgium, and the United Kingdom), and rather than spurring additional political action on local tensions, it mostly increased the funds available to nongovern mental organizations working on bottom-up conflict resolution.

Within the Swedish embassy, Lena Sundh – who, as an ambassador, ranked high in the foreign ministry's hierarchy – spearheaded the initiative. When Sundh was dispatched to MONUC, she remained in contact with the Swedish foreign ministry and managed to convince her diplomatic colleagues to finance the grassroots conflict-resolution initiative she supervised. Her legacy persisted after she left MONUC, probably in part because she became Sweden's Ambassador for Conflict Prevention and continued to advocate for bottom-up peacebuilding in the Congo and elsewhere. Sweden was the only embassy with a small fund expressly designated for grassroots conflict resolution, and the embassy's cooperation department made a special effort to finance local conflict-resolution projects like those of the Life and Peace Institute. The Swedish embassy was also the only diplomatic mission to include a political affairs officer whose tasks specifically involved supporting bottom-up peacebuilding initiatives. Despite these efforts, local conflict resolution was just one among the mission's many concerns, and even for the diplomat tasked with grassroots peacebuilding, this issue ranked significantly behind the organization of elections. Additionally, Sweden was a small diplomatic mission, with only two or three diplomats. As a result, its overall contribution to local peacebuilding remained relatively marginal.

In the Belgian political establishment, two figures engaged in most of the contestation of the traditional diplomatic approach. The first, Reginald Moreels, was a senator and former minister of cooperation. Moreels lobbied his colleagues to adopt a different approach to the Congolese crisis, which would include bottom-up peacebuilding. However, Moreels was never influential, partly because his colleagues often derided him as a maverick with psychological problems and impracticable ideas. On the issue of local involvement, the Belgian diplomatic establishment sidestepped and marginalized him. The second main contester was the Belgian Consul based in Lubumbashi (Belgium had a diplomatic presence in Katanga due to historical legacies and the presence of a large Belgian community in the province). The Consul lobbied for a much greater Belgian involvement in Katanga, constantly pushed MONUC to intervene in local conflicts, and relentlessly warned his colleagues about the importance of continued violence in the province. His actions did have some influence at the provincial level, but he never managed to convince his superiors to adopt a comprehensive strategy to address local tensions.

Within the British embassy, the few advocates of bottom-up peacebuilding succeeded in launching an initiative that made a significant financial contribution to grassroots conflict-resolution efforts. The United Kingdom became a key donor for local peacebuilding organizations such as International Alert, Life and Peace Institute, Search for Common Ground, and Christian Aid. However, the initiative was located within the United Kingdom's Department for International Development and it did not involve the political, economic, or military sections of the embassy in its efforts.

All other Western and African diplomats relied on the presence of the international peacekeeping troops as a deterrent to quell local violence. Diplomatic actions were mostly nonexistent at the local level. There were no meetings to mediate between local parties in conflict, no pressure applied to local spoilers, no mention of local conflict resolution in Security Council resolutions or in reports of diplomats' visits to Central Africa, and no political support for grassroots peacebuilders. As mentioned in chapter 3, local-level political intervention took place only at times of severe crises. In these rare instances, a few diplomats called on the main local warlords, as well as the provincial political and religious authorities, and tried to mediate between them. The only other diplomatic political action at the grassroots level occurred during the rare visits that diplomats made to the eastern Congo. On these occasions, diplomats usually reminded all of their interlocutors of the necessity to participate faithfully in the transition process. Additionally, the U.S., Norwegian, and Belgian governmental aid agencies also financed a handful of bottom-up peacebuilding projects, but there were very few initiatives of this kind, and the donors considered them to be apolitical solutions to apolitical problems. Otherwise, diplomats insisted that MONUC was the primary actor responsible for local conflict resolution – while, as explained earlier, MONUC believed that nongovernmental organizations should be in charge of bottom-up peacebuilding.

The Standard Approach of Other International Organizations

There was virtually no contestation within the UN system in general, or within other international organizations, despite many opportunities. In 2002, for example, following one of the recommendations of the Brahimi Report (the landmark document that led to major reforms in UN peacekeeping at the beginning of the twenty-first century), the UN leadership tried to ensure that its humanitarian, political, and military responses to the Congolese crisis reinforced one another. This new strategic orientation could have led various UN agencies to decide that they would adopt a bottom-up approach to complement the top-down work of MONUC and other political or military interveners. Development and humanitarian organizations were especially well prepared to adopt this bottom-up strategy, given their familiarity with intervention at the local level, their repeated interaction with subnational actors, and the potential of aid programs to contribute to local conflict resolution.[31]

However, this potential for increased attention to grassroots peace-building never materialized. In 2003 and 2004, virtually all UN humanitarian staff members based in the field and whom I interviewed claimed that their work was purely neutral, apolitical, and removed from any peacebuilding imperative. If aid was part of the broader response to the Congolese crisis, it was according to the logic presented in chapter 3: as an apolitical solution to an apolitical problem.

In early 2005, the UN attempts at implementing the recommendations of the Brahimi report led to the formation of a "semi-integrated mission" in the Congo. The new deputy head of MONUC would now coordinate the work of all UN agencies to ensure that they all worked toward the same objective: the stabilization of the country and, predictably, the preparation and implementation of elections. This macro-level development, however, impacted local conflict resolution only negligibly. Most humanitarian and development programs remained devoid of a peacebuilding dimension. In the eastern provinces, they focused on emergency relief such as food distribution and primary care, and almost all UN aid workers took pains to ensure that their projects remained as apolitical as possible.

There were only very few exceptions. The UN Development Program had a Disarmament, Demobilization, and Reintegration project that intended to include micro-level initiatives, although it very rarely led to concrete action, mainly due to funding and coordination problems. The UN Office for the Coordination of Humanitarian Affairs implemented a few local peacebuilding initiatives. For example, in a workshop on the return of Congolese refugees from Tanzania, it discussed the mechanisms necessary to peacefully settle the intercommunal conflicts that this return might produce. However, the UN office designed these projects as a way to facilitate the provision of humanitarian services, not to help with the political or military stabilization of the country. Its staff consistently stressed that they were neutral and their work and mandate had nothing to do with conflict resolution.

---

[31] See Anderson 1999, and Prendergast 1996 on the peacebuilding potential of development and humanitarian aid programs.

Beyond the UN, even the World Bank's actions in the Congo showed a total lack of involvement at the local level, which was surprising given the organization's projects to address local conflict in other contexts.[32] To World Bank employees, along with other staff members of international organizations whom I interviewed, local peacebuilding fell within MONUC's purview and was, therefore, not their concern.

The Ituri Case

Each of these actors, however, shared one exception: the approach to violence in the small district of Ituri. Ituri enjoyed significantly more international attention and resources than did any other eastern province. It was also the theater of most of the micro-level peacebuilding initiatives implemented in the Congo.

Ituri was given its own decentralized pacification process, led by its own transitional administration, and financed by its own international trust fund. When the International Criminal Court took on the Congo as its first task in July 2003, it decided to focus its efforts on the Ituri district and, as of this writing, the court's four cases on the Congo all involve defendants who operated in Ituri. The nongovernmental organizations working on grassroots conflict resolution were more numerous and more active in this district than in any other Congolese province. UN agencies endowed Ituri with a specific disarmament program, independent from the national program. The UN Development Program even implemented close to one hundred micro level projects aimed at facilitating community reconciliation by reestablishing trust between former enemies and enabling them to work together toward a common goal. Although this program remained very limited in scope and was hampered by a lack of resources, weak support from the Kinshasa hierarchy, and inadequate coordination with broader conflict-resolution initiatives, it reduced violence in its areas of intervention.[33]

Foreign states involved in the Congolese peace process similarly focused on this district. After the departure of Ugandan troops

[32] See, for example, Barron, Smith, et al. 2004, for a presentation of World Bank grassroots projects in Indonesia.
[33] Samset and Madore 2006.

unleashed an explosion of violence in Ituri in May 2003, the EU deployed its first military operation outside of Europe, Operation Artemis, to the district capital of Bunia. This intervention stood out both for the fact that the peacekeeping force was composed of Western troops (while MONUC troops were exclusively from non-Western countries) and, as a Western diplomat strikingly put it, for the "exceptional rapidity with which Europe implemented an intervention for a small part of a country in Central Africa." Furthermore, in a 2003 resolution, UN Security Council members authorized "MONUC to use all necessary means to fulfill its mandate in the Ituri district and, *as it deems it within its capabilities*, in North and South Kivu."[34] While the mandate placed no restrictions on action in Ituri, it did specify limitations for the Kivus. Later on, incidents of violence in the district often generated strong international condemnation, especially from the International Committee in Support of the Transition (the forum of fifteen foreign states and international organizations supervising the Congolese peace process). Finally, following a specific request from Belgium, the Congolese government deployed its Belgian-trained first brigade, which was considered the best in the integrated army, to Ituri.[35]

MONUC treated Ituri, similarly, with special care. In the words of a high-ranking MONUC official, after Ituri "blew up" in May 2003, "it became a mission within the mission, and it was such a big problem that it definitely had its own strategy." Throughout the entire transition, the Secretary-General's Reports on MONUC to the Security Council always considered the security situation in Ituri before that in the Kivus, even in the reports covering the 2004 large-scale fighting in Bukavu and Kanyabayonga.[36]

Additionally, MONUC devoted many more resources to Ituri than to the other eastern provinces, despite the fact that violence in the Kivus and Katanga caused more casualties. In September 2003, the mission deployed almost half of its available troops (4,800 out of 10,800) to secure Ituri. Until November 2004, the small district benefited from as many soldiers as did the two large Kivu provinces combined.

---

[34] UN Security Council 2003b, para. 26, my emphasis.
[35] Author's interview with Jozef Smets, Belgian Ministry of Foreign Affairs, Africa department, Brussels, May 2005; and Wolters and Boshoff 2006.
[36] UN Security Council 2003–2006a.

During the last two years of the transition, while other MONUC brigades used arms exclusively to defend UN staff and properties, the Ituri brigade started to fight militias proactively, searching for and attacking them when necessary. The overall MONUC military strategy at that time was to tackle the Ituri problem first, and then focus its efforts on the Kivus once Ituri had been pacified. Likewise, on MONUC's civilian side, the head of office for Ituri was of a higher rank than all the other heads of offices. Finally, MONUC's public information department devoted a disproportionately large number of its press releases, as well as many of its weekly press briefings, to the situation in Ituri even when large-scale fighting was occurring elsewhere in the country.

Understanding the Exceptions

How can we understand these exceptions? Why did a few organizations, and a few people within other organizations, escape the dominant peacebuilding culture, contest the dominant narrative on the causes of continued violence during the Congolese transition, and reconceptualize their role as not exclusively focused on the macro levels? Why did even diplomats and MONUC officials make an exception to their general strategy for the small Ituri district? Building on existing research on resistance to dominant cultures, this section considers two sets of explanations, one drawing on the influence of organizational subcultures and the other on the occurrence of shocking events.[37]

Organizational Subcultures

The existence of specific subcultures cannot explain as much as organizational theorists might predict; it can account for only a handful of the exceptions to the dominant narratives and practices. It is true that various actors (such as nongovernmental organizations) and various subunits within each organization (such as MONUC's different departments and offices, and a diplomatic mission's assorted

---

[37] Barnett 2002; Barnett and Finnemore 2004; Carpenter 2006; Eden 2004; Holohan 2005; and March and Olsen 1984 provide the most helpful approaches to this topic and the inspiration for this section.

divisions) had unique ideas, customs, beliefs, rules, and standard operating procedures. Because some of these factors varied from those of the broader culture detailed in chapters 2 and 3, a few of the subcultures were more attuned to intervention at the local level.

Humanitarian, human rights, and development actors were perfectly at ease with the idea of local-level involvement. In the Congo, as in all places where they intervene, they conceptualized their role as including continual interactions with subnational actors to negotiate access to affected populations or engage the local communities in their projects. Likewise, during interviews and informal conversations, staffs of nongovernmental organizations involved in relief and development, MONUC's human rights and humanitarian sections, and the development and cooperation departments of diplomatic missions mentioned micro-level tensions more than did other international interviewees.

MONUC officials deployed in the eastern provinces, in contrast to UN political staff and diplomats based in Kinshasa or in foreign capitals, similarly conceptualized their role as including regular interactions with provincial officials to gather and transmit information to their hierarchy. These individuals also reportedly wrote numerous memos warning of impending local crises throughout the three years of the transition.

The existence of these subcultures with enhanced sensitivity to local issues, however, did not necessarily mean that the majority of humanitarian actors or UN and diplomatic officials based in the field identified micro-level conflicts as a critical source of violence or advocated for stronger international involvement at the grassroots level. As detailed earlier, in fact, only a few did so. The others usually only briefly mentioned local tensions and interactions with subnational representatives, while otherwise reproducing the dominant narrative. The determining element, therefore, seemed to be not a specific field or humanitarian subculture, but rather the particular organizational culture of the few agencies and units that focused on bottom-up peacebuilding.

Life and Peace Organization and Search for Common Ground, for example, defined their identity in a very different way than did the diplomatic missions and the international peacebuilding organizations studied in chapter 3. The staff members working for these specific nongovernmental organizations perceived their central task as requiring, at least in part, work at the grassroots level with civil society actors.[38] This identity and strategic focus predated the agencies' arrival in the Congo. Indeed, the Life and Peace Institute is famous for its bottom-up peacebuilding initiative in Somalia during the 1990s, and Search for Common Ground was similarly involved in local peacebuilding in South Africa during the demise of the apartheid.

It is beyond the scope of this book to document how these specific identities developed, but the organizational consequences are clear: Because the role of the organization focused on bottom-up conflict resolution, top managers recruited experts interested in or knowledgeable about local peacebuilding. At the same time, just as diplomatic missions and international organizations tend to attract people interested in macro-level approaches, these agencies attracted staff members attuned to micro-level action. For example, one of the most active international actors working on grassroots conflict resolution during the Congolese transition, Hans Romkema, recalls that his previous involvement in the Congo led to his decision to serve as Life and Peace Institute's head of mission. While working for a humanitarian agency in the Kivus during the war, Romkema noticed that "there were always windows of opportunity remaining for peace at the local level," even in the places most affected by violence. At that time, he tried to support bottom-up conflict-resolution initiatives but had only limited means. With the help of his largest donor, the Swedish International Development Cooperation Agency, he started looking for an organization that wished to support local peace initiatives and discovered the Life and Peace Institute.[39] Once inside these types of organizations, staff members such as Romkema developed new expertise and reinforced the agencies' identity as focused on grassroots conflict resolution. This process led to an increased focus on local tensions and a deeper organizational expertise on the topic, perpetuating both the organization's identity and its strategic orientation toward decentralized peacebuilding.

The United Kingdom's development branch presents a slightly different case from these nongovernmental organizations, although the logic remains similar: The focus on local issues predated the Congolese transition; it resulted from the United Kingdom's broader political orientation during the Congolese wars of the 1990s. As various UK

---

[38] For publicly available sources, see the websites of these agencies.
[39] Romkema's personal communication to author, 2008.

officials and foreign observers explained to me, until the transition began, the United Kingdom refused to "engage with the Congo until there was a government that represented the whole country," and not only a third of it. Unable to implement its usual top-down approach to development, the United Kingdom's Department for International Development sought an alternative strategy. It decided to "focus on the area where the conflict was the worst" – the eastern provinces – and on the issue where it could "add value" – local conflict resolution. During the transition, the reunification of the Congo eliminated the United Kingdom's reluctance to work with the Congolese government, and the entire diplomatic mission switched its primary focus to the national peace process. However, local conflict resolution remained one of the development branch's priorities. This legacy most likely persisted, in part, because the unit now had a different view of its role as well as a stock of expertise and standard operating procedures for local conflict resolution.

The process seems to have been similar for the Swedish diplomatic mission, although in this case, it was the legacy of a specific individual and not of a broader political orientation that was most influential. Because of her prominent position before and during the Congolese transition, Lena Sundh helped to redefine Sweden's role in the Congo as not exclusively focused on macro-level issues. This effort contributed to the development of various tools to address local conflict resolution and a strengthened belief in the legitimacy of this new strategic orientation.

More research on each of these organizations is necessary to understand how their internal cultures could develop in a way so distinct from the dominant narrative on the role of international interveners. More investigation is also indispensable to understanding why, within international organizations and diplomatic missions, a few exceptional individuals such as Lena Sundh or Reginald Moreels escaped the dominant organizational culture and advocated for an increased involvement at the local level. Reasons probably include local knowledge, personality, personal and professional background (including, for Moreels, a long exposure as a humanitarian aid worker to the consequences of decentralized violence), and other idiosyncratic characteristics.[40]

---

[40] For more on these hypotheses but applied to other cases, see Barnett 2002, conclusion; and Holohan 2005.

Even without such further research, one conclusion is clear: The presence of specific organizational cultures can solve only one part of the puzzle. This line of analysis can help explain why a few agencies and units focused on local conflict resolution while most others did not. It does not, however, help explain why various MONUC officials and diplomats, who usually shared and repeated the dominant narrative on the causes of violence and the role of international actors, nevertheless occasionally became involved in local conflict resolution, as they did in Ituri. To understand this phenomenon, we must examine the influence of shocking events.

Shocking Events and Increased Intervention

During the transition, five kinds of events proved so shocking that they grabbed international attention and inspired increased intervention even from those actors otherwise apathetic to decentralized peacebuilding: (1) when supposedly peaceful areas suddenly flared up; (2) when a crisis started to look like a potential genocide; (3) when violence was particularly gruesome or spectacular; (4) when local militias targeted international peacebuilders; and (5) when it was readily apparent that local conflict jeopardized the national and regional settlements.

The Ituri district provides a textbook example of this phenomenon. As detailed in chapters 2 and 4, violence continued in Ituri, as in the other eastern provinces, mostly because of unresolved local conflicts over land and mineral resources. In contrast to these other provinces, however, a series of shocking events led international actors to consistently categorize the Ituri situation as a crisis and, therefore, to provide unparalleled support to decentralized peacebuilding, as detailed in the earlier section on the Ituri case. Even though localized violence was ongoing in Ituri from 1999, international interveners often saw the district as more "peaceful" than other parts of the eastern Congo. The rapid flare-up of tensions in 2002 and 2003 thus took them by surprise and attracted their attention to Ituri. UN, U.S., and EU officials also perceived the deteriorating situation as a potential genocide. This perception was extremely influential in compelling the EU to launch Operation Artemis in Bunia and in encouraging the UN to station significantly more civilian and military staff members in the Ituri district than in any of the other eastern provinces.[41] Additionally, militias killed several peacekeepers and kidnapped several others (notably in 2003, 2005, and 2006), further inciting high-level UN management to launch extensive military actions. Finally, throughout the transition, the presence of very graphic horrors (such as massacres by machete and torture) seemed to function as a catalyst for intervention. Whenever MONUC was about to step up its military action in the district, its press conferences usually detailed such horrors at length. For example, just before a large MONUC offensive in May 2005, the weekly MONUC press conference broadcast an interview with an Ituri woman who had been horribly tortured and maimed and witnessed her tormentors chopping up, grilling, and eating her children.

In other parts of the Congo, the shocking nature of specific instances of violence also played a large role in attracting international interveners' attention. In the Kivus, for example, violence had been endemic for a long time; international peacebuilders thus perceived it as "chronic" and localized. Then, in May to June 2004, the violence suddenly became acute around Bukavu, drawing the attention of intervention forces. When renegade troops attacked and killed a few UN peacekeepers, during the first few days of the fighting, the perception of the crisis rapidly went from being a local, unimportant problem to a disaster worthy of the highest diplomatic action.

Likewise, the gruesome nature of some of the massacres that rebel Rwandan Hutu militias committed in South Kivu was instrumental in bringing international attention to these events. In early July 2005, for instance, one of these many slaughters provoked a MONUC armed intervention, a trip by high-ranking diplomats and UN officials to the targeted village, and many press articles. The only difference between this and previous massacres, which had mostly gone unreported, was its spectacular and horrific nature; Rwandan rebels had burned people alive or cut them to pieces with machetes.

One last factor proved effective in focusing increased attention on ongoing violence in the eastern provinces: the realization that local conflict could jeopardize the national and regional settlements. As

---

[41] For public sources, see Cowan 2004; Thomas Hofnung, "Comment l'ONU A Évité un Génocide dans cette Région à l'Est de la République Démocratique du Congo – Ituri au Bord du Gouffre," *Libération*, June 20, 2005; and Alain Barluet, "Enquête sur une Mission de Paix au Congo – Arte / Dans les Arcanes de l'ONU," *Le Figaro*, June 20, 2005.

I explain throughout this book, international peacebuilders usually did not acknowledge the interaction between the micro- and macro-level dimensions of the conflict. However, whenever a direct link between local issues and the national and regional peace processes became apparent, significant international involvement immediately followed. For example, in the Kivus, international actors focused on the tensions between indigenous and Kinyarwanda-speaking communities mostly because regional and national actors constantly reaffirmed the link between the bottom-up and top-down dimensions of this conflict. The fighting in Bukavu and Kanyabayonga (in May and December 2004, respectively) likewise perfectly illustrates this pattern. In both cases, international peacebuilders left local issues to fester for months, even though a crisis was inevitable. Only when these local issues erupted in massive violence, which was followed both by Rwandan threats to reinvade the Congo and by fear of possible fighting between Kabila and RCD-G troops, did international peacebuilders finally focus their attention on situations that they had previously neglected.

The post-transition pattern of violence and intervention is also particularly illuminating in this regard. In August 2008, the North Kivu tensions between the Mai Mai, units of the integrated army, and people of Rwandan descent (now supporting General Nkunda) escalated yet again into large-scale fighting. In the following months, it caused displacement of more than 500,000 people as well as several massacres and numerous horrific human rights violations. Nkunda threatened to march across the Congo to seize power in Kinshasa, Rwanda's support of Nkunda's group became increasingly clear, and Angola offered to return to the Congo in support of President Kabila. As the specter of a renewed regional and national war loomed larger, international interveners switched their focus from the Ituri district to the Kivus. MONUC redeployed 90% of its troops – including some previously based in Ituri – to the Kivus, and the UN Secretary-General requested that the EU send a multilateral force to help stabilize the situation, a request that the EU seriously considered fulfilling. This change in focus is especially interesting because violence escalated in Ituri at the exact same time as it did in the Kivus. In Ituri, local militias launched military operations that caused the displacement of more than 250,000 people, as well as extensive fighting. However, there was virtually no media coverage of the Ituri situation and no mention of a multilateral force because, in contrast to the situation in the Kivus, the Ituri fighting had no clear regional and national dimensions.

It is important to note that these shocking events had only a limited and temporary impact during the period of the transition. They generated increased international involvement, attention, and resources – including some support of bottom-up conflict resolution – in response to these specific situations, but they did not yield broader revisions of the dominant narratives. Analyzing the failed attempts at contestation documented earlier in this chapter helps explain why the shocking events failed to trigger a reinterpretation of the environment as a whole and of the role of international actors within it.

Understanding Failures

The Defeat of Contestation

A host of converging and mutually reinforcing elements account for the failure of contestation.[42] Most fundamentally, the reform attempts threatened entrenched organizational interests. For diplomats and UN staffers, conceding that local peacebuilding was a priority would have ultimately required undergoing extensive training in bottom-up conflict resolution. Alternatively, they would have had to admit that their expertise was insufficient and that their superiors needed to hire new people who might eventually replace them. For the entire organization, this concession meant embarking on an extensive process of change – creation of new departments, new standard operating procedures, new funding and operating patterns – which would be challenging and time-consuming, especially when staff members already felt overwhelmed by their daily work. Finally, for bureaucracies such as the UN and embassies, considering work on local conflicts would have signified something paramount: It would have challenged their very identity, which (as detailed in chapter 3) centered on the notion that they were macro-level international organizations.

Resistance to change also persisted because the alternative strategy outlined earlier (focusing on micro-level conflicts in addition

---

[42] This analysis builds on the research on resistance to change in Barnett and Finnemore 2004; Eden 2004; Weaver 2008; and Weick 1995.

to macro-level tensions and prioritizing security building over the organization of elections) fundamentally clashed with existing cultural norms. As detailed in chapter 3, the norm of nonintervention in a state's domestic affairs, especially if that state is a former colony, became very powerful on the international scene in the second half of the twentieth century. Most international actors therefore found the idea of micro-level intervention outrageous, to such an extent that they often disparaged its advocates, designating them "paternalists," "neocolonialists," and "neoimperialists." Similarly, elections had become so closely equated with democracy in the late twentieth century that international interveners immediately perceived a contestation of swift elections as a rejection of the very idea of democracy.

Considering the focus on elections, Western peacebuilders' fear of other options also probably played a critical role. A Western diplomat explained what many of his diplomatic and UN colleagues had implied: The belief that "there is no alternative [to democracy through elections] to consider" is "still deeply embedded in many Western cultures." Western actors never questioned the electoral principle because doing so would have "open[ed] a Pandora's box" and led them to consider strategies such as installing a benevolent dictator, which clashed with their most ingrained values. This interviewee emphasized that, if his colleagues accepted the possibility that elections might not be the solution to war, their "whole worldview," their "paradigm for understanding the world," would disintegrate, and they would have nothing to replace it with. To prevent such a plight, diplomats and UN staff repeated the same refrain throughout the entire transition, as if they meant to convince themselves as much as their Congolese counterparts that "there [was] no alternative" to elections.

The significance of these organizational stakes in maintaining the dominant narrative explains why contestation could succeed only in small, young agencies, where the organizational culture and structure were still fluid (such as Life and Peace Institute or Search for Common Ground); in the much larger and older bureaucracies, the structures, identities, and expertise were firmly ingrained and taken for granted. The considerable organizational and normative stakes these bureaucracies had in preserving the status quo also help illuminate the significant personal antagonisms against advocates of increased international involvement in local peacebuilding, such as Lena Sundh, Reginald Moreels, or Hans Romkema, though nothing in their personalities appeared to invite it. These enormous stakes similarly help explain why the contesters' actions bred such resentment when flaws in their plans, though significant, were reparable. Finally, acknowledging these stakes elucidates why, during my research, probing the issue of what UN and diplomatic actors concretely did to end local violence often generated defensive or aggressive reactions. A diplomat who had been polite and respectful during most of the interview became increasingly and outwardly bored when I began asking follow-up questions about his embassy's actions on local violence. Several others started laughing. In many cases, diplomats and UN officials who had been friendly eventually became annoyed at my questions about local efforts. The few people I know who tried to raise the same issue with UN officials encountered similar reactions.

In these circumstances, only very powerful advocates could have managed to induce a movement for reform. But those who contested the focus on macro developments, the elections fetishism, the postconflict label, and the view of violence as innate to the Congolese were far from being the dominant actors within their organization or on the global stage. Congolese civil society members have historically been marginalized and deprived of access to discursive space on the international scene.[43] Nongovernmental agencies, the other main source of contestation, have much less power than diplomats or international organizations. Within embassies, the dissenting voices came mainly from the development branches, which are always much less regarded and thus overshadowed by the political or economic departments. The same held for MONUC. The UN valued MONUC's electoral and political affairs sections more highly than the mission's humanitarian, human rights, or civil affairs departments, as evidenced by the number of people deployed in each unit and their ranks. In the field, the head of the political affairs or the electoral section was often the number two, just below the head of office, whereas the heads of the humanitarian, human rights, or civil affairs sections were much lower in the hierarchy. Along the same lines, the few MONUC political affairs officers who did highlight the role of local conflict were always junior members and often newcomers. The only exception was Lena Sundh, who held the second highest position in the mission. Yet, according to many accounts, she did not benefit from the credibility,

---

[43] Dunn 2003.

power, and influence usually attached to such a rank. Many interviewees said that this was because she was a woman, and because she
did not have a traditional family with children, something that might
have redeemed her in her male colleagues' eyes.

The Limited Impact of Shocking Events

At this point in the analysis, it becomes easier to understand why
the five types of shocking events had only a limited and temporary
impact. They removed the organizational incentives to maintain the
status quo, but they did not affect the existing cultural norms.

The shocking events, in fact, changed only one of the elements of
the peacebuilding culture analyzed in this book: the categorization of
the Congo as a "postconflict" situation. As the only element that had
been formed through practice during the transition, it was still fluid
and not yet fully taken for granted. Congolese civilians, humanitarian
and human rights activists, and some journalists reverted to the word
"war" when referring to each of the aforementioned striking cases.
The effect was particularly significant to the UN. Whereas recatego-
rizing the Congo as a war situation did not in any way jeopardize the
continued existence of embassies, foreign ministries, or nongovernmental agencies, it did threaten MONUC's and the UN's Department
of Peacekeeping Operations' organizational survival. Because the
existence of relative peace is one of the essential criteria for the deployment of UN peacekeeping missions (UN missions are supposed, quite
literally, to keep the peace, not to make it), in times of crises many
MONUC officials worried that the UN Security Council would withdraw the mission from a country where there was, as they put it, "no
peace to keep." Furthermore, the resources that the UN expended on
the Congo were so massive that in many Western capitals diplomats
voiced similar admonitions: The Congo was a test case for UN peacekeeping; member states would see war resumption there as a proof
that, even when given a strong mandate and enormous resources, UN
missions were ineffective.[44] The stakes of failure were so high for the
UN that they partly explain the divergence of responses to the murder
of peacekeepers in Rwanda in 1994, which prompted withdrawal,
and in the Congo in the mid-2000s, which prompted increased intervention. (Other reasons for the more aggressive response in the Congo

---

[44] For public sources, see the documents cited in chapter 1, footnote 25.

probably include the presence of a different leadership – in both the field and headquarters – and the influence of the "lessons learned" from Rwanda and Somalia).

The specter of genocide, the horrific violence, and the acknowledgment of the micro–macro relationships demonstrated to international actors that their overall strategy was failing and, therefore, provoked a greater degree of local involvement. However, these shocking events did not affect the elements of the peacebuilding culture that predated the international engagement in the Congo and fueled the resistance to change: the norms of nonintervention, the promotion of democracy through elections, and the understanding of extensive violence as "normal" for the Congo. Rather, the shocking events reinforced some of these norms and ideas. As happens in most instances of social life, international actors often interpreted the new information provided by shocking events as a confirmation of existing beliefs.[45] They attributed large-scale fighting to regional and national leaders, thus further justifying their action at the macro level. They also perceived horrific violence in Ituri or the Kivus as further evidence of the "barbaric" character of the Congolese people. Therefore, the goal of their increased international involvement was merely to bring the situation back to "normal" – meaning, to a level of violence they considered normal for a peaceful Congo.

Constructing Constraints

The defeat of contestation allowed a vicious circle to continue, as this section explains. Constraints, interests, and dominant collective understandings mutually constituted and reinforced one another. In the process, international actors perceived constraints on action at the local level as insurmountable obstacles to bottom-up peacebuilding. This perception perpetuated the view of local conflict resolution as an ineffective, illegitimate, and unmanageable task. It also reinforced the international actors' tendency to rely on what was familiar: the checklist approach to postconflict settlement detailed in chapter 3, with its predefined tasks, organizational guidelines, and standard operating procedures that failed to deal with local conflict. The view of local

---

[45] See chapter 1, p.30 for more details on this widespread psychological phenomenon.

peacebuilding as ineffective and the resort to a checklist approach to intervention, in turn, heightened the perceived constraints on local-level involvement.

Bureaucratic Structures and Available Expertise

To understand the process at stake, a comparison of the local conflict-resolution efforts with the organization of the elections is illuminating. Similar degrees of logistical, security, financial, and human resource constraints confronted the two endeavors. However, perceptions of elections and local conflict resolution, and the resulting intellectual and material toolkits available to work on both issues, differed so significantly that international actors deemed the constraints manageable in the case of the former and insurmountable in the case of the latter.

As detailed in chapter 3, in the case of elections, international actors could rely on a body of knowledge, standard operating procedures, preexisting bureaucracies, and predefined indicators; these tools enabled peacebuilders to consider the existing constraints on organizing elections as difficulties they could overcome. By contrast, no such intellectual and material toolkits were available for local conflict resolution. The process was thus the opposite of that which developed around the organization of elections.

None of the international bureaucracies involved in peacebuilding, such as the UN and the diplomatic missions, had ever developed any organizational capacity to address local conflicts. None had any specialized unit for grassroots peacebuilding, standard operating procedures to address bottom-up problems, and predefined indicators to measure the successful completion of the task. Nor was there any ready-made analytical framework to understand decentralized conflict; the only available tools were the inapt "postconflict" model, the greed framework, and the idea of Congolese as barbarians. Finally, UN staff and diplomats had no training for work at the local level. MONUC staff, for example, lacked basic skills in conflict resolution – even more so in *local* conflict resolution – and the UN offered no instructional program to compensate for its staff's lack of expertise.[46] According to several MONUC officials, even their political affairs officers lacked

---

[46] See Staibano 2005, p. 17, for a public source.

proper analytical and information-gathering skills. Diplomats, be they from European, American, or African countries, were not much better prepared. During my interviews, whenever I asked a diplomat if he had received training on local peacebuilding, either before or after entering his foreign ministry, he always replied in the negative.

This lack of familiarity with local conflict analysis shaped diplomats' and international organization officials' interpretation of continuing violence. As detailed in chapters 2 and 3, they found (or privileged) information indicating that conflict in the eastern provinces was a top-down problem. The lack of organizational capacity for local peacebuilding also shaped the diplomats', UN staffers', and nongovernmental organization officials' perception of local conflict resolution as an unmanageable task. During interviews, they often complained that bottom-up peacebuilding was a very complicated endeavor that required "experts" and specialized instruments – which most interviewees believed their organizations lacked – and yielded results that could not be properly evaluated. Finally, and most important, the international peacebuilders' unfamiliarity with local conflict analysis, and the lack of organizational capacity for local peacebuilding, led them to see constraints on grassroots action as insurmountable obstacles rather than conquerable hurdles.

Congolese Sovereignty

Consider one of the main constraints international actors claimed they would face if they decided to engage in local conflict resolution: the sovereignty of the Congolese state. Diplomats and UN staffers argued that local conflicts were an internal matter (all the more so when interveners viewed decentralized violence as a mere criminal problem). From this point of view, as in any sovereign country, national authorities had the greatest legitimacy to address such internal issues. As a result, in the words of a MONUC official, it was "not necessary, [or] even legitimate," for interveners to deal with questions other than the national peace process.

However, Congolese sovereignty was not an absolute constraint. To begin with, the UN charter specifies that the noninterference principle "shall not prejudice the application of enforcement measures under Chapter VII." (Chapter VII details what the UN can do to manage threats to international peace and security and legitimates peacekeeping missions such as the one deployed in the Congo.) As ongoing local conflicts were precisely a threat to international peace and security, as argued in chapter 4, the UN Charter allowed interference in these circumstances. Most significant, as explained in chapter 3, UN staff and diplomats overlooked Congolese sovereignty whenever they deemed it necessary. They closely supervised the writing of the new constitution, the organization of elections, and various legislative processes – all principally matters of national sovereignty. The international work on the constitution gives a good sense of the degree of interference this supervision entailed. Throughout the first year of the transition, international actors held regular meetings with their Congolese counterparts to spell out the donors' expectations. They "corrected" the various drafts judged too undemocratic; they ensured that Congolese representatives duly followed international "advice" (including threatening to cut off all aid should Congolese politicians remain firm on their positions), and they posted "experts" in various institutions to help with the technical side of the process.

International actors did not interpret state sovereignty as inhibiting their involvement in electoral and constitutional matters for two reasons. First, as explained in chapter 2, they could fulfill their task through interactions with state elites. Second, the dominant discourse on sovereignty evolved in the twentieth century and, progressively, humanitarian goals became legitimate reasons for ignoring state sovereignty, especially in Africa.[47] As a result, in the 1990s the UN designed a new generation of peace operations, labeled "multidimensional," to work in "areas long thought to be the exclusive domain of domestic jurisdiction."[48] In the case of the Congo, this evolving discursive construction enabled international actors to legitimize overlooking Congolese sovereignty to address what they saw as the cause of the humanitarian and security problems of the region (for example, Mobutu in the late 1990s and the lack of elected – and thus legitimate – leadership in the 2000s). By contrast, because international actors did not acknowledge the critical role of local conflict in causing humanitarian problems or in threatening international peace and security, they viewed sovereignty as an insurmountable obstacle to their involvement at the grassroots level.

[47] Finnemore 1996a; and Dunn 2003.   [48] Doyle, Johnstone, et al. 1997.

Mandate "Constraints"

The same argument applies for mandate constraints, which MONUC staff members often presented as another primary reason why they could not work on local conflict resolution. In interviews, UN officials explained that peacekeeping missions derive their authority from a peace agreement, and that the Congolese accord focused on regional and national reconciliation, not on local politics. They also emphasized that the UN Security Council had never given MONUC the right or the duty to work on grassroots peacebuilding and argued that they therefore could not legitimately do so.

In fact, the topic of local conflict resolution never even reached the agendas of high-level meetings. The UN Security Council resolutions specifying MONUC's mandate neither supported nor proscribed local peacebuilding; they did not even mention the issue. During interviews, diplomats and UN officials based outside the Congo presented local conflict resolution as an unimportant initiative exclusively in the domain of field officers.

More important, the mandates defining the roles of peacekeeping missions are always vague; they provide a broad orientation for the mission but do not go into much detail. They require interpretation, which gives the missions' political leaders and the various peacekeeping contingents substantial leeway.[49] For example, in its resolution 1493 (July 2003), the UN Security Council initially stated MONUC's role was "to provide assistance, during the transition period, for the reform of the security forces, the reestablishment of a state based on the rule of law and the preparation and holding of elections, throughout the territory of the Democratic Republic of the Congo."[50] This definition was so ambiguous that, a year later, the Secretary-General admitted in one of his reports on MONUC that "the interpretation of Security Council Resolution 1493 (2003) ha[d] been a major challenge for MONUC over the past year." He also lamented "the lack of specifics as to [MONUC's] tasks under [this] resolution."[51]

Furthermore, throughout the transition, different MONUC leaders and military commanders interpreted the same mandate in dissimilar

---

[49] For a public source, see Holt and Berkman 2006.
[50] UN Security Council 2003b, para. 5.
[51] UN Security Council 2004d, paras. 58 and 59.

ways. The Nepalese battalion stationed in Ituri in 2006, for example, interpreted the MONUC mandate as requiring direct military action against militias to protect the population. The Pakistani battalion stationed in North Kivu simultaneously interpreted the same mandate as allowing military involvement to protect the population only on an ad-hoc basis. Meanwhile, the Indian battalion stationed in South Kivu interpreted the mandate as forbidding direct engagement with militias and only allowing the support of Congolese troops.

The flexibility in deciphering the mandate was the same concerning local conflict resolution.[52] Although most MONUC officials blamed mandate constraints for their lack of action, other actors regularly interpreted MONUC's mandate as including local peacebuilding. As detailed earlier in this chapter, virtually all of the diplomats I interviewed, including representatives (or colleagues of representatives) to the UN Security Council, considered local initiatives as part of MONUC's role. Several UN Secretary-General's Reports on MONUC, written just before the beginning of the transition and during its early stages, also mentioned local reconciliation as one of MONUC's responsibilities. And a high-ranking MONUC officer based in New York similarly agreed that his field colleagues were in charge of grassroots peacebuilding efforts.

All in all, MONUC's mandate was no more an absolute constraint on its local-level involvement than was Congolese sovereignty. What transformed a vague mandate into an insurmountable obstacle was the way in which field implementers perceived and interpreted their instructions. Except for a few individuals, the interveners saw their mandate as proscribing MONUC involvement in local conflicts because, under the influence of dominant peacebuilding culture, they considered grassroots peacebuilding to be an ineffective, unfamiliar, and illegitimate task for international actors.

Contextual "Constraints"

Contextual constraints, which international actors presented as yet another significant obstacle to their involvement at the local level, were not absolute either; rather they were constructed differently depending on whether the peacebuilders were considering elections

---

[52] See also Staibano 2005; and Sundh 2004.

or decentralized conflict resolution. Regional and national actors, including spoilers, could (and sometimes did) derail the electoral process in the same way as they could (and sometimes did) disrupt micro-level peacebuilding projects. The collapse of the state bureaucracy in many eastern provinces hampered any kind of initiative that required state support, be it the organization of elections or local conflict resolution. The unceasing security problems affected the electoral process by preventing freedom of campaigning, endangering candidates, and limiting access to unstable areas. To a similar extent, lack of security affected local peacebuilding initiatives by imperiling local peacebuilders and restricting access to unstable locales. The lack of roads and communication infrastructure limited travel in a way that was equally problematic for both the organization of elections and local peacebuilding. International interveners had to surmount the overwhelming complexity of the politicomilitary situation in the case of both elections (to ensure the "fairness" of the electoral process) and local peacebuilding (to find solutions acceptable to all parties). Finally, Congolese society was so polarized (as discussed in chapter 3) that the population saw electoral agents with about the same level of suspicion as they perceived local peacebuilders.

However, because international actors viewed elections as the top priority of any postconflict environment, they devoted massive logistical, financial, and human resources to their implementation and thus surmounted many logistical constraints. Had international actors only realized the critical need to address local tensions, they could have redistributed their logistical, financial, and human resources toward local peacebuilding projects. These additional resources would have helped overcome many obstacles to local peacebuilding.

The views on the organization of elections as a technical engineering task – and not as a multidimensional, abstract concept like local peacebuilding – were also influential in helping interveners manage contextual constraints. With the technical approach to elections, there was no need to know too much about the context or to interact with the Congolese population. It was also possible to work in a top-down manner, at the regional and national levels, and thus to stay in safe places like Kinshasa or the neighboring capitals. Finally, it was feasible to design a simple and straightforward answer (the organization of elections) to a very complex question (how to build democracy in the Congo). This is not to say that international actors should have approached local conflict resolution as a technical endeavor. Doing so would have negated the point of local conflict-resolution initiatives, just as seeing elections organization as simply a technical engineering problem decreased the potential benefits of the electoral process. Rather, this observation serves to emphasize how appreciably the peacebuilding culture shaped the constraints that actors perceived as external and insurmountable. Though it would not be preferable, international interveners *could* have approached local peacebuilding in a technical manner and developed template projects and predefined indicators to use in any conflict environment. Doing so would have enabled them to design at least some simple, manageable solutions to complex problems, and thus to overcome to some extent what they perceived as insurmountable contextual obstacles to micro-level involvement.

A Vicious Circle

The various processes documented in this section helped perpetuate the dominant narratives on the causes of violence and the role of international actors. The international perception of the sovereignty, mandate, and contextual constraints as insurmountable obstacles reinforced a dominant historical frame: that of Africa as a hopeless place where nothing can be done to improve the situation.[53] International peacebuilders developed a "sense of 'powerlessness' that led them to deny their capacity for action."[54] Despite their apparent influence over the country, they felt increasingly unable to end the decentralized violence they witnessed. In these circumstances, two distinct psychological processes combined to construct violence as normal. As I observed through years of interactions with expatriates stationed in the Congo, and as I myself experienced, after seeing or hearing about many human rights violations, international actors became numb to them. Foreign interveners also intellectually deflected violence, as detailed in chapter 2, by understanding it as long-standing.

---

[53] See Shaw 2007 on this historical frame.
[54] This development builds on the analysis of UN inaction in Rwanda in Barnett 2002 (quotation from p. 10). For a public source on the Congo, see "Congo – Un entretien exclusif avec le responsable des opérations de maintien de la paix de l'ONU Guéhenno: 'Si on réussit, c'est toute l'Afrique qui repart'," *Le Soir*, April 23, 2005.

This latter mechanism reinforced the dominant international perception of local violence as a normal feature of life in a peaceful Congo. In turn, the view of violence as an insignificant matter led many intermediaries to filter out data on local conflicts when they transmitted information from UN field offices to the UN headquarters (and the information was filtered even further between the UN field offices and the various embassies and foreign ministries). This lack of information reinforced the international actors' difficulties in analyzing local conflict and their puzzlement over which solutions they could implement.

The view of decentralized conflict as secondary also bolstered the tendency to base virtually all diplomats and high-ranking UN staff members in the capital. This course was problematic because diplomats could not build on their experiences of life and work in Kinshasa to understand the violence that marred the eastern provinces. Kinshasa was, in fact, a completely different world. The physical distance between the two places is immense (1,500 kilometers or 930 miles, the same distance as between Munich and Madrid, or between Boston and Atlanta). This problem is compounded by a very poor transport infrastructure; because there is no road, the only way to go from the capital to the eastern provinces is either by foot or by plane. During the transition, Kinshasa felt like a well-developed, lively city. It had relatively good roads, public lighting, well-equipped soldiers and police officers, and classy shops, bars, and restaurants. By contrast, the eastern provinces looked shabby, miserable, and utterly underdeveloped. The Congolese population in both locations also focused on very different issues. Kinshasa's inhabitants discussed elections, economy and employment, and the popular political debates of the time, while eastern Congolese talked about violence, Rwanda's threats, and the presence of Rwandan Hutu militias.[55] Furthermore, although Kinshasa was the stage of large-scale fighting in the earliest phases of the generalized conflicts, the war barely affected the capital after 1998, apart from some disruptions in food supplies. As a result, Kinshasa was mostly peaceful during the transition, while the eastern provinces were not, and the overall experience of the wars was quite dissimilar for the two populations.

[55] See Vinck, Pham, Baldo, and Shigekane 2008, for a comprehensive analysis of the different perspectives on the various conflicts that residents of Kinshasa and the eastern provinces held.

The UN staff's and diplomats' lack of first-hand knowledge of violence strengthened their tendency to underestimate both the consequences of local tensions in the eastern provinces and the need for intervention. For example, an internal inquiry into the UN's failure to prevent the May 2004 generalized fighting in South Kivu faulted, in part, the Kinshasa staff's tendency to dismiss field reports as overly alarmist.[56] More broadly, according to many interviewees, the lack of intimate knowledge of decentralized violence led diplomats and UN management staff to misjudge the difficulties inherent in local conflict resolution in the eastern Congo. They therefore miscalculated the logistical, security, financial, and human resources necessary for such action.[57] According to several interviewees, the diplomats' lack of familiarity with the situation in the eastern provinces also fueled the already existing funding constraints on Congolese agencies involved in grassroots peacebuilding, because donors had difficulties discriminating between promising and faulty projects. This problem, along with the lack of interaction between donors and nongovernmental organizations based in the eastern Congo (as opposed to those agencies based in Kinshasa), resulted in the financing of many more projects around the capital than in the eastern provinces. Most important, all of these elements reinforced the international interveners' feeling of powerlessness, resistance to contestation, and tendency to focus on macro-level developments.

Conclusion

Adding a bottom-up component to the top-down strategy would have been possible, and it would have contributed tremendously to building peace in the Congo. However, a combination of deeply entrenched cultural norms and organizational interests made most international peacebuilders highly resistant to change that would facilitate their increased involvement in local conflict resolution. Contestation (from inside and outside the main peacebuilding bureaucracies) and shocking events therefore failed to prompt staff members to update their understanding of the causes of violence and their roles.

[56] UN Mission in the Democratic Republic of Congo (MONUC) 2005b.
[57] For a public source, see Samset and Madore 2006, section 3.1.3.

Throughout the transition, most international actors continued to perceive local tensions as a secondary cause of violence and grassroots conflict resolution as an unfeasible and illegitimate task. This collective understanding shaped not only the overall intervention strategy away from micro-level involvement, but also the international actors' perception of the obstacles they would have faced had they tried to become involved at the grassroots level. They viewed the institution of sovereignty, as well as mandate, financial, logistical, and human limitations as absolute constraints instead of manageable problems. As a result, interveners let local tensions fester to the point where they jeopardized the macro-level settlements many times both during and after the transition.

6 | *Beyond the Congo*

The e-mail signature of Kemal Saiki, the spokesperson of the United Nations Mission in the Congo (MONUC) during most of the transition, included a fitting – and quite clichéd – quotation attributed to the British leader and political theorist Edmund Burke: "All that's necessary for the forces of evil to win in the world is for enough good men to do nothing." Saiki probably did not recognize the irony. During the Congolese transition, the "good men" staffing his organization, the diplomatic missions, and most nongovernmental agencies did nothing to assuage local tensions. As a result, the "forces of evil" – or, in modern language, the perpetrators of massive human right violations – won the eastern Congo.

This book started with a puzzle: Even though the Congo is the stage of intense international peacebuilding efforts, and even though it recently experienced a transition from war to "peace and democracy," it continues to be plagued by the deadliest conflict since World War II. Why did the international intervention fail to help the Congo achieve lasting peace and security? I proposed a straightforward answer. Bottom-up rivalries over land, resources, and political power explain, in large part, why organized violence persisted in the eastern provinces after the Congo was supposedly at peace, and why war resumed in late 2008. However, a dominant peacebuilding culture shaped the intervention strategy in a way that precluded action on local conflicts. Most international actors interpreted "postconflict" fighting as the consequence of regional and national tensions alone. United Nations (UN) staff and diplomats viewed intervention at the macro levels as their only legitimate responsibility. Local peacebuilding was such an unimportant, unfamiliar, and unmanageable task that even the magnitude of the disaster could not impel international peacebuilders to augment their efforts at the local level.

By way of conclusion, this chapter first provides an appraisal of the international intervention and the prevailing explanations for

its relative failure. I then synthesize the argument presented in the
book and emphasize its theoretical significance: a new explanation
for peacebuilding failures. The first section recapitulates the argument on the Congo; the next demonstrates that attention to the dominant peacebuilding culture and local-level dynamics helps illuminate
multiple cases of international intervention success or failure beyond
the Congo, in Africa and elsewhere. The chapter ends by detailing
key policy recommendations to improve international interventions
in civil wars.

Why Did the International Intervention Fail to Help the Congo Build Peace and Democracy?

The Intervention's Meager Results

In December 2006, the Congo inaugurated newly elected President
Joseph Kabila, thus "bringing the transition process envisaged by the
Global and All-Inclusive Agreement of 2002 to a formal conclusion."[1]
At that time, the media overflowed with jubilant statements such as
"the Congo is at peace" or "the Congo is a democracy" from journalists, Congolese leaders, foreign diplomats, and staff of international
and nongovernmental organizations. A few months later, in his first
report on MONUC written after the end of the transition (March
2007), the UN Secretary-General presented a less optimistic appraisal
of the situation. Despite a positive tone, he noted few successes:

The Transitional Government, with massive support from the United
Nations and the international community, made considerable progress
towards the objectives of the 2002 Global and All-Inclusive Agreement,
particularly regarding the reunification of the country; the initial integration of [the Congolese army]; the adoption, through a national referendum,
of the new Constitution; and the holding of national elections. However,
significant aspects of the transition agenda remain to be completed, particularly with respect to [Congolese and foreign] armed groups [mostly in
Ituri, the Kivus and Katanga], local elections, transitional justice and the
promotion of reconciliation relating to ethnic tensions and serious human
rights violations.[2]

---

[1] UN Security Council 2007c, para. 2.   [2] Ibid., para. 23.

Grim as this appraisal already was, it was still overly bright. It is true that, in 2007, the country was no longer divided into several areas of control as it was during the war, but pockets of rebellions remained in the eastern provinces – under the control of Nkunda's forces in North Kivu, Rwandan Hutu rebel groups in North and South Kivu, and various local Congolese militias in the Kivus, Katanga, and Ituri. Moreover, the "initial integration of the Congolese Army" that the report praises was just that – a project in its preliminary stages.

We can actually credit the international intervention during the Congolese transition with two major accomplishments. The first was the organization of general elections and the installation of the elected officials. These elections provided the demoralized Congolese population with a source of pride and a newfound belief in their political system, and they introduced an element of competition and democracy to the Congo's previously dictatorial politics. They also provided international financial institutions and bilateral donors with a governmental partner that they perceived as reliable, ultimately leading to a significant increase in international funds for the Congo after 2007.

The second accomplishment was the general easing of macro-level tensions. Most of the fighting between regional and national factions ended, and MONUC prevented the Congo from sliding back into a full-scale national and regional war during the transitional period. The elite actors' manipulation of local armed groups also decreased. As a result, the living conditions for the majority of the Congolese population improved significantly. Even in the eastern provinces, some of the fighting-related displacement, forced conscription, and violence against civilians disappeared. In time, many women came to no longer fear rape (or murder) on the way to their fields. Trade resumed between areas formerly closed to one another because competing armed groups had controlled them. Farmers restarted small-scale investment, particularly in livestock. Displaced people began to return to their villages. Humanitarian access expanded in most of the provinces, and many places formerly inaccessible for security reasons finally opened to humanitarian organizations.

However, the international intervention failed to achieve its two main objectives: building peace and installing democracy in the Congo. The security situation remained extremely precarious in certain parts of the eastern provinces. Despite the noteworthy improvement mentioned here, all UN and nongovernmental organizations' reports during the transition still told of much fighting, population displacement, massacres, cannibalism, rape, torture, killing, looting, extortion, and other serious violations of human rights, especially in the eastern Congo. Toward the end of the transition, violence in North Kivu reached "a scale and intensity not seen since the height of the war in 2000."[3] In the year following the elections, fighting and riots occurred in Kinshasa, Ituri, the province of Bas-Congo, and the Kivus. Unceasing, large-scale fighting resumed in 2007 and persisted in the Kivus and Oriental Province until the time of this writing in late 2009.

Furthermore, the elections did not give birth to democracy but instead to a competitive autocracy, a system with relatively competitive elections but autocratic governance in the interim.[4] In the Congo, the new administration neglected public matters, tightly controlled the justice system, and appointed highly corrupt officials to top positions. Kabila also set out to bribe part of the opposition into joining him and physically eliminate the rest. In March 2007, his presidential guard shelled the house of Jean-Pierre Bemba, a former rebel leader and the runner-up to the presidential seat in the 2006 elections. Bemba had to flee to Europe shortly afterward, and many of Bemba's suspected supporters were subject to arrest and torture. In the subsequent years, the Bureau of the National Assembly excluded opposition members, and in the provinces Kabila's allies set out to harass and slowly destroy their rivals.[5]

The broader socioeconomic conditions did not improve much either during the transition. In his first report on MONUC after the 2006 elections, the UN Secretary-General noted:

Social indicators are dismal. Life expectancy stands at 43 years, and mortality of children under 5 years of age is above 220 per thousand. An estimated 16 million people suffer critical food needs. Gross domestic product per capita stood at about $120 in 2005, and 75 percent of the

---

[3] Quotation from International Crisis Group 2007a, p. 1.
[4] Stephen Smith, "Conflict in the Congo: Prospect for Peace," Seminar Series, New School, April 2008.
[5] Human Rights Watch 2007 and 2008b. See also Fédération Internationale des Ligues des Droits de l'Homme 2009 for a broad overview of the Kabila regime's drift toward authoritarianism.

population lives on less than one dollar a day. The Democratic Republic of the Congo ranked 167th out of the 177 countries in the [UN Development Programme's] *Human Development Report 2006*.[6]

As a result, and despite the previously expressed wishes of most UN member states to withdraw the peacekeeping mission once elections occurred, the level of international support to the UN operations in the Congo actually increased after the vote transpired. In late December 2006, the Security Council authorized the deployment of 916 additional MONUC soldiers tasked primarily with ending the persisting violence in the eastern provinces. In his March 2007 report, the UN Secretary-General requested the same extensive mandate, at the same level of force, and with the same budget, to fulfill almost exactly the same duties that MONUC had undertaken during the transition – including a focus on organizing local elections. Despite reservations, the UN Security Council decided to provide MONUC with this mandate and these resources for fear that otherwise the Congo might slide back into a full-scale war. Even with this assistance, late in 2008 fighting in North Kivu escalated to such a point that the UN Special Representative of the Secretary-General for the Congo requested a still more dramatic increase in troop numbers. Everyone – journalists, Congolese leaders, foreign diplomats, Congolese civilians – lamented that the Congo was back at war. In November 2008, the Security Council approved yet another increase of 3,000 troops to stabilize the Kivus. As of this writing in late 2009, the UN mission is much larger than it was during the transition, and the UN Security Council has granted it an even stronger mandate.

Was the International Intervention Truly a Failure?

This renewed fighting and the return to authoritarian control do not necessarily establish the international intervention as a failure. Two sets of arguments support the view that, at least in the eyes of the interveners, the intervention was a success. During professional conferences, political scientists emphasized that the foreign interveners may have ended up with just what they desired: a functioning government, legitimate in the eyes of its international partners (since it was

---

[6] UN Security Council 2007c, para. 38.

"democratically elected"), both willing and able to meet international obligations. Congolese civilians were often even more cynical; they said that the international interveners were, in fact, happy to see that instability persisted in the Congo, because it enabled them to exploit Congolese natural resources more easily.

If the international peacebuilders' only goal had been to set up a functioning government in the Congo, however, they would have withdrawn the peacekeeping troops after the 2006 general elections. If foreign interveners had wanted to maintain disorder in the eastern provinces, they would also have pulled out the UN troops. Yet, not only did MONUC stay but, as explained previously, donors even expanded and strengthened the mission. The strategy developed by the UN in 2007 and 2008, and later approved by the Security Council, also demonstrated that the states most involved in the Congolese peace process wanted much more than a legitimate government and were not pleased about the continued instability. Under this new plan, MONUC had to remain until most Congolese fighters were either integrated into the army or disarmed and demobilized, until the Congolese army and police were able to "assume responsibility for the country's security," and until local elections were organized.[7]

How politicians presented and understood their countries' interests during the Congolese transition also confirmed that the states most involved in supporting the Congolese peace process were not just trying to establish a functioning government or to perpetuate the instability in mineral-rich provinces. It is true that, in the mid-1990s, few Western states believed that it was in their economic or political interests to maintain a stable Congo. However, this position changed radically in 1998.[8] By the time the transition started in 2003, the states and international organizations most involved in the Congo – Belgium, the European Union (EU), France, South Africa, the United Kingdom, the UN, and the United States – understood their national interests as requiring a stable and peaceful country for several reasons. They could not afford to let the Congolese territory become a safe haven for terrorists. They needed to create an environment that would enable their national companies to conduct profitable business. They had to prevent the Congolese conflict from destabilizing their allies in central and southern Africa. Moreover, Belgium, the EU, France, the

[7] Ibid.   [8] See, for example, Gambino 2008, p. 12; and Willame 2007.

United Kingdom, and the UN wished to demonstrate that UN peace operations could be successful.

Despite this interest in the stability of the Congo, there was an important caveat. During the transition, the richest and most powerful countries placed the Congo as a low priority on their agenda, and the remaining countries and international organizations lacked the resources necessary to support the Congo fully in its peacebuilding efforts.[9]

The Bush administration considered the Congo to be a "low-intensity conflict" that did not threaten U.S. national interest, which, after 9/11, was defined mostly with respect to the risk of terrorism.[10] The U.S. government merely wanted to avert another collapse into chaos to ensure that the Congolese war would not continue to threaten African states of significance to U.S. foreign policy (especially Angola, Sudan, Uganda, Tanzania, and Rwanda). Ensuring a degree of stability in the Congo was also a way to preserve mining access for U.S. corporations, particularly in Katanga.[11] These concerns stimulated some U.S. interest in the Congo, but not enough to make it a high-priority issue. The Congolese conflict was similarly a low-profile issue on the British agenda, linked mostly to the fear that a renewed crisis would destabilize several of the United Kingdom's close African allies, in particular Rwanda and Uganda. Along the same lines, the demographic weight of the Congo and its strategic position in Africa rendered it a crucial diplomatic partner for France and a key channel for French influence in Africa. However, the Congo remained less important to French foreign policy than former colonies such as Ivory Coast and Congo-Brazzaville.

In contrast, the African Union, South Africa, Belgium, and the EU perceived the Congo as critical to their foreign policy goals, but they lacked the financial, military, or diplomatic resources to follow through on their ambitions. The African Union could have carried a lot of weight during the Congolese transition, but massive difficulties in financing any kind of operation, as well as internal rivalries within the organization (most members sponsored or supported one of the Congolese combatant groups), thwarted this potential influence.

[9] See Prunier 2008, and Willame 2007 for public sources providing many details and evidence for the claims developed below.
[10] For a public source, see Willame 2002.
[11] For a public source, see Gambino 2008, p. 14.

South Africa wanted to create a stable environment in the Congo where its companies could easily trade – and, whenever possible, be favored. The government also wanted to affirm Thabo Mbeki's role as a peace broker and South Africa's position as a regional hegemon. However, South Africa's economic situation did not allow it to finance many actions outside its borders. President Mbeki also had to work on many other domestic and international crises (notably South African economic development and ending the war in Ivory Coast), which made the Congo only one among many foreign and domestic priorities.

Belgium had a different view: The Congo was a clear priority. Belgian politicians felt that they had inherited a moral debt toward the country because of their colonial past. They also considered themselves responsible for ensuring the well-being of the large Belgian diaspora living in Congolese territory, and for maintaining and sustaining the strong economic ties between the two countries. Belgium thus devoted massive political and financial resources to the Congo. However, its limited diplomatic and economic weight severely restricted the scale and impact of these contributions.

The EU did have the financial power necessary to be a key player, as it was the largest multilateral donor to the Congo. However, reluctance to share a common foreign and defense policy coupled with radically divergent positions on the Congo among the most influential member states hindered the EU delegation's ability to weigh in on potentially sensitive political issues. The EU representatives thus had to focus on consensual projects, such as financing the elections, or on issues that its member states perceived as less political, like humanitarian and development aid.

Finally, the UN's interest in the stabilization of the Congo was clear. As explained in chapter 5, the transitional Congo had become a test case for UN peacekeeping. During the transition, many UN officials dreaded a potential peacebuilding failure that would endanger the future of their organization. The UN therefore devoted considerable efforts and resources to the Congo, although, as detailed throughout the book, UN member states imposed significant financial and human resource limitations on the peacekeeping mission.

It is true that all states and organizations may have had hidden agendas. Various bureaucracies may have had different beliefs about what mattered most for their country and how to most effectively achieve the goals of peace and democracy building. Yet, one thing is clear: Such a high level of continuing violence in the eastern provinces was against the perceived interests of all of the countries or organizations most involved in the Congolese peace process. Why then did they fail to help the Congo achieve at least relative stability?

International peacebuilders are clearly not exclusively, or even predominantly, responsible for the failure of the Congolese peace process. The most blameworthy are certain Congolese actors at all levels, certain regional leaders, and certain individuals and companies involved in arms trafficking and the illegal exploitation of natural resources. Nonetheless, the international peacebuilders missed an excellent opportunity. With their financial, military, and human resources – limited, but nonetheless significant – and their willingness to overcome logistical and normative constraints whenever they considered the stakes high enough, international actors could have contributed much more significantly to establishing a sustainable peace and an emergent democracy in the Congo.

The Drawbacks of the Electoral Tool

The most convincing explanation for the failure of democracy building faults the swift organization of elections. Previous experience in states emerging from war has largely shown that elections organized within a few years of a peace settlement rarely promote democracy, whether they are organized at the national level (as during the transition) or at the local level (as might be done in 2011).[12] Two or three years are sufficient to arrange the technical and logistical aspects of the elections – such as registering electors, moving ballot boxes, and so on – and to ensure that voting can safely take place. In the Congo, these procedural tasks were accomplished successfully, and no major violence occurred on voting day. However, organizing voting is only one of the many tasks that must be completed to build democracy.[13] A democratic state requires strong political parties, local governments, a judicial system, and civil society. Elections also never address the

---

[12] Paris 2004 provides a book-length, multicase study demonstration of this point. Carothers 2002 also provides a compelling explanation of why elections do not guarantee democracy.

[13] Dahl 1989; and Diamond 1996.

structural problems, such as the unequal distribution of wealth, that create a gap between political elites and citizens and thus hinder both democracy and social cohesion; specific programs to address these issues are therefore required in addition to organizing the voting.[14]

Furthermore, elections can be fair, and thus provide legitimacy, only when certain preconditions exist, such as freedom of the press, of association, of expression, and of the judiciary.[15] These conditions take years to develop, and are rarely present in the immediate aftermath of a militarized conflict. The transitional Congo, for example, never enjoyed most of these freedoms. The ongoing insecurity and ethnic hatred made it impossible for many candidates, especially those from the population of Rwandan descent, to campaign freely and safely throughout the country. UN reports and Congolese interviewees documented many cases of intimidation and harassment of opposing presidential and provincial candidates by the dominant party.[16] Numerous arbitrary arrests of journalists and opposition supporters, as well as the torture of detainees, marred the electoral campaign. Voters were also vulnerable to intimidation by armed forces devoted to specific candidates.[17] Additionally, most parties refused to accept the finality of the electoral process, reserving the use of violence or corruption if results were unfavorable. In practice, they used both corruption and violence, and Kabila's allies proved the main offenders. Kabila's troops attacked opponent Bemba when the electoral commission named him as the runner-up for the presidential seat, and Kabila's party bought off provincial representatives in Kinshasa and Bas-Congo to ensure that the governorship of both provinces would go to men loyal to the president.[18]

Moreover, in a country where the population has never enjoyed democracy, civic education is essential to make the vote meaningful. It is a lengthy endeavor that, in a country devoid of infrastructure

---

[14] Carothers 2002.
[15] De Zeeuw 2005; Diamond 1996; Mansfield and Snyder 2005; and Snyder 2000.
[16] See most Secretary-General's reports on MONUC to the Security Council, 2005–2007, in particular, UN Security Council 2006e, para. 69. These sources also include data on some of the events mentioned in the rest of this paragraph.
[17] International Crisis Group 2006a, pp. 8–9; and Turner 2007, pp. 175–180.
[18] International Crisis Group 2007c, pp. 6–7 and 9–10.

like the Congo, requires much more than two or three years. As a result, the vote was largely meaningless in many rural areas, where approximately 70% of Congolese live. Up to the eve of the voting day, most rural interviewees did not know the objective of the elections or what was expected of them as voters. A series of interviews that I conducted with rural inhabitants of South Kivu in May 2005, just before the referendum on the new constitution, gives an idea of the extent of the problem. At that time, the presidential and legislative polls were still scheduled for the following month, June 2005. Most of my interviewees had never heard about the upcoming vote. The few who had heard of it possessed incorrect information. For example, one interviewee believed the elections would select the traditional chief for the southern part of Lemera territory, where she lived, and that all traditional chiefs would later elect the president. Another had heard that the elections would determine "the governor's advisor." Neither interviewee planned to participate in this round of elections; as illiterate women, they did not believe they were entitled to vote. I heard similar misconceptions in all of the interviews that I conducted with people living in rural areas throughout the eastern Congo between 2004 and 2006.

Not only did the international obsession with quick elections fail to ensure democracy, but it also jeopardized peace. The democratic reconstruction model presented in chapter 3, which was used in the Congo, disregards existing evidence that elections, especially when they occur immediately after a civil war, often increase tensions.[19] Electoral campaigns require the candidates to mobilize support by differentiating themselves from one another and criticizing their opponents, a process that contributes little to reconciliation between former enemies. In the Congo, as detailed in chapter 2, many candidates disparaged the "nonindigenous" to mobilize their followers, and their electoral campaigns served to enlarge the audience and power base of extremists. This strategy strongly increased the localized tensions in the Kivus.[20] Furthermore, in many provinces, the elections led to "a major power reconfiguration based on ethnicity and demography, which created a new imbalance" and increased the minorities' fears.[21]

[19] Paris 2004; Sisk and Reynolds 1998, pp. 150–151; and Snyder 2000.
[20] Boas 2008; and Kayser 2008.
[21] Quotation from International Crisis Group 2007a, p. 5.

In turn, these effects renewed instability in the Kivus and Kasai and destabilized Bas-Congo.

Even more important, the international peacebuilders' fixation on organizing voting and their unfounded belief that rapid elections would somehow improve the situation prevented them from devoting their resources to other critical peace- and state-building measures. For example, a consensus has emerged among policy analysts who study the transition, that international interveners should have done more to support security-sector reform.[22] From this point of view, the massive resources allocated to the electoral process would have made a significant difference had they been redistributed to this task.

Congolese and international actors, indeed, consistently faulted lack of funding for the slow progress in the reform of the security sector. They also blamed numerous logistical problems, which they believe MONUC could have overcome if it had used its capacities to help with army restructuring rather than organizing elections. Likewise, they noted that, though it was true that former armed group leaders lacked the motivation to integrate their troops, which slowed the integration of the army, this process nonetheless drastically accelerated after diplomats adopted the issue and increased pressure on their Congolese counterparts from late 2004 onward. Similarly, the diversion of funds for the army at all levels of the hierarchy was a major problem, but the situation improved tremendously once the EU started to supervise the disbursement process. Lack of candidates for military integration (since most soldiers chose to demobilize) would likely have remained problematic, but former militia members may have been more motivated if they could have expected regular payment and respectable living conditions on enrollment. Along the same lines, the massive resources devoted to the elections would have made a tremendous difference if they had been devoted to the police and the justice systems.

Beyond this retrospective consensus on the importance of the security-sector reform, one can also argue that the focus on elections distracted international attention from other key regional and national issues. For example, although MONUC repatriated more

[22] See, for example, Gambino 2008; International Crisis Group 2009; and Wolters and Boshoff 2006, among the many public sources available on the topic.

than 13,000 foreign combatants and their dependents, foreign militias – especially those from Rwanda – continued to wreak havoc in the eastern Congo and to poison the Rwanda–Congo relationship long after the transition ended.[23] Stronger security institutions in the Congo, additional pressure from countries able to influence Rwanda (such as the United States, the United Kingdom, and South Africa), and more resources for MONUC's Disarmament, Demobilization, Repatriation, Reintegration, and Resettlement program would probably have helped diminish this problem.

There were, in fact, many ways to spend international resources to make them more conducive to peace and democracy in the Congo, even given the existing constraints. In addition to the consensual suggestions detailed earlier, international actors could also have devoted their time, resources, and energy to protecting the Congolese population in immediate danger, or to building up a local human rights capacity. In truth, there were so many options that one may wonder how international peacebuilders could have decided among them.

Toward a New Understanding of Peacebuilding Failures

This book has suggested another way these resources could have been used, in a manner more conducive to peace than disproportionately focusing on elections, security-sector reform, or the repatriation of foreign militias. International peacebuilders should have devoted part of their time, efforts, and resources to local conflict resolution, because local tensions were crucial. Bottom-up conflict was, in fact, the main reason why violence continued during the transition, elections increased violence in several provinces, Congolese officers and soldiers resisted the security-sector reform so vigorously, and foreign militias continued to thrive in the Congo.

During the transition, just as before and during the war, violence was motivated not only by regional or national causes (such as the illegal exploitation of the Congolese natural resources by foreign armed groups or the struggle for power in Kinshasa), but also by longstanding bottom-up conflicts, whose main instigators included villagers, local traditional and administrative chiefs, and grassroots militia leaders. Even issues considered purely regional or national problems,

---

[23] Statistics from UN Security Council 2006e, para. 57.

such as the presence of foreign armed groups on Congolese territory
or the tensions between indigenous and Kinyarwanda-speaking communities, had important local dimensions. Grassroots agendas have
fueled micro- and macro-level violence throughout modern Congolese
history, and they continued to do so during the transition, eventually
jeopardizing the national and regional peace settlements. In parallel,
in the transitional period, some local conflicts became increasingly
autonomous from top-down developments, notably in South Kivu,
Katanga, and Ituri.

In these circumstances, why did international actors not devote as
much time, effort, and resources to assuaging decentralized tensions
as they did to solving the macro-level problems? When asked this
question, most interviewees mirrored the existing scholarly explanations for peacebuilding failures. International actors emphasized the
massive contextual, financial, legal, political, security, and human
resources constraints that they faced. However, they could have overcome these obstacles. In fact, they faced similarly daunting constraints
when organizing elections, but managed to rise above them.

As mentioned earlier, Congolese interviewees had a different point
of view, maintaining that international actors perpetuated violence
to ease access to Congolese natural resources, while in fact only a
few foreign individuals and companies did so. The vast majority of
international organizations and foreign countries were truthful in
their claims that their main goal was to support the Congo in its
transitional efforts. Their staff implemented what they genuinely considered the best strategy to help the Congo on the path toward peace
and democracy.

Members of diplomatic missions, international organizations, and
nongovernmental agencies overlooked decentralized conflict because
the dominant international peacebuilding culture shaped their understanding of violence and intervention in a way that precluded their
involvement at the local level. This culture included norms arising
from the world polity, notably the belief that the Congo was inherently violent and the view that elections were the best peacebuilding
mechanism. It also incorporated understandings shared only by the
actors of the international peacebuilding field, including, among others, the definition of the Congo as a postconflict situation, the conception that war and postwar violence resulted from top-down causes,
and the belief that the strategies used in violent environments (such

as direct negotiations with local actors) were unsuited to postconflict situations. Finally, this dominant culture included elements that were rooted in the specific identities of various international organizations, especially the UN and diplomatic staff's conception of their role as concerned exclusively with the macro level.

This prevailing peacebuilding culture shaped the international understanding of violence during the Congolese transition. Most international actors interpreted continued fighting as the consequence of regional and national tensions. They understood the hostilities that they could not relate to any regional or national antagonisms as consequences of the lack of state authority in the eastern provinces, a result of decades of poor management by the central government. The interveners viewed micro-level conflicts as private and criminal and extensive grassroots violence as a normal feature of life in a peaceful Congo.

The dominant peacebuilding culture also oriented the international actors' understanding of their roles. This culture constructed intervention at the regional and national levels as the only "natural" and "legitimate" task for diplomats and UN staff. It elevated the organization of elections as the most effective peacebuilding mechanism and established humanitarian and development programs as the most appropriate answer to grassroots tensions. It also shaped the international view of decentralized conflict resolution as an unimportant, unfamiliar, and unmanageable task. It led international actors to interpret contextual hurdles and a lack of resources as absolute constraints on their involvement at the local level. In turn, these constraints fueled the lack of interest in grassroots conflict, as well as the perception of bottom-up peacebuilding as a task unworthy of international attention. All told, the peacebuilding culture oriented international actors toward an intervention strategy that permitted, and at times even exacerbated, fighting, massacres, and massive human rights violations during and after the transition. Furthermore, it enabled these actors to view their intervention as a success, until war resumed in late 2008.

Various Congolese and international actors contested the main elements of the dominant peacebuilding culture and the strategies that they enabled. These individuals argued that decentralized agendas did, indeed, fuel violence, that grassroots conflicts were not purely criminal, and that extensive violence was not a normal feature of life in a peaceful Congo. They also maintained that the international role in a civil war situation could include local-level intervention and that organizing elections shortly after the war ended would fuel violent conflict rather than assuage it. However, these dissenting voices had little influence within their organizations and on the international scene. Moreover, the strategy for which they advocated clashed so fundamentally with existing cultural norms, and so threatened key organizational interests, that the contesters were derided and marginalized. Even the occurrence of shocking events was insufficient to prompt diplomats and UN staff to reevaluate their understanding of violence and intervention. As a result, though they achieved some limited successes, the international actors' intense peacebuilding efforts failed to build lasting peace and security.

The patterns of violence and intervention during the years after the transition had many similarities to those of the previous period. In 2007, 2008, and 2009, violence escalated again, and the Kivus and Oriental Province returned to all-out war.[24] The few existing local conflict-resolution structures intensified their efforts, but continued to meet the same obstacles as before. There was one noteworthy development, though. A number of international interveners started acknowledging the significant role of local tensions, in large part thanks to the efforts of the various individuals who contested the status quo as described in the previous chapter (and perhaps also due to the various articles I published and the many briefings I conducted while preparing this book).[25] In January 2008, for example, the Congolese government, with strong diplomatic and UN support, organized a peace conference in Goma to find a solution to the specific problems of the Kivus. Afterwards, under the leadership of a new special representative, Alan Doss, MONUC established several initiatives that would contribute to bottom-up peacebuilding, in particular, the Eastern Stabilization Commission and the Joint Protection Teams. In December 2009, for the first time ever in a MONUC mandate, the UN Security Council mentioned that the UN mission should help address violence in the Kivus through the "establishment of mechanisms for resolving local disputes."[26]

---

[24] See Autesserre 2008 for an analysis of the post-transition dynamics of violence.

[25] Ibid., seems to have influenced at least a few key policy makers.

[26] UN Security Council 2009, para. 36.

However, these developments were far from sufficient. For instance, during the 2008 peace conference in Goma, participants had a chance to discuss their grievances over local political power, land expropriation, and mining resources, but these topics were not a priority. The conference focused instead on neutralizing the most prominent warlords, such as Laurent Nkunda and the major Mai Mai chiefs. A cease-fire agreement was signed, but the gathering's main accomplishment, a nonbinding "act of engagement," proposed no concrete solutions for local antagonisms. More important, the fighting never stopped, not even during the conference.[27] Similarly, the mention of local peacebuilding in the December 2009 MONUC mandate was just a passing reference in the middle of a lengthy resolution and it went mostly unnoticed.

As of this writing, the dominant understanding of the causes of violence remains top-down, and so does the dominant strategy to end this violence. "Local involvement" is a buzzword for international interveners in the eastern Congo, but it still refers mostly to involvement with the Congolese national elite. When this phrase does refer to grassroots action, it concerns primarily humanitarian and development agencies, not peacebuilding or peacekeeping structures. More broadly, there is still no acknowledgment that bottom-up tensions contribute extensively to sustaining violence and no admission that widespread and systematic local peacebuilding efforts are needed.

Beyond the Congo, Beyond Africa

The scope of this argument is not limited to international intervention in the Congo. The approach suggested in this book is valuable to understanding international peacebuilding success or failure in many unstable environments around the world.

Recent research emphasizes the importance of local tensions in fueling violence in most war and postwar situations.[28] Civilians, civil society organizations, religious institutions and leaders, as well as state and nonstate agencies have also initiated bottom-up peacebuilding projects in various places and contexts. These initiatives have

[27] This brief analysis of the Goma conference already appeared in ibid., p. 108.
[28] Kalyvas 2003 and 2006. See also Dennys and Zaman 2009; Fujii 2008; Krämer 2006 and 2007; Klopp and Kamungi 2007/2008, and Straus 2006.

been quite scattered, but the few researchers who have evaluated them share one conclusion: "In order for peace agreements between warring parties to lead to durable peace, there needs to be, alongside top-down implementation of the peace agreement, concurrent bottom-up processes aimed at constructing a new social contract and healing societal divisions."[29]

Achieving Peacebuilding Success: The Need for Bottom-Up Approaches

Somalia in the 1990s and 2000s provides a perfect illustration of the need for bottom-up processes.[30] In Puntland and Somaliland, in the north of the country, indigenous attempts at bottom-up peacebuilding succeeded in generating a relatively peaceful and stable situation. Grassroots conferences used indigenous methods of reconciliation, which included mediation by traditional elders and elites, and eventually managed to quell clan conflicts and neighborly disputes. These locally driven programs expanded to provincial inter-clan dialogues, which led to the successful disarmament and demilitarization of most of the area, as well as to the creation of a reliable police force. In Somaliland, bottom-up efforts also succeeded in reconstructing functioning state institutions and selecting political representatives that the population accepts as legitimate.

By contrast, in the central and southern part of the country, the international peacebuilders' top-down peacebuilding strategy was largely a failure. The UN peacekeeping mission, the United States, and regional peace brokers mainly focused on organizing elite conferences to reconcile the leaders of the main factions, initiatives that proved consistently unsuccessful. In fact, the UN attempt to quickly reconstruct a central government arguably promoted fragmentation and prolonged

---

[29] Prendergast and Plumb 2002, p. 327. See also Anderson and Olson 2003; Lederach 1997; and all the case studies of the project Reflecting on Peace Practices (http://www.cdainc.com/cdawww/project_profile. php?pid=RPP&pname= Reflecting%20on%20Peace%20Practice).

[30] This and the following paragraphs are based on Adam 2004 and 2008; Cassanelli 1997; Duffey 2000, pp. 160–162; Farah 2002; Farah and Lewis 1993; Lederach 1997, pp. 52–53; Lewis 1993; Menkhaus 1997; Terlinden and Debiel 2004; Wallis 2009; and Jeffrey Gettleman, "A new approach to bringing order in Somalia," *International Herald Tribune*, August 18, 2008.

the civil war.[31] This macro-level strategy also failed to coordinate with complementary grassroots actions of the kind that had been successful in the northern part of the country. The UN's support of a decentralization process in Somalia was ad-hoc and incongruent; it remained mostly top-down and implemented from the capital Mogadishu. Efforts at promoting local peace and reconciliation remained minimal and lacked coherence: Peacebuilders oscillated between macro-level initiatives and a few weak micro-level policies, eventually implementing rushed and inefficient procedures that destroyed any long term bottom-up peace- and state-building process. While many other factors, such as the diverse nature of conflicts across the country, as well as international, regional, organizational, and domestic interests were also significant, most Somalia experts agree that the presence of sustained bottom-up peacebuilding initiatives largely explains the success of the peace process in the northern region while large-scale violence continued in other parts of the country.

Several other recent examples confirm the effectiveness of bottom-up conflict-resolution approaches. In 2003, U.S. officers in Iraq started to complain that they lacked information on the local population necessary to stabilize their areas of deployment.[32] In 2006, under General Petraeus's supervision, the U.S. Department of Defense drafted a new counterinsurgency manual that emphasized the importance of local knowledge for successful combat operations. The same year, the U.S. military initiated a pilot program, called, in military lingo, the "Human Terrain Team." This initiative would embed anthropologists and other social scientists within combat units in Afghanistan and later in Iraq, to help the army analyze grassroots dynamics.

The new program quickly made a significant difference. For example, in Afghanistan, an anthropologist joined the 82nd Airborne Division to enable better understanding of the complex tribal and land conflicts of the Shabak Valley. On arrival, he convinced the U.S. army

---

[31] Adam 2004, p. 274.

[32] The following three paragraphs are based on Kipp, Grau, et al. 2006; David Rohde, "Army enlists anthropology in war zones," *New York Times*, October 5, 2007; Anna Mulrine, "The culture warriors," *US News and World Report*, November 30, 2007; Michel Sauret, "Human terrain team: Regaining the human touch in the midst of war," *Savannah Morning News*, October 28, 2008; and Steve Featherstone, "Human quicksand for the US Army, a crash course in cultural studies," *Harper's Magazine*, September 2008.

to facilitate the organization of local councils to resolve long-standing disputes in the area. In the first eight months of this experiment, the Division saw a 60% reduction in its combat operations. Likewise, Operation Khyber (2007) successfully fought off hundreds of Taliban insurgents and significantly reduced suicide attacks on U.S. troops and their allies in Paktia Province, in part thanks to bottom-up peace-building efforts. Here, anthropologists devised a job-training program to relieve economic pressures on young men who otherwise would be tempted to join well-paying insurgents. The embedded scholars also helped to thwart a Taliban attempt at dividing the Zadran tribe, which, when united, was powerful enough to prevent Taliban operations in the area. Combat teams throughout Afghanistan similarly reported a decrease in the need for combat operations once a local conflict expert joined their ranks.

The military use of social scientists is controversial. It presents many risks to academics conducting fieldwork in conflict situations, since it increases the local population's tendency to see them as intelligence gatherers for various armies. Nevertheless, the success of this program emphasizes a crucial lesson: Addressing grassroots tensions is critical to pacifying a violent area, be it in Afghanistan, Iraq, or the Congo.

The remarkable improvement of the Northern Ireland situation in 2006 and 2007 is similarly illuminating.[33] A network of interrelated initiatives by local, national, and international actors dramatically decreased violence during these years. In this process, local civil society organizations proved fundamental in laying the groundwork for high-level reconciliation. They were the only actors with "a low enough profile and sufficient credibility to make contact, build trust, and convene discussions across the divide with prisoners, paramilitaries, government ministers, community leaders, and civil servants."[34] Along the same lines, in El Salvador in the early 1990s, provincial UN officers (military and political) promoted reconciliation processes between landlords and landless peasants by, for example, convening meetings between the two enemy groups in given localities. Such actions significantly contributed to the success of the overall peace process.[35]

---

[33] Fitzduff and Williams 2007; and Knox and Quirk 2000, chapters 2 and 3.
[34] Fitzduff and Williams 2007, p. 31.
[35] Personal communication from Elisabeth Wood, Yale University, 2006.

Burundi provides yet another compelling example, illustrating both the effectiveness of bottom-up peacebuilding and the consequences of an incomplete local strategy.[36] One of the main reasons certain areas in Burundi remained peaceful during the war was precisely because of the efforts of grassroots military and political elite, who convinced local populations not to follow national calls to violence.[37] More broadly, a review of the peace process between 1993 (at the beginning of the large-scale civil war) and 2007 (a time of relative peace) concluded that bottom-up initiatives, which grassroots organizations implemented and international actors supported, were "key in supporting the transition, in preparing the disposition of the various parties for talks, and in the negotiations themselves, as well as in the electoral processes, and especially in transforming people's outlooks at every level."[38]

Despite this involvement in local peacebuilding, the national and international response to the conflict in Burundi contained flaws similar to those of the Congolese peace process, in particular, a lack of attention to land conflict, local reintegration of demobilized soldiers, and reconstruction of a functioning justice system. As a result, as of this writing, Burundi remains at risk of destabilization. At the national level, the underlying conflicts around national political power persist. At the local level, access to land remains an important source of deadly disputes and poses a central obstacle to the return of displaced people and refugees. Many supposedly demobilized soldiers, especially those formerly part of rebel militias, have not turned in their weapons and continue to wreak havoc on their communities. Although Burundi no longer experiences large-scale fighting, an increase in both bottom-up and top-down conflict resolution is necessary to make the relative peace sustainable in the long term.

---

[36] The next two paragraphs are based on confidential sources, as well as Sebudandi and Icoyitungye 2008; Lemarchand 2008, chapter 11; a BBC news report on Burundi by Robert Walker, broadcast on December 26, 2005 on *BBC World News*; a news item in *Burundi Réalités,* May 18, 2007, and reproduced in Jean-Claude Willame's *Ephémérides Grand-Lacs* (distributed by e-mail); and personal communications from Mcghan Lynch, PhD candidate, Yale University, 2009.

[37] Personal communication from Lynch, 2009, on the main findings of her ongoing fieldwork.

[38] Sebudandi and Icoyitungye 2008, p. 41.

The case of South Africa similarly illustrates the usefulness of grassroots efforts and the consequences of persisting local tensions.[39] In 1991, the National Peace Accord established a network of subnational – notably local – peace committees to promote grassroots reconciliation, as South Africans recognized that the peace process could not succeed without it. During the next three years, thousands of citizens promoted political and racial cooperation at the local level, thus assuaging many sources of conflict and preventing ongoing violence from escalating and jeopardizing national reconciliation. Along with top-down initiatives, these bottom-up efforts were critical in enabling the country to proceed with the 1994 democratic elections and to prevent the resumption of war. However, they remained insufficient, especially in KwaZulu-Natal. Although the national cleavages ceased to generate organized large-scale violence in postapartheid South Africa, power struggles within local political parties of KwaZulu Natal continued to motivate significant fighting and to prevent the pacification of the entire country.

Even when incomplete, these initiatives are important developments compared to the routine absence of bottom-up peacebuilding programs. Indeed, just as local tensions are a recurrent source of violence in war and postwar environments, the UN staff members' and diplomats' neglect of local conflict resolution is a recurrent pattern of third-party interventions. According to a number of UN officials, none of the UN peacekeeping missions around the world implement any comprehensive bottom-up peacebuilding program. Only a handful of diplomats have tried (without success) to advocate for a better approach to local issues. This dearth of locally oriented programs should not be surprising, since most elements of the dominant peacebuilding culture documented in this book come from the world polity, the peacebuilding field, or the internal culture of international organizations, and are therefore not Congo specific.

Top-Down Understanding, Local "Criminality," and the Normality of Widespread Violence

As detailed in chapter 2, the media, policy makers, and even academics usually portray war and postwar violence as resulting exclusively

---

[39] This paragraph builds on Knox and Quirk 2000; Krämer 2006; and Marks 2000.

from top-down causes, and they therefore ignore critical bottom-up dynamics. Despite evidence to the contrary, manipulation of the masses by ethnic entrepreneurs is still the dominant explanation for the 1994 Rwandan genocide and the ethnic cleansings of the 1990s in the former Yugoslavia. Likewise, media outlets and policy makers often portray Muslim combatants in Iraq, Afghanistan, and the "global war on terror" as mere puppets of terrorist masterminds, such as religious extremists and Al-Qaeda executives, while they are, in fact, often part of small, unconnected networks of fighters who do not report to a higher authority.[40]

The international understanding of the war in Darfur presents particularly insightful parallels to that of the Congo.[41] Violence there is the joint product of regional disputes (between Chad, Eritrea, and Sudan), national tensions (notably between Khartoum and both the Sudan Liberation Movement and the Justice and Equality Movement), and micro-level antagonisms around land, livestock, water, and local authority. Land ownership in particular has been a significant source of tensions in recent Darfuri history, and it has become one of the primary motivations for the horrific intercommunal fighting in recent years. However, top-down representations of the Darfur conflict as an ethnic, Arab versus African war, and as a simplified, good versus evil battle have long prevented international interveners from acknowledging the grassroots dynamics of violence. Views of fragmented militias as criminal bandits, in addition to lingering perceptions of a high level of violence as a normal aspect of the nature and culture in this part of the world, also allowed international interveners to often neglect the political dimensions of grassroots tensions.

Likewise, the dominant narrative on the causes of the 2008 post-election violence in Kenya emphasized the national political cleavage between President Mwai Kibaki and opposition leader Raila Odinga, and the national ethnic cleavage between Kikuyus and other ethnic groups. In fact, a closer look at the patterns of violence reveals that many clashes centered on land issues, which fed into intercommunal

---

[40] Hoffman 2008; Sageman 2008; Sageman and Hoffman 2008; and author's field research in Afghanistan, 2002.

[41] This paragraph builds on De Waal 2005a, 2005b, and 2007; Ismail and Fick 2009; Lie and de Carvalho 2008; Mamdani 2007 and 2009; International Crisis Group 2007b; and De Waal's interview with Nima Elbagir, *London's Frontline Club*, September 3, 2008 (www.frontlineclub.com).

tensions.[42] Macro-level problems did trigger the civil unrest, but the violence would have been much less widespread and much less deadly in the absence of grassroots conflicts.[43]

Just as in the Congo, the top-down understanding of violence in conflicts around the world often accompanies a view of local tensions as unimportant, criminal, and apolitical. In *The Logic of Violence in Civil Wars*, Kalyvas provides numerous illustrations, spanning continents and centuries, of the widespread perception that local conflict is negligible as a cause of war hostility.[44] Another example is Haiti, where most interveners understand violence as purely criminal, although it has broader and more encompassing implications. In Chad, EU peacekeepers view local militias as "bandits" and bands of "roaming thugs," although these groups have identifiable political, social, and military agendas.[45] In Uganda, international interveners portray the Lord's Resistance Army as a ragtag gang with purely criminal objectives, overlooking the armed group's political claims.[46] In the United States and parts of Europe, policy makers and journalists often frame terrorism as mere criminality, although its political and economic motivations are evident.

The understanding of organized violence as a normal feature of life, as opposed to an indication of the continuation of war, has also influenced the analysis of conflict situations beyond the Congo. Woodward documents such a process of normalization of violence against the population during the Balkan wars of the 1990s.[47] Above all, this understanding prevails for Africa as a whole.[48] The Russian

---

[42] See Klopp and Kamungi 2007/2008, and Klopp and Zuern 2007 for a fascinating analysis of the various dynamics of violence during the 2008 postelectoral clashes.

[43] Human Rights Watch 2008a; and Marx 2008. See also Klopp 2002 for a broader analysis of grassroots conflicts in Kenya, and Branch 2009 for a short opinion piece emphasizing the role of bottom-up antagonisms during the 2008 crisis.

[44] Kalyvas 2006, chapter 2.

[45] See Vincent Hugeux, "Tchad. L'EUFOR a des faiblesses," *Le Vif / L'Express*, October 3, 2008, on the EU mission, and Debos 2008 for an excellent analysis of these combatants.

[46] Perrot Forthcoming; and Sandrine Perrot, "Northern Uganda: a forgotten conflict again? The role of external actors in the Northern Uganda conflict resolution," Seminar delivered at Columbia University, April 17, 2008.

[47] Woodward 1995 (pp. 19–20) and 1997.

[48] See Shaw 2007 for a public source making a similar claim.

president once claimed, for instance, that cannibalism belonged to African traditions and culture.[49] In informal settings, Western diplomats use very different criteria to evaluate "normal" levels of violence depending on their geographical focus, and often voice the idea that violence is normal in daily African life.[50]

Combined with the understanding of war and peace as a dichotomy, rather than a continuum, this normalization of violence for certain parts of the word allows international interveners to confer the label "peaceful" or "postconflict" to many violent situations (based on the view that signing a peace agreement indicates a transition from war to peace). Although Uganda, for instance, is usually categorized as "postconflict," its situation is relatively similar to that of the Congo. A large part of the territory is stable, but the Lord's Resistance Army continues to perpetrate tremendous violence in the districts of Arua, Gulu, Pader, Kitgum, Lira, and Adjumani. Similarly, although Nigeria is widely considered to be at peace, the country is actually partly at war.

Top-Down Understanding of the Interveners' Role

The widespread top-down understanding of the causes of violence reinforces the foreign interveners' conception of their role as "naturally" focused on the international and national realms. Accordingly, foreign peacebuilders usually adopt a state- or capital-centered approach. They interact almost exclusively with national and international actors and work solely on macro-level issues, often producing terrible consequences.

In Rwanda in 1993, for example, international peacebuilders focused their efforts on pressuring the state's political elites to negotiate with each other and on organizing peace talks in Arusha, Tanzania. As the subsequent eruption of genocide proved, this top-down intervention not only failed to reconcile the elites, but also did nothing to assuage the bottom-up tensions that fueled violence in many Rwandan towns and villages.[51]

---

[49] David Wooding, "Putin's 'cannibals' gaffe," *The Sun*, June 14, 2005.
[50] Roland Marchal, researcher at Sciences-Po/CERI (France) made a similar observation (personal communication, January 2004).
[51] Jones 2001; Paris 2004, chapter 4; and personal communication from Jean-Claude Willame, 2006. See Fujii 2008, and Straus 2006 for the grassroots dynamics of violence during the genocide.

The picture that Johnston and Reno paint of international peace-builders in Sierra Leone also closely resembles the analysis developed in this book. UN and British peacekeeping staff, as well as diplomats and aid workers attached to embassies, lived in a "bubble," refused to go out of their safe "enclaves," and had "very little knowledge" of the rest of the country beyond the capital. They therefore held "very disturbing misconceptions of the reality."[52] As could be expected, given these circumstances, the interveners neglected the key local dimension of the Sierra Leonean crisis, and thus promoted only a very tenuous reconciliation.[53]

Other examples abound. According to numerous personal communications from researchers and practitioners, conflicts as dissimilar as Afghanistan, Nepal, East Timor, and northern Uganda share one significant characteristic: Extensive violence continues, in part because national and international pacification programs fail to address the critical role of contested land ownership. Similarly, in Cyprus in the early 2000s, the lack of grassroots reconciliation between Turkish and Greek Cypriots, and the lack of large-scale bottom-up peace initiatives among Greek Cypriots, thwarted important progress at the international and national levels.[54] In Darfur, after four years of large-scale violence and failed diplomatic and UN efforts, the International Crisis Group still urged (in vain) the African Union and UN mediation team to include in the peace talks "the core issues that drive the conflict," such as "land tenure and use" and "the role of local government and administrative structures."[55] In the rest of Sudan, the North–South peace process has also continually ignored critical grassroots tensions over livestock, natural resources, and political and social power, despite the success of pilot projects in locally driven reconciliation and disarmament.[56] In Kenya, the 2008 peace settlement brokered by the UN and African Union included an investigation into the electoral dispute

---

[52] Johnston 2005, and William Reno's comments on Johnston's paper, 49th Annual Meeting of the African Studies Association Conference, Washington, D.C., 2005.

[53] Englebert and Tull 2008, citing Bruce Baker and Roy May, "Reconstructing Sierra Leone," pp. 50–51.

[54] Hadjipavlou and Kanol 2008.

[55] International Crisis Group 2007b (quotation from p. 4). Berger 2009 similarly emphasizes the detrimental ignorance of local issues by UN and African Union peacekeepers.

[56] For a public source, see Brewer 2008.

and a power-sharing arrangement between the two main political parties, but no bottom-up component. As in the Congo, the bulk of local peacebuilding work was left to certain grassroots organizations and authorities, which were too few to address all of the problems. Land disputes and cattle rustling therefore continued to sustain numerous pockets of violence and constantly threatened to unravel the fragile peace.[57] This widespread focus on the macro level at the expense of the local also characterized the Ethiopian–Eritrean peace process.[58]

To make matters worse, in many cases, just as in the Congo, the categorization of a situation as "postconflict" or "peaceful" triggers the routine adoption of tools and procedures inappropriate for still unstable environments. The main such strategy, the obsession with holding elections, has already been extensively documented. In the post-Cold War era, elections took place in all postconflict environments in which international actors played a leading role, such as Afghanistan, Angola, Bosnia, Cambodia, Croatia, Kosovo, Iraq, Liberia, Nicaragua, and Sierra Leone, even before the necessary preconditions were established, such as security for all candidates and supporters, civic education, or freedom of speech.[59] In many contexts, such as Liberia, South Africa, and several East European countries, there was also a pervasive belief that, somehow, elections would bring about not only peace and democracy but also economic prosperity.[60] Even worse, this obsession with elections often transpired at the expense of true peacebuilding and, as in the Congo, led to further disregard of the root causes of continued violence and to an exacerbation of existing tensions.[61] In South Sudan for example, the label "postconflict" led to an unawareness of ongoing clashes between rebel groups in the South, of continued fighting between the North and South along oil-rich border areas, and of critical bottom-up tensions.[62]

[57] Human Rights Watch 2008a; Klopp 2009; Klopp, Githinji, et al. 2009; and Marx 2008.

[58] Terlinden and Debiel 2004.

[59] Author's field observation in Kosovo (2000) and Afghanistan (2002), and personal communication from Susan Woodward (2004). For public sources on these topics, see Coles 2007; Lyons 2002 and 2004; Ottaway 2002; Paris 2004; Snyder 2000; Stedman 1997, p. 50; and Youngs 2004.

[60] Personal communication from Christine Cheng, PhD candidate, Oxford University, 2008.

[61] See, for example, Paris 2004, chapters 4 to 7.

[62] See Brewer 2008, pp. 17–18 for a public source on this topic.

Just as in the Congo, the postconflict label yields other repercussions. After the signing of the peace agreement in Sierra Leone for instance, according to a Western diplomat, the German cooperation agency, GTZ, sent a postconflict team that did not even coordinate with the existing "conflict" team in-country. This omission unsurprisingly created major problems for GTZ projects. There, as in many other places, the staffs of international organizations and diplomatic missions typically use a checklist approach to postconflict reconstruction, as they did in the Congo. Whether in Afghanistan, Bosnia, the Congo, Iraq, Kosovo, or Liberia, they view each situation as requiring the use of a preexisting toolkit that includes the deployment of peacekeepers; the disarmament, demobilization, and reintegration of combatants; the repatriation of refugees; and, of course, elections.[63] This approach limits the development of the context-specific response that would be required to be truly effective; it also precludes action on the underlying political, social, and economic micro-level tensions.

Liberia illustrates the consequences of many of the aforementioned processes. In the 1990s, the collapse of the state led to a devolution of sovereign power from the capital into the hinterlands of the different rebel-held areas. However, the United States, the UN, and the regional peacekeeping mission failed to recognize the centers of effective power and the people who controlled them. Instead, the international interveners "kept up the fiction of the Liberian State" and failed to relate adequately to subnational actors.[64] Throughout the two wars of the 1990s–2000s, media, diplomats, international organizations, and nongovernmental agencies also attributed most of the violence to national dynamics, in particular to manipulation by Liberian leader Charles Taylor.[65] The peace process therefore focused on these macro levels: Its foreign overseers labeled Liberia as a "postconflict" situation as soon as the national power-sharing agreement commenced in 2003, and they quickly led the country through the 2005 general

[63] For public sources, see Ellis 2005; Gilbert 2008; and International Crisis Group 2004b (quotation from p. 1).

[64] Alao, Mackinlay, et al. 1999.

[65] The rest of this paragraph, as well as the following one, build on Boas 2009; Ellis 2002; personal communications from Morten Boas, Oslo, 2008 and from Christine Cheng, e-mail communication, 2009; and newspaper coverage of Liberian politics.

elections. The dominant narrative on Liberia now considers the country to be at peace.

In fact, Liberia has long been, and remains, in a gray zone between war and peace. Now, as during the war and the transition to peace, the population of some parts of the country continues to support local warlords because of grassroots antagonisms concerning contested land ownership, which is inextricably linked with national citizenship. Far from acknowledging the economic, political, and social dimensions of this decentralized violence, UN peacekeepers have instead mostly considered it a normal feature of life in the area and a mere problem of criminality. This shared understanding has reinforced the peacekeepers' propensity not to become involved at the local level. As a result, tensions over land and citizenship persist and, as of this writing, Liberia remains highly susceptible to large-scale conflict.

Vicious Circles and Shocking Events

As this book documents for the Congo, these collective understandings often initiate a vicious circle. Because of their top-down interpretation of the causes of violence and the role of international interveners, diplomats, and UN managers are stationed in the capitals and rarely travel outside them. In many cases, this means that they have little direct contact with the consequences of ongoing violence, which are often greater in rural than in urban environments.[66] The limited exposure to violence leads to, (1) a tendency to focus mostly on events in the capital; (2) an underestimation of continuing conflict in the countryside; and (3) additional difficulties in understanding subnational dynamics and acting on them.[67] As in the Congo, these three elements worsen the financial, logistical, and resources constraints on intervention at the subnational level and in rural areas.

---

[66] Kalyvas 2006, chapter 2, provides extensive evidence that violence is higher in rural areas for most conflicts.

[67] On the first element: Johnston 2005; Staibano 2005; author's interview with Smets, 2005; personal communication from Thorsten Benner, researcher at the Global Public Policy Institute in Berlin, May 2008; and William Reno's comments on Johnston's paper, 49th Annual Meeting of the African Studies Association Conference, Washington, D.C., 2005. On the second: Kalyvas 2006, chapter 2. On the third: public sources include Bigo 1996; Badie 1995; and Alao, Mackinlay, et al. 1999.

As a result, in many cases, only the presence of shocking events prompts an international reaction to decentralized violence (although, thus far, this response has not included increased support to local peacebuilding). The example of Sudan best illustrates this process. For two decades, South Sudan was the theater of a major humanitarian crisis in which an estimated 2 million people died. However, the UN, the United States, and the African organizations that supervised the peace process gradually became inured to this violence; they did not do enough to assuage the tensions and let the peace efforts waste away. Then, in the first few months of 2003, massive killings took place in Darfur, a region that foreign interveners considered "peaceful." The sudden escalation of the conflict there, combined with a subsequent framing of the killings as genocide and media coverage emphasizing their gruesome nature, succeeded in overcoming the international actors' habituation to violence against the Sudanese population. Although the number of victims in Darfur remained six times lower than that in South Sudan, the shocking nature of the crisis absorbed many international actors, in particular African regional organizations, the UN, and the United States. It therefore managed to generate an unprecedented level of foreign involvement to end the Darfuri conflict.

The strong international response to the 2008 postelectoral violence in Kenya is another example of how shocking events can lead to interventions. For several decades, donors had perceived Kenya as an oasis of stability in Africa, one of the only peaceful and democratic countries on the continent; it was also a popular tourist destination. In fact, tensions and low-level violence were pervasive.[68] Then, in early 2008, violence suddenly escalated. Though the hostilities were far less deadly than combat in neighboring countries, the abrupt and therefore shocking nature of the violence incited European and U.S. journalists to cover the crisis on a daily basis. It also prompted the UN and various Western and African states to immediately send peacemaking teams to the ground.

The Ugandan case ultimately best illustrates how graphic violence can influence the level of international involvement. In Uganda, most humanitarian and development agencies focus on the northern part of the country (notably the Gulu area) and on the victims of the Lord's Resistance Army, at the expense of many other parts of the

[68] See, for example, Klopp and Kamungi 2007/2008.

territory plagued by various armed groups. According to an experienced researcher, the dissimilar nature of violence in diverse areas largely accounts for these differing reactions: The Lord's Resistance Army uses knives and machetes, whereas the other groups use Kalashnikovs, which are just as or more deadly, but produce much less horrific killings.[69]

This brief overview is not meant to be exhaustive but rather to open areas for further research. We need to analyze the aforementioned examples in much greater depth and consider the relevance of the explanation proposed in this book in these and other contexts. Even more important, we need to understand the process by which some actors escaped the dominant narratives on the causes of violence and the role of foreign interveners, acknowledged the significance of grassroots conflict in places like Northern Ireland or Somaliland, and convinced their colleagues and hierarchies to implement a comprehensive bottom-up peacebuilding strategy.

Of course, the attention to or neglect of local conflict does not and cannot explain all cases of international intervention success or failure. The influence of micro-level versus macro-level tensions varies across time and space, in the Congo and elsewhere. In certain countries, disregard of bottom-up antagonisms may not lead to a resurgence of full-scale national or international war. In other places, national actors and institutions are sufficiently strong to implement grassroots peacebuilding projects, and international action at the local level may be unnecessary. Overall, however, decentralized agendas often play a critical role in sustaining peace or violence, and grassroots actors often need international support. It is therefore important to further our understanding of the factors that facilitate or hinder sustained international efforts at the local level.

Policy Recommendations

While awaiting further research results, this section presents practical ways for policy makers and practitioners to better address the micro-level dynamics of violence. In brief, policy makers should revise their approach to local peacebuilding. This change would be most effective if they also reconceptualized their approach to state reconstruction.

---

[69] Personal communication from Sandrine Perrot, New York, May 2008.

This reconceptualization, in turn, would be much easier if they reevaluated their entire approach to postconflict intervention.

The whole process will be difficult, costly, and lengthy, and it will face a great deal of organizational resistance. Yet, it is the only way to ensure that international interveners will finally be able to address bottom-up causes of violence and thus build sustainable peace.

Facilitate Cultural Change

Most immediately and importantly, academic and policy researchers must begin to question the widespread understandings of violence and intervention that make local peacebuilding appear irrelevant or inappropriate. This book already takes a first step toward denaturalizing such understandings. Other researchers should analyze other war or postwar environments, evaluate whether their results are similar to mine, and circulate their findings to policy makers and practitioners. This questioning and further research would make it easier for international peacebuilders to listen to alternative framings of the situations they encounter. It would make interveners more receptive to the idea that micro-level tensions are a critical cause of peacebuilding failures. It would help them recognize that the relationship between war and peace is continuous, not dichotomous, and mass violence is never a "normal" feature of life. It would assist them in acknowledging that elections are a poor peacebuilding mechanism. Finally, it would aid them in accepting the appropriateness and legitimacy of the diplomats', donors', and peacekeepers' support of bottom-up conflict resolution.

Additionally, high-ranking policy makers should disseminate this new information to help overcome resistance by staff members on the ground. Directives from the top hierarchy within foreign ministries and international organizations (including, for the UN, from the Department of Peacekeeping Operations, the Security Council, and the leadership of each field mission) should emphasize the dangers of grassroots tensions and the staffers' responsibility in local conflict prevention and resolution.

Media outlets also have a significant role to play. Many interviewees acknowledged that their organizations often paid more attention to issues that were widely covered in the press. Publicizing the risks posed by decentralized antagonisms and the valuable impact of bottom-up peacebuilding projects would help reinforce nascent interest on these topics. International nongovernmental organizations and think tanks that already advocate for local peacebuilding are best equipped to start raising interest among journalists, who could then induce other actors and media outlets to consider further action.

Once policy makers and practitioners have acknowledged the importance of local issues during postwar reconstruction, and once they have recognized that they should implement extensive peacebuilding programs at all levels, it will be easier for them to take further steps. Peacebuilders should next work to develop expertise, bureaucratic structures, and training programs for local conflict resolution. These initiatives would, in turn, further denaturalize the ideas that local tensions are unimportant and that bottom-up peacebuilding is an illegitimate task for international actors, thereby decreasing resistance to organizational change.

Develop Expertise and Bureaucratic Structures for Local Peacebuilding

Foreign ministries, international organizations (especially the UN), and nongovernmental agencies specialized in peacebuilding should apply the same rigor and preparation to local conflict resolution that they harness for the organization of elections. Within their headquarters, they should create offices or departments devoted to this effort, and staff them with newly hired specialists on bottom-up peacebuilding. These experts should develop a body of knowledge and a set of potential strategies that their field colleagues could use. One way to do this would be to conduct a comparative review of existing grassroots conflict-resolution programs, within or outside of one's bureaucracy, and determine which approaches work best, which tools are most useful, and what the limits of such programs are. The experts would also have to evaluate ways to overcome the problems that the few international actors supporting local peacebuilding organizations usually encounter and ways to manage the resistance to bottom-up conflict resolution within their respective bureaucracies.

In parallel, the local peacebuilding experts should develop and implement a training program to share their knowledge with all existing staff. The experts should especially teach all diplomats and UN officials deployed to unstable settings how to analyze subnational dynamics, interact with local warlords, and partner with decentralized peacebuilders to work on grassroots conflict-resolution projects.

Additionally, foreign ministries and international organizations should create local peacebuilding offices in all of the countries where they support or implement conflict-resolution initiatives. Embassies should have many more consulates based in unstable provinces, and they should post to those consulates at least one person specifically devoted to decentralized conflict resolution. Diplomats based in the capital should also travel to the field much more frequently to better understand local tensions and grassroots opportunities for peace, and thus be better prepared to support their field colleagues.

Likewise, for each observation site, peacekeeping missions (from the UN, the EU, or the African Union) should deploy, alongside the military, a civilian staff member responsible for monitoring local tensions and providing suggestions for resolution. He or she should have the authorization to draw on military, diplomatic, or development resources to achieve local peace. When selecting new hires, human resources managers should give priority to those with anthropological training or interests, particularly those who enjoy traveling to remote places rather than settling in capital cities. Managers should deploy these local peacebuilding point persons for at least two or three years (and not just six months, as is the current standard practice for expatriates working in unstable environments), allowing them time to build networks in the field and gain the trust of their local counterparts. Before each new assignment, these point persons – and if possible, all of their colleagues as well – should have the opportunity to acquire extensive knowledge of the country in which they will work. Such an education would include, for example, extended briefings and time to read and research before setting out for the field, opportunities that are usually very rare in UN and diplomatic missions. Finally, on their arrival on the ground, the point persons should benefit from an extended hand-over period during which their predecessor would introduce them to local contacts and help them gain local trust more quickly.

Work through Local Actors Whenever Possible; Intervene Directly if Necessary

The first task of the local peacebuilding point persons deployed to the field should be to develop an in-depth analysis of grassroots conflicts in their area of operation. They should pay particular attention to the local underpinnings of national (and potentially regional or international) tensions, as well as to the distinctively local agendas that fuel decentralized violence, to counteract the tendency to interpret violence as a top-down problem. Policy makers should then draw on this analysis in designing their macro-level intervention strategy. The local peacebuilding point persons should also develop an in-depth knowledge of the history, agenda, culture, goals, and leaders of each significant local group, clan, or militia. This work is difficult for a foreigner, but it can be greatly facilitated by setting up a partnership with grassroots researchers and civil society organizations. Based on the research they conduct, the local peacebuilding point persons should identify the conflicts most likely to erupt into violence or to threaten the macro-level settlement, and determine a strategy to address these conflicts.

Although interveners must tailor local peacebuilding projects to each specific context, several measures are likely to be among the top priorities in each setting. Contested land ownership is a major source of tension and violence in most of Africa as well as in parts of Southeast Asia and Central and Latin America, so reforms and programs to resolve land disputes, such as those suggested for the Congo in chapter 5, are often necessary. Reconciliation projects among families, clans, communities, militias, or social groups that have fought one another during the war are also likely to be appropriate. In particular, wars often create deep resentment over past injustices and human rights violations, so peacebuilders should enable the population to decide how to handle war criminals. Finally, because wars often destroy local and national judicial structures, reconstructing these institutions is necessary to enable communities to peacefully manage and prevent current and future conflicts.

Whenever possible, the strategy should put local actors in control for several reasons. Grassroots organizations and indigenous authorities know the local context best, and they already have extensive contacts. They are therefore most effective at designing and implementing bottom-up peacebuilding projects. Furthermore, by letting local partners make decisions, international actors can support critical micro-level projects while still upholding the dominant norms of noninterference and respect for state sovereignty. Empowering these partners also helps ensure that foreign ministries, international agencies, and nongovernmental organizations do not use the new peacebuilding approach to advance neocolonial agendas. Finally, working primarily through grassroots partners would minimize the amount of work and staff needed for the foreign interveners' local peacebuilding offices in the field. Thus, whenever possible the main role of the local peacebuilding point person should be to enable the local population, authorities, and organizations to decide which micro-level tensions and priorities to address, which actions would be most effective, which partners are reliable, and how international actors can best support their efforts.[70]

In many war and postwar environments, local peacebuilding structures most desperately need (in order of decreasing importance) financial, logistical, and technical support. Increasing the total budget for peacebuilding would be the easiest way for states and international organizations to contribute the required resources. However, this is not the only solution. An alternative option would be to improve the distribution of existing assets. To begin with, the massive funds generally allocated to organizing elections in the immediate aftermath of a war rarely promote either peace or democracy. Such electoral processes can have some positive externalities, such as symbolizing a new beginning and providing demoralized populations with a renewed belief in their political systems, but these benefits are limited compared to their tremendous direct and opportunity costs. The funds usually devoted to organizing immediate postwar elections would, therefore, be better spent on stabilizing the country, reconstructing the other institutions indispensable for democracy (judicial systems, political parties, local governments, and civil society), and creating the necessary preconditions for meaningful elections (freedom of the press, of association, and of expression). In this process, local peacebuilding should receive part of these resources.

The massive amount of money spent on development and humanitarian programs can also help advance bottom-up conflict resolution. Some emergency relief projects clearly cannot and should not include peacebuilding measures, because such measures would compromise the projects' effectiveness or the aid workers' access to the population, and therefore cost numerous lives. Nonetheless, many

---

[70] Anderson and Olson 2003, chapters 5 and 11, provide very detailed guidelines for the relationships between local and foreign peacebuilders.

other humanitarian initiatives, as well as virtually all development programs, can and should include such measures.[71] Including a peace-building dimension in most development and humanitarian programs would not only help increase resources for local conflict-resolution endeavors, but would also maximize their impact. By all accounts, conflict-resolution initiatives, such as reconciliation workshops and peace education programs, work best when combined with develop-ment or relief undertakings. For example, building a market, a school, or a health center shared by two communities in conflict helps rees-tablish social and commercial links between them, thus assuaging the tensions born of distrust and lack of communication and perpetuat-ing the benefits of reconciliation workshops. Combining development projects with local peacebuilding work is also a way to respond to the requests of many targeted communities. These communities often emphasize that they can enjoy the benefits of reestablished peace only after their basic day-to-day needs are met. They also often underscore that providing alternative survival strategies for existing or potential militia members, as well as those who stand to lose their political, economic, or social power when the war ends, is vital to creating sus-tainable peacebuilding programs. These alternative survival strategies could include food security and livelihood projects as well as educa-tion and job-training programs.

States and international organizations should develop funding instruments that are sufficiently flexible to channel money directly to local actors, and ask their respective local peacebuilding point per-sons to monitor the distribution of these funds. Large "new philan-thropy" institutes such as the Gates, Clinton, and Buffet foundations could also play a critical role in this process, because their fundrais-ing, monitoring, and accountability mechanisms are easier for small organizations to navigate than those of traditional funders.[72] All state, international, and private donors should also conceive of their fund-ing instruments as long-term budgets, instead of disbursing funds for the short term in war and postwar environments, as is the standard practice. This approach would ensure that the local peacebuilding projects are effective (because most require a multiyear commitment)

---

[71] See Anderson 1999; and Prendergast 1996 for a thorough discussion of this topic.

[72] I thank Colin Thomas-Jensen of the *Enough* project for this suggestion.

and local partners have time to gradually build up their capacity. Finally, donors, international organizations, and nongovernmental organizations should closely coordinate their grassroots efforts to avoid overlap. Though coordination is often a major problem in international interventions, using the UN Office for the Coordination of Humanitarian Affairs' cluster system to share information and identify a primary organization in charge of each geographic area would be an important step forward.

Increased support for nongovernmental organizations that specialize in local conflict resolution would help those who are already active in this field, who often lack the necessary logistical and financial resources to implement all of the programs they deem necessary. The increased availability of funds would also be an incentive to create new grassroots peacebuilding agencies. In the long term, it would generate a strong network of experienced local peacebuilding staff, who could help further develop the expertise and best practices necessary to make bottom-up conflict resolution an integral part of the international interventions template.

In addition to working through grassroots partners whenever possible, international political and military interveners should also acknowledge that their direct involvement is sometimes required. Civil society actors cannot address all of the decentralized causes of violence, such as many of the political or military issues over which armed groups often fight. Local combatants also usually listen only to actors who have some kind of coercive capacity over them, such as provincial, national, or international officials. When, as often happens, peace agreements install in power the provincial and national leaders who fueled local tensions during the war and continue to do so during the transition to peace, only one option is left: International political and military actors must step in to end organized violence. The intervention of diplomats and political or military UN staff in decentralized conflict would, on the one hand, deter local warlords and, on the other, signal to these warlords a possibility for assistance, thus increasing the estimated peace dividends.

These interventions should use peaceful methods, such as diplomatic pressure or aid projects, to convince local combatants to end violence, but if these incentives fail, as a last resort, interveners should not shy away from coercive military action. Therefore, in addition to reforming the civilian side of their bureaucracies, states and organizations should also review peacekeeper deployment practices. The most necessary change requires deploying special operations forces, which, as explained in chapter 5, are better qualified for action at the local level than traditional units. Such an approach would enable peacekeepers to hunt down and arrest spoilers when all other options have failed. It would also allow foreign interveners to better protect the population; to prevent, deter, or respond to violence more strongly; and to more effectively impose existing embargoes on the traffic of arms and resources. Additionally, member states should allow the UN to develop an intelligence capacity, which its special operations forces could use. Finally, the UN should revise its existing rules to minimize the bureaucratic obstacles to rapid deployment. These adjustments would contribute to a more effective military response, which would in turn help create the environment necessary for the success of nonviolent grassroots peacebuilding.

Conceive of Local Peacebuilding as a Part of the Broader Task of Peace- and State-Building

The overall strategy for local peacebuilding would work best if integrated into broader peace- and state-building efforts. Focusing more on local conflict resolution, indeed, does not mean that international actors should neglect national and regional tensions. Doing so would lead to a settlement as unsustainable as that produced by neglecting local conflicts. Rather, the new strategy should approach all levels at the same time, concentrate on the grassroots dimensions of violence as much as international actors currently focus on national and regional tensions, and link all initiatives together.

In particular, the bottom-up conflict-resolution strategy should become a central element of state-building efforts so that local peacebuilding can be sustainable. The ultimate goal is not to suppress conflicts, which exist in all societies, but to ensure that these conflicts do not lead to violence. To do so, international interveners must help construct or reconstruct institutions that allow for the peaceful management of tensions at all levels, with the consent of the citizens, and in a way sufficiently fair that the losing side does not resort to violence. Electoral processes are one such mechanism, but they are only one among many, and they can assuage conflict over authority only when the necessary preconditions are in place.

It is also critical to form coherent, disciplined, and effective coercion forces that respect human rights, protect the population, and can tackle spoilers as soon as possible. Another essential step toward resolving political, economic, and social antagonisms is to rebuild a stable judiciary, as well as other state structures such as a cadastre that can register real estate.

While state building can thus perpetuate the benefits of local peacebuilding projects, bottom-up conflict-resolution initiatives can also contribute to state reconstruction. Having village- or district-level authorities whom local populations accept and consider legitimate will help ensure that state authority extends beyond the provincial capitals. These local officials can then be the vehicle for bottom-up demands for better accountability from provincial and national leaders. Finally, resolving violent local conflicts is the only way to ensure true pacification and, therefore, to guarantee that the preconditions for meaningful presidential and legislative elections (such as freedom of speech, association, and campaigning for all voters and candidates) exist throughout the country.

Consider a New Approach to Postconflict Intervention

To implement this new local peacebuilding approach and facilitate a meaningful state reconstruction strategy, policy makers should update their understanding of postconflict interventions. To begin with, they should acknowledge that postwar environments are inherently dangerous postings for international peacekeepers, that fighting with spoilers might be necessary, and therefore that casualties and material losses are likely. This revised understanding would help change standard operating procedures in times of crisis. It would enable commanders on the ground to conduct real combat operations, so that, for example, UN troops could hunt down spoilers or protect the population in immediate danger instead of giving disproportionate attention to shielding UN buildings and equipment.

Above all, as many other scholars have advocated, decision makers should plan peace processes over longer periods.[73] Two or three years may be enough to engineer the technical aspects of elections, but they are rarely sufficient to ensure that the voting process will be free, fair,

---

[73] See Ottaway 2002; and Paris 2004 among many others.

and meaningful to the population. Neither is it an adequate amount of time to ensure that local and national state institutions can peacefully contain the exacerbation of rivalries inherent to electoral processes. Finally, two or three years is not sufficient time to address the root causes of violence at all levels – local, national, and international.

Maintaining longer transitions would give peacebuilders more opportunity to build sustainable peace and democracy. It would give them time to address the local underpinnings of conflict. It would enable them to adopt a long-term vision of the problems, as opposed to the usual short-term, crisis-management approach that has proved so detrimental in the Congo. Planning transitions over a longer period would allow interveners to focus on establishing the preconditions for peace and democracy in the immediate aftermath of a conflict, organizing elections only when the prerequisites for a free and fair process are in place. These benefits would eventually ensure that elections promote reconciliation and democratization instead of fuel tensions and reignite violence.

Conclusion: Transforming the Peacebuilding World

Disruptions in peace processes often have catastrophic consequences, as in Afghanistan in 1992, Rwanda in 1994, Sierra Leone in 1996, Israel and Palestine in 2000, Sri Lanka in 2005, and Darfur in 2006. In the Congo, the violent transition to peace caused, directly and indirectly, 2 million deaths in addition to the 3 million victims of the generalized conflicts, and war resumption in 2008 produced tens of thousands more casualties. International interventions can help prevent such disruptions, but they often fail to do so. The dominant international peacebuilding culture often orients intervention strategies away from local conflict resolution and toward popular, but harmful, tactics such as the rapid organization of elections.

A few international peacebuilders, along with many grassroots activists, have attempted to challenge the dominant narratives on the causes of violence and the role of foreign interveners in war and postwar situations. Although their contestation has thus far been unsuccessful, this book seeks to amplify their voices. Questioning the central elements of the prevailing peacebuilding culture – notably the propensity to understand and approach violence in a top-down manner and to conceive of local tensions as an unimportant issue – is a first step integral to designing new, more efficient intervention strategies. Nevertheless, much more remains to be accomplished.

International peacebuilders will need to act in novel ways that are likely to challenge deeply entrenched cultural norms and jeopardize numerous organizational interests. They will have to learn how to support grassroots conflict-resolution efforts. They will have to integrate bottom-up and top-down strategies to fully address the local, national, and international sources of tensions. This transformation will be a challenging, extensive, and costly process that at times may even seem futile.

And yet, only when international interveners address the micro-foundations of peace settlements will they become Burke's "few good men," able to defeat the perpetrators of massive human rights violations. To emphasize one last time why this process is so vital, we must return to Georges and Isabelle, the interviewees with whom this book opened. It is only when these changes occur that Georges's "humanoids" will become less disoriented. And it is at this point, and at this point only, that they will be able to help people like Isabelle, so that affected populations all over the world may stay near their land without being raped, tortured, or killed.

Appendix – Chronology

16th–19th centuries	Central Africa divided into small kingdoms. The Luba, Lunda, and Chokwe are successively the most powerful. Significant slave trade takes place.
1884–1885	Berlin Conference. European nations approve Belgian King Leopold II's claim to the Congo basin.
1908	Belgian parliament takes over the Congo in response to criticisms of harsh treatment of African population.
1960	Congo's Independence. Patrice Lumumba named prime minister. Joseph Kasavubu elected president.
	Secession of Katanga (until January 1963) and brief secession of South Kasai. Fighting between Kasavubu, Lumumba, and Joseph Mobutu over central power.
	Deployment of l'Opération des Nations Unies au Congo, the first United Nations (UN) peacekeeping operation in the Congo, until 1965.
January 1961	Assassination of Lumumba.
1964–1965	Rebellion in Bandundu and throughout the eastern provinces.
November 1965	Coup d'état by Mobutu.
November 1973	Zairianization policy, including expropriation of foreign-owned businesses and property and their subsequent distribution to Congolese government officials.
1977–1985	Four successive rebellions in Katanga.
April 1990	Mobutu promises national multiparty elections for 1991.

May 1990   Massacre of student protesters at University of
                            Lubumbashi. Belgium, the European Economic
                            Commission, Canada, and the United States cut
                            off all but humanitarian aid to the Congo.

1991–1992   National conference on political reform.

August 1992   National conference establishes new govern-
                            ment, names Etienne Tshisekedi prime minis-
                            ter. Subsequent conflict between Tshisekedi and
                            Mobutu over control of government.

March 1993   Mobutu names new prime minister; the Congo
                            has two rival governments.

May 1993   Large-scale fighting between "indigenous" com-
                            munities and Congolese of Rwandan descent in
                            North Kivu.

April–July 1994   Rwandan genocide. Approximately 800,000
                            Tutsis and moderate Hutus killed. 2 million
                            Rwandan Hutus flee the advance of the forces of
                            the new Tutsi-led government, and take refuge in
                            the Kivus. Rwandan Hutu militias use refugee
                            camps as bases to attack Rwandan territory and
                            to strike Congolese Tutsis.

Wars of the 1990s

October 1996   First Congo War begins. Fighting between Mobu-
                            tu's troops and the Alliance of the Democratic
                            Forces for the Liberation of Congo-Zaire (ADFL)
                            supported by Angola, Burundi, Rwanda, Uganda,
                            and South Sudanese rebel forces.

May 1997   ADFL takes over Kinshasa. Laurent-Désiré
                            Kabila declares himself president. End of the
                            First War.

August 1998   Second Congo War begins, led by the Congolese
                            Rally for Democracy (RCD). Rwanda, Uganda,
                            and Burundi support the RCD; Zimbabwe, Angola,
                            Namibia, Chad, and Sudan side with Kabila.

September 1998   Creation of the Congo Liberation Movement
                            (MLC).

July 1999   Lusaka Agreement: ceasefire among all national
                            and regional warring parties, except the RCD,
                            and plan for return to peace.

February 2000	UN Security Council authorizes UN peacekeeping mission in the Congo, Mission de l'Organisation des Nations Unies au Congo (MONUC).
May 2000	First split within the RCD. Uganda supports one faction, now based in Kisangani; Rwanda supports the other based in Goma.
January 2001	Assassination of Laurent-Désiré Kabila. His son Joseph Kabila replaces him as president.
March 2001	Beginning of UN peacekeepers' deployment to the Congo.
April 2002	Beginning of Inter-Congolese Dialogue in Sun City, South Africa.
July 2002	Pretoria Agreement between Rwanda and the Congo.
August 2002	Luanda Agreement between Uganda and the Congo.
October 2002	Withdrawal of most regional armies from Congolese territory completed.
December 2002	Participants in the Inter-Congolese Dialogue sign Global and All-Inclusive Agreement.
April 2003	Final Act of the Inter-Congolese Dialogue.
May 2003	Departure of the last remaining regional army in the Congo, the Ugandan troops stationed in Ituri, followed by an explosion of violence in the district.
June 2003	European Union's Operation Artemis begins its deployment to Bunia, where it stays for three months.

Transition to Peace and Democracy

June 30, 2003	Nomination of Transitional Government led by President Joseph Kabila; official beginning of transition.
July 2003	Four vice presidents inaugurated: Jean-Pierre Bemba (MLC), Abdoulaye Yerodia Ndombasi (government), Arthur Z'ahidi Ngoma (Political Opposition), and Azarias Ruberwa (Congolese Rally for Democracy Goma, RCD-G).

August 2003	Installation of Transitional Parliament.
September 2003	Installation of general staff of the army.
March 2004	Failed coup d'état in Kinshasa.
May 2004	Seven Ituri militias sign agreement on disarmament and participation in transition.
	Nomination of the provincial governors.
May–June 2004	Bukavu crisis (South Kivu). Units of the integrated army loyal to Kabila clash with dissident Banyamulenge and Banyarwanda units, led by Laurent Nkunda and Jules Mutebutsi. Dissidents occupy and pillage Bukavu. At least 87 people killed and 3,700 displaced. International pressure eventually forces withdrawal of dissidents. Nkunda's troops retreat to Minova, Mutebutsi's to Rwanda.
	Second failed coup d'état in Kinshasa.
August 2004	Massacres of Congolese Banyamulenge refugees in Gatumba (Burundi). 152 killed, 106 wounded. In protest, Vice President Ruberwa suspends Congolese Rally for Democracy Goma's (RCD-G) participation in transition, but resumes involvement after four days.
September 2004	After a week of heavy fighting, units of the integrated army loyal to Kabila occupy Nkunda's stronghold of Minova. At least 150,000 people displaced.
December 2004	Kanyabayonga crisis (North Kivu). Pro-RCD-G units of the integrated army clash with pro-Kabila units allied with Mai Mai over status of Kinyarwanda-speaking Congolese in the army and in civilian life. Over 200,000 people displaced.
	Parliament adopts census law.
January 2005	Riots in Kinshasa following mention of a potential postponement of the elections.
February 2005	Nine UN military observers killed in Ituri.
April 2005	Independent Electoral Commission requests that parliament extend transition.

May 2005	Parliament adopts constitution and law on referendum (for population to approve constitution).
June 2005	Parliament votes for six-month extension of transition. Census begins.
	Late June: violent protests in major Congolese cities over management of transition.
December 2005	Referendum: 84% of voters approve new constitution. Parliament extends transition by another six months.
January–February 2006	Rutshuru crisis (North Kivu). Nkunda's troops fight against government and Mai Mai forces; at least 70,000 people displaced.
July 2006	Legislative elections and first round of presidential elections. Kabila receives 45% of vote; opposition leader Bemba (MLC) receives 20%.
August 2006	Fighting in Kinshasa between troops loyal to Bemba and troops loyal to Kabila; 23 people killed.
October 2006	Provincial elections and second round of presidential elections. Kabila receives 58% of vote, Bemba 42%. Elections receive general approval from international monitors.
November 2006	Sake Crisis (North Kivu). Nkunda's troops take over the town of Sake and prepare to attack Goma. MONUC forcefully intervenes to defend Goma and pushes the rebels back to their original positions.
December 6, 2006	Inauguration of President-elect Joseph Kabila. Official end of the transition.

Post-Transition

January–February 2007	Fighting in Minembwe (South Kivu) between Congolese army and Banyamulenge dissident group following disagreement over elections results. At least 200 people killed, including 50 soldiers on both sides; 20,000 people displaced.
	Fighting between Congolese security services and members of the Bunda dia Kongo religious movement in Bas-Congo province; 134 people killed.

March 2007	Fighting in Kinshasa between Bemba's guards and Kabila's troops; 200–500 people killed. Bemba goes into exile three weeks later.
January 2008	Goma Peace Agreement attempts to end continued fighting between various armed groups in the Kivus. Subsequent implementation fails.
August 2008	Renewed large-scale fighting in North Kivu, South Kivu, and Ituri. At least 500,000 additional people displaced and hundreds of civilians killed over the next six months.
December 2008– January 2009	Ugandan troops reenter the Congo with agreement of Congolese government to fight the Lord's Resistance Army, a Ugandan rebel movement. Rwanda arrest Nkunda, then Rwandan troops reenter the Congo to fight alongside the Congolese army and capture Rwandan Hutu militias in the Kivus.
2009	Rwandan and Ugandan troops withdraw from Congolese territory.
	Congolese army conducts large-scale military operations against Rwandan Hutu militias in the Kivus; Congolese, Rwandan, and Ugandan militias launch regular attacks against civilians throughout the eastern Congo; and heavy fighting erupts over local fishing rights in Equateur province. In total, at least 2,700 people are killed and 1,500,000 additional civilians are displaced in 2009.

Bibliography

Abdullah, Ibrahim. 1997. "Bush Path to Destruction: The Origin and Character of the Revolutionary United Front." *Africa Development* 22 (3/4): 45–76.

Adam, Hussein. 2004. "Somalia: International Versus Local Attempts at Peacebuilding," in *Durable Peace: Challenges for Peacebuilding in Africa*, eds. M. Ali Taisier and Robert O. Matthews (pp. 253–281). Toronto: University of Toronto Press.

Adam, Hussein. 2005. "Peace Making and Peace Building in Somalia: A Tale of Two Political Cultures." Paper presented at the 49th Annual Meeting of the African Studies Association Conference, November, Washington, D.C.

Adam, Hussein M. 2008. *From Tyranny to Anarchy: The Somali Experience*. Trenton, NJ: Africa World Press.

Adler, Emanuel. 1997. "Seizing the Middle Ground: Constructivism in World Politics." *European Journal of International Relations* 3 (3): 319–363.

Alao, Abiodun, Olonisakin, Funmi, and Mackinlay, John. 1999. *Peacekeepers, Politicians and Warlords: The Liberian Peace Process*. New York: United Nations University Press.

Amnesty International. 2003. *On the Precipice: The Deepening Human Rights and Humanitarian Crisis in Ituri*. New York: Amnesty International.

2005. *Democratic Republic of Congo: Arming the East*. New York: Amnesty International.

Anderson, Mary B. 1999. *Do No Harm: How Aid Can Support Peace – or War*. Boulder, CO: Lynne Rienner Publishers.

Anderson, Mary, and Olson, Lara. 2003. *Confronting War: Critical Lessons for Peace Practitioners*. Cambridge, MA: The Collaborative for Development Action.

Autesserre, Séverine. 2006. "Local Violence, National Peace? Post-War 'Settlement' in the Eastern D.R. Congo (2003–2006)." *African Studies Review* 49 (3): 1–29.

2007. "Explaining Peace Building Failures: A Study of the Eastern D.R. Congo (2003–2006)." *Review of African Political Economy* 34 (113): 423–442.

2008. "The Trouble with Congo – How Local Disputes Fuel Regional Violence." *Foreign Affairs* 87 (3): 94–110.

2009. "Hobbes and the Congo. Frames, Local Violence, and International Intervention." *International Organization* 63: 249–280.

Avruch, Kevin. 2004. "Culture as Context, Culture as Communication: Considerations for Humanitarian Negotiators." *Harvard Negotiation Law Review* 9: 391–408.

Baaz, Maria Eriksson, and Stern, Maria. 2008. "Making Sense of Violence: Voices of Soldiers in the Congo (DRC)." *Journal of Modern African Studies* 46 (1): 57–86.

Badie, Bertrand. 1995. *La Fin des Territoires: Essai sur le Désordre International et sur l'Utilité Sociale du Respect*. Paris: Fayard.

Banégas, Richard, and Jewsiewicki, Bogumil (eds.). 2000. "RDC, La Guerre Vue D'en Bas. Special Issue." *Politique Africaine* 84.

Bangura, Yusuf. 1997. "Understanding the Political and Cultural Dynamics of the Sierra Leone War: A Critique of Paul Richards's Fighting for the Rain Forest." *Africa Development* 22 (3/4): 117–148.

Barnett, Michael N. 2002. *Eyewitness to a Genocide: The United Nations and Rwanda*. Ithaca, NY: Cornell University Press.

Barnett, Michael N., and Finnemore, Martha. 2004. *Rules for the World: International Organizations in Global Politics*. Ithaca, NY: Cornell University Press.

Barron, Patrick, Smith, Claire Q., and Woolcock, Michael. 2004. *Understanding Local Level Conflict in Developing Countries: Theory, Evidence and Implications from Indonesia*. Social development papers. Conflict prevention and reconstruction series. Washington, DC: World Bank.

Barston, R. P. 1988. *Modern Diplomacy*. New York: Longman.

Bax, Mart 2000. "Warlords, Priests and the Politics of Ethnic Cleansing: A Case-Study from Rural Bosnia Herzegovina." *Ethnic and Racial Studies* 23 (1): 16–36.

Bayart, Jean-François. 1989. *L'Etat en Afrique: la Politique du Ventre*. Paris: Fayard.

1996. *L'illusion Identitaire*. Paris: Fayard.

Behrend, Heike. 1999. *Alice Lakwena & the Holy Spirits: War in Northern Uganda, 1985–97*. Oxford: James Currey.

Benson, Rodney. 2006. "News Media as a 'Journalistic Field': What Bourdieu Adds to New Institutionalism, and Vice Versa." *Political Communication* (23): 187–202.

Berger, Carol. 2009. "The Unintended Consequences of UN Peacekeeping in Post-War Southern Sudan: Why Everyone Wants a Uniform." Paper presented at the Symposium on Imperfect Duties? Humanitarian

Intervention in Africa and the Responsibility to Protect in the Post-Iraq Era, March, De Pauw University, Indiana.

Berger, Peter L., and Luckmann, Thomas. 1967. *The Social Construction of Reality; a Treatise in the Sociology of Knowledge.* Garden City, NY: Doubleday.

Berkeley, Bill. 2001. *The Graves Are Not Yet Full: Race, Tribe and Power in the Heart of Africa.* New York: Basic Books.

Bigo, Didier. 1996. "Guerres, Conflits, Transnational et Territoire," in *L'international Sans Territoire*, eds. Bertrand Badie, Marie-Claude Smouts, and Wladimir Andreff (pp. 397–418). Paris: L'Harmattan.

2006. "Globalized (in)Security: The Field and the Ban-Opticon," in *Illiberal Practices of Liberal Regimes – the (in)Security Games*, eds. Didier Bigo and Anastasia Tsoukala (pp. 5–49). Paris: L'Harmattan.

Boas, Morten. 2008. "'Just Another Day' – the North Kivu Security Predicament after the 2006 Congolese Elections." *African Security* 1 (1): 53–68.

2009. "Funérailles Pour un Ami: des Luttes de Citoyenneté dans la Guerre Civile Libérienne." *Politique Africaine* (112): 36–51.

Boshoff, Henri. 2005. *Update on the Status of Army Integration in the DRC.* Pretoria, South Africa: Institute for Security Studies.

Bourdieu, Pierre. 1979. *La Distinction: Critique Sociale du Jugement.* Paris: Éditions de Minuit.

Boutros-Ghali, Boutros. 1992. *An Agenda for Peace. Preventive Diplomacy, Peacemaking and Peace-Keeping.* New York: United Nations.

Braeckman, Colette. 1999. *L'enjeu Congolais: L'Afrique Centrale Après Mobutu.* Paris: Fayard.

2003. *Les Nouveaux Prédateurs: Politique Des Puissances En Afrique Centrale.* Paris: Fayard.

Branch, Daniel. 2009. *The Normalisation of Violence.* Oxford Transitional Justice Research Working Paper Series, Oxford University.

Brewer, Cecily. 2008. "Good Intentions: The UN's Integrated DDR Dilemmas in Southern Sudan." Unpublished Manuscript, Johns Hopkins University, on file with author.

Brittain, Victoria, and Conchiglia, Augusta. 2004. *EU Security: The Great Lake.* Study Group on Europe's Security Capabilities. London: London School of Economics – Center for the Study of Global Governance.

Bush, Robert A. Baruch. 2003. "Realizing the Potential of International Conflict Work: Connections between Practice and Theory." *Negotiation Journal* (January): 97–103.

Carayannis, Tatiana. Forthcoming. *Pioneers of Peacekeeping: The Story of the UN Operation in the Congo 1960–1965.* Boulder, CO: Lynne Rienner Publishers.

Carayannis, Tatiana, and Weiss, Herbert F. 2003. "The Democratic Republic of Congo: 1996–2002," in *Dealing with Conflict in Africa: The Role of the United Nations and Regional Organizations*, ed. Jane Boulden (pp. 253–303). London: Palgrave.

Carothers, Thomas. 2002. "The End of the Transition Paradigm." *Journal of Democracy* 13 (2): 5–21.

Carpenter, R. Charli. 2003. "Women and Children First: Gender, Norms, and Humanitarian Evacuation in the Balkans 1991–5." *International Organization* (57): 661–694.

2006. *Innocent Women and Children: Gender, Norms and the Protection of Civilians*. Burlington, VT: Ashgate.

Cassanelli, Lee V. 1997. "Somali Land Resource Issues in Historical Perspective." In *Learning from Somalia*, ed. Walter Clarke and Jeffrey Herbst (pp. 42–63). Boulder, CO: Westview Press.

Cellule Provinciale d'Appui à la Pacification and Programme des Nations Unies pour le Développement. 2008. *Rapports de l'Exercice Participatif d'Analyse des Conflits et Capacités de Paix pour la Planification du Développement dans la Province du Nord-Kivu*. Goma: Programme des Nations Unies pour le Développement.

Chrétien, Jean-Pierre. 1995. *Les Médias du Génocide*. Paris: Karthala.

Coles, Kimberley. 2007. *Democratic Designs. International Intervention and Electoral Practices in Postwar Bosnia-Herzegovina*. Ann Arbor: University of Michigan Press.

Conrad, Joseph. 1971 [1902]. *Heart of Darkness*. New York: Norton.

Cowan, Paul. 2005. *The Peacekeepers*. Montreal: National Film Board of Canada.

Curtis, Devon. 2001. *Politics and Humanitarian Aid: Debates, Dilemmas and Dissension*. HPG Report. London: Overseas Development Institute.

Daase, Christopher. 1999. "Spontaneous Institutions: Peacekeeping as an International Convention," in *Imperfect Unions: Security Institutions over Time and Space*, eds. Helga Haftendorn, Robert O. Keohane, and Celeste A. Wallander (pp. 223–258). Oxford: Oxford University Press.

Dahl, Robert Alan. 1989. *Democracy and Its Critics*. New Haven, CT: Yale University Press.

De Goede, Meike, and Van Der Borgh, Chris. 2008. "A Role for Diplomats in Postwar Transitions? The Case of the International Committee in Support of the Transition in the Democratic Republic of the Congo." *African Security* 1 (2): 115–133.

De Wall, Alenander. 1997. *Famine Crimes: Politics & the Disaster Relief Industry in Africa*. Bloomington: Indiana University Press.

2005a. "Counter-Insurgency on the Cheap." *London Review of Books* 26 (15).

2005b. "Who Are the Darfurians? Arab and African Identities, Violence and External Engagement." *African Affairs* 104 (415): 181 205.

2007. "Prospects for Peace in Darfur," in *War in Darfur and the Search for Peace*, ed. Alex De Waal (pp. 367–392). Cambridge and London: Global Equity Initiative, Harvard University, and Justice Africa.

De Zeeuw, Jeroen 2005. "Projects Do Not Create Institutions. The Record of Democracy Assistance in Post-conflict Societies." *Democratization* 12 (4): 481–504.

Debos, Marielle. 2008. "Fluid Loyalties in a Regional Crisis: Chadian 'Ex-Liberators' in the Central African Republic." *African Affairs* 107 (427): 225–241.

Deng, Francis M. 1995. *War of Visions: Conflict of Identities in the Sudan.* Washington, DC: Brookings Institution.

Denich, Bette. 1994. *"Dismembering Yugoslavia: Nationalist Ideology and the Symbolic Revival of Genocide." American Ethnologist* 21 (2): 367–390.

Dennys, Christian, and Zaman, Idrees. 2009. *Trends in Local Afghan Conflicts – Synthesis Paper.* Kabul, Afghanistan: Cooperation for Peace and Unity.

Des Forges, Alison. 1999. *Leave None to Tell the Story: Genocide in Rwanda.* New York: Human Rights Watch.

Diamond, Larry. 1996. "Democracy in Latin America: Degrees, Illusions, and Directions for Consolidation," in *Beyond Sovereignty: Collectively Defending Democracy in the Americas*, ed. Tom Farer (pp. 52–104). Baltimore: Johns Hopkins University Press.

Dimaggio, Paul, and Powell, Walter. 1983. "The Iron Cage Revisited: Institutional Isomorphism and Collective Rationality in Organizational Fields." *American Sociological Review* 48 (2): 147–160.

Doom, Ruddy, and Gorus, Jan F. J. 2000. *Politics of Identity and Economics of Conflict in the Great Lakes Region.* Brussels: VUB University Press.

Doom, Ruddy, and Vlassenroot, Koen. 1999. "Kony's Message: A New Koine? The Lord's Resistance Army in Northern Uganda." *African Affairs* 98: 5–36.

Downs, George, and Stedman, Stephen John. 2002. "Evaluation Issues in Peace Implementation," in *Ending Civil Wars. The Implementation of Peace Agreements*, eds. Stephen John Stedman, Donald Rothchild, and Elizabeth M. Cousens (pp. 43–69). London: Lynne Rienner Publishers.

Doyle, Michael W., Johnstone, Ian, and Orr, Robert C., eds. 1997. *Keeping the Peace: Multidimensional UN Operations in Cambodia and El Salvador*. New York: Cambridge University Press.

Doyle, Michael W., and Sambanis, Nicholas. 2000. "International Peacebuilding: A Theoretical and Quantitative Analysis." *American Political Science Review* 94 (4): 779–801.

Doyle, Michael W., and Sambanis, Nicholas. 2006. *Making War and Building Peace: United Nations Peace Operations*. Princeton, NJ: Princeton University Press.

Drew, Elizabeth. 1994. *On the Edge: The Clinton Presidency*. New York: Simon & Schuster.

Duffey, Tamara. 2000. "Cultural Issues in Contemporary Peacekeeping." *International Peacekeeping* 7 (1); 142–168.

Duffield, Mark R. 2001. *Global Governance and the New Wars: The Merging of Development and Security*. New York: Zed Books.

Dunn, Kevin C. 2003. *Imagining the Congo: The International Relations of Identity*. New York: Palgrave Macmillan.

Eden, Lynn. 2004. *Whole World on Fire: Organizations, Knowledge, and Nuclear Weapons Devastation*. Ithaca, NY: Cornell University Press.

Ellis, Stephen. 2002. "Cautions on Macro-Political Peacebuilding." Paper presented at the symposium Democratization after War: State-Of-the-Art Thinking about Governance and Peacebuilding, Tinas J. Watson Jr. Institute for International Studies, Brown University, Providence, Rhode Island.

2005. "How to Rebuild Africa." *Foreign Affairs* 84 (5): 135–148.

Englebert, Pierre, and Tull, Denis. 2008. "Postconflict Resolution in Africa: Flawed Ideas About Failed States." *International Security* 32 (4): 106–139.

Fahey, Dan. 2009. "Guns and Butter: Uganda's Involvement in Northeastern Congo 2003–2009." Paper presented at the 52nd Annual Meeting of the African Studies Association Conference, November, New Orleans.

Fanthorpe, Richard. 2001. "Neither Citizen nor Subject? 'Lumpen' Agency and the Legacy of Native Administration in Sierra Leone." *African Affairs* 100: 363–386.

Farah, Ahmed Yusuf. 2002. *African Conflicts, Their Management, Resolution and Post Conflict Reconstruction*. CODESRIA, Addis Ababa,   http://unpan1.un.org/intradoc/groups/public/documents/cafrad/unpan009239.pdf.

Farah, Ahmed Yusuf, with Lewis, I.M. 1993. *Somalia: The Roots of Reconciliation*. London/Hargeisa: Action Aid.

Farah, Ahmed Yusuf, with Lewis, I.M. 1997 "Making Peace in Somaliland." *Cahiers d'Études Africaines* 37 (146): 349–377.

Fearon, James D., and Laitin, David D. 2003. "Ethnicity, Insurgency, and Civil War." *American Political Science Review* 97 (1): 75–90.

Fearon, James, and Wendt, Alexander. 2002. "Rationalism Versus Constructivism: A Skeptical View," in *Handbook of International Relations*, eds. Walter Carlsnaes, Thomas Risse, and Beth Simmons (pp. 52–72). London: Sage Publications.

Fédération Internationale des Ligues des Droits de l'Homme. 2009. *République Démocratique du Congo: la Dérive Autoritaire du Régime*. Paris: Fédération Internationale des Ligues des Droits de l'Homme.

Ferguson, James. 1990. *The Anti-Politics Machine: "Development," Depoliticization, and Bureaucratic Power in Lesotho*. New York: Cambridge University Press.

Fetherston, Betts and Nordstrom, Carolyn. 1995. "Overcoming Habitus in Conflict Management: UN peacekeeping and Warzone Ethnography." *Peace and Change* 20 (1): 94–119.

Finnemore, Martha. 1996a. "Constructing Norms of Humanitarian Interventions," in *The Culture of National Security: Norms and Identity in World Politics*, ed. Peter J. Katzenstein (pp. 107–126). New York: Columbia University Press.

  1996b. "Norms, Culture, and World Politics: Insights from Sociology's Institutionalism." *International Organization* 50 (2): 325–347.

Fitzduff, Niall, and Williams, Sue. 2007. *How Did Northern Ireland Move toward Peace?* Collaborative Learning Project. Cambridge, MA: Reflecting on Peace Practice Project.

Fortna, Virginia Page. 2004a. "Where Have All the Victories Gone? War Outcomes in Historical Perspective." Paper presented at the 99th Annual Meeting of the American Political Science Association Conference, September, Chicago.

  2004b. *Peace Time: Cease-Fire Agreements and the Durability of Peace*. Princeton, NJ: Princeton University Press.

  2008. *Does Peacekeeping Work? Shaping Belligerents' Choices after Civil War*. Princeton, NJ: Princeton University Press.

Fujii, Lee Ann. 2008. "The Power of Local Ties: Popular Participation in the Rwandan Genocide." *Security Studies* (17): 568–597.

Gambino, Anthony W. 2008. *Congo. Securing Peace, Sustaining Progress*. Washington, DC: Council on Foreign Relations Press.

Gilbert, Andrew. 2008. *Foreign Authority and the Politics of Impartiality in Postwar Bosnia-Herzegovina*. PhD diss., University of Chicago.

Gilligan, Michael, and Stedman, Stephen John. 2003. "Where Do the Peacekeepers Go?" *International Studies Review* 5 (4): 37–54.

Global Witness. 2005. *Under-Mining Peace. Tin: The Explosive Trade in Cassiterite in Eastern DRC*. Washington, DC: Global Witness.

Grove, Brandon. 2005. *Behind Embassy Walls: The Life and Times of an American Diplomat.* Columbia: University of Missouri Press.

Guilhot, Nicolas. 2005. *The Democracy Makers: Human Rights and International Order.* New York: Columbia University Press.

Hadjipavlou, Maria, and Kanol, Bülent 2008. *Cumulative Impact Case Study. The Impacts of Peacebuilding Work on the Cyprus Conflict.* Collaborative Learning Project. Cambridge, MA: Reflecting on Peace Practice Project.

Hamilton, Keith, and Langhorne, Richard. 1995. *The Practice of Diplomacy: Its Evolution, Theory and Administration.* New York: Routledge.

Hansen, Lene. 2006. *Security as Practice: Discourse Analysis and the Bosnian War.* New York: Routledge.

Held, David. 2006. *Models of Democracy.* Cambridge, UK: Polity.

Hergé. 1930–1931. *Tintin au Congo.* Paris: Casterman.

Hochschild, Adam. 1998. *King Leopold's Ghost: A Story of Greed, Terror, and Heroism in Colonial Africa.* Boston: Houghton Mifflin.

Hocking, Brian. 2004. "Privatizing Diplomacy? (ISP Policy Forum: The Privatization of Diplomacy and Security)." *International Studies Perspectives* 5 (2): 147–152.

Hoebeke, Hans, Carette, Stéphanie, and Vlassenroot, Koen. 2007. *EU Support to the Democratic Republic of Congo.* Paris: Centre d'Etudes Stratégiques. Bureau du Premier Ministre de la République Française.

Hoffman, Bruce. 2008. "The Myth of Grass-Roots Terrorism. Why Osama Bin Laden Still Matters." *Foreign Affairs* 87 (3): 133–138.

Holbrooke, Richard C. 1998. *To End a War.* New York: Random House.

Holohan, Anne. 2005. *Networks of Democracy: Lessons from Kosovo for Afghanistan, Iraq, and Beyond.* Stanford, CA: Stanford University Press.

Holt, Victoria K., and Berkman, Tobias C. 2006. *The Impossible Mandate? Military Preparedness, the Responsibility to Protect and Modern Peace Operations.* Washington, DC: The Henry L. Stimson Center.

Howard, Lise Morjé. 2008. *UN Peacekeeping in Civil Wars.* Cambridge, UK: Cambridge University Press.

Human Rights Watch. 1999. *Democratic Republic of Congo: Casualties of War: Civilians, Rule of Law, and Democratic Freedoms.* New York: Human Rights Watch.

2000. *Eastern Congo Ravaged: Killing Civilians and Silencing Protest.* Washington, DC: Human Rights Watch.

2002. *The War within the War – Sexual Violence against Women and Girls in Eastern Congo.* Washington, DC: Human Rights Watch.

Human Rights Watch. 2004. *End Arm Flows as Ethnic Tensions Rise.* Brussels: Human Rights Watch.

Human Rights Watch. 2005. *République Démocratique Du Congo – Attaque Contre Des Civils au Nord Kivu.* Brussels: Human Rights Watch.

2007. *Human Rights Watch World Report 2007: Events of 2006.* New York: Seven Stories Press.

2008a. *Ballots to Bullets: Organized Political Violence and Kenya's Crisis of Governance.* New York: Human Rights Watch.

2008b. *We Will Crush You: The Restriction of Political Space in the Democratic Republic of Congo.* New York: Human Rights Watch.

Huntington, Samuel P. 1993. "The Clash of Civilizations?" *Foreign Affairs* 72 (3): 22–49.

Hutchinson, Sharon. 2001. "A Curse from God? Religious and Political Dimensions of the Post-1991 Rise of Ethnic Violence in South Sudan." *The Journal of Modern African Studies* 39 (2): 307–331.

International Crisis Group. 1999. *The Agreement on a Cease-Fire in the Democratic Republic of Congo: An Analysis of the Agreement and Prospects for Peace.* Democratic Republic of Congo Report. Brussels: International Crisis Group.

2000a. *Indonesia's Maluku Crisis: The Issues.* Brussels: International Crisis Group.

2000b. *Scramble for the Congo. Anatomy of an Ugly War.* Africa Report. Brussels: International Crisis Group.

2001. *The Inter-Congolese Dialogue. Political Negotiation or Game of Bluff?* Africa Report. Brussels: International Crisis Group.

2002. *Storm Clouds over Sun City. The Urgent Need to Recast the Congolese Peace Process.* Africa Report. Brussels: International Crisis Group

2003a. *Congo Crisis: Military Intervention in Ituri.* Africa Report. Brussels: International Crisis Group.

2003b. *The Kivus: The Forgotten Crucible of the Congo Conflict.* Africa Report. Brussels: International Crisis Group.

2004a. *Back to the Brink in the Congo.* Africa Briefing. Brussels: International Crisis Group.

2004b. *Liberia and Sierra Leone: Rebuilding Failed States.* Africa Report. Brussels: International Crisis Group.

2004c. *Maintaining Momentum in the Congo: The Ituri Problem.* Africa Report. Brussels: International Crisis Group.

2005a. *The Congo's Transition Is Failing: Crisis in the Kivus.* Brussels: International Crisis Group.

2005b. *Congo: Deal with the FDLR Threat Now.* Brussels: International Crisis Group.

2006a. *Congo's Elections: Making or Breaking the Peace.* Brussels: International Crisis Group.

2006b. *Escaping the Conflict Trap: Promoting Good Governance in the Congo.* Brussels: International Crisis Group.

2006c. *Katanga: The Congo's Forgotten Crisis.* Brussels: International Crisis Group.

2007a. *Bringing Peace to North Kivu.* Brussels: International Crisis Group.

2007b. *Darfur's New Security Reality.* Brussels: International Crisis Group.

2007c. *Congo: Consolidating the Peace.* Brussels: International Crisis Group.

2008. *Congo: Four Priorities for Sustainable Peace in Ituri.* Brussels: International Crisis Group.

2009. *Congo: Five Priorities for a Peacebuilding Strategy.* Brussels: International Crisis Group.

International Rescue Committee. 2003. *Mortality in the Democratic Republic of Congo: Results from a Nationwide Survey.* New York: International Rescue Committee and Burnet Institute.

2004. *Mortality in the Democratic Republic of Congo: Results from a Nationwide Survey. Conducted April–July 2004.* New York: International Rescue Committee and Burnet Institute.

2005. *Mortality in the Democratic Republic of Congo: Results from a Nationwide Survey.* New York: International Rescue Committee and Burnet Institute.

2007. *Mortality in the Democratic Republic of Congo: An Ongoing Crisis.* New York: International Rescue Committee and Burnet Institute.

Ismail, Omer, and Fick, Maggie. 2009. *Darfur Rebels 101.* Washington, DC: Enough Project.

Jackson, Stephen. 2000. "'Nos Richesses Sont Pillées!' Economies de Guerre et Rumeurs de Crime au Kivu." *Politique Africaine* 84: 117–135.

2006. "Sons of Which Soil? The Language and Politics of Autochthony in Eastern D.R. Congo." *African Studies Review* 49 (2): 95–123.

Johnston, Patrick. 2005. "Dynamics of Post-War and Peacekeeping in Sierra Leone." Paper presented at the 49th Annual Meeting of the African Studies Association Conference, Washington, D.C.

Jones, Bruce D. 2001. *Peacemaking in Rwanda: The Dynamics of Failure.* Boulder, CO: Lynne Rienner Publishers.

Jönsson, Christer, and Hall, Martin. 2005. *Essence of Diplomacy.* New York: Palgrave Macmillan.

Kalere, Jean Migabo. 2002. *Génocide au Congo? Analyse des Massacres de Populations Civiles.* Brussels: Broederlijk Delen.

Kalyvas, Stathis N. 2001. "'New' and 'Old' Civil Wars, a Valid Distinction?" *World Politics*, 54 (1): 99–118.

2003. "The Ontology of 'Political Violence': Action and Identity in Civil Wars." *Perspectives on Politics* 1 (3): 475–494.

2006. *The Logic of Violence in Civil War*. New York: Cambridge University Press.

Kaplan, Robert. 1994a. "The Coming Anarchy." *The Atlantic Monthly*, February.

1994b. *Balkan Ghosts: A Journey through History*. New York: Vintage Books.

1996. *The Ends of the Earth: A Journey at the Dawn of the 21st Century*. New York: Random House.

Kasongo, Missak, and Sebahara, Pamphile. 2006. *Le Désarmement, la Démobilisation et la Réinsertion des Combattants en RD Congo*. Note d'Analyse. Brussels: GRIP.

Katz-Lavigne, Sarah. 2008. "Partial Peacebuilding and the Failure of Civilian Protection in the Democratic Republic of Congo, 2003–2006." MA thesis, London School of Economics, on file with author.

Kayser, Christiane. 2008. *La Conférence De La Dernière Chance ? Et Après ?* Echos de Goma et d'Ailleurs. Goma: Pole Institute.

Kim, Cheryl M. Lee, and Metrikas, Mark. 1997. "Holding a Fragile Peace: The Military and Civilian Components of UNTAC," in *Keeping the Peace*, eds. Michael W. Doyle, Ian Johnstone, and Robert C. Orr (pp. 107–133). New York: Cambridge University Press.

Kipp, Jacob, Grau, Lester, Prinslow, Karl, and Smith, Don. 2006. "The Human Terrain System: A Cords for the 21st Century." *Military Review* (Sept-Oct).

Klopp, Jacqueline. 2002. "Can Moral Ethnicity Trump Political Tribalism? The Struggle for Land and Nation in Kenya." *African Studies Review* 61 (2): 269–294.

2009. "Kenya's Unfinished Agendas." *Journal of International Affairs* 62 (2): 143–158.

Klopp, Jacqueline, Githinji, Patrick, and Karuoya, Keffa. 2009. "Internal Displacement and Local Peace-Building in Kenya: Challenges and Innovations." Unpublished Manuscript, Columbia University/Internal Displacement Policy and Advocacy Center, on file with author.

Klopp, Jacqueline, and Kamungi, Prisca. 2007/2008. "Violence and Elections: Will Kenya Collapse?" *World Policy Review* 24 (4): 11–18.

Klopp, Jacqueline, and Zuern, Elke. 2007. "The Politics of Violence in Democratization." *Comparative Politics* 39 (2): 127–146.

Klotz, Audie, and Lynch, Cecelia. 2007. *Strategies for Research in Constructivist International Relations*. Armonk, NY: M.E. Sharpe.

Knox, Colin, and Quirk, Pádraic. 2000. *Peace Building in Northern Ireland, Israel and South Africa. Transition, Transformation and Reconciliation.* New York: Palgrave Macmillan.

Krämer, Mario. 2006. "The Relations between Center and Periphery. Dynamics of Violence in Kwazulu-Natal, South Africa." Paper presented at the Order, Conflict, and Violence Speaker Series, Yale University.

2007. *Violence as Routine. Transformations of Local-Level Politics and the Disjunction between Centre and Periphery in Kwazulu-Natal (South Africa).* Köln: Rüdiger Köppe Verlag (Siegener Beiträge zur Soziologie, vol. 8).

Kuper, Adam. 1999. *Culture: The Anthropologists' Account.* Cambridge, MA: Harvard University Press.

Lapid, Yosef, and Kratochwil, Friedrich V. 1996. *The Return of Culture and Identity in IR Theory.* Boulder, CO: Lynne Rienner Publishers.

Lederach, John Paul. 1995. *Preparing for Peace: Conflict Transformation across Cultures.* Syracuse, N.Y.: Syracuse University Press.

1997. *Building Peace: Sustainable Reconciliation in Divided Societies.* Washington, DC: U.S. Institute of Peace Press.

Lemarchand, René. 1995. "Rwanda: The Rationality of Genocide." *Issue: A Journal of Opinion* XXIII: 12–17.

2008. *The Dynamics of Violence in Central Africa.* Philadelphia: University of Pennsylvania Press.

2009. "Reflections on the Crisis in Eastern Congo," in *L'Afrique Des Grands Lacs – Annuaire 2008 – 2009,* eds. Filip Reyntjens and Stefaan Marysse (pp. 105–123). Paris: L'Harmattan.

Lesch, Ann Mosely. 1998. *The Sudan: Contested National Identities.* Bloomington: Indiana University Press.

Lewer, Nick. 1999. *International Non-Government Organisations and Peacebuilding – Perspectives from Peace Studies and Conflict Resolution.* West Yorkshire, UK: University of Bradford. Department of Peace Studies. Centre for Conflict Resolution.

Lewis, I. M. 1993. *Understanding Somalia: Guide to Culture, History and Social Institutions.* London: Haan.

Licklider, Roy. 1995. "Consequences of Negotiated Settlements in Civil Wars, 1945–1993." *American Political Science Review* 89 (3): 681–687.

Lie, Jon Harald Sande, and De Carvalho, Benjamin 2008. *A Culture of Protection? Perceptions of the Protection of Civilians from Sudan.* Oslo: Norwegian Institute for International Affairs (NUPI).

Life and Peace Institute. 2004. *Atelier de Planification des Partenaires de l'Institut Vie et Paix.* Bukavu: Life and Peace Institute.

2006. *Analyse des Dynamiques Locales de Cohabitation avec Groupes Armés FDLR à Bunyakiri, Hombo Nord, Hombo Sud et Chambucha.* Bukavu: Life and Peace Institute.

Lyons, Terrence. 2002. "The Role of Postsettlement Elections," in *Ending Civil Wars. The Implementation of Peace Agreements,* eds. Stephen John Stedman, Donald Rothchild, and Elizabeth M. Cousens (pp.215–237). Boulder, CO: Lynne Rienner Publishers.

2004. "Post-Conflict Elections and the Process of Demilitarizing Politics: The Role of Electoral Administration." *Democratization* 11 (3): 36–62.

2005. *Demilitarizing Politics: Elections on the Uncertain Road to Peace.* Boulder, CO: Lynne Rienner Publishers.

Macrae, Joanna, and Leader, Nicholas. 2000. *Shifting Sands: The Search for 'Coherence' between Political and Humanitarian Responses to Complex Emergencies.* HPG Report. London: Overseas Development Institute.

Maindo Monga Ngonga, Alphonse 2000. "Survivre à la Guerre des Autres. Un Défi Populaire en RDC. RDC, la Guerre Vue d'en Bas." *Politique Africaine* 84: 33–58.

2007. *Des Conflits Locaux à la Guerre Régionale en Afrique Centrale: Le Congo-Kinshasa Oriental 1996–2007.* Paris: L'Harmattan.

Mamdani, Mahmood. 1996. *Citizen and Subject: Contemporary Africa and the Legacy of Late Colonialism.* Princeton, NJ: Princeton University Press.

2001. *When Victims Become Killers: Colonialism, Nativism, and the Genocide in Rwanda.* Princeton, NJ: Princeton University Press.

2007. "The Politics of Naming: Genocide, Civil War, Insurgency." *London Review of Books* 29 (5): 5–8.

2009. *Saviors and Survivors: Darfur, Politics, and the War on Terror.* New York: Pantheon Books.

Mampilly, Zachariah Cherian. 2007. Stationary Bandits: Understanding Rebel Governance. PhD diss., University of California–Los Angeles.

Mansfield, Edward D., and Snyder, Jack L. 2005. *Electing to Fight: Why Emerging Democracies Go to War.* Cambridge, MA: MIT Press.

March, James, and Olsen, Johan. 1984. "The New Institutionalism: Organizational Factors in Political Life." *American Political Science Review* 78 (3): 734–749.

Marchal, Roland, and Messiant, Christine. 2002. "De l'Avidité des Rebelles. L'analyse Economique De La Guerre Civile Selon Paul Collier." *Critique Internationale* 16: 58–69.

Marks, Susan Collin. 2000. *Watching the Wind: Conflict Resolution During South Africa's Transition to Democracy.* Washington, DC: U.S. Institute of Peace Press.

Marx, Benjamin. 2008. "Elections, State Collapse, and Local Conflict in the Rift Valley. Kenya 2008." Unpublished Manuscript, Columbia University, on file with author.

Mathieu, Paul, and Willame, Jean-Claude. 1999. *Conflits et Guerres au Kivu et dans la Région des Grands Lacs: Entre Tensions Locales et Escalade Régionale*. Paris: L'Harmattan.

Médecins Sans Frontières. 2005. *Rien de Nouveau en Ituri: La Violence Continue*. Geneva: Médecins Sans Frontières.

Menkhaus, Ken. 1997. "International Peacebuilding and the Dynamics of Local and National Reconciliation in Somalia," in *Learning from Somalia*, eds. Walter Clarke and Jeffrey Herbst (pp. 42–63). Boulder, CO: Westview Press.

Mitchell, Timothy 2002. *Rule of Experts: Egypt, Techno-Politics, Modernity*. Berkeley: University of California Press.

Moore, Barrington. 1966. *Social Origins of Dictatorship and Democracy; Lord and Peasant in the Making of the Modern World*. Boston: Beacon Press.

Mortimer, Edward. 1998. "Under What Circumstances Should the UN Intervene Militarily in a 'Domestic' Crisis?," in *Peacemaking and Peacekeeping for the New Century*, eds. Olara A. Otunnu, Michael W. Doyle, and International Peace Academy (pp. 111–142). Lanham, MD: Rowman & Littlefield.

Muana, Patrick. 1997. "The Kamajoi Militia: Violence, Internal Displacement and the Politics of Counter-Insurgency." *Africa Development* 22 (3/4): 77–100.

Mugangu Matabaro, Séverin. 2008. "La Crise Foncière à l'Est de la RDC." In *L'Afrique des Grands Lacs – Annuaire 2007–2008*, eds. Stefaan Marysse, Filip Reyntjens, and Stef Vandegiste (pp. 385–414). Paris: L'Harmattan.

Nest, Michael, Grignon, François, and Kisangani, Emizet F. 2006. *The Democratic Republic of Congo. Economic Dimensions of War and Peace*. Boulder, CO.: Lynne Rienner.

Neumann, Iver B. 2002. "Returning Practice to the Linguistic Turn: The Case of Diplomacy." *Millennium: Journal of International Studies* 31 (3): 626–651.

   2008a. "Discourse Analysis: From Meta to Method," in *Qualitative Methods in International Relations*, eds. Audie Klotz and Deepa Prakash (pp. 61–77). New York: Palgrave.

   2008b. "Globalisation and Diplomacy." Unpublished Manuscript, Norwegian Institute for International Affairs, on file with author.

Ngbanda Nzambo, Honoré. 2004. *Crimes Organisés en Afrique Centrale. Révélations sur les Réseaux Rwandais et Occidentaux*. Paris: Duboiris.

Nicolson, Harold. 1988. *Diplomacy*. Washington, DC: Institute for the Study of Diplomacy School of Foreign Service, Georgetown University.

Ottaway, Marina. 2002. "Rebuilding State Institutions in Collapsed States." *Development and Change* 33 (5): 1001–1023.

2003. "Promoting Democracy after Conflict: The Difficult Choices." *International Studies Perspectives* 4: 314–322.

Paris, Roland. 2003. "Peacekeeping and the Constraints of Global Culture." *European Journal of International Relations* 9 (3): 441–473.

2004. *At War's End: Building Peace after Civil Conflict*. Cambridge, UK: Cambridge University Press.

Patrick, Stewart, and Rice, Susan. 2008. *Index of State Weakness in the Developing World*. Washington, DC: Brookings Institute.

Perrot, Sandrine. 2008. "Les Sources de l'Incompréhension. Production et Circulation des Savoirs sur la Lord's Resistance Army." In *Politique Africaine* 112: 140–160.

Forthcoming. "Northern Uganda: A Forgotten Conflict, Again? The Role of External Actors in the Northern Uganda Conflict Resolution," in *The Lord's Resistance Army, War, Peace and Reconciliation in Northern Uganda*, eds. Tim Allen and Koen Vlassenroot. London: Zed Books.

Pole Institute. 2004. *Une Plaie Encore Ouverte: La Problématique des Violences Sexuelles au Nord Kivu*. Regards Croisés. Goma: Pole Institute.

Pourtier, Roland. 2004. *L'Economie Minière au Kivu et ses Implications Régionales (Version Provisoire) – Rapport Suite à Une Mission au Nord Kivu, au Sud Kivu, et au Rwanda*. Paris: OCDE – Initiative for Central Africa / Initiative pour l'Afrique Centrale.

Power, Samantha. 2002. *"A Problem from Hell:" America and the Age of Genocide*. New York: Basic Books.

Prendergast, John. 1996. *Frontline Diplomacy: Humanitarian Aid and Conflict in Africa*. Boulder, CO: Lynne Rienner Publishers.

Prendergast, John, and Plumb, Emily. 2002. "Building Local Capacity: From Implementation to Peace Building," in *Ending Civil Wars. The Implementation of Peace Agreements*, eds. Stephen John Stedman, Donald Rothchild, and Elizabeth M. Cousens (pp. 237–349). London: Lynne Rienner Publishers.

Prunier, Gérard. 1995. *The Rwanda Crisis: History of a Genocide*. New York: Columbia University Press.

2008. *Africa's World War. Congo, the Rwandan Genocide, and the Making of a Continental Catastrophe*. Oxford: Oxford University Press.

Przeworski, Adam. 1999. "Minimalist Conception of Democracy: A Defense," in *Democracy's Value*, eds. Ian Shapiro and Casiano Hacker-Cordon (pp. 12–17). Cambridge, UK: Cambridge University Press.

Putnam, Robert D., Leonardi, Robert, and Nanetti, Raffaella Y. 1993. *Making Democracy Work: Civic Traditions in Modern Italy*. Princeton, NJ: Princeton University Press.

Rajasingham-Senanayake, Darani. 2003. "Sri Lanka and the Violence of Reconstruction." *Development* 48 (3): 111–120.

Rassemblement Pour Le Progrès. Undated, probably 2001. *Pour Que L'On N'Oublie Jamais*. Brussels: Rassemblement pour le Progrès.

Refugee International. 2008. *DR Congo: Give Peacekeepers Political Support and an Achievable Mission*. May. http://www.humansecuritygateway.com/documents/RI_DRC_GivePeacekeepers PoliticalSupport.pdf (accessed December 2009).

Regan, Patrick M. 2002. "Third-Party Interventions and the Duration of Intrastate Conflicts." *Journal of Conflict Resolution* 46 (1): 55–73.

Reno, William. 1998. *Warlord Politics and African States*. Boulder, CO: Lynne Rienner Publishers.

Reyntjens, Filip. 1999a. "Briefing: The Second Congo War: More Than a Remake." *African Affairs* 98 (391): 241–250.

    1999b. *La Guerre des Grands Lacs: Alliances Mouvantes et Conflits Extraterritoriaux en Afrique Centrale*. Paris: L'Harmattan.

    2007. "Democratic Republic of Congo: Political Transition and Beyond." *African Affairs* 106 (423): 307–317.

    2009. *The Great African War: Congo and Regional Geopolitics, 1996–2006*. New York: Cambridge University Press.

Richards, Paul. 1996. *Fighting for the Rain Forest: War, Youth & Resources in Sierra Leone*. Oxford: International African Institute and James Currey.

    2005. *No Peace, No War: An Anthropology of Contemporary Armed Conflicts*. Oxford: James Currey.

Richmond, Oliver P. 2002. *Maintaining Order, Making Peace*. New York: Palgrave.

    2005. *The Transformation of Peace*. New York: Palgrave Macmillan.

    2008. *Peace in International Relations*. New York: Routledge.

Rieff, David. 2002. *A Bed for the Night: Humanitarianism in Crisis*. New York: Simon & Schuster.

Romkema, Hans. 2004. *Update on the DRC Transition: The Case of the Kivu Provinces*. Pretoria, South Africa: Institute for Security Studies.

Rothchild, Donald. 1997. *Managing Ethnic Conflict in Africa: Pressures and Incentives for Cooperation*. Washington, DC: Brookings Institution Press.

Rubinstein, Robert A. 2008. *Peacekeeping under Fire: Culture and Intervention*. Boulder CO: Paradigm Publishers.

Sageman, Marc. 2008. *Leaderless Jihad: Terror Networks in the Twenty-First Century*. Philadelphia: University of Pennsylvania Press.

Sageman, Marc, and Hoffman, Bruce. 2008. "Does Osama Still Call the Shots? Debating the Containment of Al Qaeda's Leadership." *Foreign Affairs* 87 (4): 163–166.

Samset, Ingrid, and Madore, Yvon. 2006. *Evaluation of the UNDP/ UNOPS Peacebuilding and Community Development Project in Ituri, the Democratic Republic of Congo*. Bergen, Norway: Chr. Michelsen Institute.

Samset, Ingrid, and Suhrke, Astri. 2007. "What's in a Figure? Estimating Recurrence of Civil War." *International Peacekeeping* 14 (2): 195–203.

Satow, Ernest Mason. 1979. *Satow's Guide to Diplomatic Practice*. New York: Longman.

Schraeder, Peter. 2003. "Sapphire Anniversary Reflections on the Study of United States Foreign Policy Towards Africa." *Journal of Modern African Studies* 41 (1): 139–152.

Sebudandi, Christophe, and Icoyitungye, Juliette Kavabuha. 2008. *Impact Cumulatif des Efforts de Paix au Burundi: Avancées et Fragilités*. Collaborative Learning Project. Cambridge, MA: Reflecting on Peace Practice Project.

Sells, Michael. 1996. *The Bridge Betrayed: Religion and Genocide in Bosnia*. Berkeley: University of California Press.

Shaw, Ibrahim Seaga. 2007. "Historical Frames and the Politics of Humanitarian Intervention: From Ethiopia, Somalia to Rwanda." *Globalisation, Societies and Education* 5 (3): 351–371.

Silber, Laura, and Little, Allan. 1996. *The Death of Yugoslavia*. London: Penguin Books.

Simpson, Smith. 1972. *Instruction in Diplomacy: The Liberal Arts Approach*. Philadelphia: American Academy of Political and Social Science.

Sisk, Timothy, and Reynolds, Andrew (eds.). 1998. *Elections and Conflict Management in Africa*. Washington, DC: U.S. Institute of Peace Press.

Snyder, Jack L. 2000. *From Voting to Violence: Democratization and Nationalist Conflict*. New York: Norton.

Staibano, Carina. 2005. "Enhancing the UN Capacity. Part Two: The Democratic Republic of Congo: Enhancing UN Peacekeeping Capacity – Some Operational Aspects." Unpublished Manuscript, Department of Peace and Conflict Research, Uppsala University, Uppsala.

Stedman, Stephen John. 1997. "Spoilers Problems in Peace Processes."
    International Security 22 (2): 5–53.
    2002. "Introduction," in *Ending Civil Wars. The Implementation of
    Peace Agreements*, eds. Stephen John Stedman, Donald Rothchild,
    and Elizabeth M. Cousens (pp. 1–40). London: Lynne Rienner.
Stedman, Stephen John, Rothchild, Donald S., and Cousens, Elizabeth
    M. (eds.) 2002. *Ending Civil Wars: The Implementation of Peace
    Agreements*. Boulder, CO: Lynne Rienner Publishers.
Straus, Scott. 2006. *The Order of Genocide: Race, Power, and War in
    Rwanda*. Ithaca, NY: Cornell University Press.
Sundh, Lena. 2004. "Making Peace Keeping Missions More 'Prevention
    Aware.'" Paper presented at the Stockholm International Forum
    2004: Preventing genocide, Stockholm, Sweden.
Swidler, Ann. 1986. "Culture in Action: Symbols and Strategies." *American
    Sociological Review* 51 (2): 273–286.
Synergie Vie. 2004. *Mémoire sur les Entraves au Rapatriement des
    Groupes Armés Hutu Étrangers dans le Kivu*. Bukavu, D.R. Congo:
    Synergie Vie.
Terlinden, Ulf, and Debiel, Tobias. 2004. "Deceptive Hope for Peace?
    The Horn of Africa between Crisis Diplomacy and Obstacles to
    Development." *Peace, Conflict and Development* (4): 1–20.
Thayer, Charles Wheeler. 1974. *Diplomat*. Westport, CT: Greenwood
    Press.
Touval, Saadia, and Zartman, I. William. 1985. *International Mediation
    in Theory and Practice*. Boulder, CO: Westview Press.
Trefon, Theodore. 2004. *Ordre et Désordre à Kinshasa: Réponses
    Populaires à la Faillite de l'Etat*. Paris: L'Harmattan.
Tull, Denis M. 2005. The Reconfiguration of Political Order in Africa. A
    Case Study of North Kivu (DR Congo). PhD diss. Hamburg: Institut
    fur Africa-Kunde.
Tull, Denis, and Mehler, Andreas. 2005. "The Hidden Costs of Power-
    Sharing: Reproducing Insurgent Violence in Africa." *African Affairs*
    104 (416): 375–398.
Turner, Thomas. 2007. *The Congo Wars: Conflict, Myth and Reality*. New
    York: Palgrave Macmillan.
Turner, Thomas and Young, Crawford. 1985. *The Rise and Decline of the
    Zairian State*. Madison, WI: University of Wisconsiu Press.
UN Best Practice Unit. 2003. *Handbook on United Nations
    Multidimensional Peacekeeping Operations*. New York: United
    Nations.
UN Mission in the Democratic Republic of Congo (MONUC). 2004. *Kivu
    Strategy and Kivu Offices Action Plans*. Kinshasa (D.R. Congo): United
    Nations, Department of Peacekeeping Operations.

UN Mission in the Democratic Republic of Congo (MONUC). 2005a. *Inter-Agency Internal Displacement Division (IDD) – Mission to the Democratic Republic of the Congo (12–20 May 2005) – Final Report.*

2005b. *MONUC and the Bukavu Crisis.* Department of Peacekeeping Operations, Best Practices Unit.

UN Office for the Coordination of Humanitarian Affairs. 2009. *Population Movements in Eastern DR Congo, April–June 2009. http://www. reliefweb.int/rw/RWFiles2009.nsf/FilesByRWDocUnidFilename/ LSGZ-7UKHCF-full_report.pdf/$File/full_report.pdf,* accessed in October 2009.

UN Panel of Inquiry. 2001a. *Report of the Panel of Experts on the Illegal Exploitation of Natural Resources and Other Forms of Wealth of the Democratic Republic of the Congo.* S/2001/357. New York: United Nations.

2001b. *Report of the Panel of Experts on the Illegal Exploitation of Natural Resources and Other Forms of Wealth of the Democratic Republic of the Congo.* S/2001/1072. New York: United Nations.

2002a. *Report of the Panel of Experts on the Illegal Exploitation of Natural Resources and Other Forms of Wealth of the Democratic Republic of the Congo.* S/2002/565. New York: United Nations.

2002b. *Report of the Panel of Experts on the Illegal Exploitation of Natural Resources and Other Forms of Wealth of the Democratic Republic of the Congo.* S/2002/1146. New York: United Nations.

2003. *Report of the Panel of Experts on the Illegal Exploitation of Natural Resources and Other Forms of Wealth of the Democratic Republic of the Congo.* S/2003/1027. New York: United Nations.

UN Secretary-General. 1998. *The Causes of Conflict and the Promotion of Durable Peace and Sustainable Development in Africa.* Report of the Secretary-General to the Security Council. New York: United Nations.

UN Security Council. 2002. *Twelfth Report of the Secretary-General on the United Nations Mission in the Democratic Republic of Congo.* New York: United Nations.

2003a. *Fourteenth Report of the Secretary-General on the United Nations Mission in the Democratic Republic of Congo.* New York: United Nations.

2003b. *Resolution 1493 (2003).* New York: United Nations.

2003c. *Second Special Report of the Secretary-General on the United Nations Mission in the Democratic Republic of Congo.* New York: United Nations.

2003d. *Thirteenth Report of the Secretary-General on the United Nations Mission in the Democratic Republic of Congo.* New York: United Nations.

2003–2006a. *Fourteenth to Twenty-Third Report of the Secretary-General on the United Nations Mission in the Democratic Republic of Congo.* New York: United Nations.

2003–2006b. *Resolutions 1711, 1671, 1653, 1649, 1635, 1621, 1616, 1596, 1592, 1565, 1555, 1552, 1533, 1522, 1501, 1499, 1493, 1489.* New York: United Nations.

2004a. *Fifteenth Report of the Secretary-General on the United Nations Mission in the Democratic Republic of Congo.* New York: United Nations.

2004b. *Report of the Group of Experts Submitted through the Security Council Committee Established Pursuant to Resolution 1533 (2004) Concerning the Democratic Republic of the Congo.* New York: United Nations.

2004c. *Sixteenth Report of the Secretary-General on the United Nations Mission in the Democratic Republic of Congo.* New York: United Nations.

2004d. *Third Special Report of the Secretary-General on the United Nations Mission in the Democratic Republic of Congo.* New York: United Nations.

2005a. *Eighteenth Report of the Secretary-General on the United Nations Mission in the Democratic Republic of Congo.* New York: United Nations.

2005b. *Nineteenth Report of the Secretary-General on the United Nations Mission in the Democratic Republic of Congo.* New York: United Nations.

2005c. *Report of the Group of Experts Submitted through the Security Council Committee Established Pursuant to Resolution 1596 (2005) Concerning the Democratic Republic of the Congo.* New York: United Nations.

2005d. *Report of the Security Council Mission to Central Africa, 4 to 11 November 2005.* New York: United Nations.

2005e. *Resolution 1592 (2005).* New York: United Nations.

2005f. *Resolution 1621 (2005).* New York: United Nations.

2005g. *Resolution 1635 (2005).* New York: United Nations.

2005h. *Resolution 1649 (2005).* New York: United Nations.

2005i. *Seventeenth Report of the Secretary-General on the United Nations Mission in the Democratic Republic of Congo.* New York: United Nations.

2005j. *Special Report of the Secretary-General on Elections in the Democratic Republic of the Congo.* New York: United Nations.

2005k. *Twentieth Report of the Secretary-General on the United Nations Mission in the Democratic Republic of Congo.* New York: United Nations.

2006a. *Report of the Group of Experts Submitted through the Security Council Committee Established Pursuant to Resolution 1616 (2005) Concerning the Democratic Republic of the Congo.* New York: United Nations.

2006b. *Resolution 1671 (2006).* New York: United Nations.

2006c. *Resolution 1711 (2006).* New York: United Nations.

2006d. *Twenty-First Report of the Secretary-General on the United Nations Mission in the Democratic Republic of Congo.* New York: United Nations.

2006e. *Twenty-Second Report of the Secretary-General on the United Nations Mission in the Democratic Republic of Congo.* New York: United Nations.

2006f. *Twenty-Third Report of the Secretary-General on the United Nations Mission in the Democratic Republic of Congo.* New York: United Nations.

2007a. *Report of the Group of Experts Submitted through the Security Council Committee Established Pursuant to Resolution 1698 (2006) Concerning the Democratic Republic of the Congo.* New York: United Nations.

2007b. *Resolution 1771 (2007).* New York: United Nations.

2007c. *Twenty-Third Report of the Secretary-General on the United Nations Mission in the Democratic Republic of Congo.* New York: United Nations.

2008. *Report of the Group of Experts Submitted through the Security Council Committee Established Pursuant to Paragraph 18(d) of Security Council Resolution 1807 (2008) Concerning the Democratic Republic of the Congo.* New York: United Nations.

2009. *Resolution 1906 (2009).* New York: United Nations.

Union Paysanne Pour Le Développement Intégral and Life and Peace Institute. 2007. *Violence et Insécurité à Nindja / Kaniola – Le Phénomène "Rasta."* Bukavu: Life and Peace Institute.

Uvin, Peter. 1998. *Aiding Violence: The Development Enterprise in Rwanda.* West Hartford, CT: Kumarian Press.

Van Acker, Frank (ed.) 1999a. *L'Afrique Des Grands Lacs. Annuaire 1998–1999.* Paris: L'Harmattan.

Van Acker, Frank. 1999b. "La 'Pembénisation' Du Haut-Kivu: Opportunisme Et Droits Fonciers Revisités," in *L'Afrique Des Grands Lacs. Annuaire 1998–1999,* ed. Stefaan Marysse (pp. 1–35). Paris: L'Harmattan.

Van Acker, Frank, and Vlassenroot, Koen. 2000. "Youth and Conflict in Kivu: 'Komona Clair'." *Journal of Humanitarian Assistance.* Previously available at http://www.jha.ac, first accessed April 2002.

Van Hoyweghen, Saskia, and Vlassenroot, Koen. 2000. "Ethnic Ideology and Conflict in South Saharan Africa. The Culture Clash Revisited," in *Politics of Identity and Economics of Conflict in the Great Lakes Region*, eds. Ruddy Doom and Jan F. J. Gorus, Jan F. J., (pp. 93–118). Brussels: VUB University Press.

Veit, Alexander. 2008. "Figuration of Uncertainty: Armed Groups and 'Humanitarian' Military Intervention in Ituri (Dr Congo)." *Journal of Intervention and Statebuilding* 2 (3): 291–307.

2009. "Intervention as Indirect Rule: The Politics of Civil War and State-Building in Ituri (Democratic Republic of Congo)." PhD diss., Humboldt University, Berlin.

Verhaegen, Benoît. 1967. *Rebellions Au Congo*. Brussels: Centre de Recherche et d'Information Socio-Politiques.

Vincent, John. 1974. *Nonintervention and International Order*. Princeton, NJ: Princeton University Press.

Vinck, Patrick, Pham, Phuong, Baldo, Suliman, and Shigekane, Rachel. 2008. *Living with Fear. A Population-Based Survey on Attitudes About Peace, Justice, and Social Reconstruction in Eastern Democratic Republic of Congo*. Human Rights Center, University of California, Berkeley / Payson Center for International Development, Tulane University / International Center for Transitional Justice.

Vlassenroot, Koen. 2000. "The Promise of Ethnic Conflict: Militarization and Enclave Formation in South Kivu," in *Conflict and Ethnicity in Central Africa,* ed. Didier Goyvaerts (pp. 59–109). Tokyo: Institute for the Study of Languages and Culture of Asia and Africa.

2002. "Citizenship, Identity Formation & Conflict in South Kivu: The Case of the Banyamulenge." *Review of African Political Economy* 93/94: 499–516.

Vlassenroot, Koen, and Raeymaekers, Timothy. 2004a. *Conflict and Social Transformation in Eastern D.R. Congo*. Ghent, Belgium: Academia Press Scientific Publishers.

2004b. "The Politics of Rebellion and Intervention in Ituri: The Emergence of a New Political Complex?" *African Affairs* 103: 385–412.

Vlassenroot, Koen, and Romkema, Hans. 2002. "The Emergence of a New Order? Resources and War in Eastern Congo." *Journal of Humanitarian Assistance*. Available at http://www.jha.ac/articles/a111.htm.

Walls, Michael. 2009. "The Emergence of a Somali State: Building Peace from Civil War in Somaliland." *African Affairs*. Available at http://africacenter.org/2009/12/the-emergence-of-a-somali-state-building-peace-from-civil-war-in-somaliland/, accessed December 2009.

Walker, R. B. J. 1984. *Culture, Ideology, and World Order*. Boulder, CO: Westview Press.

Walter, Barbara F. 2002. *Committing to Peace: The Successful Settlement of Civil Wars*. Princeton, NJ: Princeton University Press.

Watson, Adam. 1991. *Diplomacy: The Dialogue between States.* London: Routledge.

Weaver, Catherine 2008. *Hypocrisy Trap: The World Bank and the Poverty of Reform.* Princeton, NJ: Princeton University Press.

Weick, Karl E. 1995. *Sensemaking in Organizations.* Thousand Oaks, CA: Sage Publications.

Weinstein, Jeremy M. 2005. *"Autonomous Recovery and International Intervention in Comparative Perspective."* Unpublished Manuscript, Center for Global Development, Washington, DC.

Willame, Jean-Claude. 1997. *Banyarwanda et Banyamulenge: Violences Ethniques et Gestion de l'Identitaire au Kivu.* Brussels: Institut Africain – CEDAF.

2002. *L'accord de Lusaka: Chronique d'une Négociation Internationale.* Tervuren: Institut Africain – CEDAF.

2007. *Les Faiseurs de Paix au Congo. Gestion d'une Crise Internationale dans un État sous Tutelle.* Brussels/Paris: Editions Complexes.

Wolters, Stephanie. 2004. *Continuing Instability in the Kivus: Testing the DRC Transition to the Limits.* Pretoria, South Africa: Institute for Security Studies.

Wolters, Stephanie, and Boshoff, Henri. 2006. *The Impact of Slow Military Reform on the Transition Process.* Pretoria, South Africa: Institute for Security Studies.

Wood, Elisabeth Jean. 2000. *Forging Democracy from Below: Insurgent Transitions in South Africa and El Salvador.* New York: Cambridge University Press.

Woodward, Susan. 1995. *Balkan Tragedy: Chaos and Dissolution after the Cold War.* Washington, DC: Brookings Institution.

1997. "Violence-Prone Area or International Transition? Adding the Role of Outsiders in Balkan Violence," in *Violence and Subjectivity*, eds. Veena Das, Arthur Kleinman, et al., (pp. 19–45). Berkeley: University of California Press.

2006. *Why State-Building? Toward a Conceptual Framework.* Program on States and Security. New York: City University of New York.

Young, Crawford. 1967. "Significance of the 1964 Rebellion," in *Footnotes to the Congo Story*, ed. Helen Kitchen (pp. 526–543). New York: Walker and Company.

1994. *The African Colonial State in Comparative Perspective.* New Haven, CT: Yale University Press.

Youngs, Richard. 2004. "Democratic Institution-Building and Conflict Resolution: Emerging EU Approaches." *International Peacekeeping* 11 (3): 526–543.

Zartman, I. William. 1989. *Ripe for Resolution: Conflict and Intervention in Africa.* New York: Oxford University Press.

Zartman, I. William, and Rasmussen, J. Lewis. 1997. *Peacemaking in International Conflict: Methods and Techniques.* Washington, DC: U.S. Institute of Peace Press.

Zartman, I. William, and Touval, Saadia. 1996. "International Mediation in the Post-Cold War Era," in *Managing Global Chaos*, eds. Chester Crocker, Fen Osler Hampson, and Pamela Aall (pp. 445–461). Washington, DC: U.S. Institute of Peace Press.

Index

Note: Page numbers in italics indicate figures; those with a "t" indicate tables; those with an "n" indicate footnotes.

Cambridge Studies in International Relations